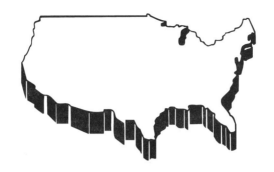

AMERICA IN THE 21ST CENTURY

CHALLENGES AND OPPORTUNITIES IN DOMESTIC POLITICS

EDITED BY

KUL B. RAI
SOUTHERN CONNECTICUT STATE UNIVERSITY

DAVID F. WALSH
SOUTHERN CONNECTICUT STATE UNIVERSITY

PAUL J. BEST
SOUTHERN CONNECTICUT STATE UNIVERSITY

W9-CLL-066

PRENTICE HALL, UPPER SADDLE RIVER, NEW JERSEY 07458

Library of Congress Cataloging-in-Publication Data

America in the 21st century: challenges and opportunities in domestic
    politics/edited by Kul B. Rai, David F. Walsh, Paul J. Best.
        p.   cm.
    Includes bibliographical references and index.
    ISBN 0-13-570946-6
    1. Political planning—United States.   2. United States—Politics
and government—1989–   I. Rai, Kul B.   II. Walsh, David F.
III. Best, Paul J.
JK468.P64A53   1997
320.973—dc21   97-13590
                                                                        CIP

Editorial director: Charlyce Jones Owen
Editor-in-chief: Nancy Roberts
Acquisitions editor: Michael Bickerstaff
Editorial assistant: Kathryn Sheehan
Editorial/production supervision
    and electronic page makeup: Kari Callaghan Mazzola
Interior design: John P. Mazzola
Cover design: Bruce Kenselaar
Buyer: Bob Anderson

This book was set in 10/12 New Baskerville by Big Sky Composition
and was printed and bound by Courier Companies, Inc.
The cover was printed by Phoenix Color Corp.

 © 1998 by Prentice-Hall, Inc.
Simon & Schuster/A Viacom Company
Upper Saddle River, New Jersey 07458

Printed in the United States of America
10   9   8   7   6   5   4   3   2   1

ISBN 0-13-570946-6

PRENTICE-HALL INTERNATIONAL (UK) LIMITED, *London*
PRENTICE-HALL OF AUSTRALIA PTY. LIMITED, *Sydney*
PRENTICE-HALL CANADA INC., *Toronto*
PRENTICE-HALL HISPANOAMERICANA, S.A., *Mexico*
PRENTICE-HALL OF INDIA PRIVATE LIMITED, *New Delhi*
PRENTICE-HALL OF JAPAN, INC., *Tokyo*
SIMON & SCHUSTER ASIA PTE. LTD., *Singapore*
EDITORA PRENTICE-HALL DO BRASIL, LTDA., *Rio de Janeiro*

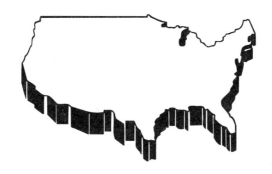

Contents

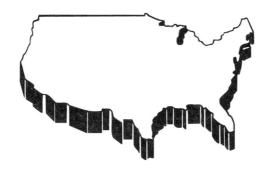

FOREWORD

This series of essays, like its companion volume (*America in the 21st Century: Challenges and Opportunities in Foreign Policy*), provides an exemplary model of how research can be intertwined with teaching. Both are essential elements of the enterprise of scholarship.

The faculty members of the four universities that comprise the Connecticut State University system are engaged in scholarship in the broad sense in which the late Ernest Boyer described it: They are involved in the *discovery* of knowledge, the *integration* of research from a narrow discipline into larger patterns of understanding, the kind of *teaching* that at the same time stimulates student learning and creates new paths of inquiry, and the *application* of theory to practical problems that may also inspire new research. (See, especially, Ernest L. Boyer, *Scholarship Reconsidered* [Princeton: The Carnegie Foundation for the Advancement of Teaching, 1990], Chapter 2.) The model of the universities that fosters their scholarly work is not the Germanic research university. That outdated model seeks to subjugate practice to theory, to focus on the inculcation of research methods in graduate instruction, and to clearly distinguish one discipline from another. Instead, the contemporary CSU model is one in which active researchers try to relate their work both to other disciplines and to practical problems, and also push their students to grapple with issues that beset them everyday.

It accordingly should come as no surprise that these essays—whose authors are faculty members from the CSU universities—address issues of public policy across disciplinary lines and place contemporary problems within their historical context. They then provide recommendations for the future in such a way that the intended readers—students in an introductory course in American government or public policy—must wrestle with the alternatives in order to arrive at a conclusion that makes sense to them.

We often say that contemporary students, in order to be adequately prepared for the "knowledge work" society of the twenty-first century, must develop the capacities to (1) define, clarify, and solve problems; (2) engage in critical thinking; (3) work in teams across disciplines; (4) cope with complex realities and rapid change; (5) tolerate and deal with uncertainty and ambiguity; (6) make sense of disjointed and contradictory data; (7) assess risks; (8) choose among competing values; and (9) communicate ideas clearly. A student using these essays under the guidance of a teacher-mentor can develop precisely those competencies.

The issues considered here seize the imagination of students, just as they demand the attention of the country:

To both promote democratization and locate final authority to determine policy, should a constitutional amendment be adopted to permit the President or either house of Congress to submit a policy issue to a national referendum?

Should health care be rationed, or—perhaps better stated—*how* should health care be rationed?

What should be incorporated into school curricula to improve education? Can higher standards in the classroom alone enable American education to meet world-class criteria?

Should market-oriented methods be used to protect the environment, or do such solutions as emissions trading programs facilitate its degradation?

Is a national identification card an appropriate way to curb illegal immigration? Should employment-based immigration be given a higher priority than the reunification of families? Should English be the official language, for purposes of legal transactions as well as instruction?

Is the development of telecommunications best stimulated through regulation or competition?

Should public policy accommodate differences between men and women? Are there differences that should be accommodated?

How much should be spent to provide for an adequate national defense now that the Cold War has ended?

Can an effective government be reconciled with contemporary anti-government bias?

This volume of essays is designed to push its readers, including students, to *think*. These essays, these questions, reach out to draw the reader into the consideration of policy recommendations to resolve problems facing this country. They ask students to play the role of legislators or active citizens. They demand full participation in considering policy options, a kind of active engagement that citizenship theorists of democracy have always contended is educational, increasing the participant's capacity to resolve issues of a higher order of difficulty. In doing so, they fulfill the highest tradition of scholarship.

William J. Cibes, Jr., Ph.D.
Chancellor, Connecticut State University system

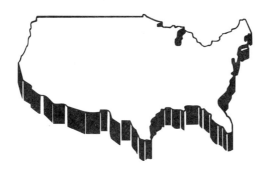

PREFACE

The end of the Cold War and the existence of some persistent social and economic problems in the United States have thrust the domestic agenda to the forefront, with the result that most Americans consider it more important than the foreign policy agenda. We examine the challenges and opportunities brought forth by this change. We consider major issues of the domestic agenda and not only discuss public policy formulated in response to the new challenges and opportunities, but also make recommendations for the twenty-first century.

The issues analyzed in this book are the economy, health care, education, the environment, immigration, the electronic revolution, the changing role of women in American politics, and American force posture. In addition, an introductory chapter provides a background to the political and economic context of current American policy making. Finally, a concluding chapter considers recent criticisms of American political institutions and political culture and assesses their adequacy to deal with the problems of the twenty-first century.

We employ political economy as our major approach in analyzing the issues discussed in the book. Simply stated, political economy is the interaction of economics and politics. Economic forces influence political institutions and political behavior. On the other hand, the political process and political decisions not only regulate private enterprise, but they also affect—and in many cases determine—the allocation of scarce economic resources. For example, the chapter on health care demonstrates the relationship between economics and politics. The rising cost of health care in the United

States created a political environment that made the introduction of a universal health care bill in Congress inevitable during President Clinton's first administration. The bill's defeat in turn determined the type of health care available, the groups served by it, and, equally important, the distribution of cost. Wherever appropriate, the following four major headings are used in the chapters: "Historical Background"; "Challenges, Opportunities, and Constraints"; "Policy Options: The Current Debate"; and "Recommendations for the Twenty-First Century."

A majority of the contributors to this volume are political scientists from three of the four campuses—Southern, Central, and Western—of the Connecticut State University system. The other contributors also are faculty members at Connecticut State University campuses and are from the departments of economics, public health, and education.

The book is suitable as a supplementary text in an introductory U.S. Government course. The text may also be adopted in courses in American public policy and economics.

ACKNOWLEDGMENTS

The editors gratefully acknowledge the assistance of the Connecticut State University Research Grants Committee and the Faculty Development Office at Southern Connecticut State University—especially its director, James Newman—in the preparation of this manuscript. While we owe thanks to many individuals, we wish to single out Jean Polka, the Secretary of the Political Science Department at Southern Connecticut State University, for her endeavors in the completion of this project. Jean went far beyond the call of duty and worked with us even when she was tired or sick. Additionally, we thank Mrs. Kathleen Walsh, without whose help some of the chapters would not have been completed. We also thank Rosemary Yanosik and Lisa Dupler for typing sections of the manuscript. Finally, we would like to thank William E. Kelly of Auburn University and Howard P. Lehman of the University of Utah for reviewing the manuscript.

Kul B. Rai wishes to express appreciation to Paul Holmer of the Southern Connecticut State University Library for his assistance in obtaining books, articles, documents, and other materials through the interlibrary loan network.

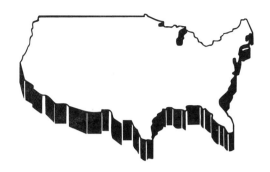

CONTRIBUTORS

Kul B. Rai, Ph.D. University of Rochester (1969), is professor and chairman of the department of political science at Southern Connecticut State University. He is a co-author of four books, *America in the 21st Century: Challenges and Opportunities in Foreign Policy* (1997), *Governing Through Turbulence* (1995), *Politics in Three Worlds* (1985), and *Political Science Statistics* (1973), and a co-translator of another, *Politics Among Nations* by Hans Morgenthau, into Hindi (1976). Rai has published articles in scholarly journals in the United States, Europe, and India, notably in *International Organization, Polity, Comparative Political Studies, Journal of Peace Research*, and *Indian Journal of Politics*. He served as president of the Northeastern Political Science Association in 1990–1991.

David F. Walsh, Ph.D. University of Connecticut (1975), is professor of political science at Southern Connecticut State University. He is a co-author of three books, *America in the 21st Century: Challenges and Opportunities in Foreign Policy* (1997), *Governing Through Turbulence* (1995), and *Politics in Three Worlds* (1985). Dr. Walsh is a frequent participant in professional conferences.

Paul J. Best, Ph.D. New York University (1965), is professor of political science at Southern Connecticut State University. He is a co-author of three books, *America in the 21st Century: Challenges and Opportunities in Foreign Policy* (1997), *Governing Through Turbulence* (1995), and *Politics in Three Worlds* (1985), and has published articles in several scholarly journals, notably *The Polish Review* and the *Journal of European Economic History*. Dr. Best served as Managing Editor of *The Polish Review* for twenty-three years (from 1969 to 1992).

John W. Critzer, Ph.D. University of Delaware, is associate professor of political science at Southern Connecticut State University.

Russell G. Fryer, Ph.D. New York University, is professor of political science at Western Connecticut State University.

Antonia C. Moran, J.D. University of Connecticut, is associate professor of political science and director of the Center for Social Research at Central Connecticut State University.

Arthur C. Paulson, Ph.D. University of Colorado, is associate professor of political science at Southern Connecticut State University.

Leah G. Stambler, Ph.D. University of Connecticut, is professor of education at Western Connecticut State University.

Moses Stambler, Ph.D. New York University, is professor of public health at Southern Connecticut State University.

James A. Thorson, Ph.D. University of Illinois at Chicago, is associate professor of economics and finance at Southern Connecticut State University.

Robert S. Workman, M.S. City University of New York, is associate professor of computer science at Southern Connecticut State University.

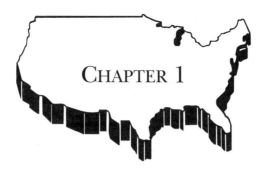

CHAPTER 1

AMERICAN POLITICS IN TRANSITION

THE 1980s AND 1990s

DAVID F. WALSH

For the United States, as for most major states in the world, the 1980s and 1990s were a time of change and challenge. During this period the effects of recent transformations, both within American society and at the international level, acted as catalysts for change in many areas of life, including economics and politics. Although these transformations had been underway since the late 1960s, their intensity and pervasiveness increased significantly as America was exposed to a succession of new factors and conditions—global shocks and recessions, increased foreign economic competition, the end of the Cold War and the demise of the Soviet Union, the development of revolutionary new technologies, the achievement of post-industrial society within the United States, slower rates of domestic economic growth, and demographic changes within American society. As always, the political response to these economic and social changes was filtered through the values and beliefs of the American political culture and mediated by the legal and political institutions of the American political system. Nonetheless, by the mid-1980s new conditions had given rise to a powerful new conservative political movement, new ideas and values had been added to the national debate on America's future, and important developments had occurred within interest groups, political parties, and the general electorate. In addition, political discourse in the 1980s and 1990s also featured prolonged national debates on America's future in the post–Cold War world, the state of America's economic competitiveness, American culture and morality, and the proper relationship between state and society. These political developments have been subject to a wide range of interpretations, including that politics in the 1980s and 1990s was an era of

1

antigovernment sentiment demonstrating considerable continuity with the past, that a decisive realignment had occurred in American politics complete with critical elections, and that these decades constituted an important transitional period, although no decisive realignment had occurred. A proper understanding of the pattern of politics of the 1980s and 1990s must begin with the development of a framework for analysis that includes six points: (1) the basic nature of the American political system, (2) the sources of political change since the late 1960s, (3) the conservative renewal and the new conservative agenda, (4) the Reagan-Bush legacy in politics and public policy, (5) the new political and economic constraints in the era of divided government, and (6) the public policy environment of the 1990s.

THE POLITICAL SYSTEM IN COMPARATIVE PERSPECTIVE

The United States leaves the twentieth century with a constitution that is more than 200 years old and a political system that is unique among the advanced industrial states. Born out of the American Revolution, the political and constitutional order has been shaped by a combination of cultural, geographic, and socioeconomic factors that many sources argue are unique, giving rise to a theory of American exceptionalism. At the core of American political culture is support for the values of liberty, egalitarianism, individualism, populism, and laissez-faire—the elements of the American Creed.[1] As defined in the United States, this creed gave expression to eighteenth and nineteenth century conceptions of government and society emphasizing the voluntary nature of society, the glorification of the individual, and the rejection of conservative theories of organic society, hierarchy, and natural aristocracy. It also fostered a strong distrust of government, an anti-power ethic, reinforced by the belief that the essence of democracy was popular control of government to be achieved through strict adherence to constitutionalism and the rule of law.[2] Despite some modifications over time, the significance of the core values of the American Creed can hardly be overestimated. Historically the creed has received broad support from most elements of American society, and it has played a central role in the definition of American national identity.[3] As one study has argued, being an American means accepting this liberal-democratic creed, while those who reject it are considered to be un-American.[4]

America's political evolution has also been shaped by the continental scale of the American state, 3.6 million square miles, and by America's legacy as a nation of immigrants. Periods of large-scale immigration occurred in the 1840s, 1850s, 1870s, 1890s, and between 1900 and 1921. Between 1860 and 1929, 32.5 million people immigrated to the United States, with more than 10 million arriving in the peak years, from 1900 to 1921.[5] The most recent influx of immigration has occurred since the mid-1960s and for the first time has included more non-Europeans than immigrants of European ancestry. The result has been an extraordinary mixture of ethnic, racial, and religious groups spread across a continent-wide expanse that contributed historically to strong religious, racial, and regional cleavages. In addition, America's abundant natural resources, climatic variations, and diverse economic activities contributed to the development of regionally specific economic traditions and interests. The largest sectors of the economy were commercial agriculture, mercantile capitalism, mining, and heavy (capital goods) industry, but each of these was also subdivided and diversified into separate product-specific areas. As the adoption of modern technology spread from east to west, the corporate form of business was born. By 1900 America's economy was the largest in the world, and by the end of World War I America's economic leadership was acknowledged around the globe. Even before World War I the environment of comparative affluence, the fluidity of social relations, and the abundance of free land produced a belief in the United States as a "land of opportunity" and gave rise to a relentless pursuit of material success.[6] The ethic of work and achievement fused with the Democratic Creed to produce the nation's operative ideology, and "the American dream of success" became a magnate for generations of immigrants from around the world.[7] Collectively, the cultural, geographic, and socioeconomic factors had a profound effect on America's political development because they reinforced trends towards decentralization and localism that had already been established in the political and legal domains by the constitution of 1789.

THE POLITICAL SYSTEM

The United States constitutional/legal order created the most decentralized political system of any major state in the world. At the national level, under the separation of powers principle, the executive, legislative, and judicial branches operate as co-equal parts of the national government in the absence of any constitutionally prescribed hierarchy or scheme of coordination. This "non-system" of government not only facilitates institutional conflict, but also makes it inevitable. In addition, the division of authority between the states and the national government under the principles of federalism further contributes to the complexity and decentralization of the system of government. The relationship between the subunits, the states, and the national government in the American federal system is the reverse of that found in other federations; the U.S. Constitution assigned only enumerated powers to the national government while reserving all residual powers for the states.[8] Historically, the effect of the federal system was to prevent the development of a single locus of political power such as that found in Japan and most European states.[9]

A distinct pattern of politics and public policy also developed in the

United States. The absence of legal or cultural barriers to political participation, the diversity of interests (economic, regional, and ethno-religious), and the availability of money for political causes produced the most open and complex political system in the world. Both political party and interest group conflict flourished in the American environment and, aided by modern communications technology, this trend continues today. Interest groups have historically articulated an extremely wide range of issues, including moral and religious positions, economic and political concerns of specific regions of the country, and economic demands of single sectors of the economy. Although a two-party system developed early in American history, it was organized at the state and local levels and retained a local focus. This local focus was continually reinforced by the fact that every political office in the country was elected at the state or local level except that of the president and vice president. The political parties were, therefore, unable to perform a strong integrating function to overcome the severe structural decentralization created by the separation of powers at the national level and the division of powers between the states and the national government. Throughout U.S. history parties served as conduits for local and state interests, as was so often demonstrated by the lack of discipline and coherence in the actions of persons elected to Congress. Although in most periods of American history the consensus on the Democratic Creed precluded conflict over basic values, such as the proper form of government or the legitimacy of the Constitution, beyond that the political process became a sprawling and complex arena for the interaction of every conceivable societal interest.

The pattern of public policy was also shaped by the strength of antigovernment sentiments and by the influence of local groups. Public policy at the national level followed a distinctive course, being slow to develop until the New Deal (1933–1940), and then having lower levels of taxation and welfare, and less developed health care and income policies than those in Europe.[10] U.S. public policy has also been characterized by cycles of growth and retrenchment in the scope of national government policy, reflecting the relative strength of the forces of nationalism and localism during different periods. Episodes of retrenchment of the scope of Washington's policy role, including the present one, have frequently been accompanied by virulent antigovernment rhetoric and claims that such a retreat was necessary to save the Constitution.

THE 1970S AND 1980S: THE POLITICAL RESPONSE TO ECONOMIC AND SOCIAL CHANGE

Like other advanced industrial states, the United States was exposed to strong international and domestic pressures for change in the 1970s and 1980s. Foremost among these were the emergence of the global economy, the end of the Cold War, and domestic demographic and social changes. Although the United States was still the most powerful state in the world during this period, new economic and social conditions acted as catalysts for a series of important political changes. Established economic and political relationships that had existed for most of the postwar period were altered, including industrial relations between unions and businesses and the relationship between the two major parties and their constituent interest groups. The environment of change also altered the partisan electoral balance between the Democratic and Republican parties, although the extent of this change remains open to interpretation. Certain political ideas, institutions, and political groups were empowered in the new environment while others were disempowered. In general, ideas associated with economic laissez-faire and the reduction of the role of government were empowered, while Keynesian economic theory and national government institutions were disempowered. Similarly, groups advocating an expanded role for government or the development of large-scale national government programs saw their influence diminish. Most important, the new conditions were conducive to efforts at agenda change, the imposition of a new set of national priorities by a political party seeking to attract the support of major interest groups and to build a new majority electoral coalition. Political actors perpetually seek to exploit the conflicts in society, and by identifying major problems and proposing solutions to them that are preferred by the majority of the politically relevant population, they gain financial, moral, and electoral support.[11] The political history of the last two decades demonstrates, however, that discrediting the previous agenda is not the same thing as imposing a new one, and that attempts at agenda construction do not always succeed. Several decades may be needed before the elements of a new agenda can be ordered, prioritized, and sold to the public.

The forces for change that developed during the 1970s occurred at a time when the previous pattern of politics, dating to the 1930s, was already in the process of disintegration. This pattern, frequently referred to as the New Deal Order, was America's response to the crisis of industrialization that manifested itself during the Great Depression of 1929. Although loosely constructed, the New Deal Order was built around a set of ideas, a unique political and electoral alignment, and a distinct pattern of public policy. The ideal foundation of the New Deal included the beliefs that a limited, pragmatic reform of certain economic practices was necessary to save the capitalist system, and that Keynesianism, the economic theory of John Maynard Keynes and his followers, offered the appropriate means. Under Keynesianism the state's spending and monetary powers would be used to maintain a healthy macroeconomic environment by stimulating mass consumption (assuring aggregate demand) and by distributing the benefits of capitalism on a larger scale.[12] Thus, America's acceptance of Keynesianism created both commercial and social commitments that resulted in an expanded regulatory role for the national government, national legislation that created a limited social safety net, and increased political influence for public sector institutions—especially those in Washington. The agenda of the New Deal was constructed and implemented by the Democratic party, which dominated American politics from 1933 to 1968. Support to sustain Democratic party control of the national government was supplied by an electoral coalition made up of blue-collar workers, Southerners, urban dwellers, and certain cultural and religious minorities—including Catholics, Jews, and blacks. By the 1970s electoral support for the New Deal Order had seriously eroded, as major constituent groups perceived a series of gaps between its promises and accomplishments. Three problems in particular accelerated the decline of the New Deal consensus: the poverty-stricken status of many blacks, the moral and foreign policy conflicts surrounding the Vietnam War, and the growing alienation of the middle class from the high levels of bureaucratization in both public and private sectors.[13] Thus, the post-1973 catalysts for change appeared at a time when the coherence of public policy and the direction of the electoral alignment were in a state of flux.

Throughout the postwar period from 1945 to the mid-1970s, two conditions shaped the international system: the Cold War competition between the United States and the Soviet Union and the economic dominance of the United States. The Cold War had both domestic and international consequences of great import. Domestically, the military and political threat of the Soviet Union produced a bipartisan (Democratic and Republican) consensus on the foreign policy of containment of communist influence on a worldwide basis, as well as majority support for the development of what has been called the "National Security State." The National Security State was a political system of big government, military conscription, and high levels of defense spending and taxation. In the environment of the Cold War the opponents of the expansion of the scope of government activity, as well as of the increasing power of the president and the executive branch, were successfully marginalized. Internationally, the Cold War provided the justification for American military and political leadership of the Western Alliance. During this period, potential economic competitors, including Japan and Germany, were reduced by their defeats in World War II to a position of complete military and economic dependence on the United States. Although after the mid-1950s, the changing nature of the Cold War permitted America's allies more freedom of action, Washington was still able to dominate most of the West's foreign and defense policies well into the 1980s.

With the end of the Cold War in the years between 1985 and 1990, Japan and the states of Western Europe asserted new independence and assumed a more competitive role in their relationship with the United States.

This new posture was most obvious in trade relations, which included both prolonged and bitter disputes. The end of the Cold War also produced increased partisan conflict over foreign policy—especially foreign economic policy—as candidates, interest group representatives, scholars, and pundits rushed to join the debate over America's post-Cold War role and the related debate over America's economic competitiveness. Although the consensus on America's foreign policy had broken down during the Vietnam War, the new conditions after 1990 permitted the articulation of a wide range of foreign policy alternatives, including sharply decreased defense spending to achieve the so-called "peace dividend," an end to military interventions, and even the general expression of neo-isolationist sentiments.

The changes in the global economy impacted the United States even more profoundly than the end of the Cold War. In 1945 the United States possessed more than half of the world's supplies of gold and convertible currencies, and its gross national product exceeded that of all other nations combined.[14] The disproportionate size of the U.S. economy, and the fact that access to American consumers was desired by every non-communist state (through the granting of most-favored-nation status), gave the United States the power to shape the international economic order according to American interests. The result was the Bretton Woods system, an international economic order promoting free trade, opposing economic nationalism, and establishing the U.S. dollar as the medium of international exchange. Although compatible with the traditional values of American capitalism, the advocacy of free trade was clearly based on practical political and economic considerations. For the country with the most modern economy and employing the highest level of technology, an open international economy provided maximum opportunity for profit from investment and trade. Throughout the first three decades after World War II, American corporations became increasingly dependent on profits from international transactions, with the value of exports reaching 10 percent of the GNP by 1981.

By the late 1970s America's economic advantage had been seriously eroded. Although experts remained divided about the extent and cause of America's comparative economic decline, America faced unprecedented competition from Japan, the states of the European Union, and several newly industrialized countries (NICs) in Asia and elsewhere. This competition included increasing penetration by foreign imports of domestic consumer markets. The triple revolutions in global communications, new production technologies, and transportation did much to nullify the American economic advantage of the early postwar period. By 1990 it was also unclear which of the three major powers, the United States, Japan, or the European Union, was best situated in the trajectory of new technology development to lead the world in the twenty-first century.[15] It was certain, however, that the era of absolute American dominance had come to an end, and that the encounter with global competition had contributed to several negative developments for the domestic American economy, including the following: (1) The rising prices of some natural resources, especially oil in the 1970s, contributed to several bouts of inflation; (2) by the early 1970s America's trade balance was in deficit, and had ballooned to $129 billion by 1989;[16] (3) many traditional industries failed in the face of low-wage foreign competition, contributing to a major episode of deindustrialization; and (4) in the 1980s and 1990s workers faced declining wage growth, an increasing gap between high and low earners, and job insecurity unprecedented in the postwar era. Although many of these problems had their ultimate origins in the early postwar period, their visible effects in the 1970s and 1980s created a political opening for groups that opposed Keynesianism, the scope of public sector activity, existing levels of government spending and taxation, and specific social programs.

DEMOGRAPHIC AND SOCIAL CHANGE

Between the 1960s and 1980s a series of demographic and social changes transformed American society and created the social foundations for the politics of the 1980s and 1990s. The changes included separate socioeconomic, cultural, and demographic developments, but their collective impact was to make American society more affluent, more economically unequal, and more culturally diverse than at any time in American history. In terms of socioeconomic development, the period from 1945 to 1970, often referred to as the "golden age of capitalism," was a period of nearly uninterrupted growth that positively impacted the lives of the majority of the population. During this time the United States was transformed from an industrial society to a postindustrial one in which a majority of the population was engaged in providing services to people. Beyond the dichotomy between industrial and service sector workers, the foundations of the "knowledge society" were established at this time, which subsequently resulted in the proliferation of many types of service sector job categories distinguished by their level of sophistication and importance to society. The economic transitions of the period produced five outcomes of special import:[17] (1) The majority of the population was removed from the condition of scarcity of the Depression era to the condition of mass affluence in which basic needs—like housing, food, and medical attention—were taken for granted; (2) in the environment of mass affluence, the importance of materialist values—such as having a job and being protected against the economic hazards of life—declined, while postmaterialist values—such as concern for the environment and quality-of-life issues—were added to the national political agenda; (3) poverty became a condition that was confined to a distinct segment of the population, disproportionately consisting of racial and ethnic minorities; (4) society was economically stratified on the basis of the possession of higher education or specialized knowledge of new technology; and (5) traditional class conflict over economic resources was increasingly supplanted by status conflicts involving single group demands for special benefits or the recognition of a special status in society.

Certain geographic and demographic developments also had important political ramifications. The movement of middle class and upper middle class whites to the suburbs that started in the 1950s not only created a physical condition in which races and classes lived apart, but also shattered the principle that some broad public interest existed in the rapidly growing urban areas of the country.[18] The race issue proved to be destructive to the New Deal coalition. Its dimensions included black frustration with the perceived failure of the civil rights movement of the 1960s, the persistent problem of racially segmented labor markets, blue-collar resentment of black economic demands, conflict over symbolic racial issues like affirmative action, and the deliberate exploitation of racial antagonisms in political campaigns and advertisements.[19] Collectively, these socioeconomic and demographic changes were the social prerequisites for the three wedge issues: race, taxes, and the reaction to the granting of special rights to certain groups, which shattered the New Deal coalition and made possible the victory of conservative groups in the 1980s.[20]

Finally, since the mid-1960s an important increase in immigration has occurred, a by-product of the increased mobility of the global market and changes in U.S. immigration rules in the 1960s. For the first time in U.S. history the majority of the new immigrants are non-Europeans, with Asians and Hispanics constituting 85 percent of the new arrivals. This influx is the largest since the 1920s and has had a significant impact on the composition of the population. For example, in the decade after 1970 the Hispanic component increased by 61 percent, for a total of 14.6 million,[21] and by the early 1990s groups classified as "minority" constituted 25 percent of the population.[22] As always, the immigrant population was unevenly distributed, being clustered in the border states of Texas, California, and Florida, and in selected urban centers such as Los Angeles, Miami, Chicago, and New York City. The political and social impact of the new immigration was thus extremely uneven and gave rise to demands by certain states and localities for special federal assistance to help with the costs of education, public health, and other services. The new immigration contributed to the development of a number of contentious political issues, including school curriculum; the rights of immigrants; community-police relations; the availability of government services in the Spanish language; the impact of the North American Free Trade Agreement on immigration; a national language policy, with demands by conservatives for "English First"; and conflicts over specific pieces of legislation, like the Immigration Reform and Control Act of 1986.

THE RENEWAL OF CONSERVATISM AND THE NEW CONSERVATIVE AGENDA

The decades of the 1970s and the 1980s witnessed the emergence of an unusually militant and self-conscious conservative movement. This movement resulted from the fusion of several distinct traditions of conservatism, including traditional conservatism, neoconservatism, the New Right, and the New Religious Right. Traditional conservatives, oriented almost exclusively toward economic issues, emphasized the values of limited government, economic freedom, and individualism. As critics of New Deal programs and the higher levels of government spending and taxation, they had been relegated to a minority position within the Republican party in the 1940s and 1950s. In the environment of increasing inflation and slowing economic growth after 1973, however, traditional conservatives renewed their attack on the Keynesian state. The credibility of these attacks was enhanced by the fact that many social programs of the 1960s had been directed at minorities or "special needs" groups rather than a numerical majority of the population. These programs were much more costly on a per capita basis than the older social programs aimed at the general working-age population, and they were unable to equal the impressive results of the earlier programs in promoting economic productivity and national welfare.[23] The second group, the neoconservatives, were small in number but included some prominent intellectuals and professionals who were well placed in society to influence public opinion. Some of the most important neoconservatives had previously been part of the anticommunist right wing of the Democratic party, but had become dissatisfied with what they considered the insufficiently firm foreign policy positions of George McGovern and Jimmy Carter.[24] Although they still supported the core programs of the New Deal enacted during the Roosevelt and Truman eras, they disapproved of such programs as affirmative action and were equally opposed to the perceived cultural trends of "permissiveness" and "anti-Americanism" of the 1960s. The support of the neoconservatives was significant because it broadened the intellectual base of the conservative movement and also contributed to an ideological realignment of the two major parties which increased the strength of the Republicans.

Both the New Right and the New Religious Right had roots in the populist tradition. Members of the New Right, frequently described as "Middle Class Radicals," were primarily lower-middle-class people who felt that they were being forced to bear the burden of social change, including benefits demanded by the poor and minorities.[25] Since the mid-1970s, conservative activists had sought to organize this segment of the population while conservative think tanks and single-issue organizations had structured and communicated their political demands. The issues articulated by the New Right included opposition to the following: the Equal Rights Amendment, school busing to achieve integration, gun control, sex education in schools, the modern school curriculum, government poverty programs, legalized abortion, softness on crime, existing levels of immigration, and perceived media bias.[26] They were also critics of unions and the growth of government bureaucracy. The demands of the New Right included defense of traditional social and cultural values, stringent measures against crime, policies to preserve the traditional family, and compulsory work for welfare recipients. Finally, the New Religious Right consisted largely of evangelical Protestants who had also mobilized in reaction to social, cultural, and legal developments, including the legalization of abortion, prohibition of prayer in school, emergence of the gay and feminist movements, availability of pornography, and specific acts of federal legislation that froze some licenses for religious radio and television programming and ended the tax-exempt status of private schools that practiced racial discrimination.[27]

The fusion of economic and social conservatives created a dynamic new force in American politics that transformed the partisan political alignment in favor of the Republican party. As one source has argued, a movement that was radical, majoritarian, lower-middle class, and conservative at the same time was completely unprecedented in modern American politics.[28] Specifically, the electoral accomplishments of the new conservative movement had four components: (1) The populist impulse was completely reoriented away from resentment of the rich to resentment of elected officials, judges, and government bureaucrats who had implemented unpopular social policies; (2) the social and cultural issues raised by the New Right cut across the most important constituencies of the Democratic party, including blue-collar workers and Southerners, and accelerated the electoral disintegration of the New Deal coalition; (3) the influx of the Religious Right produced a shift to presidential Republicanism in the South and Southwest;[29] and (4) across the United States, social and cultural issues helped the Republicans make unprecedented electoral gains in middle-class suburbs. It must be emphasized that the conservative movement benefited greatly from the skillful use of communications technology, as well as the political potential of public policy resource centers or think tanks that helped to create a new "politics of conservative ideas."[30] Ronald Reagan's victories in the presidential elections of 1980 and 1984 were clear demonstrations of the strength of the conservative movement. By 1984 a new conservative national agenda had been developed that emphasized both economic and social issues. In practice, however, the Reagan administrations were dominated by economic conservatives whose top priority was the implementation of supply-side economic policies. The public policy record of the Reagan administrations is open to a wide variety of interpretations, but it is clear that they relentlessly pursued the domestic goals of cutting taxes, reducing government spending, and sharply increasing defense spending.

THE REAGAN-BUSH LEGACY

The two administrations of Ronald Reagan dominated the politics of the 1980s and achieved a fundamental reorientation of the domestic political discourse toward conservative economic and social issues. As a political project, Reagan Republicanism was an unqualified political success, but the Reagan and Bush administrations left behind a complex and confusing legacy of populist politics and contradictory policies. In the economic area, the combination of large tax reductions for corporations and those in the highest income brackets, combined with the largest increases in defense spending in history, produced an unprecedented burgeoning of the public debt and made the United States government the world's largest debtor. More than three-fourths of the cumulative federal debt in American history was incurred during the twelve years of the Reagan-Bush administrations, some $3,549 billion.[31] By 1990, two items—servicing the debt and entitlement spending—accounted for 66.9 percent of federal budget appropriations.[32] While this development rendered untenable a return to the traditional Democratic approach of creating new federal programs to benefit minorities and the disadvantaged, it also had a negative impact on low- and middle-income working families. The incomes of the lowest 80 percent of the population stagnated throughout the 1980s and 1990s, while at the same time reform of Social Security placed heavy new tax burdens on the middle class, and the recession that began in 1989 increased unemployment among all income groups.[33] At the same time, the income of the top 1 percent of the population doubled during the Reagan-Bush years, as the level of income inequality reached a sixty-year high.[34] Voter dissatisfaction with these economic outcomes surfaced most clearly in 1992 after Bush was forced to raise taxes, and this dissatisfaction led to his defeat in the presidential election of that year.

The success of Reagan's populist appeal was indicated in both public opinion surveys and electoral outcomes. Nearly 70 percent of the general public expressed approval of his performance as president at the end of his second term. Despite his personal popularity, no permanent electoral realignment occurred to make the Republicans the majority party during the Reagan-Bush years. As one source has argued, "Reagan left behind neither a permanent Republican majority nor a stronger Republican party nationally and no apparatus to extend the so-called Reagan Revolution."[35] Finally, Reagan's legacy in the social policy area is also unclear. Although Reagan captured the social conservatives of the New Right and the New Religious Right for the Republican party, Reagan's social agenda had stalled by 1985 in several key areas, including ending federal employment quotas, reintroducing school prayer, and outlawing abortion. In general, the entire social agenda was de-emphasized after the 1984 election, but social conservatives were pacified by the fact that Reagan was able to appoint over 300 federal court judges—including three members of the Supreme Court—and to promote

William Rehnquist as the Court's Chief Justice.[36] Thus, outcomes in the social policy area were left to be resolved at a later date. In retrospect, the decade of the 1980s proved to be a significant transition period, but not a decade in which a new direction for the nation was decisively established.

THE 1990S: DIVIDED GOVERNMENT AND NEW CONSTRAINTS

The 1990s revealed the full scope of the constraints operative in the new American political environment. Public frustration with "political gridlock," the persistence of divided government at the presidential and congressional levels, and the declining capacity of the economy to generate high-paying jobs were but the most visible manifestations of a complex syndrome of economic, fiscal, electoral, and political constraints that were unprecedented in modern American history. The full impact of these became clear in the patterns of political and economic behavior during the Bush and Clinton administrations, as did the reality that in all probability these constraints would persist into the twenty-first century.

The economic environment was increasingly shaped by the openness of the United States to the forces of the global market. The admonitions of those in the 1970s who argued that the American economy as a self-contained system had come to an end were validated. The reality of "stateless" corporations, the hypermobility of capital as investors moved their funds to foreign sites, and the need of businesses to downsize to retain global competitiveness became increasingly evident.[37] The most visible impact of the development of global capitalism on the American population was the shortage of well-paying jobs and the growing mass job insecurity that involved workers in all categories, including college-trained professionals. By 1992, 20 percent of working college graduates were employed in low-skill jobs, and small business, the only sector of the economy not involved in job retrenchment, paid the lowest wages and benefits.[38] In addition, the recovery from the recession of March 1991 to February 1993 produced job growth of less than 1 percent, compared to job growth of 5 percent to 7 percent in previous postwar recessions.[39] The general electorate responded to the growing threat to their economic status by punishing incumbent candidates deemed to have failed to reverse the nation's economic fortunes, first George Bush in 1992, then the Democratic Congress in 1994, and soon after House Speaker Newt Gingrich, whose standing in public opinion surveys plummeted within a year after the 1994 election, although the Republicans did retain control of Congress in 1996.

The fiscal constraints inherited from the 1980s made any large-scale government response—like the stimulus packages of the Keynesian era—impossible, even if this should be desired. Both the Bush and Clinton administrations were forced to accept that the range of feasible options had been narrowed, that budget reduction was a top priority at both the congressional and mass levels, and that any new government initiatives must be small-scale and based on new principles, at least until the end of the century.[40] The new reality was that America had become the "zero-sum society" in which any new government program that was created must be paid for by the termination of an existing one.[41] In addition, there was a more fundamental problem. Most existing large-scale government programs dated from the New Deal era and had been developed to serve an industrial society that no longer existed. As has been recently argued, such programs demonstrated "an industrial-era comprehension of social policy," based on the concepts of national community, a two-tiered workforce of skilled and unskilled workers, bureaucratization of both the public and private sectors, and entitlements as the most appropriate form of social program.[42] By contrast, a postmodern formulation of social policy must take into account the new realities of global commerce, the hypermobility of capital, the trends of restructuring and privatization, and the need for investments in human capital rather than static social entitlements.[43] Consequently, the expansion of New Deal programs, if it were possible, was unlikely to produce important and positive improvements in the nation's social and economic condition.

Throughout the period from 1990 to 1996, the most visible political constraints continued to be divided government and party dealignment. The control of the White House and at least one house of Congress by different parties contributed further to the trends of excessive partisanship, the diffusion of power, and policy incoherence that had historically existed in American politics. These problems were acute in election years and in the interactions between the Clinton administration and the Republican-controlled Congress (House and Senate) during 1994 to 1996. The outcome of the 1996 election, in which Bill Clinton was re-elected as president while the Republicans retained control of both houses of Congress, assured that the status quo, divided government, would continue at least until the end of 1998. In addition, institutional constraints involving the decline of parties and the growing influence of lobbying and research organizations also worked to limit the options of presidents, members of Congress, and party leaders. The trend of party decline, evident for three decades, accelerated in the 1990s. This trend was obvious in the declining percentage of citizens who actually voted (except in 1992), the growing number of unaffiliated voters, and public opinion surveys indicating dissatisfaction with the two major parties. All of these developments were part of the process of political dealignment at work in the political system. The most visible manifestation of the disconnection of a growing number of voters from the two major parties was the strength of the Perot bloc, which gained 19 percent of the popular vote in the 1992 presidential election by employing a populist, anti-establishment theme.[44] As the candidate of the new Reform party in the 1996 election, Perot's share of the vote was 8 percent.

As the strength of the two major political parties declined, the influence of interest groups increased to an unprecedented degree. By 1992, 92,000 registered lobbyists operated in the nation's capital, with a corresponding increase in the number of advocacy organizations (think tanks and research organizations), lawyers, consultants, and policy-minded people who numbered in the tens of thousands.[45] By 1993, 100 advocacy organizations operated in the Washington, DC, area, with the largest carrying out yearly activities budgeted at more than $10 million.[46] As the political system came to resemble a supply-side marketplace of political ideas, the contributions and activities of lobbyists and think tanks contributed to the growth of what has been called "an enormously complex conversation centered on shaping the national agenda."[47] Critics of this process point to the fact that the groups involved possessed unequal resources and that their ultimate objective was the "mobilization of bias" against measures they opposed, regardless of the effect this might have on efforts to solve national problems.[48] While the merits of this clash of rival ideas can be debated from a number of perspectives, the growth of interest groups and the influence of think tanks contributed to a number of developments that shaped the pattern of politics in the 1990s, including permanent campaigning, the rising influence of media and policy specialists, elite domination of the policy process, the growth of the influence of big money, and the proliferation of rival ideas, images, and advertisements. Democrats and Republicans alike were forced to confront the new political constraints, as the difficulty of avoiding gridlock and accomplishing even incremental gains continued to increase.

Finally, the fragmentation of the electorate continued to constitute an important constraint on the two major parties and their elected officials. Between 1992 and 1996 both polls and elections demonstrated that neither of the two major parties could claim the support of more than one-third of the electorate, and that neither had dominated the electoral era from the late 1980s to the mid-1990s.[49] None of the three prevailing projects, New Deal Keynesianism, Reaganomics, or the neoliberalism of Bill Clinton and the moderate Democrats had won the support of a majority of voters. Public opinion surveys consistently reported that 60 percent of the electorate would vote for an independent candidate for president if an appropriate person could be found.[50] Further, the complexity and volatility of election outcomes was also attributable to the fact that two different and countervailing majorities appeared to exist simultaneously.[51] One majority, formed around economic and social insurance issues, favored the Democrats. In elections in which the dominant strategic context revolved around economic concerns— as the election of 1992 did—the Democratic party was likely to win. On the other hand, on issues of culture and nationalism, a second electoral majority could be identified that favored the Republicans. The cultural and national dimension included such issues as prayer in school, peace through military strength, strengthening the police, opposition to immigration, banning pornography, and barring homosexuals from the military.[52] Ironically, although the existence of these two majorities would seem to dictate an electoral strategy in the direction of a party's strength, partisan activists in each party insisted on the development of a different agenda. Democratic activists continued to push to the forefront such issues as gay rights and affirmative action—issues on which their party was in the minority—while economic conservatives within the Republican party continued to overestimate popular support for conservative themes on economic matters.[53]

THE PUBLIC POLICY ENVIRONMENT: THE 1990S AND BEYOND

Contemporary public policy is made in a political-economic environment that has been described as post-hegemonic, postindustrial, and post-Keynesian. To this list could be added post-Reagan. The meaning of these descriptions is clear. The ability of the United States to shape the global economic order according to its interests is no longer assured, and today American society is a complex technological entity increasingly open to the forces of the global market. Such a society is no longer susceptible to easy management by domestic policy makers. Similarly, the postwar consensus on domestic policy has collapsed and a new conservative project has been advanced to fill the ideological and political vacuum. Central to this project are a series of ideas about the role of government and the relationship between state and society, which are in direct opposition to Keynesian principles. These include privatization, deregulation, tax reduction, welfare retrenchment, and the commodification of services such as health care, which would make them subject to the laws of supply and demand. Despite the existence of these principles, the current setting is also post-Reagan in that the limits and shortcomings of the economic policies of the Reagan Revolution in both the economic and electoral dimensions have been revealed. The stimulus package for the wealthiest Americans, which was the core of the Reagan program, failed to generate sufficient economic growth to compensate for tax cuts, to assure the creation of adequate numbers of high-paying jobs, and to protect the middle class from the threat of downward mobility. It is also clear that there has not been a decisive political-electoral realignment in favor of Reagan Republicanism.

The absence of a political and electoral project with majority support is nothing new in American politics, but it is a major factor in the lack of coherence and excessive partisanship that characterize the contemporary policy process. As has been noted, in the short-term, American policy makers at the national level are constrained by the weakness of national parties, the growing influence of interest groups, the ability of the media to define political issues, the existence of dual and countervailing electoral majorities, and the most severe federal budget constraints in modern American history. The most severe constraint of all, however, may be the general cynicism and hostility toward government and elected officials, a legacy of two decades of negative campaigning and high-powered opinion manipulation. The debate over public policy in America also occurs in an international environment in which conservative political and economic principles are dominant throughout the Western world, but it continues to demonstrate some uniquely American characteristics. In the country with the smallest public sector, the lowest overall tax burdens, and the highest level of economic productivity, the antitax and antigovernment impulse remains the strongest. In addition, the importance that Americans assign to social issues with religious overtones—such as opposition to abortion, establishment of prayer in school, and censorship of pornography—is also unique in the Western world.

The public policy records of the Bush and Clinton administrations suggest the course that America may take in the immediate future. Both administrations demonstrated a comparatively low set of policy expectations, a minimalist or non-interventionist style of leadership, and a tendency to risk aversion.[54] Both increasingly sought to narrow the range of their legislative agendas and to seek cooperative or shared leadership with Congress, a condition that was not easy to achieve in an era of divided government. George Bush was constrained by the popularity of his predecessor, Ronald Reagan, which precluded any expansion of federal government powers to address national problems, while the increasing visibility of those hurt by the program cuts of the 1980s also made new efforts at program retrenchment politically costly.[55] The first Clinton administration experienced not only the opposition of Republicans, but also occasional resistance from liberals within the Democratic party on anticrime measures and NAFTA. The defeat of Clinton's health care reform plan of 1993 was a serious setback to the legislative program of the moderate Democrats, and with the victory of Newt Gingrich and the House Republicans in the 1994 midterm elections, the political initiative passed temporarily to the Republicans.[56] Within a year, however, Gingrich's style, and a better understanding of his ten-point "Contract with America" by groups that would suffer from its terms, assured that most of the contract would never be enacted. Finally, both the Bush and Clinton administrations demonstrated the overwhelming primacy of partisan political calculations in the current political environment. Both displayed a constant sensitivity to public opinion ratings, a tendency to engage in symbolic rather than substantive acts, an inability to counter negative images depicted by the media, and a compulsion to submit every action to calculations of future electoral success.

Despite the existence of political and institutional constraints, the United States continues to face the policy challenges of a complex and interdependent society and of a rapidly changing post–Cold War international environment. Although there is currently a clear lack of consensus on the proper direction of future policy and on the greater question of what model American society should seek to emulate in the future, there has been sub-

stantial agreement at both the mass and elite levels concerning which problems must be confronted. Public opinion surveys consistently demonstrate a
high level of concern over management of the economy, job security, crime,
and health care. There is also substantial concern over immigration, education, the environment, and defense. Each of these issues exists in a distinct
political and social context that includes the following elements: objective
factors regarding the scope of the problem, the history of past policy initiatives, the current subjective definition of the problem in terms of other issues
on the national agenda, the alignment of political forces regarding specific
program alternatives and the choice of instruments for addressing the problem, and the general environment of political opportunities and constraints
for successful resolution. Five alternative instruments are available for
addressing each public policy issue: the four governmental options of formal
legislation, administrative regulation, budgetary allocation, or legal adjudication, as well as nongovernmental initiatives by the private sector.[57] It is important to realize that a distinct pattern of politics may prevail in each issue-area
and that opportunities for cooperation between institutions and across party
lines may differ significantly from case to case. In our current understanding
of the process, public policy making is equated with political development
and collective learning by society as it copes with new problems. The process
is, therefore, of great importance for both the present and the future.

In the nine chapters that follow, area specialists examine some of the
major issues confronting the United States as it approaches the twenty-first
century. The issue-areas are the economy, health care, education, immigration, the environment, defense policy and force posture, the electronic revolution, and the role of women in society and politics. A concluding chapter
considers recent criticisms of American political institutions and political culture and offers a tentative assessment of their ability to meet the challenges
of decision making and governance in the twenty-first century. Collectively,
the chapters indicate the diversity of the challenges facing the United States
at century's end, as well as the wide range of potential alternatives that are
available for their resolution if sufficient resources and political will can be
found. The studies also demonstrate that there is nothing inevitable about
American political or economic decline and that the country can draw inspi-
ration from its history of accomplishments and successful problem solving.

NOTES

1.   Seymour Martin Lipset, *American Exceptionalism: A Double-Edged Sword* (New York:
     W. W. Norton & Company, 1996), p. 31.
2.   Samuel P. Huntington, *American Politics: The Promise of Disharmony* (Cambridge:
     Harvard University Press, 1982), pp. 33–39.
3.   Ibid., p. 14.
4.   Lipset, p. 31.

5. Everett Carll Ladd, Jr., *American Political Parties: Social Change and Political Response* (New York: W. W. Norton & Company, 1970), p. 140.

6. Tom Kemp, *The Climax of Capitalism: The U.S. Economy in the Twentieth Century* (New York: Longman, 1990), p. 18.

7. David M. Potter, *People of Plenty: Economic Abundance and the American Character* (Chicago: The University of Chicago Press, 1954), pp. 75–127.

8. Rod Hague, "The United States," in Martin Harrop, ed., *Power and Policy in Liberal Democracies* (Cambridge: Cambridge University Press, 1992), p. 99.

9. Ibid.

10. Ladd, p. 2.

11. Steve Fraser and Gary Gerstle, "Introduction," in Steve Fraser and Gary Gerstle, eds., *The Rise and Fall of the New Deal Order 1930–1980* (Princeton, NJ: Princeton University Press, 1989), pp. xiv–xx.

12. Ibid., p. xviii.

13. See Theodore Geiger, *The Future of the International System: The United States and the World Political Economy* (Boston: Unwin Hyman, 1988), pp. 9–17.

14. This crucial issue is discussed by Borrus and Zysman, "Industrial Competitiveness and American National Security," in Wayne Sandholtz, et al., *The Highest Stakes: The Economic Foundations of the Next Security System* (New York: Oxford University Press, 1992), pp. 7–52.

15. David P. Calleo, "America's Federal Nation State: A Crisis of Post-imperial Viability?" in John Dunn, ed., *Contemporary Crisis of the Nation State?* (Cambridge: Blackwell Publishers, 1995), p. 20.

16. These points are presented by Ladd, pp. 243–311.

17. Sidney Plotkin and William E. Scheuerman, *Private Interest, Public Spending: Balanced-Budget Conservatism and the Fiscal Crisis* (Boston: South End Press, 1994), pp. 124–125.

18. Noel Jacob Kent, "To Polarize a Nation: Racism, Labor Markets, and the State in the U.S. Political Economy, 1965–1986," in Crawford Young, ed., *The Rising Tide of Cultural Pluralism: The Nation-State at Bay?* (Madison: The University of Wisconsin Press, 1993), pp. 56–63.

19. This is the thesis of Thomas Edsall with Mary D. Edsall, *Chain Reaction: The Impact of Race, Rights, and Taxes on American Politics* (New York: W. W. Norton and Company, 1992), pp. 99–153.

20. Rodolfo O. de la Garza, "Immigration Reforms: A Mexican-American Perspective," in Gillian Peele, Christopher J. Bailey and Bruce Cain, eds., *Developments in American Politics* (New York: St. Martin's Press, 1992), p. 310.

21. Crawford Young, "The Dialectics of Cultural Pluralism: Concept and Reality," in Young, ed., *The Rising Tide of Cultural Pluralism*, p. 5.

22. Geiger, pp. 42–47.

23. For an excellent analysis of the neoconservatives, see Lipset, pp. 193–200.

24. Ibid., p. 199.

25. Donald Warren, cited by Linda J. Medcalf and Kenneth M. Dolbeare, *Neopolitics: American Political Ideas in the 1980s* (New York: Random House, 1985), p. 166.

26. William C. Berman, *America's Right Turn: Richard Nixon to Bush* (Baltimore: Johns Hopkins University Press, 1994), p. 28.

27. Ibid., p. 62.

28. Medcalf and Dolbeare, p. 166.

29. Berman, p. 62.

30. For a theoretical explanation of the influence of these organizations, see David M. Ricci, *The Transformation of American Politics: The New Washington and the Rise of the Think Tanks* (New Haven: Yale University Press, 1993), especially pp. 182–207.

31. David Stoesz, *Small Change: Domestic Policy Under the Clinton Presidency* (New York: Longman Publishers, 1996), p. 196.

32. Stoesz, pp. 196–197.

33. Stanley B. Greenberg, *Middle Class Dreams: The Politics and Power of the New American Majority*, rev. ed. (New Haven: Yale University Press, 1995), p. 286.

34. Ibid., pp. 286–287.

35. Larry Berman, "Looking Back on the Reagan Presidency," in Larry Berman, ed., *Looking Back on the Reagan Presidency* (Baltimore: Johns Hopkins University Press, 1990), p. 5.

36. Walter F. Murphy, "Reagan's Judicial Strategy," in Larry Berman, ed., *Looking Back on the Reagan Presidency*, p. 210.

37. Stoesz, pp. 23–25.

38. Plotkin and Scheuerman, pp. 11, 13.

39. Ibid., p. 10.

40. Bert A. Rockman, "Leadership Style of George Bush," in Colin Campbell, S. J., and Bert A. Rockman, eds., *The Bush Presidency: First Appraisals* (Chatham, New Jersey: Chatham House Publishers, 1991), pp. 4–5, 11; and Stoesz, pp. 15–22.

41. For the arguments that comprised this thesis, see Lester Thurow, *The Zero-Sum Society: Distribution and the Possibilities for Economic Change* (New York: Penguin Books, 1980).

42. Stoesz, p. 24.

43. Ibid.

44. Greenberg, p. 231.

45. Stoesz, p. 195.

46. Ricci, p. 208.

47. Ibid.

48. Ibid., pp. 198–202.

49. Greenberg, pp. 6–7.

50. Ibid., p. 7.

51. This is the thesis of Byron E. Shafer and William J. M. Claggett, *The Two Majorities: The Issue Content of Modern American Politics* (Baltimore: Johns Hopkins University Press, 1995), pp. 1–9, 168–192.

52. Ibid., pp. 14–24.

53. Ibid., pp. 118–150, 189.

54. Colin Campbell and Bert Rockman, "Conclusion," in Campbell and Rockman, eds., *The Bush Presidency: First Appraisals*, pp. 291–294.

55. For a discussion of the problem of the political costs of retrenchment in the U.S. and Britain, see Paul Pierson, *Dismantling the Welfare State?: Reagan, Thatcher, and the Politics of Retrenchment* (Cambridge: Cambridge University Press, 1995), pp. 1–9, 27–52, 131–163.

56. For a discussion of the 1994 election and the "Contrast with America," see Clyde Wilcox, *The Latest American Revolution?: The 1994 Elections and Their Implications for Governance* (New York: St. Martin's Press, 1995), pp. 1–63.

57. Rod Hague, "The United States," in Martin Harrop, pp. 112–115.

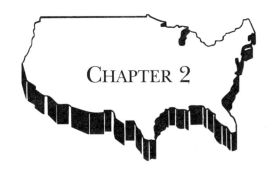

CHAPTER 2

THE POLITICAL ECONOMY
OF POSTINDUSTRIAL AMERICA

ARTHUR C. PAULSON

In the American popular mind, and probably for elites as well, the end of the Cold War, the fall of the Berlin Wall, and the dissolution of the Soviet Union all represent something of a "final" triumph of democracy. A "New World Order," we have been told, is being achieved, slowly perhaps, but inexorably, which involves democratization, economic development, and the globalization of market economies and the American way of life.

Yet, if we are living through the global triumph of democracy and markets, why do we see evidence of a decline of public confidence in American political institutions here at home? The 1992 campaign provided the stage for disquiet about serious economic problems: "It's the economy, stupid," the Clinton campaign reminded itself. But the political distemper extended to a perception, promoted by scandal and "gridlock," that American government was not working the way it should. The campaigns for Jerry Brown and Ross Perot, the movement for term limits, the public reluctance toward any new program involving new taxes, the landslide defeat of the Democrats as the incumbent party in the 1994 mid-term elections, and the partial shutdowns of the federal government over budget disputes, all seem to be an expression of this distemper.[1]

This chapter presents the argument that the current subjective distemper is a reflection of a very serious objective disequilibrium in the American political economy, as well as in the political economies of other advanced capitalist democracies. The evidence of the last two decades suggests that low rates of economic growth in advanced capitalist economies stretch across waves of the business cycle, and have become a long-term structural reality.

Low growth presents a severe problem for political elites in pluralist or consociational democracies, as bargaining over a static pie becomes a zero-sum game. Simultaneously, low growth and rapid technological change increase rates of structural unemployment. A breakdown of political consensus among elites, along with growing social inequality, combine to promote a decline in elite-mass consensus. At the same time, to combat low growth, the need for the exertion of political authority to accumulate capital for private investment increases. But the difficulty of coalition building in a zero-sum game increases the likelihood of policy stasis, just as concerted policy initiatives are most required.

The postindustrial capitalist state would seem to face the dilemma of becoming either more dysfunctional or more authoritarian. Our contemplation of global democratization in the twenty-first century must include serious consideration of the fate of democracy here at home.

HISTORICAL BACKGROUND

The current agnostic political temper is hardly typical of the American experience. Indeed, America has often been considered "exceptional" for a political culture marked by pride in its political structures, and its virtually universal support for classic liberal ideology and a capitalist economy.[2] As recently as thirty years ago, the tenor of American politics was considered remarkable for its degree of consensus at both elite and mass levels of the mainstream culture, grounded in a public confidence in American political institutions and in a rapidly growing economy. "Postindustrial society" was presented as an age in which affluence would spread through an increasingly egalitarian division of a growing economic pie. Within the academic discipline of political science, pluralist theories of democratic capitalism seemed to justify, as well as to explain, the operation of the American political economy.

PLURALIST DEMOCRACY AND CAPITALISM

Pluralist theory acknowledges that democratic capitalist societies, including the United States, are not purely democratic; that is, they do not operate by pure majority rule. But, according to pluralism, democratic capitalist societies offer about as much political democracy as is practical in a modern, organizationally and technologically complex world.

The limits on majority rule are evident. First, while capitalism produces unprecedented wealth, it also produces disparities of wealth. Citizens are not equal in their economic resources, and economic resources are also political resources. Therefore, pluralist theory concedes that economic inequality at least limits political equality and majority rule.[3]

Second, according to pluralist theory, modern capitalist societies are not organic communities that can be ruled by any single majority. Rather, they are technologically complex, specialized societies, organized around competing economic, social, and political interests. Desirable or not, rule by a majority in such societies is structurally unlikely, if not impossible.[4]

Finally, constitutional structures of government in democratic capitalist societies facilitate or limit majority rule to varying degrees. In the United States, the Constitution was designed to prevent "majority tyranny" for the purpose of protecting liberty and property rights. The result was a separation of powers among the executive, legislative, and judicial branches of government. Political structures such as the Electoral College and staggered elections limited popular influence even on the elected branches of government, while the judicial branch was insulated almost entirely.[5]

Thus, pluralist theory views modern democracy as constitutionally limited government which arrives at policy through a process of conflict and compromise among competing interests. Capitalism facilitates political democracy, according to the pluralist analysis, because it avoids the command economies of fascist and socialist states, thus preserving a degree of liberty necessary to democratic citizenship. While capitalism does not provide social equality, it is capable of approximating political equality and equality of economic opportunity.

If pluralists acknowledge that modern democracy is not majority rule, they argue that it is, at least, government by consent of the governed. Certainly elites hold the power to make policy decisions, but they gain and hold their position by "competitive struggle for the people's vote."[6] And, in their exercise of power, political elites are representing the masses. While individuals, acting alone, have little power to shape the policy agenda, they gain power when they organize. For example, David B. Truman argued that power in democratic capitalist societies resides with an "intervening structure of elites," and that masses of ordinary people "cannot act except through organization and in response to the initiative of small numbers of leaders."[7]

Thus, according to pluralist theory, despite the fact that citizens are not all politically equal, popular movements can—and do—make a difference. Although the Constitution of the United States limits majority rule by design, organized movements representing, for example, abolitionism, populism, labor, feminism, and civil rights, have all contributed to the democratization of the American political system over two centuries. But placing issues on the public agenda requires elite initiative.

PLURALISM AND CONSENSUS

Generally speaking, for a generation after World War II, the pluralist model of democracy seemed not only to explain American politics, but also to function as a stable system of democratic governance. While political scientists who subscribed to pluralism claimed to be free of bias, pluralist theory provided a justification for political consensus. Its power in the postwar period can be traced to two factors: the ideological hegemony of classic liberalism in American political culture, and extended economic growth at unprecedented rates.

The ideological hegemony of classic liberalism in America has been widely noted.[8] Despite the efforts of the framers of the Constitution, Alexis de Tocqueville warned of the "tyranny of the majority" in American society. As he put it:

> I know of no country in which, speaking generally, there is less independence of mind and true freedom of discussion than in America....
>
> In America, the majority has enclosed thought within a formidable fence. The writer is free inside that area, but woe to the man who goes beyond it....
>
> Under the absolute government of a single man, despotism, to reach the soul, clumsily struck at the body, and the soul, escaping such blows, rose gloriously above it; but in democratic republics, that is not at all how despotism behaves; it leaves the body alone and goes straight for the soul.[9]

In his classic work *The Liberal Tradition in America*, Louis Hartz agreed:

> This then is the mood of America's absolutism: the somber faith that its norms are self-evident. It is one of the most powerful absolutisms in the world.... American absolutism ... lacked even the passion that doubt might give.
>
> It was so sure of itself that it hardly needed to become articulate.... American pragmatism has always been deceptive because, glacierlike, it has rested on miles of submerged conviction, and the confirmation ethos which that conviction generates has always been infuriating because it has refused to pay its critics the compliment of an argument.[10]

In the postwar period, the hegemony of liberalism in the context of the Cold War took the form of a virulent anticommunism, reaching the level of hysteria in McCarthyism. But rather than being the isolated pathology of an individual, Joe McCarthy was more the product of an ideological hegemony which, at least periodically, "encloses thought within a formidable fence," and "refuses to pay its critics the compliment of an argument."[11] It was in this ideological environment that pluralist democracy flowered. The leaders of a variety of interest groups, however they may have differed over policy issues, shared in the consensus that capitalism, political democracy, and personal liberty all go hand in hand.

High rates of economic growth and the relatively strong political consensus of the mid-twentieth century are not coincidental. Dealing with a growing pie, political elites were able to negotiate economic issues on the basis of a distribution of benefits. On these issues, at least, coalition building could be treated as a win-win proposition.

At the mass level, affluence fed the belief that the American system provides equitably for freedom, economic opportunity, and upward social mobility. Ironically, ideological hegemony plus affluence led to observations of an "end of ideology."[12] According to this vision, mature capitalist societies had become "postindustrial" societies, service economies in which industrial class conflict was being resolved by the spread of affluence.[13] The apparent result was a growing "working class conservatism," in which the working class had come to support capitalism as vigorously as the owners of capital.[14]

THE RISE AND FALL OF THE HIGH-GROWTH ECONOMY

The construction of American prosperity in the years after World War II required massive government policy innovation. It was accomplished with a high degree of elite consensus and bipartisan support, and it promoted a high degree of mass consensus on the legitimacy of the system of political authority. The result was a social bargain that would endure uninterrupted in the United States and other advanced capitalist democracies for a generation after World War II: The public sector would provide social investments and fiscal stimulus; the private sector would profit; and the mass population would benefit from increased employment and real incomes.

The conceptual and structural framework for postwar economic policy emerged in two initiatives. The Bretton Woods Agreement of 1944 provided the dollar standard for exchange rates in the international economy. With the Employment Act of 1946, the United States government made its official commitment to use fiscal policy to stimulate economic growth and employment. Fiscal policy was based on the economic theory of John Maynard Keynes, who had argued as early as a decade before that government should set its budgets to influence and respond to the business cycle.[15] In times of depression or recession, according to Keynes, government should run budget deficits to stimulate economic growth. By the 1960s, the United States government was optimally using budgets that would be in balance at "full employment." When unemployment was more than four or five percent, the federal budget would run a deficit, stimulating economic growth and jobs; when unemployment was less than that, a budget surplus would serve to fight inflation and service the debt left by the deficits. Even when a budget deficit was planned, the budget might balance because economic growth would increase incomes and tax revenues.[16]

The full employment budget was adopted officially with the tax cut of 1964. Soon thereafter, it was not uncommon for Keynesian economists to proclaim that the business cycle had been neutralized by fiscal policy, and that the managed economy had been achieved.[17] Their claims were supported by real rates of economic growth, which averaged around 5 percent annually in the 1960s.[18]

Fiscal policy, of course, is not content neutral. The structure of an affluent society was developed on three fronts, all based on a system of public investment and private profit. On all three fronts, policies facilitated not only economic growth, but also political legitimation.

Most important, perhaps, to postwar economic growth was the reality that the war economy was never dismantled. The Cold War made defense spending a very high priority, and a policy of "military Keynesianism" facilitated the development of a military-industrial complex that became a central feature of the American economy.[19] The bipartisan foreign policy signaled the elite consensus behind a Cold War economy. In the early 1960s, defense spending represented half of federal expenditure and almost 10 percent of the gross domestic product (GDP).[20]

Second, the national government took the lead in the construction of a social infrastructure that would promote profits and jobs. The centerpiece to the new infrastructure was the Federal Highway Act of 1956, which fueled the sprawl of suburbs in metropolitan areas. The result was an economy structured around automobiles, oil, and highways. By the 1960s, the automobile and highway industries accounted for one of every six businesses and almost one of every five American jobs.[21] The institutional benefit extended to labor unions, whose membership peaked with the growth of jobs in these industries.[22] An indicator of the elite consensus behind the Federal Highway Act is that, as much as it restructured the economy, it passed the House of Representatives on a voice vote, and the Senate by 89 to 1.[23]

Finally, affluence was extended by the welfare state. Much of the welfare state, including Social Security, unemployment insurance, and Medicare, was structured initially to support middle-class and working class life. Later, economic growth promoted both new jobs and public budget revenues to redistribute income incrementally. Between 1959 and 1973, the proportion of the American population living in poverty was reduced by half, from 22 percent to 11 percent.[24] In addition to the material benefits it provided, the welfare state supported the legitimacy of the social order by building mass consensus on the system of political authority, and by disciplining poor recipients of state services.[25]

To a large extent because of the success of the Bretton Woods/Keynesian policy regime, changes in the structure of the international economy made its collapse inevitable. By 1971, when President Nixon floated the dollar to effectively end the Bretton Woods system, the Vietnam War had fueled a major inflation; the automobile culture had rendered the United States dependent on foreign oil; and the United States was a competitor, rather than the dominant force, in international trade. The oil embargo of 1973 ended the long postwar economic expansion, and with it, elite consensus on the social bargain.[26] A decade of stagflation and oil shocks was then followed by the tax cuts of Reaganomics in the 1980s.

But the economic growth of the 1980s was not as sustained as in the 1960s, and it did not spread affluence. Rather, Reaganomics was based on an upward redistribution of wealth by shifting the tax burden. Despite the market rhetoric of the Reagan administration, economic growth was promoted by massive federal budget deficits related to tax cuts and the reintroduction of "military Keynesianism."[27] Meanwhile, the proportion of the population living in poverty increased from about 11 percent in 1978 to about 14 percent in 1990.[28] If the Reagan administration had accomplished anything beyond short-term economic growth, it was a fundamentally political objective: The accumulated federal budget deficits and national debt of the 1980s would severely constrain the capacity of the federal government to act on economic issues, deeply influencing the policy agenda well into the twenty-first century.

CHALLENGES, OPPORTUNITIES, AND CONSTRAINTS

If, as the preceding analysis indicates, political consensus is linked to economic growth and affluence, democratic capitalism faces a triple challenge. First, capitalist economies in postindustrial societies are structurally low-growth economies. Second, low economic growth (or no growth) threatens political consensus in democratic capitalist systems. Finally, the combination of low growth and declining consensus presents a threat to political democracy. Each challenge will be addressed in turn.

CHALLENGE 1: CAPITALIST ECONOMIES IN POSTINDUSTRIAL SOCIETIES ARE STRUCTURALLY LOW-GROWTH ECONOMIES

Economic growth has been systematically lower in advanced capitalist societies since the early 1970s than it was between the end of World War II and that time. In the United States, economic growth averaged almost 5 percent annually during the boom of the 1960s, with unemployment as low as 3.5 percent. During a period of similar duration in the 1980s, annual economic growth averaged closer to 3 percent, with unemployment never lower than 5 percent. Unemployment reached 7 percent during the recession in 1991, and stubbornly remained there well into the subsequent recovery.[29] At this writing, after about three years of low but persistent economic growth, unemployment is reported to be a little under 6 percent, still half again as large as the unemployment rate that represented "full employment" in the 1960s.

While Keynesian economists claimed to have arrived at a method for managing the business cycle, low economic growth, declining rates of profit, and higher unemployment in postindustrial societies are now more structural than cyclical. Following, we discuss five structural limits to growth in postindustrial societies: affluence, the changing structure of work and the workforce, the changing structure of the international economy, the environment, and the fiscal crisis of the state.

First, the aggregate size and affluence of the American economy help explain low rates of growth in the gross domestic product and a generally declining rate of private profit since the mid-1960s. In 1993, the GDP increased by about $146 billion (measured in real 1987 dollars) over the previous year, almost exactly the same increase as had been enjoyed in the boom year of 1966.[30] But in 1966, that increase represented a 6 percent rate of growth; in 1993, in an economy twice as large, the rate of growth was only 3 percent.

The same is the case with private profits: While profit has increased, the rate of profit has decreased. Despite rising profits, the declining rate of profit is a severe problem because it is rate of profit, not absolute profit, which measures the capacity of a business to reinvest as it grows. Corporate profit, as a percentage of private wages and salaries, peaked in the mid-1960s. The rate of profit began to decline slowly after 1966, then declined more rapidly and structurally as the oil shocks of the 1970s increased energy costs. After the energy readjustment and the Reagan tax cuts, the aggregate rate of corporate profit increased briefly, then settled down in the mid-1980s, about one-third lower than it had been in the 1960s. If capital investment is included in the calculations, the same shifts in rate of profit are observed.[31]

Second, the changing structure of work and the workforce limits growth rates. "Fordism" in the early and mid-twentieth century had been a brand of capitalism that operated on the premise that a well-paid workforce could afford to consume what it produced, thereby increasing profits.[32] But while rising labor compensation provides rising incomes and profits, it also threatens the rate of profit. Even if corporate earnings rise dollar for dollar with labor compensation, the rate of profit falls, which explains the need for accelerating aggregate growth in a capitalist economy. This is the classic problem described by Karl Marx, but the business accountant might understand it as the law of diminishing returns.[33]

Whether or not Marx was correct that a declining rate of profit is a central characteristic of industrial capitalism, it may prove to be an important element of postindustrial modernization in the twenty-first century. Today, a majority of the workforce is in services and information-related employment in all of the advanced capitalist societies, including the United States, where the proportion is about 75 percent.[34] Around 1970, the growth of white-collar employment was evidence of increasing incomes, affluence, and a declining rate of corporate profit. Corporate responses to the declining rate of profit led to an employment picture that is more discouraging, with the consistent decline of employment in manufacturing since 1966, and the growth of low-paying service jobs.[35] The decline of middle-income employment, if it continues, would leave us with two types of employees whose numbers would be growing in the postindustrial economy: one whose employment threatens the rate of profit by high compensation, and one whose employment threatens the rate of profit by low consumption.[36]

While there may be lower economic growth in the aggregate economy, pockets of growth will develop around small businesses and new technologies, emerging in waves of increasing frequency. Thus, where there is low growth, unemployment will increase, while high growth will be accompanied by waves of labor displacement. The total number of jobs may increase, but so will structural unemployment, not significantly related to the business cycle. Meanwhile, the gap between high and low pay, discussed previously, will be exacerbated.[37]

The structure of the workforce is also being altered significantly by the internationalization of production by multinational corporations. Increasingly, industrial jobs are exported by businesses to less developed countries to gain the benefits of cheaper labor. The decline in American employment is not random: It is mostly middle-income goods-producing jobs that disappear.

The structure of the new international economy is a third factor that appears likely to limit growth in postindustrial societies. American economic hegemony will not be re-created in a multipolar world. The shift in the cost of energy not only contributed to the end of postwar economic growth, but it illustrated that the advanced capitalist countries can no longer count on cheap and easy access to the raw materials of the less developed countries.

If the international politics of the postwar era was defined by security issues in East-West relations, the international politics of the twenty-first century seems likely to be defined by the economic issues of North-South relations.[38] Colonial relations dating back to the industrial revolution are a thing of the past, and efforts by the advanced capitalist countries of the north to maintain neocolonial relations, either by market or military means, will be increasingly expensive, particularly given the underdevelopment of the former colonies. Corporate investment from the north in cheap labor will almost certainly remain a structural characteristic of the international economy, but these investments carry two costs: increasing unemployment in the home countries, like the United States; and the economic necessity along with political obligation of investing in development and, in some cases, maintaining order in the host countries.[39]

Fourth, since the late 1960s, there has been a developing awareness of environmental limits to economic growth, or at least to industrial growth. This chapter is not constructed to establish where those limits are, but either environmental realities or environmental politics, or both, will be likely to retard growth.[40]

Finally, in a low-growth economy, the state sector faces a fiscal crisis of budget deficits and structurally low revenues. In the wake of the Reagan deficits, the federal government is severely constrained in making any new public investments, and in the current political environment, cannot use fiscal stimulus to increase economic growth. Thus, the end of sustained high rates of economic growth in the early 1970s also has produced an end to the social bargain central to the spread of affluence in the United States and other democratic capitalist systems in the postwar period.[41]

CHALLENGE 2: LOW ECONOMIC GROWTH (OR NO GROWTH)
THREATENS POLITICAL CONSENSUS IN DEMOCRATIC CAPITALIST SYSTEMS

There is significant evidence of a decline of political consensus in the United States, among both elites and masses. First, according to polling data, there has been a decline of public confidence in American political institutions and the incumbents of public office, going back to the 1960s.[42] Second, there has been a geometric increase in the number and power of special interest groups in the United States.[43] Finally, there has been a decline in the functions and power of political parties, indicated by declining voter turnout, decreasing voter identification with either of the major parties, increasing split-ticket voting, and frequently divided control of the executive and legislative branches of government.[44] Thus, interest groups, which perform the function of articulation of interests, have been increasing in power, while political parties, which perform the function of aggregation of interests into governing coalitions, have been declining.

Too often, however, the failure of policy initiatives in the United States is explained entirely in terms of "gridlock," the divided partisan control of the Presidency and Congress in the national government.[45] Gridlock in the separation of powers system is certainly an important factor in policy stasis, but bipartisan coalitions have often taken new policy initiatives, and proposals have often failed, even when one party controls both of the "political" branches of government. The gridlock explanation, taken alone, ignores socioeconomic structure as a variable in declining political consensus.

The thesis presented in this chapter is that structurally low economic growth undermines political consensus among elites. While low economic growth may not be inevitable, the measures that will prove necessary and sufficient to promoting growth in postindustrial societies require levels of capital accumulation that would also undermine public confidence in democratic capitalist systems of authority.

The initial decline in political consensus should not be attributed primarily to the economy. Indeed, the decline in political consensus predates the decline of the economy in the late 1960s and early 1970s. Civil rights, the domestic politics surrounding the Vietnam War, and abortion, for example, all promoted ideological polarization and a decline in political consensus.[46]

Daniel Bell, in his discussion of postindustrial society, offered an explanation that fit within his "end of ideology" model. As affluence spread, alternative choices of lifestyle would be promoted; as society became more complex, those choices would become more collective. Thus, the "end" of industrial-class ideologies did not preclude the development of new, relatively classless ideologies associated with affluence.[47]

Political scientists, observing electoral politics, agreed.[48] As Walter Dean Burnham put it:

> So long as these cultural struggles are intense "world view" conflicts, there is one thing that cannot be done with them. They cannot be treated in a "more-or-less" fashion … as if they were equivalent to conflicts over tariffs, taxes, or minimum wages. They inherently involve not questions of more-or-less, but either-or.[49]

However, with lower rates of economic growth, higher inflation, higher structural unemployment, and a higher federal budget deficit, economic issues, too, have become either-or issues. When economic issues are about the distribution of benefits in an era of growth, elite consensus is relatively easy to achieve: Policy can be constructed to satisfy the needs of both productivity and distribution. But if economic issues are about the distribution of costs, or new public investments in a static economy, politics becomes a zero-sum game: Each new investment requires some disinvestment. The priorities of productivity and distribution appear to be mutually exclusive.[50]

The economic issues on the agenda as the twenty-first century approaches, given budget deficits and the limits to growth, seem to demand fundamental change in policy instruments because the economic policy framework does not seem to offer answers: It appears to be a failed paradigm.[51] But as the necessity of policy change becomes more evident, elites respond all the more by acting to protect the vested interests of their groups and institutions.[52] Under these conditions, any substantial proposal is likely to generate more opposition than support. Thus, we are left with a discouraging conclusion: The more policy innovation is required, the less likely it becomes.

The decline in elite consensus is closely related to the decline in mass confidence in government. Here again, the decline in confidence was not initiated around economic issues. Rather, Vietnam and Watergate changed Americans' perception of government. But the decline of economic growth has certainly depreciated public confidence in government.

Some observers have attributed the source of the "crisis of confidence" problem to the people themselves, citing rising expectations and "excess democracy" leading to "system overload."[53] Whether the people can be so blamed is a subject for vigorous debate: Those very expectations supported the legitimacy of the political system when rapid economic growth was a reality.[54]

Now, in the absence of high rates of growth, the democratic capitalist state faces the necessity to perform potentially contradictory functions: capital accumulation and legitimation.[55] Capital accumulation functions include policies developed for the purpose of accumulating capital for investment, to stimulate productivity and economic growth. Legitimation refers to the process by which authorities manipulate symbols and economic outcomes to maintain the legitimacy of the system. During periods of rapid economic growth, the performance of these functions together is not necessarily contradictory. Keynesian fiscal policy, for example, promoted profits, jobs, and equality of opportunity. But during periods of low or no growth, capital accumulation amounts to upward redistribution of income and increased economic inequality, which threatens legitimation. When inequality is sufficiently visible that people feel their life chances to be declining, their confidence in political authority is inevitably reduced, and their sense of relative deprivation increased.

CHALLENGE 3: THE COMBINATION OF LOW GROWTH AND DECLINING CONSENSUS PRESENTS A THREAT TO POLITICAL DEMOCRACY

The criticism of democratic capitalism, from the point of view of classic democratic theory, has always been its social inequality. According to this criticism, the political and legal equality so central to democratic citizenship requires social and economic equality, because social and economic resources are also political resources.

Liberal democracy, historically specific to the capitalist state, has always taken political and legal equality to be adequate, while considering social and economic equality to be dangerous. Liberalism, as classic ideology, is premised on a belief in individual liberty, private property, the market economy, and limited republican government. According to this vision, a society founded on socioeconomic equality would present a major threat at least to the first three.[56] Democratic capitalism, thus, seeks legitimation by offering a compromise on the issue of equality: political and legal equality, without socioeconomic equality, but with some approximation of equal economic opportunity.

In the United States, support of classic liberalism is so strong as to severely limit majoritarian democracy. According to the framers of the Constitution, liberty and private property are threatened not only by equality, but by majority rule, which they do not distinguish from majority tyranny. James Madison and his colleagues designed a limited government, a republic in which the separation of powers and staggered elections prevent the electorate from acting in a concerted fashion on the whole of government in any given election. Thus, given the ideological hegemony of classic liberalism and the market economy, the United States is the most liberal and least democratic of liberal democracies, and the most capitalist and least democratic of the advanced capitalist democracies.

Whatever limits to democracy are inherent to capitalism, democracy and capitalism remain historically associated. The industrial revolution promoted democratization by building an economy based on capital, a much more dynamic form of property than feudal land. Industrial capitalism also promoted a new class system, with the middle class and working class both pushing for the development of their own brand of democratic political institutions.[57]

During the industrial age, an age of general economic expansion, the question of the relationship between equality and democracy could be finessed. But in the low-growth economies of the twenty-first century, the controversy is likely to be confronted again: Just how democratic can capitalism be in the presence of socioeconomic inequality, and the absence of high rates of economic growth? To the extent that the capitalist state seeks capital accumulation for growth, socioeconomic inequality will be increasingly apparent, threatening legitimation; to the extent that the capitalist state pursues legitimation, capital accumulation and economic growth are likely to be limited. In either case, the continued capacity of democratic capitalist systems to resolve the equality issue with equal opportunity based on economic growth is problematic.

Socioeconomic change has also deflated the power of democratic political institutions. As political parties have declined, and the power of interest groups increased, legislatures have lost power, and regulatory bureaucracies have gained power. Current trends into the postindustrial age indicate the expansion of technocratic policy making through a developing administrative state. Should these trends continue, the capacity of elites to build electoral and governing coalitions will continue to decrease, while specialized sectors of the elite will enjoy increased power to manipulate the state apparatus in their own interests.[58]

The question is thus presented for the twenty-first century: Will democratic capitalism, at the very moment of its apparent victory in the world, prove to be a political system historically peculiar to an industrial age now ending? If so, there is the danger that the carefully balanced liberal state will become something much more authoritarian. The tendency of political elites to favor social order over liberty in times of crisis was revealed even in Madison's advocacy of the Constitution:

> In framing a government which is to be administered by men over men, the great difficulty lies in this: you must first enable government to control the governed; and in the next place oblige it to control itself.[59]

OPPORTUNITIES

On the other hand, we are also presented with the opportunity to move toward a more genuine democracy. The rapid social change in advanced capitalist countries at the turn of the twenty-first century seems to contain a number of potentially democratizing trends.

First, affluence remains a reality in advanced capitalist countries, including the United States.[60] Indeed, without affluence, these societies would probably not be facing a period of relatively low economic growth. Thus, the resources to feed human and social needs, and the capacity to reproduce those resources, still exist. It is the management of those resources that will be on the political agenda of the twenty-first century.

Second, a service and information economy is an economy of intangibles. The need for services and information is not so tied to economic growth as are the demands for, say, automobiles. Information, for example, cannot be hoarded without a conscious effort to maintain its status as capital, which, so far, is going on: We are seeing new legal definitions of intellectual property. That does not change the fact that information and services are as materially different from industrial capital as industrial capital was from feudal land.

Finally, the early stages of the information age have already developed computer and telecommunications technologies compatible with direct democracy, in the home computer and the "information superhighway."

It does not follow from these economic and technological developments that the twenty-first century will be one of democratization, any more than it follows that the structural challenges to democratic capitalism will lead to authoritarian or totalitarian political systems. What can be concluded is that the careful balance of the industrial age between liberal democratic politics and capitalist economies is in jeopardy, and that the political economy of the twenty-first century is likely to present more extreme alternatives between democracy and authoritarianism, even in those systems we currently call "democratic," like the United States.

POLICY OPTIONS: THE CURRENT DEBATE

If the rapid economic growth of the postwar period offered a high degree of political consensus and an "end-of-ideology," an impending period of low growth or no growth would seem to present us with the end-of-the-end-of-ideology. The Reagan and Clinton economic packages, introduced in the first year of each presidency, each passed by handfuls of votes, with largely partisan alignments. Ideological polarization between the parties, dating back to the 1960s on cultural issues such as race, has passed to the parties today on economic issues. With the end of the postwar social bargain, economic policy proposals represent priorities that increasingly appear to be mutually exclusive: capital accumulation and productivity or demand and distributive policies.

CAPITAL ACCUMULATION

Policy decisions to promote capital accumulation to the diminution of distribution were made in democratic capitalist systems in the late 1970s and early 1980s, largely in response to the oil shocks and stagflation. In 1979, while Margaret Thatcher and the Conservatives were winning election in Britain, the Federal Reserve Board in the United States was imposing a tight monetary policy. By 1981, privatization in Britain and Reaganomics in the United

States were both being implemented, and the new economic policy was spreading. Soon, even the Socialist government of François Mitterrand in France was adopting conservative fiscal and monetary policies.[61]

Reaganomics was based on "supply side" economics, which, as the name implies, assigns a higher priority to productivity than to demand, and posits that economic growth is best promoted by the free market, with minimum government intervention in the economy. Economic growth, in turn, has a "trickle down" outcome, facilitating distribution better than government can.

Reduction of government intervention in the economy, however, has been more rhetoric than reality. While the Reagan administration continued reductions of government regulation, the reintroduction of "military Keynesianism" shifted government functions back toward national defense, and budget deficits actually increased the presence of the federal government in the economy. Thus, rather than reducing government intervention in the economy, Reaganomics marginally changed the nature of that intervention, away from distributive policies, toward policies facilitating capital accumulation and productivity.

Reaganomics was instrumental in leaving behind a budget deficit that severely constrains the federal government, limiting its policy options altogether, and channeling its choices away from distributive policies, toward encouraging capital accumulation for the private sector. This structural constraint is likely to shape the policy agenda well into the twenty-first century, and serves as a premise to the "Contract With America" offered by the Republicans in 1994 as they won new majorities in Congress.

DISTRIBUTIVE POLICIES

No sector of the American elite actually proposes policies that stimulate demand and economic distribution to the exclusion of the priorities of productivity and capital accumulation. As was the case with the social bargain constructed around Keynesian economics, the policy proposals of the Clinton administration are best understood as a program of public investment in economic growth. In that respect, these policy proposals are not very different from Keynesian economic policy.

The Clinton administration package included a number of items aimed at managing the changing structure of the American and international economies: budget deficit reduction, the North American Free Trade Agreement (NAFTA), a national service trust fund to allow students to use public service to help defer debts for higher education, welfare reform, national health insurance, and public investment in the "information superhighway." Of these initiatives, the national service trust fund and national health insurance were fundamentally distributive policies; deficit reduction, NAFTA, welfare reform, and the information superhighway all more directly served capital accumulation.

DISCUSSION

Despite some important differences in policy priorities, and despite evidence of declining elite consensus, a comparison of the Reagan and Clinton administration economic programs reveals less ideological difference than meets the eye. Capital accumulation and distributive policy in the current debate are competing priorities, rather than distinctly alternative policy directions.

Economic growth in capitalist societies always involves investment; investment requires capital accumulation; capital accumulation amounts, at least initially, to upward redistribution of wealth. For example, "military Keynesianism" found in both the Kennedy-Johnson and Reagan administrations, was a conversion of middle- and working-class incomes into capital for defense contractors, through taxes. But in the 1960s, economic growth was sustained at rates high enough to "trickle down" to the working class and poor in the form of high-wage industrial jobs and social programs. In the 1980s, economic growth was sustained, but not at rates high enough to "trickle down." Had growth in the 1960s been what is was in the 1980s, it is doubtful that much, if any, "trickle down" would have happened then either, despite the apparent ideological differences between the administrations.

Today, the Clinton administration is constrained by the national debt, a structural budget deficit, and a policy paradigm that holds that reducing the budget deficit is a paramount priority. But, so long as the balanced budget paradigm constrains policy, fiscal stimulus cannot be used to overcome structurally low rates of economic growth.[62] In the absence of stimulus in public budgets, economic growth will require capital accumulation in the private sector; that is, upward redistribution of wealth. The social bargain has been replaced by zero-sum politics.

RECOMMENDATIONS FOR THE TWENTY-FIRST CENTURY

If the analysis presented in this chapter is correct, the early twenty-first century is likely to be a period of low economic growth. In a capitalist society, low growth translates into a more uneven distribution of wealth, unless there is political intervention to the contrary. Such intervention, however, faces strong opposition from the owners of capital. Because the legitimacy of the system is related to a belief by the mass of the population in economic opportunity and upward social mobility, democratic capitalism is likely to arrive at a crisis sometime during the twenty-first century, perhaps sooner rather than later.

POLITICAL CULTURE AND ALTERNATIVE FUTURES

Eventually, given low growth, democratic capitalist societies will reach a turning point at which a decision will be made, either to move toward greater democracy, or toward greater capitalism. The latter choice would require greater capital accumulation, and authoritarian measures in response to declining legitimacy. Democratization would require a radically more even distribution, at least of incomes, if not of wealth.

Either way, the uneasy association of democracy and capitalism would be challenged. Postindustrial modernization in the twenty-first century is likely to present Americans, elites and masses alike, with choices that are foreign to American political culture. As Alfred DeGrazia put it:

> If America were to confront the future frankly, it would have to make decisions for which it is psychologically unprepared. Its actual risks would not increase: It is important to realize this fact; no decision that America might take to realize a new peaceful world order would require more sacrifices than the future will demand of it in any case.[63]

The emerging political economy will not permit Americans to wish the hard choices away. While the specific institutional character of economic modernization and political development in the twenty-first century remains unclear, what is visible is that the United States and other advanced democratic capitalist societies will continue to become more interdependent social systems. Social choices, particularly as they relate to the economy, will be increasingly collective choices.[64]

Collectivism is foreign to American political culture. The language of the culture is constructed on the premise that collectivism is inherently authoritarian. The framers of the Constitution supported liberty and limited government as a preferable middle ground between two collective authoritarianisms: minority tyranny and majority tyranny.

We need to remember what the framers understood, that democracy, majority rule, is political collectivism. But contrary to their fear that majority rule was a threat to liberty, two centuries later it appears that democracy is prerequisite to the survival of liberty. Given American political culture, the twenty-first century will probably see a much stronger libertarian movement in the United States than in other postindustrial societies. But, while that movement may or may not be successful in preserving rights to privacy and personal autonomy, it will not change the increasingly collective nature of the choices to be made on the economy. The unanswered question, then, is whether American collectivism will be democratic or authoritarian.

POSTINDUSTRIAL MODERNIZATION AND DEMOCRATIZATION

This chapter has argued that so long as industrial capitalist economies provided structurally high rates of economic growth, the relationship between social equality and political democracy could be rationalized. In a low-growth economy, that political luxury is no longer an option. Thus, democratic capitalist systems in the postindustrial era face the choice between more capitalism and more democracy.

Choice 1: More Capitalism A policy choice prioritizing accumulation of capital would result, at least initially, in more unequal distribution of income and wealth. In a low-growth economy, that outcome is unlikely to be self-correcting, and would move the democratic capitalist system toward a legitimation crisis. The choice for more capitalism would be initiated with free market policies. But, faced later with declining public support related to unequal distribution of income, a regime that chose to continue along the capital accumulation path would ultimately have to enforce its decisions by increasingly authoritarian measures.

In a service economy, a capital accumulation policy regime would hasten the development of an economically polarized workforce, with a relatively well-paid technocratic strata, a low-wage service strata, and a declining proportion of middle-income workers. With large businesses investing in new technologies, and in cheap labor in less developed countries, the displacement of American labor would accelerate. In a highly interdependent and technocratic society, regulatory relationships between monopoly capital and government agencies would continue to institutionalize, and the authority to make policy would centralize more in increasingly autonomous government bureaucracies.

What is particularly distressing about this scenario is that it can happen without catastrophic change in political institutions, or constitutional law. We are not talking about the formal imposition of a police state. Rather, the greater danger is the slow decline in the relevance and power of democratic institutions and an increase in the power of governmental institutions removed from electoral politics. The decline of American political parties in recent decades, the increased power of special interest lobbies, and the increased electoral power of incumbents in the U.S. House of Representatives (effectively insulating the House from the voters) all illustrate this trend in its early stages.

Ironically, this increased power of "iron triangles" in specialized policy areas does not translate into increased policy effectiveness. While the power of special interests to prevent policy innovation increases in this process, consensus among elites on positive policy alternatives declines. Thus, the scenario described above unfolds all the more: Declining policy effectiveness leads to more social disorder, promoting more authoritarian measures to restore order, and so on.

Choice 2: More Democracy The alternative to the preceding scenario is a more genuine development of democracy in advanced capitalist societies. The question must be posed: Is postindustrial democracy economically viable? Recommendations for the twenty-first century are motivated as much by a concern for political democracy as by a concern for economic outcomes. But if economic health and political democracy are to be maintained simultaneously, a policy strategy directed at building a new social bargain, even in the relative absence of economic growth, is required. The following principles are proposed to facilitate such a bargain:

1. *We can no longer worship at the altar of a balanced annual federal budget, even in theory. On the other hand, the reality of fiscal crisis means we cannot afford to retain the current structural budget deficit.* The truth of the second statement, and the accumulated deficits of the 1980s have created a political environment in which all deficits are treated as equally evil. But a constitutionally mandated balanced budget is unwise because it constrains the federal government from using fiscal stimulus during times of recession. Worse, a balanced budget amendment would require the government to raise revenues and decrease spending during recessions, exactly when taxes should be cut and spending increased. In addition, a mandated balanced budget would mean that capital accumulation would be derived entirely from an upward redistribution of wealth in the private sector, exactly the contrary condition to what we need if we are to construct a new social bargain.

Ironically, the new economy requires us to reapply the Keynesian idea central to the old social bargain: the full employment budget that balances not annually, but across waves of the business cycle. During recessions, public deficits would fuel economic growth; during booms, budget surpluses would supply the revenue to pay the debts associated with the deficits.

2. *Structural change requires either-or economic choices, and cannot be managed with incremental additions to an old institutional and technological base. We live in an age in which technologies are being displaced rapidly by new technologies, a process that requires new economic policies accompanied by new political institutions.* Currently, democratic capitalist systems, particularly the United States, are attempting to manage postindustrial modernization with industrial-age political institutions; the result is political decay, declining capacity in the face of increasing demand.[65] The predominant response by political elites over the past quarter century has been to attempt to decrease public demand placed on government, and to discard the social bargain.[66] But the problem is not public demand. Regardless of transitory shifts in public opinion, the increasing complexity and interdependence of postindustrial society puts new demands on government in any case, requiring new capacities for social management.

The need for new institutions does not, however, lead to the conclusion that government must grow indiscriminately. Fiscal constraints and political decay indicate instead that new social investments must displace the old. The choices we face are qualitatively alternative directions of social development.

The early twenty-first century will be a period of very rapid transition. Postindustrial modernization continues to displace the technologies and institutions of the industrial age. The Cold War is over, and the defense sector of the economy is declining. New technologies continue to displace labor, both in manufacturing and management. The pace of change itself continues to increase; what once took generations now takes years, and people's lives are altered radically. It is inevitable that in such an atmosphere there will be, in the long run, an increasing demand for public services and new policies. In a democratic society, only government can both manage the transition and articulate the collective choices involved.

The Clinton administration deserves credit for recognizing structural change in the economy. But its early proposals also suffered from the appearance of being simply more big government, offering as they did new programs and institutions without removing the old. If the functions of the welfare state are going to increase, its services must be offered more directly through new, more decentralized institutions. And, fiscal reality seems to demand that these new institutions displace, rather than supplement, the old.

Instead of becoming an entirely new layer of bureaucracy, comprehensive national health insurance, if ever adopted, might incorporate Medicare and Medicaid. The new National Service system might incorporate federal service corps like the Peace Corps, make the federal government an employer of last resort in the face of increasing structural unemployment, and replace the Federal Student Loan programs for higher education. Current welfare reform programs add new cost and layers of bureaucracy through their mentality of enforcement and control;[67] instead, the best welfare reform might be a guaranteed income administered through a negative income tax, not unlike the one proposed by the Nixon administration, combined with a work requirement administered by the National Service.

Unfortunately, displacement of old policies and institutions also means displacement of powerful vested interests. The problem, in terms of political consensus, is: How can we make the necessary either-or choices without playing the very zero-sum game that makes any new social bargain unlikely?

This is a challenging question, indeed. But it has been answered successfully before, not the least impressive case being the formation of the policy regime that led to the social bargain after World War II. Nothing less sweeping than that achievement will be required in the early twenty-first century.

3. *Rapid social change will require a clear definition of ultimate political authority in the policy-making process.* The information economy is both part of the problem and part of the solution for postindustrial society. Computer technologies will fuel the pace of change and the displacement of labor, even as they enhance capacities for social management. Technological change could facilitate either a centralization or decentralization of power. Computer networks forming what is now called the "information superhighway" could promote the power of "Big Brother."[68] Or they might build decentralized and democratic decision-making processes that can yield collective outcomes. Where the industrial economy required specialization in large organizations for the sake of efficiency and mass production, the postindustrial economy can yield collective results that can be customized to the needs of small decentralized units, such as business franchises, communities, and individu-

als. Whether the new technologies of the twenty-first century will be used to democratize or centralize political authority, however, is not so much a technical decision as it is a political one.

The fact that the technology capable of radically decentralizing decision-making processes already exists means that large bureaucracies are no longer functionally necessary to administer policy, and that even legislatures could be rendered obsolete in the twenty-first century. Direct democracy, which appeared to the framers of the Constitution to be both implausible and undesirable for "extended republics," is now certainly technologically plausible. The question remains as to whether a computer-based direct democracy is politically feasible or desirable.

There are reasons to doubt the political feasibility of a computer-based direct democracy. First, who would set the agenda and draft proposals? How would such proposals gain access to the ballot? Second, the home computer as the central voting mechanism would have an atomizing influence, unhealthy for democratic citizenship. Third, the vote count in a home-computer system would present threats to privacy and the secret ballot. Finally, constitutional constraints would probably prevent the emergence of a computerized direct democracy.

Nor does it seem likely that the United States would adopt a more decisive but less limited parliamentary system, such as a British type fusion of powers.[69] But however deep the constitutional separation of powers is in American political culture, it cannot long remain feasible without very significant reform: It is simply too oriented to preventing innovation and preserving the status quo to manage the increasing momentum of social change likely to characterize the twenty-first century. If the base of the American constitutional system is to be retained, a mechanism for locating the final authority to determine policy, even in the relative absence of consensus, must be added. If democracy is our organizing principle, that authority would best be determined by majority rule.

The reforms of the Fifth Republic in France provide an example of how a democratic capitalist system in crisis was maintained in the face of rapid change, and suggest a model for constitutional reform in the United States. A constitutional amendment may accomplish the goal of promoting democratization and locating final political authority simultaneously:

Amendment XXVIII

Section 1: Each house of Congress and the President shall have the unilateral power to submit legislation that has been approved by at least one house of Congress to the people in a national referendum. A referendum that is approved by a majority of voters participating shall become law.

Section 2: Such referenda shall be subject to the same limitations under this Constitution as an act of Congress.

Section 3: The right of citizens otherwise qualified to vote under this Constitution shall not be abridged at a national referendum.

Section 4: The Congress shall have the power to enforce this article by appropriate legislation.

Such an amendment preserves the separation of powers system, and defines the authority of elected officials to frame referenda, while assigning to the electorate the authority to resolve a policy deadlock by majority rule. And it enables majorities to act, even in the absence of policy consensus among elites.

The preceding proposal is not offered in the anticipation that it will produce necessarily preferable policy outcomes, even those advocated above. The reverse may often be the case when vested interests use their access to mass media in the public debate.[70] But a national referendum would locate authority clearly in the governed, and it would allow voters to stand responsible for the policy options they select, providing experience that would improve the quality of government by the people over time. Finally, while Americans seem generally to associate democracy with liberty, and liberty with limited government, the national referendum alternative would provide for strong government that is not distant, or centralized, or authoritarian, but that is capable of being decisive and authoritative. Democracy is, after all, majority *rule*.

CONCLUSION

The recommendations contained here are constrained by continuing realities that remain currently foreseeable into the twenty-first century, particularly the capitalist economy, American political culture, and the constitutional system. But the recognition of these constraints might, if anything, underestimate the possibilities for change, either for the better, or to the contrary. The reader should remember that we are talking about social change associated with the end of the industrial age in the United States, a change also associated with what the postindustrial society might become. In thinking about the political economy of the twenty-first century, we need to consider the constraining realities, but also to imagine what we might have predicted had we been alive at the dawn of the twentieth. How much would we have foreseen then? How many Americans would have foreseen the New Deal, or the world wars, or the end of *de jure* segregation? How many Americans alive at the dawn of the nineteenth century would have foreseen the Civil War, or the end of slavery, or the development of industrial America? How many would have proclaimed such visions to be "impossible"? How much do we foresee now?

NOTES

1. For a timely discussion of the current political distemper, see E. J. Dionne, *Why Americans Hate Politics* (New York: Simon & Schuster, 1991).

2. See Gabriel Almond and Sidney Verba, *The Civic Culture: Political Attitudes and Democracy in Five Nations* (Boston: Little, Brown, 1963); Alexis de Tocqueville, *Democracy in America*, J. P. Mayer, ed., George Lawrence, trans. (New York: Doubleday, 1969); and Louis Hartz, *The Liberal Tradition in America* (New York: Harcourt, Brace and World, 1955). For an excellent anthology on American exceptionalism, see Byron E. Shafer, ed., *Is America Different?* (Oxford: Clarendon Press, 1991).

3. This argument, while acknowledged by pluralists, is more central to theories of democratic elitism. See, for example, Peter Bachrach, *The Theory of Democratic Elitism* (Boston: Little, Brown, 1966); C. B. Macpherson, *The Life and Times of Liberal Democracy* (Toronto: Oxford University Press, 1977); C. Wright Mills, *The Power Elite* (New York: Oxford University Press, 1956); Gaetano Mosca, *The Ruling Class* (New York: McGraw-Hill, 1896); E. E. Schattschneider, *The Semisovereign People* (New York: Holt, Rinehart and Winston, 1960); and Joseph Schumpeter, *Capitalism, Socialism and Democracy* (New York: Harper, 1942).

4. See particularly Robert A. Dahl, "Polyarchal Democracy," in Dahl, *A Preface to Democratic Theory* (New Haven: Yale University Press, 1956).

5. See Alexander Hamilton, James Madison, and John Jay, *The Federalist Papers*, Roy P. Fairfield, ed. (New York: Doubleday, 1966). See particularly #10 and #51, both by Madison. See also Dahl, "Madisonian Democracy," in *A Preface to Democratic Theory*, note 4.

6. Schumpeter, *Capitalism, Socialism and Democracy*, p. 269.

7. David B. Truman, "The American System in Crisis," *Political Science Quarterly* 74 (1959), pp. 488–489, as cited in Bachrach, *The Theory of Democratic Elitism*, pp. 48–50.

8. In addition to theories of American exceptionalism, including de Tocqueville and Hartz, cited in note 2, there is the large body of neo-Marxist literature on the ideological hegemony of capitalism in democratic capitalist societies. See, for example, Jurgen Habermas, *Legitimation Crisis* (London, Heinemann, 1973); Philip K. Lawrence, "The State and Legitimation: The Work of Jurgen Habermas," in Graeme Duncan, ed., *Democracy and the Capitalist State* (Cambridge: Cambridge University Press, 1989); C. B. Macpherson, "Do We Need a Theory of the State?" in Duncan, ed., *Democracy and the Capitalist State*; Herbert Marcuse, *One-Dimensional Man: Studies in the Ideology of Advanced Industrial Society* (New York: Beacon Press, 1964); and Alan Wolfe, *The Limits of Legitimacy* (New York: The Free Press, 1977). For an excellent commentary, see Anthony H. Birch, *The Concepts and Theories of Modern Democracy* (London: Routledge, 1993), pp. 37–41.

9. de Tocqueville, *Democracy in America*, Vol. 1, pp. 254–255.

10. Louis Hartz, *The Liberal Tradition in America*, pp. 58–59.

11. For example, see Murray B. Levin, *Political Hysteria in America: The Democratic Capacity for Repression* (New York: Basic Books, 1971) for an excellent account of the "witch hunt" against communists conducted by Attorney General A. Mitchell Palmer after World War I. Anticommunist fervor after World War II was certainly not limited to conservative Republicans like McCarthy. Rather, it was central to elite consensus. Mayor Hubert H. Humphrey of Minneapolis, for example, purged communists in the process of forming the Minnesota Democratic-Farmer Labor Party (DFL), even while he was serving as chair of

Americans for Democratic Action (ADA) and taking the lead among liberal Democrats in the civil rights movement. See Carl Solberg, *Hubert Humphrey: A Biography* (New York: Norton, 1984), pp. 111–123.

12. See particularly Daniel Bell, *The End of Ideology: On the Exhaustion of Political Ideas in the Fifties* (New York: The Free Press, 1960).

13. Daniel Bell, *The Coming of Postindustrial Society: A Venture in Social Forecasting* (New York: Basic Books, 1973).

14. See Robert E. Lane, *Political Ideology: Why the American Common Man Believes What He Does* (New York: The Free Press, 1962; Lane, "The Fear of Equality," *The American Political Science Review* 53 (1959), pp. 35–51; Lane, "The Politics of Consensus in the Age of Affluence," *The American Political Science Review* 59 (1965), pp. 874–895; Seymour Martin Lipset, "Some Social Requisites of Democracy," *The American Political Science Review* 53 (1959), pp. 69–105; Lipset, *Political Man* (New York: Doubleday, 1960); Lewis Lipsitz, "Working Class Authoritarianism: A Re-evaluation," *American Sociological Review* 30 (1965), pp. 103–109; Herbert McClosky, "Consensus and Ideology in American Politics," *The American Political Science Review* 58 (1964), pp. 361–382.

15. John Meynard Keynes, *The General Theory of Employment, Interest and Money* (New York: Harcourt, Brace and Jovanovich, 1964).

16. See Walter W. Heller, *New Dimensions of Political Economy* (Cambridge: Harvard University Press, 1967). See also John Cornwall, *Economic Breakdown and Recovery: Theory and Policy* (Armonk, NY: Sharpe, 1994); and James D. Savage, *Balanced Budgets and American Politics* (Ithaca, NY: Cornell University Press, 1988), particularly pp. 175–179.

17. See Heller, *New Dimensions in Political Economy*; Arthur Okun, *The Political Economy of Prosperity* (New York: Norton, 1970); Savage, *Balanced Budgets and American Politics*, pp. 175–179. See also the Council of Economic Advisers' *Economic Report of the President 1966* (Washington, DC: U.S. Government Printing Office, 1966).

18. Council of Economic Advisers, *Economic Report of the President* (Washington, DC: U.S. Government Printing Office, 1994), p. 271.

19. See particularly Richard B. DuBoff, *Accumulation and Power: An Economic History of the United States* (Armonk, NY: Sharpe, 1989), pp. 100–101; and John Kenneth Galbraith, *The New Industrial State* (Boston: Houghton-Mifflin, 1967), pp. 228–230.

20. Harold W. Stanley and Richard G. Niemi, eds., *Vital Statistics in American Politics* (Washington, DC: Congressional Quarterly, 1994), p. 361.

21. DuBoff, *Accumulation and Power*, pp. 102–104.

22. Employment in manufacturing as a proportion of the American labor force peaked in the 1960s and has declined since then. Membership in unions as a share of the labor force peaked in the early 1950s at about one in four, remained relatively steady for about two decades after that, then began a decline that has continued. See *The Economic Report of the President* (1994), p. 318; and Stanley and Niemi, eds., *Vital Statistics in American Politics*, p. 190.

23. *Congressional Quarterly Almanac 1956* (Washington, DC: Congressional Quarterly, 1957), p. 406.

24. Stanley and Niemi, eds., *Vital Statistics in American Politics*, p. 381.

25. For the classic analysis of the welfare state as an exercise in political authority, see Frances Fox Piven and Richard Cloward, *Regulating the Poor: The Functions of Public Welfare* (New York: Pantheon, 1971). For a particularly interesting discussion of the pacification of the unemployed, see Kay Lehman Schlozman and Sidney Verba, *Injury to Insult: Unemployment, Class and Political Response* (Cambridge: Harvard University Press, 1979).

26. See Cornwall, *Economic Breakdown and Recovery*, particularly pp. 129–212; DuBoff, *Accumulation and Power*, particularly pp. 113–141; Peter Gourevitch, *Politics in Hard Times: Comparative Responses to International Economic Crises* (Ithaca: Cornell University Press, 1986), particularly pp. 181–217; Stephen Gill and David Law, *The Global Political Economy: Perspectives, Problems and Policies* (Baltimore: John Hopkins University Press, 1988); and Joan Edelman Spero, *The Politics of International Economic Relations* (New York: St. Martin's Press, 1977).

27. See Cornwall, *Economic Breakdown and Recovery*, pp. 213–229; DuBoff, *Accumulation and Power*, pp. 160–163; Gourevitch, *Politics in Hard Times*, pp. 208–214; and Savage, *Balanced Budgets and American Politics*, pp. 198–236.

28. Stanley and Niemi, eds., *Vital Statistics in American Politics*, p. 381.

29. Council of Economic Advisers, *Economic Report of the President 1994* (Washington, DC: U.S. Government Printing Office, 1994), pp. 270–271 and 314.

30. *Economic Report of the President* (1994), p. 270.

31. Conclusions derived from *Economic Report of the President* (1994), pp. 295 and 298.

32. For an excellent discussion of Fordism, see Michael Harrington, *The Next Left* (New York: Holt, 1986), pp. 18–46.

33. Karl Marx, *Capital: A Critique of Political Economy* (originally published in 1867).

34. *Economic Report of the President* (1994), pp. 318–319.

35. *Economic Report of the President* (1994), pp. 318. For a detailed discussion of the decline of manufacturing as a source of employment, see Barry Bluestone and Bennett Harrison, *The Deindustrialization of America* (New York: Basic Books, 1982).

36. For a discussion of the impact of this trend on working Americans and the aggregate economy, see Donald L. Bartlett and James B. Steele, *America: What Went Wrong?* (Kansas City: Andrews and McMeel, 1992), particularly pp. 2–30.

37. See Harrington, *The Next Left*, pp. 144–153.

38. Indeed, the Vietnam War may yet come to be understood as a watershed event, representing the last major war of the East-West conflict, and, simultaneously, the first major war of the North-South confrontation. While Vietnam discouraged military adventurism for a time, U.S. military operations since that time, including most notably the Persian Gulf War, but also Grenada, Panama, the bombing of Tripoli, etc., have all been in the less developed countries of the south. The same can be said of U.S. activities in Chile and Nicaragua, the British engagement in the Falkland Islands War, and French and United Nations military operations in Sub-Saharan Africa.

39. See Gill and Law, *The Global Political Economy*, particularly pp. 280–301; and Charles K. Wilbur and Kenneth P. Jameson, eds., *The Political Economy of Development and Underdevelopment* (New York: McGraw Hill, 1992).

40. See, for example, Richard J. Barnet, *The Lean Years* (New York: Simon & Schuster, 1980); Paul Ehrlich, *The End of Affluence* (New York: Random House, 1974); and Robert L. Heilbroner, *An Inquiry into the Human Prospect* (New York: Norton, 1970). See also Lester R. Brown, et. al., *The State of the World* (New York: Norton, annually since 1984), for excellent and current discussions of global and economic and environmental policy issues.

41. See Cornwall, *Economic Breakdown and Recovery*; DuBoff, *Accumulation and Power*; and Savage, *Balanced Budgets and American Politics*. See also James O'Connor, *The Fiscal Crisis of the State* (New York: St. Martin's Press, 1973), for an early classic discussion of the fiscal crisis of the capitalist state. See also Alan Wolfe, *America's Impasse: The Rise and Fall of the Politics of Growth* (New York: Pantheon Books, 1981).

42. Stanley and Niemi, *Vital Statistics in American Politics*, pp. 169–170.

43. Ibid., pp. 173–196.
44. See, for example, Paul Allen Beck and Frank J. Sorauf, *Party Politics in America*, 7th ed. (New York: HarperCollins, 1992); William Crotty, *American Parties in Decline* (Glenview, IL: Scott, Foresman, 1984); and Martin P. Wattenberg, *The Decline of American Political Parties* (Cambridge: Harvard University Press, 1990).
45. For an excellent discussion of the relationship among democracy, policy effectiveness, and the separation of powers, see James L. Sundquist, *Constitutional Reform and Effective Government* (Washington, DC: Brookings, 1986).
46. See Robert Huckfeldt and Carol Weitzel Kohfield, *Race and the Decline of Class in American Politics* (Chicago: University of Illinois Press, 1989), for a discussion of the decline of class-based electoral coalitions, and the rise of ideological polarization associated with race.
47. Bell, *The Coming of Postindustrial Society*. See also David Apter, "Ideology and Discontent," in Apter, ed., *Ideology and Discontent* (Glencoe, IL: The Free Press, 1964); Bell, *The Cultural Contradictions of Capitalism* (New York: Basic Books, 1976); Walter Dean Burnham, *Critical Elections and the Mainsprings of American Politics* (New York: Norton), pp. 135–193; Walter Dean Burnham, "American Politics in the 1970's: Beyond Party?" in Jeff Fishel, ed., *Parties and Elections in an Anti-Party Age* (Bloomington: Indiana University Press, 1978); and Ronald Inglehart, *The Silent Revolution: Changing Values and Political Styles Among Western Publics* (Princeton, NJ: Princeton University Press, 1977).
48. See Everett Carll Ladd with Charles D. Hadley, *Transformations of the American Party System: Political Coalitions from the New Deal to the 1970's* (New York: Norton, 1978); Ladd, "Liberalism Upside Down: The Inversion of the New Deal Order," in William Crotty, ed., *The Party Symbol: Readings on Political Parties* (San Francisco: Freeman and Co., 1980); Teresa E. Levitin and Warren E. Miller, "Ideological Interpretations of Presidential Elections," *The American Political Science Review* 73 (1979), pp. 751–780; Richard Scammon and Ben Wattenburg, *The Real Majority* (New York: Coward-McCann, 1970); David O. Sears, Richard R. Lau, Tom R. Tyler, and Harris M. Allen, "Self-Interest and Symbolic Politics in Policy Attitudes and Presidential Voting," *The American Political Science Review* 74 (1980), pp. 670–683; and James L. Sundquist, *Dynamics of the American Party System: Alignment and Realignment of Political Parties in the United States* (Washington, DC: Brookings, 1983).
49. Walter Dean Burnham, *Critical Elections and the Mainsprings of American Politics*, p. 141.
50. For a comparative perspective on competition between the policy priorities of productivity and distribution, see especially Robert A. Isaak, *European Politics: Policy Making in Western Democracies* (New York: St. Martin's Press, 1977); and Taketsugu Tsuritani, "Japan as a Postindustrial Society," in Leon N. Lindberg, ed., *Politics and the Future of Industrial Society* (New York: David MacKay Co., 1976).
51. The same can be said about public policy as about science: See T. S. Kuhn, *The Structure of Scientific Revolutions* (Chicago: University of Chicago Press, 1970).
52. See Theodore J. Lowi, *The End of Liberalism* (New York: Norton, 1982); *The Politics of Disorder* (New York: Norton, 1971); Mancur Olson, *The Logic of Collective Action* (Cambridge: Harvard University Press, 1971); and *The Rise and Decline of Nations* (New Haven: Yale University Press, 1982).
53. See Samuel P. Huntington, "The United States," in Michael Crozier, Samuel P. Huntington, and Joji Watanuki, *The Crisis of Democracy: Report on the Governability of Democracies to the Trilateral Commission* (New York: New York University Press, 1975), pp. 59–115.
54. The debate would hinge on a matter of emphasis. Is it the expectations, or the

reality, that has changed? Perhaps it is both. Whether they miss what they had, aspire to more, or resent what others have, many Americans seem to be suffering from what Ted Robert Gurr conceptualized as "relative deprivation." See T. R. Gurr, *Why Men Rebel* (Princeton, NJ: Princeton University Press, 1970).

55.   The legitimation problem for the capitalist state is most closely associated with the neo-Marxist theorists Jurgen Habermas and Alan Wolfe, cited in note 8.

56.   If there is a founder of classic liberalism, it is certainly John Locke. See "An Essay Concerning the True Original, Extent and End of Government," in Ernst Barker, ed., *Social Contract* (London: Oxford University Press, 1974). For perhaps the most compelling critique of Lockean liberalism, see also C. B. Macpherson, *The Political Theory of Possessive Individualism* (Oxford, England: Clarendon, 1962).

57.   See Dietrich Rueschemeyer, Evelyne Huber Stephens, and John D. Stephens, *Capitalist Development and Democracy* (Chicago: University of Chicago Press, 1992), particularly pp. 12–78.

58.   This observation, of course, makes reference to the classic "iron law of oligarchy." See Robert Michels, *Political Parties* (New York: Free Press, 1962). See also Lowi, *The End of Liberalism* and *The Politics of Disorder*, and Grant McConnell, *Private Power and American Democracy* (New York: Knopf, 1967). A common argument found in neo-Marxist theory is that while royal absolutism was the appropriate form of political authority for the development of early mercantile capitalism, and parliamentary democracy was appropriate for liberal market capitalism, monopoly capitalism requires a regulatory bureaucratic state. See Ernst Mandel, *Late Capitalism* (London: Verso Press, 1975); and Bob Jessop, *State Theory: Putting Capitalist States in Their Place* (University Park, PA: The Pennsylvania State University Press, 1990).

59.   James Madison, "The Federalist 51," in Hamilton, Madison, and Jay, *The Federalist Papers*, ed. Roy P. Fairfield, p. 160.

60.   United Nations Development Program, *Human Development Report* 1992 (New York: Oxford University Press, 1992), p. 189.

61.   See Gourevitch, *Politics in Hard Times*, pp. 181–217.

62.   See Savage, *Balanced Budgets and American Politics*, for an excellent analysis of the ideological power of balanced budgets in American political culture.

63.   Alfred DeGrazia, *Eight Bads, Eight Goods: The American Contradictions* (New York: Doubleday, 1975), p. 8.

64.   See particularly Michael Harrington, *The Twilight of Capitalism* (New York: Simon & Schuster, 1976), pp. 320–341, for an excellent discussion of the emergence of collectivism in advanced capitalist societies.

65.   The concept of political decay used here comes from Samuel P. Huntington, "Political Order and Political Decay," in Huntington, *Political Order in Changing Societies* (New Haven: Yale University Press, 1968), pp. 1–92.

66.   See, for example, Huntington, "The United States," in Crozier, Huntington, and Watanuke, *The Crisis of Democracy*, note 53. In this essay, Huntington, for all practical purposes, applies the concept of political decay to postindustrial modernization in the United States. He discusses a "democratic distemper" not unlike the attitude observed in the electorate by the current essay, and addresses the problem of rebuilding political order in the United States. Huntington characterized the distemper he observed in 1975 as an excess both of demands on government and democracy. I would argue that our political distemper has more to do with cynicism about government, and should be traced not to an excess of democracy, but to the fact that the American system is not democratic enough.

67.   Not all new institutions are good ideas. For example, the proposal made by

incoming Speaker of the House Newt Gingrich to put AFDC children in federal orphanages is a particularly wrongheaded idea, both because it would threaten families, and because it develops exactly the sort of bureaucratic management of social problems we should be trying to get away from.

68. The obvious reference is to Orwell's "Big Brother." See George Orwell, *1984* (New York: Signet, 1961).

69. It is the opinion of this writer, however, that in the twenty-first century, party government based in a parliamentary system would be preferable to the separation of powers system, both because the former offers a more democratic set of political institutions, and because policy making would be more effective and authoritative. For an excellent discussion of reform in that direction in the context of the American political system, see Sundquist, *Constitutional Reform and Effective Government*, note 45.

70. The issue of access to information technology is one of the clearest examples of authoritarian and democratic trends simultaneously found in postindustrial modernization. Certainly, ownership of capital in telecommunications yields real power to a relatively narrow elite. But disputes between broadcast and cable television reveal divisions within the capitalist class associated with new technologies. And while people with higher income have more access to personal computers, the "information superhighway" seems to be decentralizing access to information in the long run. Unlike the material capital of the industrial age, information is fundamentally intangible. Thus, information may prove to be an inherently more democratic form of property than industrial capital, just as industrial capital was more democratic than feudal land.

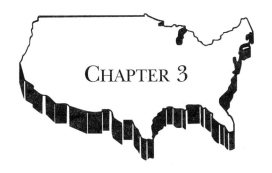

CHAPTER 3

AMERICAN INDIVIDUAL
AND PUBLIC HEALTH

CONTEXTS AND DIMENSIONS

MOSES STAMBLER

INTRODUCTION

Individual and public health are shaped within society both by external social contexts and internal health dimensions. Both individual and public health reflect the special interaction between these external contexts and internal dimensions.[1]

External contexts shape internal dimensions of health and contribute to health through general health promotion (e.g., exercise), specific disease prevention (e.g., immunization), care for illness, and rehabilitation. They shape perceptions of challenges, opportunities, and constraints, as well as acceptable future policy options for health improvement.

One external context shaping health perception and action is the values/ideology of American individualism and perspectives on the virtues of the market economy compared to social or governmental intervention.

A second significant external context is our decentralized political system featuring a separation of powers (executive, legislative, and judicial), and a division of powers (national, state, and local). The political context defines the framework of processes, relationships, and access points, and shapes debates, directions, and decisions in American health. It is through political strategies using economic resources that allocations and distribution of limited medical and other health resources are advanced. The political context also delineates an arena for resolving competing health interests, objectives, and legal structures for maximizing social and economic interests.

A third significant external context is economics. Having the most costly health care system in the world, the United States provides opportunities for advancing private or public health, as well as individual and corporate profit.

Demographics is a fourth significant external context impacting our health. Increases in the 65-plus population have resulted in expanding high-cost allocations for Medicare, Medicaid, nursing assistance, and high-tech medicine. Demographics increase traditional tensions for limited resources in society, adding the ingredient of struggles between younger and older generations to the existing social tensions.

A fifth significant external context is technological advance, impacting the political and budgetary crisis and the numbers of surviving population. Advances in technology shape debates on resource allocation, contribute to setting limits on technological intervention, and help shape powers and status structures of the health field.

Interaction with these external contexts significantly influences the functioning and significance of our internal health dimensions: organization/administration (which receives the most emphasis and medical funding); physical and social environments (stressed by environmental, public health, and social work approaches); behaviors and lifestyles (stressed by psychologists and social psychologists); and biological-genetic dimensions (stressed by molecular biologists and sociobiologists).

The following diagram illustrates spatial dimensions of interactions within and between external contexts and internal dimensions:[2]

A Model of the Interacting Influences on Individual and Public Health

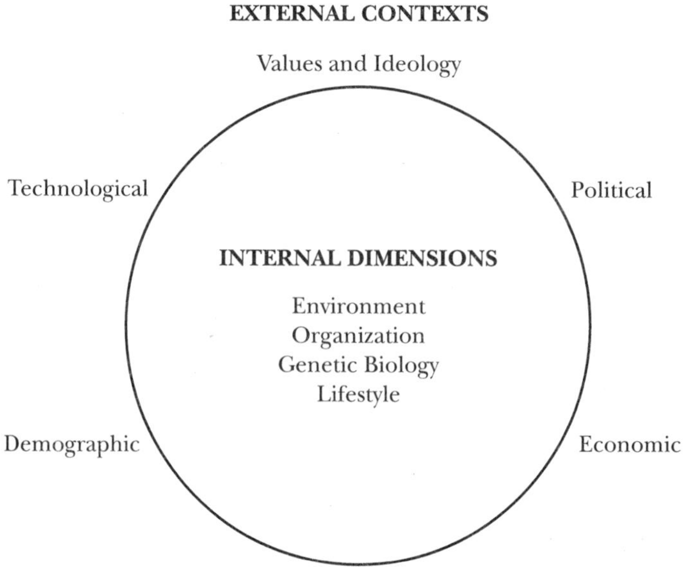

EXTERNAL CONTEXTS

Values and Ideology

Technological

Political

INTERNAL DIMENSIONS

Environment
Organization
Genetic Biology
Lifestyle

Demographic

Economic

Both contemporary and future health prospects for twenty-first century America can be better understood by looking at these health contexts and dimensions, noting past and current developments that provide foundations for twenty-first century health improvement.

CHALLENGES, OPPORTUNITIES, AND CONSTRAINTS

IDEOLOGICAL AND VALUE CONTEXT

Should health care be a social entitlement for all citizens in a political community, or should it be a commodity like food and housing, to be purchased at the discretion of the individual and on the basis of personal finances and priorities?

From the dominant American individualistic perspective, securing health services and care becomes a matter of personal choice, behavior, and personal ability to pay, characterized by terms such as "freedom to choose," "personal responsibility," and "empowerment."[3] Running counter to this traditional American perspective of health as a commodity are dominant European and Canadian views of health care as a social good to be made available on reasonably equal terms to all members of society. Basic defined health coverage for all citizens in the population is governmentally assured through taxes in those societies.

Compared to the systems that allocate health resources through national policy, the United States places heavy reliance on market forces to shape and ration medical care. Approximately 15 percent of the under-65 population in the United States do not have health insurance. In 1995, about 43.4 million Americans did not have health insurance, with the uninsured increasing at estimated rates of 1.2 million per year. Since 1989, the number of American uninsured has swelled by over 6.3 million, in addition to which we are "...facing a crisis of underinsurance. Tens of millions of Americans have seen their coverage worsen. [The increase of uninsured has been] ... a barometer of our failing health care system."[4]

In 1993, President Clinton proposed the six principles of his later defeated 1994 health reform package: security, simplicity, savings, quality, choice, and responsibility. Two of these principles, security (a guarantee of comprehensive health benefits to all, as well as transferability to 2.5 million Americans who change jobs each year) and responsibility (health as a community responsibility with everyone, including insurance and pharmaceutical companies, paying something for universally available health care), are goals for a community concept in opposition to traditional American individualistic ideology. Application of these principles was intended to halt the numbers of increasing uninsured in American health care. Approval of that plan would have been a major positive turning point for accepting community responsibility in American health, and a change in direction from American individualistic ideology.[5] Acceptance of a right to health care would have been a major break from the traditional American emphasis defining most aspects of health care as areas of individual, not public responsibility.[6]

POLITICAL CONTEXT

Our political system is a significant context influencing health dimensions. It defines our operational framework and shapes the means to advance public and private health. During the agricultural early period of this nation with only small-scale manufacturing and economic activity, effective health intervention was very limited. There was little need or value for government involvement at any level in health services and care.[7] In the contemporary period of large-scale urban society with industrial manufacturing and commerce, there is need for varying levels of governmental involvement in health through local ordinances, state laws, and federal regulations. There are extensive known health threats and potential individual and public dangers requiring governmental involvement in concerns of sanitation, pure food supply, clean water and air supply, preventive health services, toxic wastes, use of effective medical intervention and care, and other issues related to public health and safety of citizens. Large-scale corporate operations and hazardous activities by special interests and individual citizens increasingly require effective governmental involvement and appropriate regulation for the health of the citizenry.[8]

Interest groups have invested large amounts of money and other resources to shape American health care. In the fourteen years leading up to the 104th Congress, "...more than $150 million in campaign contributions helped keep health care reform off the national agenda." In the first twenty-one months of the Congress elected in 1992, "...those same interests added another $37.9 million in contributions to protect themselves from the public demand for meaningful health care reform."[9] Later, "In 1993 and 1994, hundreds of special interests spent over $100 million to influence the outcome of this public policy issue."[10] Direct contributions of $8,240,694 were made by political action committees (PACs) to members of Congress serving on five key congressional committees.[11]

In our contemporary period, we need a domestic counterweight for the disadvantaged with federal authority to maintain the public's interest. Lester Thurow, a prominent economist, points out, "With the death of Communism and, later, market socialism as economic alternatives, capitalists have been able to employ more ruthless approaches to getting maximum profits without worrying about political pressure ... capitalism is on the march."[12] In 1994–1995, there was a reassertion of states' rights in devolution attempts to overturn a central federal role in the health of Americans.[13]

There is political antagonism to federal regulation in different dimensions of health, but it is particularly pronounced in environmental areas where private profit may come into broadest conflict with public interest.[14]

The contemporary environmental health movement was ignited by the 1962 publication of Rachel Carson's *Silent Spring*. By the early 1990s, environmentalism had become more acceptable. Several federal agencies were established with responsibility to reduce environmental damage and to promote needed environmental regulations.

Pollution as a significant issue was marked by the first Earth Day proclaimed for April 22, 1970, and was followed by environmental laws enacted by Congress that brought cleaner air, water, and wetlands preservation, and an end to toxic dumping. But there are still problems to be resolved. An estimated 40 percent of the nation's rivers and lakes are still not fit for drinking or swimming. In 1994, four years after Congress passed the Clean Air Act Amendments of 1990, one out of four Americans had problems breathing when smog reached its summer peak. Researchers at the Society for Toxicology meeting noted that more people die on bad-air days, when polluted air is more likely to hasten the death of people already afflicted with diseases. Cities with small particles of pollution emitted by automobile engines, power plants, and other sources can increase the risk of reducing the life span by 15 percent more than cities with clean air. Even in cities that meet federal clean-air standards, the risk of death is higher than in the cleanest cities. Adjusting for other reasons, poor air quality in cities is resulting in human deaths an average of two years earlier than in clean air cities.[15]

The significance of environmental degradation has been reflected in higher rates of breast cancer in post-menopausal Long Island women. Dioxin has emerged as a major symbol of chemical pollutants in the age of toxins. Federal studies in 1991 blamed high levels of dioxin for numerous cancers found in chemical workers and veterans who handled Agent Orange, the dioxin-laden defoliant used in Vietnam.[16] This was reaffirmed by Congress in 1996.

On April 6, 1995, the U.S. House of Representatives approved HR9, whose main ideas included antiregulatory measures that would temporarily suspend new regulations; subject rules on health, safety, and environmental protection to intensive scientific review; and place primary focus on existing laws on economic calculations of regulatory benefits and costs rather than health considerations.[17] In 1995–96, the Senate slowed or halted the House drive to deregulate environmental controls, which would probably have faced a presidential veto because it threatened to roll back a generation of environmental progress.[18] This slowing recognized that public and business support for smaller government and decreased regulation from 1993–95 did not include carte blanche to roll back important protective regulations for clean water, clean air, and less pollution, which was supported by most Americans.

Reported contaminated food outbreaks, such as the E. coli bacteria 0157 incident at Jack-In-The-Box (a fast-food chain), chicken with salmonella, and other microbial contaminant scares have resulted in increased public restraints on political efforts to deregulate federal controls and standards on foods. These high-profile incidents have raised public concern and reemphasized the importance of food inspection controls by the Food and Drug Administration. Annually, an estimated 6.5 million Americans are sickened thorough microbes in food and bacteria in meat and poultry, and an estimated 4,000 people die. Fortunately, the Agriculture Department will gradually introduce more effective microscopic testing, known as Hazards Analysis and Critical Control points, which was originally developed for the space program.[19]

ECONOMIC CONTEXT

We have the most costly per capita health care system in the world.[20] Canadian doctors charge about half what U.S. doctors do for many of the same services. Rising health expenditures have increased the burden of federal, state, and local governments, with the federal government carrying the heaviest load.[21] There is an estimated $200 billion wasted in the American health system.[22] However, eliminating that waste and directing resources to needed areas are not adequate ways to solve the problems of expanding health needs and increased costs of our society.

Advances in technology increase the costs of health care. These advances include development of high-tech medical procedures to prolong life, development of computer-based information systems, sophisticated tests for disease, research for health promotion and disease prevention, use of gene therapy, increased numbers of transplants, the use of high-tech equipment in intensive care units, and rehabilitative therapy through mechanical and prosthetic devices.[23] Also, there is a merging of economic and demographic concerns that portend major policy readjustment needs in health care.[24]

DEMOGRAPHIC CONTEXT

The demographic context poses challenges and constraints for health in America. One demographic challenge is an increasing aging and politically active population requiring greater use of health care resources later in life. In 1994, there were 33.2 million Americans over age 65, which is projected to rise to 35.3 million in 2000 (13 percent of the population), and to 70.2 million in 2030 (20 percent of the population). An increased life span is resulting in the elderly getting even older, with the 85-plus age group among the fastest increasing segments of the population. Also, the minority aged are an increasing group in the elderly, up from 13 percent in 1990 to 25 percent of the over-65 population projected for 2030. These population changes in the elderly can be expected to increase health care costs and expand the need for diversity and ethnic/racial sensibilities in health care services.[25]

Older people account for a higher percentage of health care costs. In 1987, the 65-plus population represented 12 percent of the population, but accounted for 36 percent of all health care expenditures (an average of

$5,360 per person—more than four times the $1,290 spent per person on younger people).[26] In 2002, they will comprise 16.1 percent of the population, thereby dramatically increasing health care costs.[27] The aging population requires an adjustment in our health organization, values, and finances. Care for the elderly now consumes approximately 40 percent of our health care budget. In 1995, Medicare served about 37 million older Americans, at a federal cost of $176 billion, up from $107 billion in 1990, for an annual growth rate of 10 percent. Unless changes are made beforehand, by 2020 the annual Medicare costs for those over 65 will be $210 billion.[28]

Medicaid costs also are projected to increase greatly. By the year 2005, the Medicaid costs are expected to reach $460 billion, nearly one-fifth of the projected federal budget. The Medicaid program for those below the poverty level provided $41.1 billion in 1990, grew to $96 billion in 1995, and is projected to be $152.2 billion in 1999. Food stamps cost $15.0 billion in 1990, grew to $26 billion in 1995, and may reach $26 billion in 1999.[29] The 104th Congress, elected in 1994, was expected to deal with the Medicaid problem by giving the states block grants. However, budgetary conflicts between President Clinton and the Republican-dominated Congress, and involvement by both Democratic and Republican governors, will probably result in a compromise between state decisions for block grants and federal government safety nets of minimum services.

Costs in the Medicare and Medicaid systems are anticipated to be budget busters, and Medicare funding is projected to break down by 2002 unless Congress is able to cut back on expenditures.[30] In 1995, the costs for Social Security, Medicare, and Medicaid benefits to seniors 65-plus were approximately $300 billion. In 2030, the annual costs for seniors are expected to swell to $3.9 trillion.[31] Cutting back on elderly entitlements, however, poses a problem for politicians dependent on the high percentage of elderly voters.[32]

Close to 30 percent of Medicare spending goes to treat elderly in the final year of life, with most of that money spent during the last month of life.[33] Our technology is exceptional, but we don't know when to stop.[34] At one time, the term "competency" reflected on the doctor's skill in saving a person's life or fighting off disease and death. Now, more and more, competency is being defined as knowing when to stop the futile use of technology and expenditure of resources.

The use of resources by the elderly portends increased conflict and age-cohort warfare between older and younger generations. The third millennium will probably experience conflict between people born after 1960 and the American Association of Retired Persons (with a reported current membership of about 37 million, and a very high percentage of voting citizens), representing competing interests for the available resources.[35] Bill Strauss and Neil Howe, authors of *Generations*, complain that "The Democrats have allowed Social Security and Medicare to become giant pyramid schemes, siphoning tax money away from young people at ever rising rates—even though today's younger generations stand no chance of getting anywhere near the deal dished out to today's seniors."[36] In 1965, there were four workers for every Medicare beneficiary. Soon after the year 2000, there will be only two workers for every Medicare beneficiary.[37] In 1960, there were 5.1 workers paying social security for every retiree receiving social security. In the year 2000, it is estimated there will be only 3.2 workers paying Social Security for every Social Security recipient.[38] This will mean an increasing burden on young people to provide for the elderly.

The children of America also pose demographic health challenges. Health conditions for infants and toddlers in the United States are very poor. This is noted in a 1994 Carnegie report on the condition of children under 3 years of age—years critical for developing children's brain cells and biochemical connections vital for proper growth and development. Up to 3 million American children below the age of three (nearly one-fourth of this age group) live in poverty. Of the industrialized nations, the United States ranks near the bottom for providing such services as universal health care, subsidized child care, and extended work leaves for families with children under the age of three.[39]

Outbreaks of preventable childhood diseases, including measles, rubella, mumps, and whooping cough, are multiplying rapidly in the 1990s because of higher immunization costs, insufficient resources in public clinics, inadequate access to regular health care, and less affordability for children's health services. The United States is a backward nation when it comes to protecting its children from disease.

A resurgence of childhood diseases took place between 1988 and 1991, with over 60,000 mostly preschool American children stricken. According to Marian Wright Edelman of the Children's Defense Fund, every dollar invested in immunizing a child saves $10 in later health care costs.[40] However, spending up front for preventive health services, such as immunization needs of children, can pose higher personal political costs to politicians running for reelection, than shifting those costs to the future.

Differences between rich and poor in the United States are very wide and increasing. "We are the most unequal country in terms of income and wealth." In the United States, the richest 1 percent of the people (net worth of at least $2.3 million each) control nearly 40 percent of the nation's wealth, and the top 20 percent (households worth $180,00 or more) have more than 80 percent of the nation's wealth, "a figure higher than in other industrialized nations." This "...tilts the system toward those who have more resources, and ... [undermines] the sense of community and common purpose."[41]

TECHNOLOGICAL CONTEXT

Technological advances pose a cost as well as a potential benefit for health improvement. In 1992, $30 billion—almost half of the increase in the national health care bill—came from using new technology, particularly valuable with older people and with premature births.[42] The medical community often prefers the more costly technology than relevant drug therapy because of a technological arms race that leads hospitals to match their competition machine for machine. The choice of whether to prescribe heart drugs at lower cost, or to perform heart bypass surgery at approximately $40,000 is often made with bias toward higher technology and costlier solutions.

Major challenges arising from powerful new technologies are changing reproductive methods, the procreation process, and definitions and status of parenthood, children, and family. Of the 3 million annual births in the United States, more than 300 fertility clinics dealing with technological conception are responsible for approximately 30,000–40,000 births, with an industrial revenue of $2 billion. (More such births can be expected as new technologies develop, genetic screening grows, and the demand to end infertility increases.)[43]

POLICY OPTIONS: THE CURRENT DEBATE

IDEOLOGY AND VALUES

Current debates on policy options in health care are shaped by external contexts of health dimensions. Ideology and values shape our views and the debate on policy options. In the ideological context of the U.S. health culture and control, we take a more aggressive approach to health than other Western nations, and incorporate a "can do" spirit of the frontier. American doctors want to do something—preferably as much as possible.[44] The contemporary public generally views a return to a state of healthiness by a sick person very optimistically; not only as desirable but possible, if one only finds a competent physician.[45]

Our views on individual economic opportunity are extended to include good health and the alleviation of disease and disability. In our commitments to individual choice and autonomy, sickness and disease are more threatening to our sense of selfhood and self-assurance than they would be in societies that are less committed to individualism and less worried about using personal achievement as a measure of a person's worth. Our ideological emphasis on the individual contrasts, and at times conflicts, with community needs and concerns to extend insurance for basic health care to all in the community. It is important to harmoniously negotiate this frequent conflict between ideological concepts of individualism in our market economy, expressed through individual freedom and individual-targeted medicine, and the concept of societal and civic responsibility, as expressed in the public's need for community-wide basic health care.[46]

POLITICAL POLICY OPTIONS

Political policy options in the current health care debate include decisions on procedure for advancing health care reform. Two major procedural options are a comprehensive system reform, as attempted unsuccessfully by

President Clinton in 1994, or incremental pragmatic reform of the type our society has been engaged in following defeat of the Clinton health reform plan.[47] In 1996, budget cuts are shaping health care policy rather than health care policy shaping budget cuts, and the use of federal block grants for states to use in a manner they choose will further advance this trend.[48]

Ancillary groups outside the formal governmental organization play a vital role in the current American health care debate, using their access as financial contributors, consultants, and bill writers to advance their vital concerns in governmental decision making. The American political system relies heavily on interest groups to help define legislation and policy. Interests and health care groups—including insurance associations; business and labor groups; pharmaceutical companies; associations of hospitals, nursing, medical, allied and public health; as well as consumers—have significant input in health policy development. Their perception of health concerns, contributions to congressional races and political parties, and activation of their Washington-based lobbies influence the political debate, the agenda, and decisions on health care. In the 1996 environment for scrutinizing spending, congressional budget cutters have even been considering eliminating corporate entitlements related to health, such as the $1 billion per year to pharmaceutical companies located in Puerto Rico.[49]

COSTS AND POLICY OPTIONS

Economic costs of health care have significant implications for society. The high cost of our fee-for-service health care adversely affects domestic purchasing power, reduces possible investment in non-health areas, and decreases the health potential of our workforce. Current political forces in the Republican-dominated Congress are seeking to reduce government involvement in health care, increasingly privatize the health care industry, and increase its responsiveness to market forces.

The high costs of health care have been related to the fee-for-service organization, which encourages high doctors' fees, emphasis on care rather than health promotion or disease prevention, and abuse related to excessive care and fraudulent charges. However, the organization of U.S. health care has been changing, and with it cost incentives related to abuses.

In the post–World War II period, there has been a transformation of American medical organization from small-scale, personalized doctor-patient relationship models to large-scale, for-profit corporate models.[50] The latest and most drastic change in this organizational transformation is the rapid growth of the impersonal HMO/managed care delivery services, many for-profit ventures, and the decline of the traditional personal fee-for-service relationship between doctor and patient.[51]

For decades, health care has been run as a small cottage industry rather than as what currently accounts for about one-seventh of the economy. In the corporatization of health care, HMO-type managed care plans for companies with 200 or more employees increased from 47 percent in 1991 to 65 percent in 1994, with traditional fee-for-service doctor care declining from 53 percent in 1991 to 35 percent in 1994. From 1992 to 1994, 9 million people joined HMOs, bringing total HMO participants to 50 million, about a fifth of the nation's population, and more than double the growth of 4 million in HMO membership from 1990 to 1992. In 1996, because of increasing health care costs, budgetary constraints, new technologies, and an aging population, HMOs have grown faster than the economy as a whole. In 1996, membership in HMOs soared to roughly 56 million, up from 6 million about twenty years ago.

Along with this increasing membership, there have been increased complaints and a number of horror stories about failures in the quality of the services, a probable portent of major problems in the future.[52] HMOs are changing health care incentives so that doctors who previously would over-prescribe to generate business for themselves, are now under-prescribing, thus meeting tighter spending limitations—and in some cases securing bonuses for less patient care. As a result, health care incentives have reversed the trend from over-treatment to under-treatment.[53] This is resulting in a number of consumer legal suits against HMOs. There also are hierarchical consequences of this change in terms of the status and relationship of physicians with nurses and physician assistants, and of the formerly higher status and short supply specialists with generalist physicians.[54]

Shifting the burden of health care cost decisions from public health policy makers to private interests may help politicians avoid political costs for developing public policy, but it does not necessarily advance public interest. Uwe Reinhardt, a leading health economist notes, "The whole idea of managed competition is to delegate the painful decisions into the dark corners of the HMO…. You decentralize the agony and you privatize it by saying, 'Look, whatever the HMO does….' This is a smart way of delegating painful decisions from the government to the private sector."[55] Privatization of the public health interest offers little toward an overall solution for the public's interest. Neither does cost-cutting when the average remuneration for chief executive officers of the seven biggest HMOs runs $7 million (ranging from a high of $15.5 million to a low of $2.8 million). High profit objectives and robber-barons clearly run counter to public health interests.[56] The for-profit HMOs have emerged as major lobbying groups advancing the cause of HMOs on a political level. In 1994, "…the top national managed care companies and two industry trade groups spent at least $2,023,041 on lobbying expenses and campaign contributions to key lawmakers based on an analysis of Federal Election Commission data and federal lobbying disclosure forms."[57]

As more people move to managed care, HMO costs are being reduced, but as health economist Alain Enthoven has noted, "We'll have to make some sacrifices and pay a price for less costly medical care…. That means that everybody can't have everything all the time.... In some cases, that might reduce the quality of care."[58] It is hard to predict when or how a turning point will be reached.

This restructuring continues to leave the uninsured out in the cold and does not deal with their problems. Even if costs are reduced and HMOs transform the way health care providers deliver services, the question of providing universal health care remains an unresolved social issue.[59] Privatized health insurance will "cherry pick" the healthiest people for membership and find ways to avoid insuring all in the community. There is need to balance doctor complaints of impersonal, inadequate service with HMO claims for reducing costs and maintaining quality.[60]

A debated issue relates to the way our health system should be funded. The pattern in other Western industrialized nations is for a basic level of universal health care for all its citizens funded through a centralized national taxation system into which all citizens pay.[61] In the United States, health insurance has come primarily through employment. This results in reluctance of people to leave jobs because they'd lose their health insurance, and employers seeking to reduce health care costs by hiring, where possible, temporary employees without providing benefits for them. There is an expanding area of contention between employers and workers regarding health insurance. The AFL-CIO estimates that three-fourths of the days lost to strikes in 1989 involved disputes over health care. Major employer organizations, like the large-scale employer National Association of Manufacturers and the smaller scale U.S. Chamber of Commerce, want the government to fill in gaps for health care of the elderly, the poor, and the uninsured. The job-based insurance approach in the United States distorts the economy by having workers at large corporations more likely to get good health insurance than those at small corporations, and unionized workers with better health care than the non-unionized.

Health care costs are added to the overhead and are reflected in the final product price. In 1994, companies with over 500 employees paid $3,741 per health-insured employee, and companies under 500 employees paid $4,040.[62] In 1990, 26 percent of the average net earning of American companies went for medical costs.[63] These costs create an incentive for employers to hire consultants or temporary workers without health insurance coverage, and to produce offshore, affecting America's competitive economic position. Labor unions were particularly active in securing and establishing health insurance as part of worker benefit packages during World War II and in the 1950s. The serious decline in union membership (in the 1950s private employer unions enrolled 25 percent, reduced to 11 percent in 1995; in 1995 total private and public union membership enrollment averaged only 15.5 percent of the workforce) has as a consequence reduced health care insurance for American workers. By retaining employer-based insurance in the United States, we provide incentives for employers to increase their profits by expanding hiring of consultants or part-time, minimum-wage workers who are not provided health care.[64]

The number of temporary workers employed through temporary job agencies, without health care benefits, has been increasing and in 1995 reached 2.1 million. In addition, millions of other workers were initially hired as temps, without health care insurance, and did not gain their permanent status until after one year.[65]

Another debated cost issue is whether the public should pay for needed health care when these needs result from an individual's lifestyle and behavioral choices. The challenge posed by poor lifestyle choices impacts the total cost of health care in society, costing as much as $189 billion per year. What should be the public response to this costly individual behavior?[66] America's prime enemy, substance abuse, accounted for at least $140 billion of the 1994 national health bill, and alcohol and drugs are implicated in at least three-fourths of the nation's homicides, suicides, assaults, child molestations, and rape. As much as 80 percent of state and local prisoners are incarcerated for alcohol or drug-related crimes. An individual's choice of personal lifestyle becomes a public health problem. According to the Centers for Disease Control (CDC), in 1990 tobacco was reportedly responsible for 418,690 smoking-related premature deaths, a personal choice clearly impacting the public's health.[67]

We talk a "good line" for disease prevention programs, an upstream approach, in preference to waiting until the damage is done and having to pay for care and rehabilitation downstream. However, political factors are clearly at work in the decision making and seem to override public health interest.[68] Given smoking's heavy toll, in both lives and money, it would seem that public health would benefit by banning tobacco, at least for youth. However, economic and political factors come into play. Common Cause released figures indicating that from 1985 through 1994, twelve tobacco companies and lobbying groups, along with their executives, gave $16.7 million to political action committees, which in turn gave to individual members of Congress and the two political parties.[69]

The economic and political dimensions of smoking have been clearly driven home by President Clinton's stand to establish constraints for teenage smoking. The President has endorsed plans by the FDA to block cigarette sales to teens by requiring proof of age, restricting vending machine sales, and limiting tobacco ads.[70] In response, the tobacco industry has brought suit to tie up President Clinton's regulations to reduce teenage smoking. The value and significance of tobacco for American tobacco growers and manufacturers is very high on the one hand, as is the cumulative health cost for the American public on the other.[71] The 1996 revelations of how tobacco companies manipulated nicotine levels as drugs, their targeting youth, and the withholding of deleterious research information have led to a public outcry for increased government regulation.

Either indirectly through increasing the cost of health insurance or directly through medical costs, lifestyle choices may result in significant public costs. What should be done for those who choose lifestyles which are medically disabling?[72] Should smokers be eligible for lung and heart transplants related to their smoking and should alcohol abusers be eligible for liver transplants related to their drinking?[73] The Mickey Mantle and Larry Hagman cases in the summer of 1995 focused on this issue as related to liver transplants for alcoholics in the context of scarce resources.[74]

Libertarians argue that individuals have the right to do what they want with their own bodies. But this avoids the broader problem. In complex societal interrelationships, unhealthy actions of individuals may well affect the costs and resources of society to provide needed health care for others. How should we balance the freedom to foolishly punish one's own body, with society's right to restrict an activity that affects public health and societal costs? This issue of setting criteria for resource allocation is of significance in the current debate, and a portent of major ethical health issues as we advance toward the twenty-first century.

Another lifestyle debate relates to risk factors related to AIDS, heart disease, cancer, and other health concerns. There are many competing interests for the increasingly limited health care dollar, including competition between different diseases, (e.g., heart disease, diabetes, AIDS), and different economic and age groups (e.g., the poor, the children, the aged).[75] Prevention strategies are more useful and cost-effective if they can be directed at risk factors, a difficult problem for our political system that rewards and punishes actions taken at the next election rather than for the next generation. Prevention strategies with AIDS are clearly more cost-effective than care for AIDS victims.[76]

Given limited available funds, are specific health concerns getting too much or not enough money, and should each be getting more or less? Deaths from AIDS now exceed accidents as the leading cause of death of adults ages twenty-five to forty-four. In 1993, there were 38,500 reported deaths from AIDS—the eighth largest killer disease in the United States. In that year, AIDS killed 28,090 people in the twenty-five to forty-four age group, while accidents accounted for 25,960 deaths.[77] However, the leading cause of death in 1993 was heart disease, with 739,860 deaths, and the second leading cause of death was cancer at 530,870, with cerebrovascular disease killing 149,740 people.[78] How much public funding should be allocated to deal with specific diseases, given the limits of available funds? In mid-1992, there were about 218,000 cases of AIDS and approximately 130,000 deaths from AIDS in the United States. Yet research money for AIDS was $1.5 billion, approximately twice the amount for heart disease.[79] There is a clear need to set a fixed-sum limit of available spending for all diseases, but allocating funds for specific diseases and care poses a political problem of priority selection. With limited funds available, whose "ox should be gored"?

DEMOGRAPHICS AND POLICY OPTIONS

Current health debate relates to a number of concerns with particular stress on demographics of the aging population, issues of resource allocations in futile treatment of the dying, options for providing needed health care for the disadvantaged, and health issues related to abortion.

Debate is taking place regarding costs for the treatment during the final years of life. The Health Care Financing Administration has noted that close to 30 percent of Medicare spending goes to treat people in the final year of life, with the bulk of expenditure coming in the last months.[80] How much should our society provide for final heroic care of patients? One of the options available is to limit use of resources. Should health care for the elderly be limited?[81] Organ transplants typically costing $200,000 are now covered by Medicare. Medicaid costs (approximately 75 percent of which now goes for nursing home costs for the elderly indigent) are projected to reach $460 billion, nearly one-fifth of the federal budget in 2005. With inadequate resources to go around and the elderly consuming a high proportion of the resources, one proposal is to raise the eligibility age for Medicare from sixty-five to sixty-seven or seventy. A proposal being implemented is to reduce medical costs by developing incentives to have more seniors enrolled in managed care.[82]

Long-term care is already a major issue for an aging population. One can expect that paying for long-term care, already a major problem for the disabled, their families, and society, will become an increasingly serious burden.[83]

There is growing sentiment for developing public policy that sets limits and standards on care provided both toward the end and beginning of life.[84] If limits can be set by some type of consensus, society will not have to cope with fear from those who feel futile care should be curtailed, and those who ascribe to over-treatment on the belief that life should be preserved at all costs. Health expert George Annas noted, "There is no such thing as a medical standard that says you shouldn't treat, and that's the problem. Even after we had this two-year debate about our health care system that everyone knows costs too much, we can't stop. Money is no object."[85] Current care provides intensive care for elderly when they are dying, and care for anencephalic children born without brain stems or with other terminally ill conditions like kidney disease.

Another demographic debate relates to health care for the underclass of economically disadvantaged. It has long been an accepted fact that social and economic conditions affect health, although there are other significant variables involved as well.[86] Workers at the lower end of the pay scale are least likely to have needed health insurance. (Thirty-two percent of the 10.9 million workers under sixty-five who earn below $10,000 per year do not have health insurance, while only 6 percent of the 0.9 million workers who earn between \$30,000 to \$39,000 per year do not have health insurance.)[87] Health care coverage for individuals is getting more difficult to secure.[88] With approximately 43 million Americans without health insurance in 1995, our health system faces a major challenge for providing regularized health services for that population.

A heavy proportion of the uninsured are members of minority groups. Racial and ethnic minority members do not enjoy equal health care opportunity and are disadvantaged by lack of health insurance, limited choice of providers, and the cost of getting health care. An average of 31 percent of minority adults, ages eighteen to sixty-four, are without health insurance compared to 14 percent for whites in the same age group. Adding to the health problems minority adults face are the many barriers to care: less preventive care, and additional health-affecting factors, such as fear of violence and stress.[89]

Disparities in life expectancy and quality of health care related to race contribute to blacks having higher rates than whites of heart disease, cancer, stroke, diabetes, liver disease, asthma, and tuberculosis. A number of variables can be deemed responsible for these disparities, including higher black poverty rates, discrimination, greater lack of preventive care than whites, lifestyle choices, and genetics.[90] Contributing to this health inequity is the income disparity. The average income for a black married couple in 1993 was \$35,228 compared to \$42,000 for a white couple; and 45.9 percent of black children lived in poverty compared to 17 percent of white children.[91] In the 1995 progress report called *Healthy People 2000*, it was noted that the average life span for blacks is about 69.5 years versus 76.5 for whites. Deaths from causes such as injuries and AIDS take a greater toll among Hispanics, Native Americans, and blacks, compared with whites.

TECHNOLOGICAL CHANGES AND THE CURRENT DEBATE

The current debate in health care includes issues related to genetic breakthroughs. In the technological context, remarkable changes are taking place in biogenetic areas related to the Human Genome Project, the international effort to map all 100,000 human genes by 2005. These developments are turning an increased emphasis on biological and deterministic nature and away from nurture and social intervention. Advances in knowledge and use of genetic information now pose the probability that in the near future, one may get a blood test followed immediately by a computer printout of genetic predispositions to disease. This technological and diagnostic breakthrough is fueling significant current debate about the causes and intervention strategies for illness, and portends a disruption of traditional power relationships within the health field, and within society. Genes have become a cultural icon in our time, providing a malleable image that can be used in any way, dependent on the intellectual climate of the time. Currently, genetic developments are supporting a politically conservative view of genetic essentialism/determinism.[92] However, in the future, the genetic icon has the potential to be used to support reasons and means for health improvement intervention.

Focus on genetic causation has become important as we have reduced the infectious factors causing disease and developed more sophisticated diagnostic tools and gene therapies to correct disorders. We have discovered that genetic predisposition may well shape the relevance of environmental and lifestyle factors. William Schwarz notes, "What's really ahead is stunning: A total change in the way we think about disease ... [and] the role of genes."[93]

There are three major health-related areas of particular relevance for the genetic engineering technology: genetic screening for identifying genes with disease, genetic therapy during and after birth, and genetic engineering for changing genetic composition permanently at the time of insemination.[94] All three areas are costly procedures. Dr. Paul Billings reports that "Every major disorder like heart disease and cancer is partly genetic.... That means, if you add up all the hereditary diseases, about 40 percent of the nation would be considered seriously ill."[95] Should genetic screening be available as a routine procedure? Should health care include appropriate gene therapy for related diseases?

Genetic developments raise possible health-related issues of eugenics, implications for minorities and groups, regulations for genetic testing, rules for gene banks to protect privacy, confidentiality and the use of genetic information by private insurers and employers, justice-based health care to deal with individual differences, cases for and against genetic therapy and enhancement, and the possibility of generating new social classes of the genetically inferior.[96] Intervention would include establishing prevalence figures for key human traits, identifying and counseling at-risk individuals, genetic therapy for the unequal apportionment of genes, and designing eugenic strategies. Reading genetics to foretell the future will be like the ancient practice of seeking to predict the future by reading animal entrails.[97]

Geneticists are debating whether children should know what illness or illnesses lie in their future. The development of genetic testing for health can reveal potential problems of breast cancer, melanoma, colon cancer, Huntington's disease, cystic fibrosis, Tay-Sachs disease, and sickle-cell anemia as starters in the gene wars to improve health.[98] "So far, about 900 genes have been found that can cause genetic diseases, and the heated race to identify even more continues as part of the Human Genome Project" to map genes.[99] Gina Kolata points out that it is generally no more than a year or two between the discovery of a disease gene and the development of a test to foretell whether someone is likely to develop that serious disease.[100]

Technological advances are raising debates on confidentiality in areas of health care. This issue is related to the Hippocratic oath, accepted by society and sworn to by the physician, which calls for maintaining confidentiality of information about the patient. Genetics and the information revolution have made maintaining confidentiality of vital health information difficult if not impossible. Computerized medical records, managed-care data collections, and inputs from social and health services provided by employers and the public have made the collection and sale of information to decision makers very profitable. Health information of the most private nature routinely goes into electronic files and is accessible for the right price.[101] The confidentiality issue is raised by the legal dimensions of genetic testing. The Equal Employment Opportunity Commission determined on April 7, 1995, that people with genetic predisposition to disease cannot be legally discriminated against by employers. However, *de facto* genetic discrimination will probably become a major systemic problem.[102] Confidentiality issues are also being raised regarding AIDS testing for newborn children, now required in some states. Should the right of the unborn child to have AZT therapy be given to the mother, and the right of society to effectively deal with the problem supersede that of the mother to confidentiality about her AIDS condition?[103] Does the public health interest require loss of confidentiality for the individual?

In addition to technological developments in immunization, genetics are also being used to combat diseases. Genetically modified plants may soon be delivering vaccines for Hepatitis B, and we can expect shortly the use of edible plants like bananas and potatoes to be genetically engineered to deliver vaccinations for different diseases.[104] Reflecting our bias for the use of technological interventions in health, in the United States the products of genetic manipulation and engineering may be patented, while in Europe that is not the case.[105]

RECOMMENDATIONS FOR THE TWENTY-FIRST CENTURY

On the threshold of the twenty-first century, we can anticipate major changes in telecommunications and technology to impact external health contexts and internal health dimensions. Within this framework of conceptual changes, there are numerous recommendations one can make for health in the twenty-first century, based on contexts, constraints, challenges, and current debates. My overarching recommendation is that we should develop and implement a more socially inclusive and responsible concept of health care that embraces all citizens of the American community. The following recommendations are specific related components.

RECOMMENDATION 1: ARTICULATE AND ADVANCE NATIONAL POLICY AND PRINCIPLES OF A COMMUNITY HEALTH CONCEPT TO FACILITATE HEALTH CARE FOR ALL

Dr. C. Everett Koop, former U.S. Surgeon General, noted that we can and should make our health care system far better, far more caring, and far more equitable for everyone.[106] In *Healthy People 2000*, we already have a positive vision for future health of incidence and prevalence standards, but there is a need to publicly and dramatically move beyond the individual to broad community value commitments. President Clinton's six basic principles (security, simplicity, savings, quality, choice, and responsibility) advocated in his defeated 1994 comprehensive health care reform package are valuable as national guides and as a transcending vision for public health interest. These principles are particularly important reminders of higher human priorities in our market-driven economy, where public interest can easily fall prey to profit-driven decisions based on private and corporate bottom lines. To address this we need to strengthen incentives to move from an individualistic concept of health to a concept of a shared community for health responsibility and care, and to insure the many working poor who do not currently have health insurance.[107]

The large-scale corporatization of health care suggests the need to consider possible resulting dangers to public and private health. We should note fundamental issues of control, purpose and direction of health care, and how corporate profit fits into the public's health interest. Corporate players are driven more by profit interests than by public concern and interest. We need caring and compassionate models to take care of the higher-risk needy, poor, and disadvantaged, and the mentally and physically handicapped. These groups have generally been avoided by for-profit providers because they are not as profitable. "The administrative infrastructure among corporate health care providers, let alone the value and ethics of their managers, has never developed and is unlikely ever to develop in the private sector to address widespread social health needs."[108] Bottom-line returns of private profit objectives must be carefully monitored so as not to displace publicly directed humane health care services.

As citizens pursuing our personal goals in an individualistic society, we need reminders along the way of our civic responsibilities for both the common good of public health and toward other individuals pursuing goals and personal health objectives. A sense of shared community is an important ingredient. A single-payer system based on national and equitable tax contributions can extend possibilities for good public and private health care available to all as a basic right of citizenship rather than a factor of wealth. In my opinion, a universal tax-financed, single-payer system would be both preferable and logical considering the increasingly costly and exclusionary system and the need to transcend exclusive emphasis on bottom-line profitability in public health decision making. It will not provide a perfect solution to health problems, but given public controls, it can be a better solution than the current system.[109] Universality is clearly an idea whose time has come, and an obligation contemporary society should undertake. Current organization of health care, resulting in approximately 43 million uninsured, is politically, economically, and ethically untenable in an advanced democratic society, and requires changes and ideological adjustments to serve the public interest.[110]

RECOMMENDATION 2: DEVELOP EFFECTIVE INCENTIVES
FOR HEALTH PROMOTION AND DISEASE PREVENTION,
AND MAXIMIZE ASSUMPTION OF INDIVIDUAL SELF-CARE RESPONSIBILITY

For the twenty-first century, we will have to deal more effectively with problems of lifestyle choices people make that are clearly detrimental to individual health and public health care costs. We are generating increasing knowledge defining and linking risk factors and behavior detrimental to health, and will have to operationalize this knowledge into more healthy individual behavior. However, we will have to mediate between individuals' freedom to behave as they choose, making autonomous decisions on their own bodies, and broader social responsibility to the community. Certainly, education and prevention, and socially responsible programs are basic to bringing about behavioral changes for improving health. However, if individuals continue to make choices detrimental to themselves and costly to society, appropriate community responses need to be developed and implemented.[111]

Limited resources to meet increasing needs will require heavy emphasis on effective prevention programs as a way of cutting down on the costs of self-destructive lifestyles. Although we cannot limit the freedom of individuals to self-destruct, we can make greater efforts to reduce those possibilities through appropriate education-related social norms and mores. Public policy will have to be made on the extent health behavior should affect the allocation of resources to those knowingly practicing clearly negative behaviors.[112]

A group of eighteen recognized national health experts, sponsored by pharmaceutical companies, has projected a condition by the year 2010 in which: "The promotion of health and the prevention of disease are central values in a caring society. Individual behavior, organizational behavior, the management of societal and environmental hazards, and health care for all combine to make a healthy society."[113] How should a caring society, pressed for medical cures, deal with an individual's high-risk behavior?

RECOMMENDATION 3: STRIVE FOR CLEAN AND HEALTHY
GLOBAL AND NATIONAL ENVIRONMENTS

In a recent assessment by a United Nations–sponsored panel of 2,500 international scientists on global warming, a reduction has been urged in heat-trapping greenhouse gases like carbon dioxide and the burning of coal, oil, and wood. The current projection is for the average global sea level to rise a foot and a half by the year 2100, developments that are "...likely to cause widespread economic, social and environmental dislocation over the next century."[114] With less developed nations industrializing, we can anticipate increasing environmental hazards. As a member of the global community of nations, we must be concerned with our contribution to the degradation of the global environment, and move to responsible action and leadership for world community survival in the twenty-first century.

On the national level, environmental recommendations for the twenty-first century include making individual and public health a priority, and developing reasonable environmental controls to improve health conditions. Areas of scientifically based environmental dangers to public health should clearly be targeted and regulated for the public interest. We should avoid ideological constructs of the devolutionists seeking increases in state power, and support federal regulations to protect and improve public health. Of course, modern postindustrial society requires functional national, state, and local levels of government involvement to protect public health.[115]

At the threshold of the twenty-first century, rapid technological developments are posing new threats to areas of environmental health concern. Driven by corporate bioengineering research developments and the quest for new commercially viable products, new genetic strains of plants and animals are being released into the environment. Federal regulatory agencies are under heavy commercial pressure and lobbying influence to allow release of new plants and animal life forms without long-range testing data prior to release, assuring the environmental impact of the released product. Decisions related to ecology should be made with particular caution and sensitivity, and have as their priority the avoidance of possible dangers to public health, rather than be exclusively concerned with generating corporate profits. The burden of proof for safety should be on developers seeking the environmental release, rather than on the government or public to prove there is a danger.[116]

To facilitate the development of needed health controls, we should allocate sufficient money and authority for effective research and for public regulatory agencies acting to advance the health of Americans. In September 1995, Congress eliminated the Congressional Organization for Technological Assessment, which reflects a short-sighted immediate saving of funds but jeopardizes long-term public interests. We need both research and soundly based applicable regulatory intervention to protect and advance the health of Americans in the face of threats and hazards to individual and public health. Currently we are targeting and tracking progress toward a healthier future with *Healthy People 2000*.[117] This type of study, using epidemiological descriptive and analytical research, should be enhanced and extended rather than curtailed, if we wish to develop a data base useful for improving public health.[118]

RECOMMENDATION 4: DEVELOP AN ORGANIZATIONAL STRUCTURE FOR CONSENSUS DEVELOPMENT ON RATIONED RESOURCES AND RELEVANT ETHICAL ISSUES

This recommendation would deal with value issues in public health and develop a workable consensus and value standards for looking at critical emerging issues.

There is a need to develop a consensus and public policy based on acceptable rationing, setting limits, and establishing a cap on expenditures in the health arena. As we advance to the twenty-first century, reducing costs by cutting fat will not, by itself, solve the cost problem. Even if we adopt a single-payer Canadian-style system as a model, saving $100 billion per year, and even if we eliminate many abuses of our system, we must still face the reality that there won't be enough resources to satisfy all our wishes.[119] The needs of health care are unlimited but resources are limited. Uses of advanced technology can make health care and life extension more available but limits need to be set. Rationing will be necessary to maximize public health, and the health of the greatest number of individuals. The greatest good for the greatest number will require setting public policy with an eye on limits for expendable public resources.[120]

We should debate and develop public policy that defines limits in allocation of health resources. Under current practices, responsibility for setting health care policy falls on insurance companies, hospitals, employers, and doctors on the basis of factors such as wealth, race, ethnicity, and age. In addition to the financial problems of Medicare and Medicaid, we will have to face skyrocketing home care expenditures, which have nearly doubled in the last ten years, and the issue of long-term care, a major concern for our expanding aging population.[121]

Ethical issues in health care are becoming major concerns because of questions related to technological advances, limited resources, and the increasing racial and ethnic diversity of society. Moral values on health, which underlie priorities, portend to become a major focal point for health decisions. Operationalizing values will require sensitivity to religious views, ethnic feelings, cross-cultural and diverse medical systems and perspectives, and the ability to build consensus in a heterogeneous society of value and cultural diversity. With the extension of life expectancy and the advancement of medicine, we enter into an arena requiring a melding of individualized medicine with public health, and posing value conflicts of individual interest versus public interest. Typical of those emerging and problematic health concerns are issues of reproduction (contraception, abortion, vitro fertilization, surrogate motherhood); decisions about death (assisted suicide, withholding food, medicine, or truth from dying patients); doctor-patient relationships (confidentiality, HIV health workers, providing futile treatment); public policy and bioethics (screening newborns for HIV, anencephalic organ donations, markets in body parts, limiting health care for elderly, fairness of tying health care to employment, giving health insurance companies access to genetic information, preventing the Human Genome Project from leading to abuses in genetic engineering); and issues of extent and type of health care education and resource provisions for lifestyle choices (drug and alcohol abuse, tobacco usage).[122]

In the context of growing needs and limited resources, fiscal allocation must be seen as a life-and-death issue for many people. "The poor or even the modestly affluent could not decently be consigned to illness or death merely because of inability to pay."[123] We should develop public health policy in the full light of public debate, based on the principle of the right to adequate health care, in the context of limited resources, with the target of developing an ethical consensus for allocating resources.[124]

RECOMMENDATION 5: INCLUDE THE "CARING" DIMENSION ALONG WITH TREATMENT AND COMMUNICATIONS TECHNOLOGY

We must continue to develop revolutionary technology, but also include measures to ensure caring and sensitivity. There is a need to adequately stress the caring dimension along with the treatment dimension in health care. The information and communication revolutions are growing explosively. In the twenty-first century we can anticipate institutionalization of major advances currently heralded in the organization, delivery, and scope of the health care field. Major health care reform, temporarily sidetracked in 1994, is not dead, and its reorganization is being driven incrementally by technology and economics rather than by comprehensive political planning.

We are in the process of creating portable and potentially global health care through telemedicine.[125] The traditional "house call" of yesteryear will probably be replaced by on-line (computer) appointments, with physicians making virtual reality visits.[126] Contributing to the change are the growth of communication networks, a generation of people more at ease with computers, and a shift toward patient responsibility. Internet diagnostic and therapeutic systems are already in operation. People can now plug into medical databases, input their symptoms, and interact with the system prior to getting a computer-generated diagnosis, prognosis, or therapeutic suggestion. On-line consultations between patients and doctors would help bridge the gap in low-population or rural areas. This could reduce or eliminate the need for most doctor visits. Already, patients are communicating via the Internet with doctors as well as with other people who suffer the same afflictions. Uses of telemedicine and the Internet will bring major changes in the hierarchy of health care delivery and in the different dimensions of health, changing the structure, substance, process, and power of relationships.

Electronic breakthroughs in medical care will include uses of robot physicians to perform long-distance operations, lasers to kill skin cancer cells and remove tooth decay, new methods to regenerate organs, thereby rendering a number of organ transplants obsolete, sensors attached to the body that will enable a doctor to quickly measure a person's vital signs, and analyzers to help kill bacteria in meat-packing plants, kitchens, and restaurants. Computers are currently being used as diagnostic tools for detecting and measuring breast cancer and other diseases, and to provide treatment prognoses.[127]

Given communication and technological developments that are capable of contributing to health improvement, it is critical that we retain the human dimension and develop ways to include caring and sensitivity to human needs for all segments of the population. We should institutionalize the social dimension as part of the curing process so that compassion and care are retained. One way is to further develop an appropriate focus and development of those social dimensions of society that have health implications (e.g., education, jobs, stress, opportunities, insurance, family services). Dr. James C. Hurowitz proposes that we end medicalization of social ills and change to a social model that places adequate focus on changing society to improve health. He suggests developing a National Institute of Social Health to finance research and coordinate the social science of health, and reallocate money from the medical care system to illness prevention and meaningful health promotion through a cleaner environment.[128] Ideally, that would be a positive link tying together the social areas affecting health. Barring that type of institutionalization, we should at least retain a humanistic and compassionate focus in health, and ensure that we do not lose interest or a sense of responsibility.

Included in this caring dimension should be the development of culturally sensitive health programs addressing needs of the increasingly culturally and racially diverse American population, and consequent alternative approaches in the twenty-first century. Current general health education programs are not adequate to deal with the increasingly diverse American population, and will have to be modified and targeted in culturally sensitive ways.[129]

RECOMMENDATION 6: RETAIN AND EXTEND CURRENT GLOBAL PERSPECTIVES

We must regularly review international dimensions of health care, and debate comparative organizational approaches being used in other nations to deal with specific health concerns. Given the new, and in some cases revolutionary, technological advances, demographic changes and fiscal restraints of the present and expectations for the twenty-first century, it is essential that we think globally in terms of comparative approaches used to deal with health concerns. There are no quick fixes or solutions, and actions in these different areas may bring about reactions in other dimensions and contexts of health. It is essential that we consider the data and experiences of other nations facing similar types of problems, and take into account the differing cultural contexts. The movement into uncharted waters suggests a continuing need for rolling reform, whereby the responses to changes are quickly inputted and worked through for maximum health advantage and benefit for the population.

Donald Henderson of the President's Office of Science and Technology Policy has called for a global surveillance system to provide a better global structure and staff to detect either new or emerging viral diseases.[130] With this type of comparative updating we can develop more extensive surveillance for detecting and controlling the most feared and deadly viruses of AIDS, influenza, smallpox, shingles, and other health problems that may develop. The health needs are clearly there, but the current political order will require fine tuning to be capable of responding to this challenge.

CONCLUSION

The United States in the twenty-first century will be a nation of greater diversity of race, ethnicity, and values, with a top-heavy pyramid of the elderly. Nationally, the health of our people will be buffeted by social, demographic, technological, and rationing issues of generational and population equity, and globally, by environmental, economic, and political problems related to the global village. These changes and challenges will require pragmatic responses to extend public health care to the dispossessed and to improve public and private health. Culturally sensitive and targeted responses will be needed in the dimensions of health care related to organization, environmental regulations, effective prevention of illness through lifestyle changes and biogenetics.

Our political process provides for discussion and compromise, but it would be helpful to have a leading federal agency to profile and publicize these interacting forces for the general public, the way *Healthy People 2000* progressively tracks for the professionals. The major health issue of the future—rationing of scarce resources—will require a more accessible and debatable public forum for developing public policy. A government agency needs to take the responsibility of publicizing an annual report on the state of the public's health, with information of value for public debate and discussion. The forums developed for Clinton's 1994 health plan proposal and the Oregon Plan focused for a limited period on the central issue of health, but there is need for a long-range and continuing productive public involvement in the contexts and dimensions of public health. A healthy population is a critical concern for the next century, and it should be an issue on the front burner because it is literally a matter of life and death.

NOTES

1. James C. Hurowitz, "Toward a Social Policy for Health," *The New England Journal of Medicine,* July 8, 1993, pp. 130–133.
2. The degree to which each of these dimensions is a significant cause of morbidity or mortality depends on the specific health concern. Strategy decisions relating to extent and quality of possible intervention in any of the four dimensions generally are shaped by external influences of ideology/values, political perspectives, cost, demographic changes, and technological changes.
3. Uwe Reinhardt, "Turning Our Gaze from Bread and Circus Games," *Health Affairs,* Spring 1995, pp. 33–36.
4. Keith Bradsher, "Rise in Uninsured Becomes an Issue in Medicaid Fight," *The New York Times,* August 27, 1992, p. A1.

5. White House Policy Council, *The President's Health Security Plan: The Complete Draft and Final Reports of the White House Domestic Policy Council* (New York: New York Times Books, 1993).

6. Moses Stambler, "Public Must Set Parameters on Health Care Policy," *New Haven Register*, Nov. 25, 1993, p. 15.

7. In the early American national period, the agrarian tradition of Thomas Jefferson and James Madison sought to preserve freedom by limiting the powers of government. Small government in an agrarian society of small economic units would protect the freedom of the small individual. This agrarian view contrasted with the Hamiltonian nationalist perspective, which stressed the need for strong central government to use commerce and industry to advance American economic power.

8. Henry Bamford Parkes, *The American Experience* (Westport, CT: Greenwood Press, 1982); and Richard Hofstadter, *Social Darwinism in American Thought* (Boston, MA: Beacon Press, 1992).

9. Michael Podhorzer, "Unhealthy Money: Health Reforms and the 1994 Elections," *International Review of Health Services*, 1995, p. 394.

10. The Center for Public Integrity, "Well-Healed: Inside Lobbying for Health Care Reform," Part I, *International Journal of Health Services*, p. 411.

11. See Jane Fritsch, "Tobacco Companies Pump Cash into Republican Party's Coffers," *The New York Times*, Sept. 13, 1995, p. A1.

12. Lester C. Thurow, "Companies Merge; Families Break Up," *The New York Times*, Sept. 3, 1995, p. A11.

13. The legal basis for devolution of power from the federal government to the states is a reassertion of the Tenth Amendment as applied to health, reserving those powers to the states, not given the federal government. The limiting features of the Tenth Amendment serve as levers in an attempt to restrict federal authority in the health area. See John Kenneth Galbraith, *American Capitalism: The Concept of Countervailing Powers* (New Brunswick, NJ: Transaction Publications); and John Kenneth Galbraith, "Blame History, Not the Liberals," *The New York Times*, Sept. 19, 1995, p. A21.

14. Currently, the environmental dimension has become a major area to crystallize the political conflict over challenges and constraints between those calling for central federal regulations and control standards, and those pressing for a devolution of power and authority to the states. The political economy affects environmental issues.

15. Philip J. Hilts, "Dirty-Air Cities Far Deadlier Than Clean Ones, Study Shows," *The New York Times*, March 10, 1995, p. A20.

16. Diana Jean Schemo, "L.I. Breast Cancer Is Possibly Linked to Chemical Sites," *The New York Times*, April 13, 1994, p. A1.

17. The nature of the HR 9 as it has been passed clearly reflects the hostile reaction to environmental regulations developed over the past two decades. The regulatory reform as proposed by House Republicans would have brought the regulatory process to a halt not by repealing basic laws but by making it impossible to put them into effect.

18. John Cushman, "Republicans Will Start from Scratch in Revising Law on Toxic Dumps," *The New York Times*, Jan. 31, 1995, p. A15.

19. Anita Manning, "E. Coli Poisoning Rises; Cook Meat Thoroughly," *USA Today*, Oct. 29, 1995, p. D1; and Robert Greene, "New Rules for Meat Aimed at Bacteria," *USA Today*, Feb. 1, 1995, p. 4A:6.

20. In 1992, the United States spent $3,806 per capita on health care (13.6 percent of GDP; up from 9.3 percent in 1980), compared to under $1,949 spent by Canada (10.3 percent of GDP), slightly over $1,775 spent by Germany (8.7 per-

cent of GDP), and $1,376 spent by Japan (6.9 percent of GDP). Despite the higher levels of health expenditures in the United States, health outcomes lagged behind those in many developed nations. In 1991, despite lower expenditures compared to the United States, life expectancy for males at birth was longer by 4.4 years in Japan, 2.4 years in Canada, and 0.7 years in Germany. Also in that year, despite much higher expenditures, U.S. infant mortality was twice as high as Japan's. In the United States, patients paid a hidden 10 percent surcharge on bills to provide $25 billion for the uninsured, with a large part going to hospital emergency rooms that provide higher cost care for the uninsured. The White House Policy Council, *The President's Health Security Plan: The Complete Draft and Final Reports of the White House Domestic Policy Council* (New York: New York Times Books, 1993), p. 8.

21. In 1993, U.S. national health expenditures totaled $884 billion, of which $281 billion (32 percent) was spent by the federal government, and $107 billion (12 percent) was spent by state and local governments.

22. *Consumer Reports* claims that: "The U.S. is spending enough to bring every citizen high-quality, high-tech medical care if we stop squandering our resources." (*Consumer Reports*, "Wasted Health Care Dollars," July 1992, pp. 435–448.) In Sept. 1995, the Congressional Budget Office indicated that health care waste and fraud accounted for an annual estimated $110 billion.

23. See David S. Hilzenrath, "Cutting Costs or Quality," *The Washington Post National Weekly Edition*, Aug. 28–Sept. 3, 1995, p. 6; and Erik Eckholm, "While Congress Remains Silent, Health Care Transforms Itself," *The New York Times*, Dec. 18, 1994, p. A1.

24. Costs for the elderly, the major expanding population group, will be an unsustainable burden in the future, with the proportion of U.S. gross domestic product spent on Medicare and Medicaid costs expected to triple between 1993 and 2030 from 3.3 percent to 11 percent (Robert Binstock, "Health Care Policies and Older Americans," Paper delivered at the Aug. 31–Sept. 3, 1995 Annual Meeting of the American Political Science Association, Chicago, IL.).

25. Program Resources Department-AARP, "A Profile of Older Americans: 1995," American Association of Retired Persons, Washington, DC, 1995.

26. Medicare and Medicaid are both facing economic crisis situations.

27. Richard Wolf, "Division Takes Hold in Debate on Medicare," *USA Today*, May 2, 1995, p. 4A:2.

28. Doug Levy, "Medicare Braces for Baby Boomers," *USA Today*, April 13, 1995, p. 1D:2.

29. William Welch, "Most Entitlements Due a Review," *USA Today*, Jan. 9, 1995, p. 4A:3.

30. When the Medicare/Medicaid system was designed as part of Lyndon Johnson's 1965 Great Society program, the needs of senior citizens were great because half of them lacked health insurance and 25 percent lived in poverty. In 1996, nearly all seniors are enrolled in Social Security and are covered by Medicare.

31. Peter G. Peterson, "The Budget Buster," *The New York Times*, April 9, 1995, p. E15.

32. For those over sixty-five, cutting or slowing the growth of Medicare funding will mean higher premiums, more out-of-pocket medical expenses, and possible difficulty in finding doctors who accept the assigned Medicare payment.

33. In the United States, intensive care units, where the technology is more advanced and expensive, and the patients are older, take up 15–20 percent of hospital beds. In Europe, intensive care units take up 1–5 percent of the beds.

34. Hillary Stout, "Clinton's Health Plan Must Face Huge Costs of A Person's Last Days," *The Wall Street Journal*, April 22, 1993, p. 1.

35. Richard Wolfe, "Division Takes Hold in Debate on Medicare," *USA Today*, May 2, 1995, p. 4A:2.
36. Bill Strauss and Neil Howe, "End Special Favors for Seniors," *USA Today*, Dec. 6, 1994, p. 13A:2.
37. Judy Hasson and Judy Keen, "Doctors Prescribe Health-Care Vouchers," *USA Today*, June 28, 1995, p. 6A.
38. "The worker-retiree ratio has declined dramatically from 159.1 workers to a retiree in 1940 to a projected 2.0 workers per retiree in 2030." See "Social Security System Needs an Overhaul Now," *USA Today*, March 19, 1996, p. 12A.
39. The findings were part of a 1994 report by thirty prominent members of the Carnegie Corporation (Susan Chira, "Study Confirms Worst Fears of U.S. Children," *The New York Times*, April 12, 1994, p. A1:2).
40. Marian Wright Edelman, "Yes—Providing Free Vaccinations Is a Good Idea," *USA Today*, Feb. 9, 1993, p. 11A:3. In 1990, Congress and President Bush killed a proposed $90 million expansion in the federal immunization program for children.
41. Keith Bradsher, "Gap in Wealth in U.S. Called Wildest in West," *The New York Times*, April 17, 1995, p. A1.
42. Stout, note 34.
43. Jonathan T. Lovitt and Richard Price, "Reproductive Clinic, Doctors Ran Amok, Ex-Employees Claim," *USA Today*, June 15, 1995, p. 3A:2; Geoffrey Cowley, "Ethics and Embryos," *Newsweek*, June 12, 1995, pp. 66–67; and John A. Robertson, *Children of Choice: Freedom and New Reproductive Technologies* (Princeton, NJ: Princeton University Press, 1994).
44. Lynn Payer, *Medicine and Culture* (New York: Penguin, 1989), pp. 23–35.
45. However, in reality microbiological changes are taking place faster than our capability of developing antibiotics. Prior to World War II, physicians had very little control over combating the effects of disease and disability. Following World War II, however, the introduction of antibiotics, vaccines, powerful diagnostic technologies, and technologically based therapies changed medicine from a nearly helpless profession to one with a very serious interest and capability of curing.
46. Lawrence K. Altman, "A Focus on Caring as Well as Curing," *The New York Times*, August 15, 1993, p. A1.
47. Incremental piecemeal reform in health care is easier to implement in the short run, considering interest groups in our society, but may result in long-term magnification of other health-related consequences and problems. See Robin Toner, "When Health Care Cuts Cost More," *The New York Times*, June 4, 1995, Sec. 4, p. D1.
48. See Adam Clymer, "An Accidental Overhaul," *The New York Times*, June 26, 1995, p. A1; and editorial, "Jockeying for Block Grants," *The New York Times*, July 5, 1995, p. A20.
49. "End Corporate Welfare," *USA Today*, April 20, 1995, p. 12A:1.
50. Paul Starr, *Social Transformation of American Medicine* (New York: Basic Books, 1984).
51. The corporatization of health care has been rapid and extensive. See J. Warren Salmon, "A Perspective on the Corporate Transformation of Health Care," *International Journal of Health Services*, Vol. 25, No. 1, 1995, p. 11.
52. Susan Dentzer, "Shedding Light on Managed Care," *U.S. News and World Report*, May 6, 1996, p. 70.
53. Erik Eckholm, "While Congress Remains Silent, Health Care Transforms Itself," *The New York Times*, Dec. 18, 1994, p. A1.
54. Elisabeth Rosenthal, "Young Doctors Find Specialist Jobs Hard to Get," *The New York Times*, April 15, 1995, p. A1.

55. Stout, note 34.
56. Milton Freudenheim, "Penny Pinching H.M.O.'s Showed Their Generosity in Executive Paychecks," *The New York Times*, April 11, 1995, p. D1.
57. Nancy Watzman and Patrick Woodall, "Managed Care Companies' Lobbying Frenzy," *International Journal of Health Services*, 1995, p. 403.
58. David S. Hilzenrath, "Cutting Costs or Quality?," *The Washington Post National Weekly Edition*, Aug. 28–Sept. 3, 1995, p. 6.
59. Erik Eckholm, "While Congress Remains Silent, Health Care Transforms Itself," *The New York Times*, Dec. 18, 1994, p. A1.
60. There is a growing effort to bring the 65-plus group into HMOs as a cost-saving measure, which will in turn create a need to develop more HMOs. (Milt Freudenheim, "A.A.R.P. Will License Its Name to Managed Care," *The New York Times*, April 29, 1996, p. A1.)
61. The average percentage of tax taken out by the government from wages differs. For a family in Japan, it is 30.6 percent; in Canada, it is 35.3 percent; in Britain, it is 36.5 percent; in Germany, it is 38.1 percent; and in France, it is 43.8 percent. "The USA's Tax Picture," *USA Today*, Oct. 22, 1992, p. 15A:3.
62. Wire Reports, "Companies Cut Their Health Care Costs in '94," Feb. 14, 1995.
63. Nancy Jecker, "Can an Employer-Based Health Insurance System Be Just?" in Carol Levine, ed., *Taking Sides, Clashing Views on Controversial Bioethical Issues* (Guilford, CT: Dushkin Publishing, 1994), pp. 314–320.
64. In one 1992 example, Pizza Hut paid $23 million in health care costs for 11,000 full-time workers, but employed an additional 120,000 part-time workers at close to minimum wage without health care benefits. They saved $120–200 million on health care for workers without benefits. This was added to their total profit of $370 million. (Louis Uchielle, "The Employer Mandate: Big Companies Use Little-Company Arguments to Resist Insuring Workers," *The New York Times*, Aug. 20, 1994, p. A9).
65. Peter T. Kilborn, "In New Work World, Employers Call All the Shots," *The New York Times*, July 3, 1995, p. A1.
66. A report from the American Medical Association, "Factors Contributing to the Health Care Cost Problem," notes that unhealthful habits and violence are reportedly costing the nation more than a total of $189 billion annually, if one includes direct costs and losses of productivity. The 22-page report notes that, "Violence, drugs, alcohol and tobacco are wreaking havoc in our health system" ("Rise in Health-Care Costs Is Linked to Social Behavior," *The New York Times*, Feb. 23, 1993). Former Secretary of Health, Education and Welfare Joseph Califano refers to the need to deal with issues of substance abuse and addiction involving legal and illegal drugs, alcohol, and nicotine by developing effective government policy. See Joseph A. Califano, *Radical Surgery, What's Next for America's Health Care* (New York: Times Books, 1994).
67. "Cigarette Smoking—Attributable Mortality and Years of Potential Life Lost—United States, 1990," *Journal of the American Medical Association*, Sept. 22, 1993, pp. 1408–1411.
68. Sue Rusche, "Congress Turns Its Back on Teen Smoking, Drinking," *USA Today*, August 30, 1995, p. 13A.
69. Stephen Engelberg, "Who Got Tobacco Industry Donations," *The New York Times*, March 27, 1995, p. B7.
70. Jessica Lee, "Clinton Set to Limit Tobacco Use," *USA Today*, August 10, 1995, p. 12A:1.
71. In 1993, 50 million Americans smoked 485 billion cigarettes, generating $50 billion for cigarette manufacturers and $14 billion in federal, state, and local taxes. Tobacco leaf sales generated about $3 billion for farmers—about $3,782 an

acre, compared with $352 for cotton, and $208 for soybeans. ("Mostly Smoke," *Newsweek*, July 4, 1994, p. 45.)

72. Alcohol abuse is a major health problem causing more than 19,000 auto fatalities per year, and more than one-third of the deaths from fire, drowning, spousal abuse, assault, homicide, workplace injuries, divorce, hospital admissions, and lost productivity. (Mike Brake, "Needed: A License to Drink," *Newsweek*, March 14, 1994, p. 11.)

73. Lawrence K. Altman, "A Question of Ethics: Should Alcoholics Get Transplanted Livers?," *The New York Times*, April 3, 1990, p. C3.

74. Another issue related to lifestyle developed in Great Britain when a hospital cardiologist refused to perform a heart transplant unless the patient agreed to stop smoking. "Britons Smoke at Their Own Peril," *Hartford Courant*, August 29, 1993. In the United States, we are short on livers and hearts for transplants, yet we generally do not condition the transplant on the recipient giving up smoking or drinking. Moses Stambler, "Alarms Ringing on Rationing of Health Care," *The New Haven Register*, Sept. 6, 1995, p. A11.

75. In Great Britain, the government's National Health Service regularly does not provide kidney dialysis to those over 57, a procedure made available to those in need in the United States, irrespective of age. If we establish the principle of rationing with elderly services, what will prevent us from denying these services to disadvantaged groups as well? Carol Levine, "Should Health Care for the Elderly Be Limited?," in *Taking Sides, Clashing Views on Controversial Bioethical Issues*, 6th ed. (Guilford, CT: Dushkin Publishing, 1995), pp. 40–55.

76. Gina Kolata, "New Picture of Who Will Get AIDS Is Crammed with Addicts," *The New York Times*, Feb. 28, 1985, p. C3.

77. Anita Manning, "AIDS Top Killer in Ages 25–44," *USA Today*, Feb. 1, 1995, p. D1:2.

78. John Skow, "Health," *Time*, January 30, 1995, p. 68.

79. Eileen Daniel, "Is AIDS Getting More Than Its Share of Resources and Media Attention?," in Eileen Daniel, ed., *Taking Sides, Clashing Views on Controversial Issues in Health and Society* (Guilford, CT: Dushkin Publishing, 1993), pp. 50–70; and David W. Dunlap, "The Politicians Conjure Up the Different Faces of AIDS," *The New York Times*, July 8, 1995, p. A7.

80. Stout, note 34.

81. "A Profile of Older Americans," American Association of Retired Persons, Washington, DC, 1993.

82. Only 9 percent of current Medicare patients are enrolled in a managed care plan, compared to more than 67 percent of managed care patients employed in companies with over 200 workers.

83. Joshua M. Wiener, Laurel Hixton Illston, and Raymond Hanley, *Sharing the Burden: Strategies for Public and Private Long-Term Care Insurance* (Washington, DC: Brookings Institute, June 1994).

84. Daniel Callahan, *Setting Limits: Medical Goals in an Aging Society* (Washington, DC: Georgetown Press, 1995).

85. Gina Kolata, "Battle Over a Baby's Future Raises Hard Ethical Questions," *The New York Times*, Dec. 27, 1994, p. A1.

86. At the 1992 American Public Health Conference in Boston, a study was presented that noted that an extra 17,000 people a year died from heart disease, and as many as 2,000 a year from stroke because of the weak return to economic growth after a long recession. The findings suggested that economic policies that create jobs and decrease poverty could significantly reduce fatalities due to heart attacks and strokes.

87. Louis Uchielle, "The Employer Mandate: Big Companies Use Little-Company

Arguments to Resist Insuring Workers," *The New York Times*, August 20, 1994, p. A9.

88. Doug Levy, "Ill Health Will Plague 12 of Your 76 Years," *USA Today*, April 12, 1995, p. 1A.; and Peter T. Kilborn, "In New Work World, Employers Call All the Shots," *The New York Times*, July 3, 1995, p. A1.

89. American Public Health Association, "Minority Americans Shortchanged on Health Care, Survey Shows," *Nation's Health* (Washington, DC: American Public Health Association, April 1995), Report on the Lou Harris 1995 Survey for the Commonwealth Fund.

90. Peter G. Gosselin, "Studies: Recession Bad for Health Too," *The Boston Globe*, Oct. 16, 1992, p. 21.

91. "The State of Black America: Gains But Still Lagging," *USA Today*, Feb. 23, 1995, p. 8A:1.

92. Dorothy Nelkin and Susan M. Lindee, *The DNA Mystique—The Gene as Cultural Icon* (New York: W. H. Freeman, 1995).

93. Noted by William Schwarz in Hillary Stout, "Clinton's Health Plan Must Face Huge Costs of Person's Last Days," *The Wall Street Journal*, April 22, 1993, p. 1.

94. Editorial, "The Genetic Genie," *The Christian Science Monitor*, Nov. 29, 1993.

95. Christine Gorman, "The Doctor's Crystal Ball," *Time*, April 10, 1995, p. 61.

96. Moses Stambler, "An Eighth Day or the Final Flood," and "Ethical Tunes for Gene Marching Bands," *Community College Humanities Review*, Summer 1995, pp. 63–69.

97. Timothy Murphy and Marc A. Lappe, eds., *Justice and the Human Genome Project* (Berkeley: University of California Press, 1994).

98. Christine Gorman, "The Doctor's Crystal Ball," *Time*, April 10, 1995, p. 61.

99. Gina Kolata, "Should Children Be Told If Genes Predict Illness?," *The New York Times*, Sept. 26, 1994, p. A1.

100. Ibid. Some fear that medicine is moving too fast in diagnosing problems before we develop solutions, and there is a debate on the right to know by people who are tested for a future disease.

101. Selection from Carol Levine, "Are There Limits to Confidentiality?," in Carol Levine, ed., *Taking Sides, Clashing Views on Controversial Bioethical Issues* (Guilford, CT: Dushkin Publishing, 1995), pp. 146–163.

102. Warren Leary, "Using Gene Tests to Deny Jobs Is Ruled Illegal," *The New York Times*, April 8, 1995, p. A12.

103. Peter T. Kilborn, "The Boss Only Wants What's Best for You," *The New York Times*, May 8, 1994, p. E3; and Tom Wilkie, *Perilous Knowledge: The Human Genome Project and Its Implications* (Berkeley: University of California Press, 1993).

104. "E.P.A. Clears 3 Genetically Altered Crops That Will Repel Pests," *The New York Times*, April 11, 1995, p. A23; and Warren E. Leary, "Research Hints of Immunization by Fruits," *The New York Times*, May 5, 1995, p. A18.

105. Moses Stambler, "U.S. Flirts with Disaster by Not Regulating Genetic Science," *The New Haven Register*, May 4, 1988, p. 15.

106. C. Everett Koop, "Forward," in Clement Bezold, ed., *Healthy People in a Healthy World: The Belmont Vision for Health Care in America* (Alexandria, VA: Institute for Alternative Futures, 1992), p. 1.

107. Keith Bradsher, "Rise in Uninsured Becomes an Issue in Medicaid Fight," *The New York Times*, August 27, 1995, p. A1; and Milt Freudenheim, "Health Plans That Put Cash into Workers' Pockets Are Finding Favor," *The New York Times*, August 29, 1995, p. A15.

108. J. Warren Salmon, "A Perspective on the Corporate Transformation of Health Care," *International Journal of Health Services*, 1995, Vol. 25, No. 1, p. 11.

109. The Canadian single-payer tax-based system is facing its own economic crisis

and is undergoing major cuts as "...provinces are closing and merging hospitals and scaling back universal coverage, which pays for visits to doctors and hospitals.... They have come to see now that governments can't do everything." Clyde H. Farnsworth, "Canadians Reconsider Rising Costs of Benefits," *The New York Times*, Sept. 17, 1995, p. A4.

110. Victor Fuchs, a health policy expert, has made significant projections for the future of health in the U.S. See Victor B. Fuchs, *The Future of Health Policy* (Cambridge: Harvard University Press, 1993).

111. Health behavior of substance abuse is costly to the United States. See Joseph Califano, *Radical Surgery: What's Next for America's Health Care* (New York: Times Books, 1994). In 1996, New York City reported that as much as one-fifth of every budget dollar was being expended for substance abuse related concerns.

112. In the pursuit of better health, humans have alternated in their views of disease causation from God, nature, body balance, miasma, social causation, and microbes.

113. Clement Bezold, project director, *Healthy People in a Healthy World: The Belmont Vision for Health Care in America* (Alexandria, VA: Institute for Alternative Futures, 1992), p. 1.

114. William K. Stevens, "Scientists Say Earth's Warming Could Set Off Wide Disruptions," *The New York Times*, Sept. 18, 1995, p. A1.

115. John Kenneth Galbraith, "Blame History, Not the Liberals," *The New York Times*, Sept. 19, 1995, p. A21.

116. During the fall of 1987, I worked in Washington, DC, as an office staffer in the offices of Rep. Bruce Morrison and Sen. Ted Kennedy, and sat in on numerous committee and regulatory agency meetings and hearings. One of the issues for which I submitted a congressional staff position paper was "HR-3119, A Bill to Prohibit Patenting of Animals for Two Years." There is a great degree of fragmentation of environmental health responsibility frequently with little overall control. I feel there is need for a powerful national coordinating committee that clearly has public health interest as its major concern.

117. Public Health Service, *Healthy People 2000, Review 1993*, Washington, DC: U.S. Dept. of Health and Human Services, June 1994. This report, started in September 1990 by the Secretary of the U.S. Dept. of Health and Human Services, delineated objectives in twenty-two areas of public health. Progress is noted in annual tracking data, and reports are issued on how well we as a nation are moving toward our goals of health improvement through reduction of morbidity and mortality in these twenty-two areas. (J. Michael McGinnis, "Healthy People 2000 at Mid-Decade," *Journal of the American Medical Association*, April 12, 1995, pp. 1123–1129.)

118. There is a clear need to continue funding and research; the proposed cutting back on research funding will undoubtedly affect future health. See Laurie Garrett, "Are We Ready for the Next Plague?," *USA Today*, March 9, 1995, p. 11A:1.

119. Western industrialized and welfare-oriented societies such as Sweden, Germany, France, and England have been significantly cutting back on health expenditures and social service funding because of increasingly limited resources.

120. See Moses Stambler, "Alarms Ringing on Rationing of Health Care," *The New Haven Register*, Sept. 6, 1995, p. A11.

121. The over-65 population is living longer and is in need of more care. The fastest growing age group, the 85-plus population, is the most costly age cohort, and requires the greatest expenditures for care. How much health services should society provide? See Malvin Schechter, *Beyond Medicare: Achieving Long-Term Care Security* (San Francisco: Jossey Bass, 1993).

122. Carol Levine, *Taking Sides, Bioethical Issues* (Guilford CT: Dushkin Publishing, 1995).

123. John Kenneth Galbraith, "Blame History, Not the Liberals," *The New York Times*, Sept. 19, 1995, p. A21.

124. It will be necessary to make ideological adjustments from the Darwinian approach with some individuals getting all the health care they want, while large numbers are denied reasonable amounts of health care expenditures. There will have to be social limits set on how much health care resources are distributed, and to whom. Daniel Callahan has called for setting limits for elderly care as a way of capping health costs. See Daniel Callahan, *Setting Limits: Medical Goals in an Aging Society* (Washington, DC: Georgetown Press, 1995).

　　The Oregon Plan operationalized public forums under Dr. John Kitzhaber (Oregon governor), and developed a citizen consensus to ration and limit health services under their Medicaid program. (Marilyn Chase, "Oregon's New Health Rationing Means More Care for Some but Less for Others," *The Wall Street Journal*, Jan. 28, 1994, p. B1; and Robert A. Crittenden, "Update, State Report—Oregon," *Health Affairs*, Summer 1995, Vol. 14, No. 2, p. 303.)

125. Texas Tech's MedNet program, one of twenty-five telemedicine projects in the United States, reported a net savings of 14 percent to 22 percent in the cost of health care delivery resulting from salary decreases, lower ambulance costs, and an increase in earned revenue. Not only is MedNet thriving, but patients are increasingly communicating with their doctors through E-mail. (Tim Friend, "Patients Find 'Direct Line' to Doctors," *USA Today*, Feb. 8, 1995, p. 1A.)

126. Jerome Kassirer, "The Next Transformation in the Delivery of Health Care," *The New England Journal of Medicine*, Jan. 5, 1995, pp. 52–54.

127. "Computer '2nd opinion' Catches Breast Cancer," *The New Haven Register*, March 30, 1995, p. C3.

128. James C. Hurowitz, "Toward a Social Policy for Health," *The New England Journal of Medicine*, July 8, 1993, pp. 130–133.

129. The high value American ideology places on individual autonomy and control over health care and decisions must be tempered by the recognition that in many other cultural traditions, the family rather than the individual is the critical decision-making unit in the health process. (Moses Stambler, "The Mexican-American in the Health Care System," *ERIC-RIE*, April 1984.)

130. Stephen Morse, *Emerging Viruses* (New York: Oxford University Press, 1993).

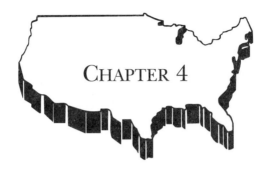

CHAPTER 4

AMERICAN EDUCATION
ON THE THRESHOLD
OF THE TWENTY-FIRST CENTURY

LEAH G. STAMBLER

HISTORICAL BACKGROUND

EDUCATION AND THE CONSTITUTION

The nature of American education is closely tied to the governmental structure of this country through the principle of federalism, as it is embedded in
the Constitution of the United States of America.[1] Nowhere in that document
is there mention of the locus of authority pertaining to education. However,
there is in the Tenth Amendment a tacit acceptance that education is the
function of the states through their reserved or residual powers. The authority of the states to provide, support, and maintain public schools and educational programs within their borders has been sustained, too, in the "Equal
Protection Clause of the Fourteenth Amendment, early local and state ordinances, educational practice, and an unbroken sequence of court findings."[2]

State governments theoretically have greater authority over education
than is exercised by any other government unit in the United States, "especially when Tenth Amendment powers and the states' constitutions legally hold
them responsible for establishing uniform systems of public education for their
citizens."[3] The states' legal responsibility for education within their borders has
been translated into the following types of actions by them: enacting legislation,
determining school taxes and financial aid to local school districts, setting minimum personnel training and recruitment standards, deciding on curriculum
and textbook lists, accrediting schools, and providing special services such as
student transportation.[4] Education laws passed by the states' legislatures apply
to nonpublic schools as well as public, in areas such as health standards, build-

ing codes, welfare of children, and student codes. However, comprehensive regulatory requirements rarely have been passed by states' legislatures, as those requirements may apply to the nonpublic sector of education.[5]

The states have created local school districts for the administration of public education within their jurisdictions, and have delegated the daily operation of the schools to those districts. American education, regarded as a state and/or local province, differs in each of the fifty states, as well as among the local districts inside the same state.[6] Compared to other countries that have national systems of education (e.g., Japan, Germany, and Great Britain), it is a unique feature of American education that the states are responsible for the quality and quantity of education that they provide for their people.[7]

The national government historically has exerted its influence on American education, and has expanded its role in education since the 1930s, through the general welfare clause of the Preamble and the First Amendment of the Constitution.

The concept of a "New Federalism" has tended to shift many educational decisions away from the national government to the states.[8] The national government still engages in three major roles vis-à-vis American education through (1) federal educational agencies (e.g., U.S. Department of Education and the Office of Educational Research and Improvement); (2) federal financing of education; and (3) the Supreme Court's decisions concerning education (e.g., cases pertaining to the desegregation of schools).[9]

GOALS AND VALUES OF AMERICAN PUBLIC EDUCATION

The governmental establishment and operation of American public schools by the various states since the ratification of the Constitution attested to the fact that public purposes were to be served by those institutions. There has been an historical discrepancy between the private goals and moral/religious beliefs of families who have sent their children to public schools and the values espoused by those institutions. Families wanted "to achieve purely intellectual goals," and were "frustrated and concerned about both the time spent on government goals for education and the content of those goals."[10]

Seven categories of fundamental American civic values, representative of the goals taught in the public schools, were stated in the Declaration of Independence, the Constitution, and the Bill of Rights: (1) the public good; (2) individual rights; (3) justice; (4) equality; (5) diversity; (6) truth; and (7) patriotism.[11] Two of these civic values, the public good and diversity, have impacted educational policy options in the past and will continue to do so in the future.

The Public Good   The founders of the American system of government borrowed from two visions of the public good: (1) the Greco-Roman republican ideal; and (2) the individual interest model espoused by Enlightenment philosophers. Government's main role in the republican prototype was understood to be the advancement of society as a whole. Late-nineteenth-century acceptance of property taxes as the funding base for public education in America was grounded in society's assent to the implementation of the republican ideal of the public good. Several terms historically have been used interchangeably with the republican model of the public good: common good, general welfare, public interest, public happiness, civic virtue, and welfare government.[12] A second view of the concept of the public good is called the individual interest model. People interpreted the public good as an aggregate of private interests and benefits, whose components included individual dignity, self-interest, interest conflicts, limited government and minimal state actions, interest advocacy, voluntarism, and business enterprise.[13] Actions by the Republican-led majority in the 104th Congress exemplified some of the seven variables characteristic of the individual interest model of the public good.[14]

Diversity   Diversity, one of this nation's civic values, forged American society from its beginnings in its social, ethnic, religious, economic, and political sectors. Intrinsic to the notion of diversity is the belief that cultural variances are beneficial in a pluralistic society: (1) interaction of a variety of ideas, outlooks, and practices enlightens the individual and society; (2) association with a range of convictions and customs enhances personal independence and expands perspectives; and (3) a single group is precluded from using its interests to dominate the society. For example, the First Amendment is notable for its protective role in allowing variations in individual thoughts and lifestyles.[15]

Historically, Western Europeans, the earliest peoples to colonize this country, were somewhat alike, sharing patterns of language, religion, national origin, and ethnic makeup. A proliferation of immigrants in the nineteenth and early twentieth centuries from Eastern, Central, and Southern Europe aroused feelings among old-stock Americans of suspicion, prejudice, persecution, and violence against the newcomers.[16] Over a period of time, American society incorporated the positive aspects of diversity and pluralism engendered by later waves of immigrants.

There is a perennial debate over how much diversity is welcome in American society without that diversity challenging national unity and identity. The future of bilingual education, curriculum that is multicultural, English as the official language, and our immigration policy exemplify controversies in the political arena about the interaction between the rewards of pluralism and maintaining common political values.[17]

WHAT INTERESTS SHOULD SCHOOLS SERVE?

The nature of American schools is impacted by contrasting viewpoints and philosophical commitments held by various segments of society. Controversies especially become noticeable when addressing educational issues that are related to (1) politics (e.g., schools' organization, operation, financing, and control); (2) religion (e.g., influence of ideologies on public schooling, relation of private religious and secular schools); (3) purposes, and (4) professional practices. "Schools are a battleground where the future of the society is at stake."[18] For example, traditionalists and progressivists display conflicting curriculum opinions pertinent to four aims of education to develop learners intellectually, as functioning citizens, as individuals in society, and as actual or potential workers.[19]

First, traditionalists believe that certain subjects are better than others to train the learner's mind, and that education is dispensed in the form of instruction. Progressivists embrace all subjects as accessories in the education of the whole child. Second, traditionalists believe that good citizenship is the result of intellectual development, while progressivists espouse the notion that functioning citizens are the result of developing good morals and useful skills through interactive living experiences. Third, according to traditionalists' perspectives, carefully prepared curricula, homogeneous grouping, and rigorous education enable learners to participate in society as individuals. Progressivists support a curriculum that is flexible, does not track the learners, and provides for the development of the learners' potential. Finally, traditionalists foster the idea that students learn work skills after the acquisition of knowledge from liberal studies, while progressivists advocate curricula that combine liberal and vocational studies, holding the vocational aspects of education in high esteem.

When confronting various schooling issues and seeking alternatives for them, Americans subscribe to one of two values to defend their choices: belief in liberty, or belief in equality. Both of these concepts were fundamental to the American Revolution, and are found in the Preamble to the Constitution. Liberty and equality may be seen as being on either end of a continuum in the American political spectrum. Those who favor liberty are viewed as being right of center, and are known as Republicans, conservatives, or libertarians. Those who favor equality are seen as left-wingers, and are known as Democrats, liberals, or egalitarians.[20]

Citizens in agreement with the libertarian position, when arguing matters of education and social policy, believe that (1) less government is better; (2) parents are responsible for finding and assisting in the education design that they want for their children; (3) government guarantees parents' and/or caregivers' freedom to choose schools for their children; and (4) government interference on behalf of those people who are less financially fortunate than others is counterproductive, in that it limits incentives of productive people and discourages industriousness of those people on the receiving end of governmental handouts.[21]

Believers in equality as a benchmark for determining answers to schooling issues differ in their perceptions of government, and its interaction with less affluent members of the community: (1) They favor government guarantees of equally good schooling for the children of the haves and the have-nots; (2) they expect the government to act in a benevolent and parental manner on behalf of all children, making sure that equality of opportunity is provided for all; (3) they believe that equality of opportunity and equality of condition are synonymous; and that (4) the government has a role to play in preventing children's unequal social and economic conditions from precluding their availing themselves of paths to equality of opportunity.[22]

A conceptual framework for understanding the interface between education and political economy is illustrated in the curriculum domain. Six major curriculum movements occurred in American education between 1860 and 1990. They were driven by the comparative political leverage of competing interest groups (1) "to establish, organize, and reorganize schools and school programs"; (2) "to open, augment, and broaden the curriculum"; (3) "to reduce, contract, concentrate, and tighten the curriculum"; (4) "to focus on children and youth as learners, and on the ways they learn"; (5) "to focus on the problems and requirements of society and culture"; and (6) "to focus on subject matter and pupils' success in learning it."[23] American education is known for its ten-year cycles of school reform that assimilate a certain number of ideas, reject others, and result in little classroom change.[24]

POLITICAL ECONOMY AND EDUCATION

The field of political economy took shape by the late eighteenth century, when political economists agreed that skilled workers and a free market system, efficiently producing goods and services, would assure economic development.[25] Charting the educational course in America has been and is tinted by the concept of political economy, or the interaction of economic factors and political policy. Economic goals and decisions about how to use scarce resources to satisfy the populace's wants are entwined with the citizenry's desired broad social goals and political choices.

Five types of economic goals frequently are germane to economic policy decisions having a wide social scope: (1) economic freedom of action in the marketplace, and its concomitant presence or lack of governmental regulation; (2) economic efficiency that yields the lowest costs in the production of the most highly desired goods; (3) full employment to avoid the presence of idle resources; (4) annual economic growth for all in society to partake of, without increasing society's numbers or diminishing the size of the shares in the growth; and (5) economic equity in the form of equal opportunity.[26]

Early in the nineteenth century, the preceding economic goals were linked to schooling in America. The common school movement, 1820 to 1860, was a struggle to establish free public schools at the same time that demands for broader types of schools were highlighted by the large numbers of immigrants coming to American shores.[27] Mid-nineteenth-century America was shifting from its rural and agricultural character to an urban and industrial one that would continue on into the twentieth century. The common school movement aimed at assisting children to make that shift, too, and to benefit from the growing economic system.[28]

By the 1890s and the turn of the century, the effects of nationally accepted economic goals on the organization of American schools had taken place.[29] Secondary education was at the center of the late-nineteenth-century debates over the form and function of public education.[30] Taxpayers disagreed as to whether or not they would finance the construction and maintenance of new public high schools. Nor were politically powerful business organizations convinced that they should pay for public secondary education programs that did not favor the needs of business and industry.[31] During the decades after 1917, various pieces of legislation signaled the policy-making presence of the federal government in education. The 1944 G.I. Bill of Rights, designed to "ease potential workers back into a peacetime economy" after World War II, guaranteed extensive educational funding for higher education to returning military service personnel.[32] A ready supply of educated workers would be available when the American economy demobilized from its wartime status and well-trained labor was needed to keep the emergent economy on a growth track.

Business leaders, social scientists, and economists in the twentieth century have maintained that economic development and social progress are linked.[33] The decades of the 1930s through the 1950s were times of improvement in the process for American youth to enter vocational positions. One effect on American education of the Cold War in the late 1940s and 1950s was the binding of national interests and schooling, exemplified by the educational sector's advocacy of rigorous scientific programs to counter the crisis brought on by the Soviet Union's launching of Sputnik in 1957.

The belief that higher education was required for occupational success emerged in the decades of the 1960s and 1970s. Advertisements provided a forum for business and industry to trumpet the benefits of scientific advancement for the growth of individual standards of living.[34] Two educational issues also emerged at this time, demonstrating the connection between national economic development and individual advancement: accessibility of equal educational opportunity as a prerequisite for securing a good job; and relevance of occupational training as a boost for employment possibilities. It generally was understood during this period that the acquisition and generation of knowledge, as well as economic success, were primary educational tasks.

Two developments in the late 1970s and early 1980s were monumental in connecting political economy and education, as well as in driving the direction of American school reform in the past two decades. Business and political leaders blamed public education institutions for not adequately preparing their graduates to assist with national economic development, as evidenced by (1) a loss of the nation's competitive edge in international trade, and (2) concurrent reports of students' academic accomplishments in other economically advancing nations being better than those of American students.[35]

Since the beginning of the 1980s, there has been a shift in the long-established educational goal that focuses on the schooling of citizens for participation in a democracy. Interest in the role of schools as educators of American workers for the future and in aiding economic development has taken priority over applying education to produce citizens versed in democracy.[36] This trend stems from a government belief that "business can show the schools how to set their house in order," since business is concerned about the employability of the populace.[37] A two-pronged premise for discussion stems from business and civic leaders' conviction that (1) national progress depends on economic growth, and (2) children are economic development resources.[38]

It is noteworthy that many analysts of the educational scene argue that business leaders should not be allowed to determine the course of American education, because their decisions are narrow and self-serving in motivation.[39] In addition, the belief that schools turn out faulty human capital responsible for declining economic growth has been criticized from the perspective that children are not raw materials to be viewed as products.

Dialogue on the state and federal levels about contemporary national school reform centers on solving unemployment problems and defining how schools should provide workers for the business sector, workers who are capable of engaging in competition for international trade. Recommendations for school reform embody plans for tougher school policies. Thirty reports, analyzing U.S. education and suggesting ways for its amelioration, were published between the 1983 release of "A Nation at Risk" by the National Commission on Excellence in Education and 1988.[40]

CHALLENGES, OPPORTUNITIES, AND CONSTRAINTS

There are multiple and complex challenges facing American education in the areas of demographics, finance, organization, access, quality and standards, race/ethnic diversity, interaction with national/state/local levels of government, and a changing economy.

Major challenges for educational decision makers are (1) how to provide equal education for economically disadvantaged children; (2) how to provide equal education for Limited English Proficient (LEP) students; (3) how to educate students for the workforce of the twenty-first century; and (4) how to best utilize the education dollar to increase its productivity and to fulfill educational reform goals.

HOW TO PROVIDE EQUAL EDUCATION
FOR ECONOMICALLY DISADVANTAGED CHILDREN

Challenges Children form the poorest segment of the American population, as evidenced by the 1993 statistic that 840,000 youngsters fell into poverty that year, and that since 1979 there had been a 26 percent increase in poverty among children.[41] In 1987, the U.S. Bureau of the Census had classified 32.5 million people as being poor, 13 million of whom were under the age of eighteen and 5 million were under the age of six.[42]

The education of children living in poverty is a challenge for the nation. In spite of the resources earmarked for education by federal and state governments, disproportionate numbers of children in poverty experience failure in their early years and in school, and more often than not will be ill-prepared for adulthood when they leave school.[43] According to James Comer, "Growing numbers of children in today's society are out of the mainstream and unprepared for school. Many schools don't have the human relationships and systematic support that will open the door to children being raised outside the mainstream."[44]

Several aspects of disadvantaged learning conditions in American schools inevitably produce negative consequences for these school-age youngsters: (1) Most low-income and minority children's schools provide less per-pupil expenditures than in higher-income areas, resulting in poorer students having less access to well-maintained facilities, smaller class size, adequate equipment, and appropriate materials; (2) less rich and demanding academic programs are provided in schools with large concentrations of low-income youngsters, providing the students with limited access to curriculum that develops inquiry and problem-solving skills; and (3) teaching vacancies and difficulties in filling positions with qualified teachers in high-poverty schools reduce low-income students' access to well-qualified teachers, compared to their more affluent peers.[45]

Poor children are disadvantaged in their pursuit of learning when they attend schools that set up barriers to high-quality education. Factors that also contribute to a disadvantaged school environment are related to the presence of high rates of mobility among the youngsters' families, a high incidence of students' emotional and/or behavioral problems, and large numbers of students with limited English proficiency.[46]

Formative interactions in the home help or hinder children when they are of school age, and are required to spend their days with other youngsters in a learning environment. The ability to interact well with their age cohorts in the school environment is mitigated for those children who are outside the mainstream in poor and broken homes, with ineffective parents.[47]

Opportunities Head Start, created in 1965 as part of President Lyndon Johnson's War on Poverty, provided educational opportunities for low-income children. A Department of Health and Human Services program of more than 1,500 individual grantees, Head Start functions as a low-budget operation, supervised by hired employees, and loosely monitored by the federal government. Children up to the ages of three and four attend Head Start centers for three to four hours daily for about eight months. It was designed as a two-generational approach to counteract the effects of socioeconomic obstacles in the development of children in low-income families. A prime tenet of the program is parental involvement. The Head Start Reauthorization Act of 1990 mirrored a concern about the quality of the program's services. The Act stipulated that 10 percent of total funding was to be used to improve the quality of services by focusing on staff salaries and fringe benefits, child and parent transportation costs, additional staff, structural improvements, and training and technical assistance.[48]

The work of James Comer in New Haven, Connecticut modeled the promotion of academic achievement among low-income children by fostering (1) the overall development of students; (2) bonding to the school; (3) staff acceptance of change in the school; (4) staff understanding of child development; and (5) improved relations between staff and parents.[49] A site-based school management team, composed of parents, teachers, administrators, and adult caretakers on the school staff, characterizes the model. Teachers in the project schools understood by 1984 the impact of home interactions on student achievement, as evidenced by students' test scores being above grade level, exemplary attendance rates, and minimal serious behavior problems. A Social Skills Curriculum for Inner City Children was produced as a result of Comer's joint efforts with parents, teachers, and administrators in the project schools.

In 1990 and 1991 Family Service Centers, substance-abuse programs, and Family Support Projects were funded for existing Head Start grantees as a way of expanding the scope of services provided for the program. Research concluding in 1992 about Head Start indicated that students' intellectual skills, emotional development, and general health met with positive results in the short run, but that the immediate impact of the program on the children disappeared within two years of their departure from receiving Head Start services.[50]

The National Center for Children in Poverty (NCCP) has recommended initiatives for supplying quality education to economically disadvantaged children. Several of these initiatives include educational opportunities, such as (1) the expansion of Head Start and other effective preschool programs to make them full-day, full-year projects; (2) the creation of educational and employment opportunities to motivate the postponement of parenthood by teenagers living in poverty; and (3) the provision of high-quality schooling and postsecondary education and training for technically demanding occupations.[51]

Constraints   Head Start has become one of the most popular domestic initiatives focusing on the early childhood development of low-income children.[52] Some supporters believe that the program should provide two years of full-day classes for every low-income child, beginning at age two and a half years.[53] Two factors limit the program's capability to effect what it was designed to do: (1) Individual Head Start grantees are provided with little motivation to maintain high levels of delivered services because of the program's funding formula; and (2) the parental involvement aspect of the program does not allow working low-income families to take full advantage of Head Start services, at the same time that it offers a disincentive for parents of children in the program to gain economic self-sufficiency (i.e., secure employment instead of collecting Aid to Families with Dependent Children—AFDC).[54]

Large amounts of federal, state, and local money have been spent over the past thirty years on the education of children diagnosed as being economically disadvantaged and educationally deficient. This has produced a controversy over whether or not taxpayers' money is being thrown at educational problems instead of finding alternative nonmonetary remedies to assist the nation's educationally needy children.

The position that there is not enough funding to rectify the economically disadvantaged learning environments of this nation is represented by Jonathan Kozol. He has suggested numerous way for closing the gap between lower- and upper-income educational institutions: (1) abolition of the property tax as the basis for funding of American education, and its equitable replacement from a single federal source; (2) provision of a funding increment for low-income inner-city and rural schools; (3) provision of a minimum increment of $10,000 for veteran/experienced teachers who agree to a lifetime of teaching in the inner city; and (4) enactment of a onetime federal school reconstruction bill to tear down all decrepit school buildings.[55] He believes that compassion toward the needy is nonexistent, and complains that "we throw money at the Pentagon," instead of allocating educational funds "to make America a democratic land."[56] This view is validated by Marian Wright Edelman, President of the Children's Defense Fund, who has characterized the decade of the 1990s as a struggle about the American conscience and the nation's future. "We need to understand that investing in our children is not investing in a special interest group or helping out somebody else—it is absolutely essential to every American's well-being and future."[57] Additionally, Comer has pinpointed unresolved systemic socioeconomic ills as mitigating monetary input and educational reform efforts on behalf of children, especially for those whom he categorizes as being outside the mainstream.[58]

HOW TO PROVIDE EQUAL EDUCATION
FOR LIMITED ENGLISH PROFICIENT (LEP) STUDENTS

Challenges Some educational visionaries believe that American schools may achieve both equity and excellence if all students are held to high common standards of world-class performance.[59] This position has wide-ranging ramifications for those students whose families report to the U.S. Census Bureau that they speak a non-English language at home.[60] Putting high common standards into operation in the nation's schools will have the effect of making the educational experience of Limited English Proficient (LEP) students "disproportionately difficult."[61]

LEP students, in meeting standards designed for monolingual English-speaking students, will have to overcome complicated cognitive and linguistic challenges in completing their learning tasks. Some of these challenges include (1) deciphering structures and functions of language before any content makes sense; (2) negotiating unfamiliar sociolinguistic/sociocultural activities when asked to contribute to group learning experiences; (3) making language express what the student knows about the content; (4) focusing on language skills while classmates focus on content acquisition when the content is known in the student's primary language; (5) carrying a heavier cognitive and linguistic burden to gain access to new concepts and vocabulary using a language that he/she is not able to read, speak, write, or understand when the content is unknown in the student's primary language; and (6) bearing a weightier cognitive and linguistic load when he/she enters school at a higher grade level.[62]

Several major issues arise when seeking to provide LEP students with the resources that they need to meet demands for compliance with high common standards of performance. First, most LEP students do not get adequate access to high-quality instruction and needed services because of a lack of systematic attention to "opportunity-to-learn standards," as formulated by professional organizations such as Teachers of English to Speakers of Other Languages (TESOL). Second, achievement by LEP students is impeded by problems having to do with programmatic and teacher preparation deficiencies, and debates over testing.[63]

Opportunities The presence of people within the American nation who do not speak English as their primary language encouraged educational policy makers to investigate options for language instruction in the public schools. Mexican Americans, Native Americans, and Puerto Ricans led the 1960s effort to have bilingual education implemented in the schools. Issues related to bilingual education are politically combustible because the culture of an ethnic group is inherent in its language. Demonstrations and boycotts in support of the classroom infusion of Spanish, teaching Mexican history and culture, providing bilingual programs, hiring of Spanish-speaking teachers, and serving Mexican food in school cafeterias led to positive political responses from Texas Senator Ralph Yarborough, Senator Edward Kennedy, and Bronx Borough President Herman Badillo in the form of the passage of the Bilingual Education Act of 1968.[64]

Several forms of bilingual education are possible to bring the learner to the point of literacy in English: (1) bilingual education—the learner becomes proficient in two languages, for example, in Lakota and English or in Spanish and English; (2) maintenance bilingual education—allows the learner to speak, read, and write in her/his primary language at the same time that the curriculum content is taught, and while the student is learning English; (3) transitional bilingual education—utilizes the learner's primary language in school until English is mastered, at which time the classes are taught in English; and (4) two-way bilingual education—combines English-speaking and non-English-speaking students in one room, the goal being to become bilingual in English and another language.

Constraints Opposition to bilingual education programs in the nation's public schools surfaced in 1986 in the form of several groups (e.g., U.S. English, Save Our Schools, and the Heritage Foundation) who espoused the use of English only on government documents, and who were favorable to legislation that would declare English the official national language.[65]

HOW TO EDUCATE STUDENTS
FOR THE WORKFORCE OF THE TWENTY-FIRST CENTURY

Challenges Work and education in the 1990s are threatened by swift, turbulent, and uncertain changes, propelled by "an electronically driven technological revolution, a competitive global market, and dangerous ecological damage."[66] In the last decade of the twentieth century, the nature of work is being transformed by the deep technological and economic changes brought on by the information-age revolution, wherein computers, robotics, and telecommunications are replacing human beings in the manufacturing, service, and knowledge sectors. Yesteryears' conventional skills are no longer adequate in the workplace.

Work in the information age is characterized by an elite technologically trained labor force, in contrast to the mass labor force of the industrial age. Worldwide, there is an expanding call for workers proficient in symbolic-analytic skills.[67] Politicians and economists have warned American educators to make the nation's youth ready to meet the ensuing changes from new technologies.

Jeremy Rifkin, president of the Foundation on Economic Trends, believes that American educators have not been fully informed about the reality of change in the global economy, and that "preparing the next generation for potential work in both the marketplace and the civil sector is, perhaps, the single most important challenge facing educators and the American school system as we make the transition into a new century and a new economic epoch in history."[68] The economy, according to Rifkin, is growing increasingly less likely to provide lasting jobs for millions of Americans seeking permanent employment. He suggests that technological and economic changes will provide the impetus for an international reconsideration of educational assumptions, in order to adapt to the needs of cyberspace.

Edward Cornish, president of the World Future Society and editor of *The Futurist*, has offered ninety-two anticipations or "futuribles" for the year 2025 that are germane to work (e.g., permanent mass employment is a serious possibility); business (e.g., buyers and sellers will make contact in cybermalls); and the economy (e.g., living standards will climb around the world) in the twenty-first century.[69]

Opportunities Educators' responses to warnings about impending challenges in the twenty-first century have been translated into a pattern of almost three decades of school reforms. Popular belief in the measurability of learning has allowed for the application of pressure on teachers to be accountable for their students' test scores.[70] Top-down change, which continued into the early 1980s of the Reagan administration, was the result. Measuring test scores was replaced by participative school restructuring at the beginning of the Bush administration. A 1988 Carnegie Foundation for the Advancement of Learning report was instrumental in the shift to restructuring, by its recounting of minimal teacher control over book selections, development of curricula, and utilization of classroom time.[71]

American education traditionally has prepared the next generation to be productive in the marketplace. Educational responses to economic imperatives, which have become increasingly strident since the publication of *A Nation at Risk* and which demand that schooling ought to better prepare workers for the twenty-first century, have taken the form of "new vocationalism."[72] This is an emerging educational concept. It has the potential of facilitating an eventual shift to a high-skills economy, allowing for a rediscovery of practices for work-based learning, and propitiating the problems of linking educational reform to vocational purposes.

There are five strands or versions of the "new vocationalism," which prove that education through occupations can incorporate the entire range of political and moral purposes of society. These five models allow students to plan for postsecondary education, employment, or both.

The first strand is a conservative approach to vocationalism. It is an outgrowth of *A Nation at Risk*'s warning that mediocrity in the educational system would cause decline in American economic competitiveness with the Pacific-Rim nations and Germany. The high school is seen as a vocational institution critical for students' employment future, academic track courses dominate the curriculum, and there are obscure connections to later employment.

Strand two is reformist in nature, responding to changing needs in the economy by incorporating new skills for future workers and new approaches to teaching. In line with recommendations from the Secretary of Labor's Commission on Achieving Necessary Skills (SCANS), high schools require a range of basic skills (e.g., reading, writing, speaking, listening, mathematics); thinking skills (e.g., decision making, problem solving, knowing how to learn); and responsibility (e.g., sociability, self-management, integrity, honesty). SCANS skills are workplace skills linked to employers' demands for educational reform. This strand continues the economic and utilitarian emphasis of *A Nation at Risk*, with educational preparation priorities that are favored by employers.

Strand three directly addresses deficiencies of the turn-of-the-century "old vocationalism" (i.e., utilitarian with a focus on specific skill training for entry-level jobs). This strand attempts to broaden the content of the curriculum by establishing connectedness to academic content, accommodating goals for postsecondary education, and is critical of the current system of employment. Calls for improvement in this strand were boosted by the 1990 Amendments to the Carl Perkins Act, which provided federally funded programs with coherent sequences of integrated academic and vocational education.

The fourth strand is reformist in its interest in school-to-work programs. Students at risk spend time in work placements without changing high school pedagogy, thereby replicating vocational education of the 1970s. It accords the least amount of financing for secondary vocational education, in comparison with appropriated funds for federal vocational education and job training.

The fifth and final strand of the "new vocationalism" is reformist in its integration of academic and vocational education and in its dependence on the restructuring of the high school for curriculum integration. Three forms of such restructuring include (1) career academies, or "schools within schools"; (2) clusters, which require students to choose career majors and promote the concept of the federal/state School to Work Opportunities Act; and (3) occupational high schools and magnet schools that allow students to focus on clear missions, pursuit of educational goals, and social contracts.

Educational institutions have remodeled and expect to continue to reform their curricula, based on the assumption that success in the cyberspace economy of the twenty-first century depends on computer literacy, technical skills, and proficiencies. What is the prospect for this assumption coming to fruition? A study conducted between 1990 and 1994 for the Software Publishers Association bolstered the belief that the key to school reform and more powerful student learning is technology. Five conclusions in the report, which was based on 133 research reviews, indicated that (1) educational technology has a significant positive impact on achievement across all subject areas, school levels, and students; (2) student attitudes are positively impacted by educational technology; (3) student population, instructional design, teacher's role, student grouping, and student access to technology influence the degree of effectively using educational technology; (4) positive results of educational technology in the classroom include increases in student-centeredness, cooperative learning, and teacher/student interaction; and (5) positive changes in the learning environment evolve over time.[73]

Constraints Changes in the workforce of the future are connected to the educational preparation of students in the remaining years of the 1990s. The role of teachers is important when calculating the prognosis for the educational technology revolution in the classrooms, and when preparing for conversion to an electronically savvy workforce.

Progress in educational technology in the schools is expected to proceed more slowly than its supporters would choose because of time and money scarcities. Costs for equipment, rewiring, and staff training will require expanded school funding. Howard Mehlinger predicts that lack of money may slow down the revolution in educational technology to an evolutionary process.[74] In addition, Arthur Wirth envisions problems coming about in educating students for the workforce of the twenty-first century as a result of two American value traditions competing for dominance in meeting the challenges of an electronically driven workplace: centralized control versus democratic concepts.[75] Jeremy Rifkin suggests that the need to rethink American ideas of politics and education may act as a constraint on the reenvisioning of work to allow displaced workers in the information age to find employment in the civil sector of society. It will be necessary to find a balance among the market, government, and civil sector forces to accomplish this task.[76]

HOW TO BEST UTILIZE THE EDUCATION DOLLAR TO INCREASE ITS PRODUCTIVITY AND TO FULFILL EDUCATIONAL REFORM GOALS

Challenges American public schools are facing multiple criticisms from (1) the business sector, with complaints that too many job applicants are illiterate and are unable to do simple computations; and (2) economists who are fearful that the nation's ability to compete in the global economy is being compromised by a weak school system. In addition, American public schools are faced with financial challenges that will decrease their ability to effectively carry out their responsibility of educating the nation's children.

Strained state budgets will lead to (1) overcrowded classrooms; (2) reduced individual student attention; (3) deferred maintenance of school facilities; (4) elimination of music, art, and sports programs; and (5) inability to pay for computers and the information technology that is necessary to prepare young Americans for the workplace of the twenty-first century.[77] How did this situation come about? Who is responsible for this sad turn of events for the nation's public schools? A major source of the financial squeeze that the schools are facing has to do with the demographics of immigration and birthrates. Southern California, New York City, South Florida, and some other areas are faced with enormous costs to the school systems as a result of their deluge of immigrants. Rising enrollments will occur concurrently with public pressure for diminished school spending. Higher pupil-teacher ratios are and will be commonplace.

Prior and current debates about funding for education have centered on the issue of whether or not the amount of money appropriated mattered in the learning of our nation's children. Two parallel trends are taking place in American education: (1) the school reform goal of raising students' achievement levels through academic standard setting; and (2) local, state, and federal retrenchment in the appropriation of funds for educational institutions.

Allan Odden contends that it is time to address what he calls "the real resource challenge of the future."[78] As he sees it, the expectation of fiscal caps for public education makes it timely to decide how to best utilize the current education dollar, so as to fulfill educational reform goals. Education reform currently is focused on improving academic standards, given the information that only 10 to 20 percent of the nation's students have mastery of mathematics, science, language arts, writing, and history.

Odden is not alone in his concern. Eric A. Hanushek indicates that society's stiff competition for limited financial resources is presenting public education with a serious challenge.[79] He, too, writes of public education's tripled "real" or inflation-adjusted spending between 1960 and 1990, at the same time that student performance "faltered" on the Scholastic Aptitude Test and the National Assessment of Educational Progress.

A trio of factors, according to Odden, contribute to the challenging situation of improving public schools productivity at current funding levels.[80] First, per-pupil spending between 1990 and 1995 has been "essentially flat" after adjusting for inflation, even though the nine decades prior to 1990 were characterized by inflation-adjusted per-pupil expenditure rises of between 25 percent and 75 percent. Second, public education's traditional dependence on the local property tax, state grants, and federal supplements for its finances is being eroded by local taxpayer revolts, reductions in state income taxes to provide property-tax relief, and the likelihood of budgetary cuts in federal funding. Third, maintenance of the public schools' fiscal integrity is being challenged by a diversion of state funds to support prison populations and to fund tax-relief plans, as well as by the need for state coffers to fill the gap when anticipated reductions in federal funding for social programs take place.

Reports on the use of funds to advance educational aspirations for increased student achievement have shown several developments: (1) Monetary outflow patterns of high- and low-spending school districts are similar; (2) funding allocated for "regular education" students has not measurably increased over the years; (3) the three-fold rise in education costs between 1960 and 1990 was connected to the labor-intense nature of education, rather than "real dollar" expenses; and (4) physically challenged and economically low-income students were the consumers of "the vast bulk of new money" spent for education.[81]

Opportunities The linchpin for long-term improvement of public education's productivity without increasing its dollar input is designing a method for boosting student achievement results and putting the money where it works. According to Odden, the key initiatives to accomplish this result are known, some of which include development of clear standards focusing on student achievement; high-quality curriculum; rigorous and full course loads for secondary students; and components of Robert Slavin's Success for All Program and Comer's School Development Program.[82]

A segment of educational policy makers, the supporters of year-round school, see the traditional school calendar as a mitigating factor for increasing student achievement levels. Also known as "continuous learning," "all-seasons learning," or "four-seasons school," year-round school reorganizes the academic calendar for continuous learning by creating instructional blocks of time and vacations.[83] In the 1994–95 academic year, 414 public school districts in thirty-five states had some form of year-round education arrangement for their students to solve the problems of vandalism of school facilities, loss of productive learning time, and unsupervised children. Year-round school is an example of the cooperation among administrators, teachers, and parents to implement continuous instruction for their children throughout the entire year. Students are monitored academically for twelve months, support services are kept in place for the students, and there is less time for students to forget the concepts and skills that they have learned. This model of school reform may well be an option for educational policy makers to consider when seeking ways to maximize the educational dollar in a period of financial retrenchment.

Constraints   The issue of increasing educational productivity (i.e., student achievement levels) within current financial parameters has yet to be addressed as a serious point of discussion by educational policy makers. Hanushek cites teacher contract restrictions for thwarting personnel adjustments, classroom reorganization, and the use of new technology. Debates about how education has been financed in the past constrain educators from engaging in discussions of how to reallocate current funds for use with strategies known to increase educational achievement.

POLICY OPTIONS: THE CURRENT DEBATE

POLICY OPTIONS AND THE CIVIC VALUE OF "THE PUBLIC GOOD"

Four policy options for attaining this civic value include (1) constitutional commands to equalize public education; (2) national goals for educational achievement; (3) promotion of parental choice; and (4) voluntary school desegregation versus court-ordered desegregation.

Constitutional Commands to Equalize Public Education   The first policy option, to use the courts to equalize public education, refers to actions by federal and state courts that have forbidden states to segregate students attending public schools by their color, or to otherwise discriminate against persons on the basis of sex, color, religion, or national origin. These cases have been based on the courts' interpretations of the Equal Protection Clause of the Fourteenth Amendment. In the landmark *Brown* v. *Board of Education* case, Thurgood Marshall, the lead attorney for the National Association for the Advancement of Colored People (NAACP), argued that schools that segregated children on the basis of color (1) were in violation of the Fourteenth Amendment's due process clause, (2) denied African-American children equality of educational opportunity, and (3) caused African-American children psychological damage.[84] The Supreme Court ruled that segregated schools were "inherently unequal and violated the Fourteenth Amendment." Subsequent rulings extended the Brown case's decision.[85]

Other decisions made by the courts, using the Equal Protection Clause, have declared that states must reasonably equalize financial resources among all their school districts, even if there must be an increase in taxes. The California Supreme Court's landmark ruling in the *Serrano* v. *Priest* case decided that the Fourteenth Amendment was violated by local property taxes that discriminated against the poor, by causing "substantial disparities among individual school districts in the amount of revenue available per pupil for the districts' educational programs."[86] Succeeding cases pertaining to the issue of financing public education found state property tax laws were in violation of the Fourteenth Amendment when there were large disparities among the districts' per-pupil expenditures.[87]

National Goals for Educational Achievement The second policy option, to create national goals for educational achievement, is connected to the public debate over the need for high-quality education and the educational reform movements that began in the 1980s. The 1989 education summit, held in Charlottesville, Virginia, and attended by President George Bush (Republican) and the fifty (mostly Democratic) state governors, exemplified a move to reach a consensus on national educational goals for the 1990s, which could result in American businesses competing in world markets.[88] The Bush Administration's school reform strategy, America 2000, favored leadership by the New American Schools Development Corporation to effect funding and guidance of research and development plans in order to "reinvent" the nation's schooling institutions. Board members of this group were CEOs of major American corporations who believed that educational practices were damaging the nation's economic growth by causing businesses to pay school taxes and the costs for literacy training of their workers.[89]

Six national education goals were drafted, setting high expectations for education performance at every stage of a learner's life, from the preschool years through adulthood.[90] Congress adopted the six goals in 1994, adding two more pertaining to teachers and parents. Generally, the goals related to improving childhood and adult literacy, graduation rates, teachers' profes-sional development, numbers of drug-free schools, and parental partnerships with schools.[91]

A 1996 commentary on the goals set at the 1989 education summit noted that the goals were "all but dead."[92] It appears that the Bush adminis-tration's effort to address school reform was frustrated by "resistance from various political interest groups in fear of the dreaded hand of Washington."[93]

Between March 26 and 27, 1996, the Second National Education Summit was held at IBM's conference center in Palisades, New York, after IBM CEO Louis V. Gerstner, Jr., publicly linked business problems to an unqualified American workforce.[94] A November 1995 report from the National Education Goals Panel reported that some positive developments had taken place relative to the America 2000 goals. However, governors and business leaders at the 1995 Governors' Conference agreed that meeting the goals' timetable was not feasible, and they decided to make "substantial and focused" efforts to "significantly accelerate student performance."[95]

The opening paragraph of the 1996 National Education Summit Policy Statement explained some of the governors' and business executives' basic premises about American education: (1) The quality of American schools is fundamental to the nation's future; (2) education's primary purpose is to enable students to "flourish in a democratic society and to work successfully in a global economy"; (3) the nation's future depends on performance at the highest level of potential for all students; (4) joint initiatives among business leaders and governors in the states is imperative; (5) the primary responsibili-ty for decisions about students' education rests with their parents (and care-givers); (6) high-quality educational experiences are the responsibility of states and localities; (7) the strengthening of schools is a top priority of the gover-nors; and (8) business leaders understand that a world-class workforce is nec-essary for the success of companies and the economic viability of the nation.[96]

The Palisades meeting was attended by forty-one governors, forty-nine corporate executive officers, thirty education experts, and President Bill Clinton. It focused on moving "from the broad goals that came out of the 1989 meetings called by President George Bush toward specific standards that would demand ... achievement."[97] It was reported that this summit was historic because the conferees acknowledged the states' control over educa-tion, as well as supported three principles for educational reform action per-taining to standards, assessment, and accountability.

A basic belief in technology as a means to give students the knowledge and skills that they will need in the workplace was expressed by the governors and business leaders: If applied thoughtfully and well-integrated into the cur-riculum, technology can assist student learning, provide access to informa-tion, and provide the workforce with a competitive edge in the global market. The leaders saw their roles as needing to be supportive of educators in over-coming the barriers that impede the effective use of technology.[98]

Summit participants committed themselves to "initiate and/or accelerate our efforts to improve student achievement" by taking various actions, some of which included the following: (1) Governors will support "internationally competitive academic standards," to be created in the states, by reallocating funds to sustain their implementation; (2) business leaders' coalitions of their peers in the various states will be used to expand support of the governors; (3) business leaders will delineate specific skills needed in the workforce, and require job applicants to verify their academic and skill proficiencies by providing documentation with academic transcripts, diplomas, portfolios, and certificates of initial mastery; (4) governors and business leaders will "be held accountable for progress in (their) respective states toward improving student achievement in core subject areas," and annually will produce reports showing the progress made by business and state officials in meeting their stated commitments; and (5) governors and business leaders will give high priority to promoting professional development for educators.[99]

The tone of the summit was considered to be hostile to federal involvement in education, unlike the 1989 meeting, which produced national goals for education that became part of the Goals 2000 legislation passed by Congress during the Clinton administration. The goals conformed with the concept of devolving federal power to the state and local levels of government for the purpose of creating standards of achievement for the nation's public schools. Jennifer A. Marshall noted that "When fifty governors get together and decide on a set of standards, those are *de facto* national standards."[100] Interestingly, a 1995 American Federation of Teachers study reported that "only thirteen out of fifty states had developed standards clear enough to be used as part of a formal curriculum."[101]

Some groups complained that the summit did not include their representatives, as was the case with the National PTA. Others criticized the prominent role of business leaders in setting the education agenda for the nation with comments such as: "Our education system should not be strictly based on preparing kids to work in those industries ... It should be on making them good citizens."[102] The Summit's focus on standards and technology was challenged with the view that "When I've got a class of kids who are tired and hungry and abused and scared, the highest standards in the world aren't going to do any good."[103]

Promotion of Parental Choice The third policy option for attaining the value of the public good concerns the controversial proposals to make public funds available for students to attend private or religious schools, or public charter schools, according to the wishes of their parents.

Proponents of the first measure favor the use of vouchers or tax credits to accomplish parental ends. The underlying theory of this policy option is that competition for students between public and private schools would encourage public schools to become more effective than their current condition. In Milwaukee, Wisconsin, State Representative Polly Williams has advocated choice for a number of years, as a way of enabling economically disadvantaged children to leave poorly functioning urban schools in her district. Critics of parental choice believe that the ideal of public education would be damaged and would result in unequal education for the children of rich and poor families.

Supporters of the second form of choice, charter schools, believe that this type of schooling (1) allows choice and options within the public school system, (2) allows for smaller, more student- and family-centered schools, (3) offers a variety of option or theme schools, (4) injects a productive level of stress into the educational system, thereby helping to stimulate needed change, and (5) provides the middle ground between the status quo and a full voucher/privatization system engulfing public education.[104]

Charter schools are independent public schools of choice, which may be authorized into existence by a local or intermediate school district, a state public university, or a state legislature. The authorizer has oversight responsibilities for the charter school, and functions as the fiscal agent by facilitating the transfer of the state's per-pupil grant to these schools. Charter schools function autonomously within the parameters of their authorizing contracts. All laws and regulations that apply to public schools apply as well to the charter schools. States vary in their authorization requirements about whether or not certified teachers must be hired for the charter schools.

Antagonists of the charter school movement see this type of organization as a threat to organized public education, as it currently exists. There is concern that inconsistency in the authorization charters, curriculum offered, standards followed, hiring of certified teachers, and themes followed in the charter schools will further damage the reform efforts that have been followed for the past fifteen years in public education. It is believed, too, that the basic premise for the foundation of the common school in the 1840s will be compromised, thereby recreating the denominational schools of pre-Revolutionary America.

Voluntary School Desegregation versus Court-Ordered Desegregation   The fourth policy option to implement the value of the public good is to effect voluntary school desegregation through a variety of measures.[105] Attendance areas may be modified to include a student population that is more desegregated than prior to the modification. Milwaukee's public schools are an example of efforts to increase the number of desegregated schools between 1976 and 1978 from 14 to 101 by (1) setting up magnet schools; (2) implementing a city-suburban transfer plan; and (3) redrawing school boundaries.

Magnet schools may be set up with specialized program offerings and personnel as a drawing point for students to enroll throughout the district. This voluntary method of desegregating students has been implemented in Boston, Buffalo, Cincinnati, Dallas, Houston, Kansas City, Minneapolis, New

Haven, Rochester (New York), and San Diego. A variety of program themes are offered in the magnet school, in anticipation that ethnic European students will be drawn to enroll in an otherwise segregated school. Schools may be paired from two adjacent areas into one larger zone. One school would be responsible for the enrollment of students from both areas in grades one through four, and the other school would handle enrollment of students from grades four to eight.

Controlled choice is a form of voluntary desegregation in a district that allows students to select the school of their choice. The choice is not supposed to result in a segregated situation.

POLICY OPTIONS AND THE CIVIC VALUE OF DIVERSITY

Policy issues involving the implementation of the civic value of diversity focus on several major areas of contention: (1) school curriculum that is multicultural; (2) busing and supervision by federal courts to achieve school integration; (3) reduction of gender bias in schools; and (4) full inclusion of students who are physically challenged.

Curriculum Content Responsibility for the development of curriculum policy for the nation's public schools is a reserved power of the fifty states. Each of the departments of education is accountable for developing curriculum guidelines, to which educators in the states' local districts are expected to be in compliance. Controversy over curriculum that is multicultural has been played out on the policy-making stage by the advocates and critics of the teaching of diversity in the schools. Public schools have been encouraged to incorporate multicultural curriculum into their programs since the early 1970s, when the American Association of Colleges of Teacher Education (AACTE) urged support for cultural diversity and global understanding. A decade later, several influential writers warned that multiculturalism was divisive for American society in the long run, and that Western civilization's cultural commonalities needed to be public education's curriculum focus. "Thus was launched the so-called culture wars, which have persisted on an educational battlefield that extends from kindergarten to graduate school."[106]

According to one of its most prominent supporters, James A. Banks, curriculum and education that is multicultural has multiple dimensions, which frequently are simplified by media commentators and some educators: (1) A variety of cultural and ethnic examples, data, and information content is integrated to demonstrate major ideas, principles, generalizations, and theories; (2) knowledge is constructed following the process utilized by social, behavioral, and natural scientists; (3) prejudice-reduction strategies assist students in the evolution of positive attitude acquisition toward diverse populations; (4) teachers follow an equity pedagogy that enables diverse students to achieve academically; and (5) the school becomes a unit of change with an empowering culture and social structure, applying evaluation methods that are fair to all groups and undoing tracking practices.[107]

In essence, advocates of multicultural curriculum support the (1) inclusion of underrepresented groups (e.g., Native Americans, Latinos, women, gays and lesbians); (2) inclusion of the history of non-European ethnic groups, who previously have been underrepresented, as a source of ethnic self-esteem; (3) de-emphasis of European history, culture, and achievements of ethnic European males; and (4) emphasis on the history, culture, and achievements of Native Americans, Latinos, Africans, and Asians.[108]

On the other hand, critics of multicultural curriculum disapprove of content that they believe (1) politicizes the curriculum by forfeiting historical accuracy; (2) "Balkanizes" the curriculum by divesting it from a common sense of civic identity for a diverse population; (3) treats Europe as a monolithic area, with undifferentiated cultures, history, and peoples; (4) overlooks the ethnic European heritage of more than 75 percent of American citizenry; and (5) exudes hostility to ethnic Europeans and Western civilization.[109] Linda Chavez, writing for the *National Review*, characterizes advocates of multiculturalism as "more affluent and assimilated native-born … most often the elite" who "hope to ride the immigrant wave to greater power and influence."[110]

School Integration   School integration of African-American and ethnic European students did not end as a diversity issue with the 1954 Supreme Court decision in the *Brown* v. *Board of Education* ruling that "separate is inherently unequal." The need for busing and federal court supervision continues as a controversial policy option to implement the civic value of diversity.[111] Defenders of court-supervised busing argue that more than forty years after the *Brown* decision, patterns of segregated education remain, and that busing should not be dropped as a policy option. Antagonists of court-supervised busing attack this policy option as a failure that should be abandoned, especially since the Supreme Court's 1991 ruling in *Board of Education* v. *Dowell* made it easier for school districts to stop busing to achieve balance among African-American and ethnic European students.

Gender Bias   The issue of whether or not discrimination against females should be reversed by governmental action has elicited policy option suggestions from various quarters since the early 1970s, when federal legislation first sought to counter gender discrimination against females involved with federally subsidized educational programs. Title IX of the Education Amendments to the Civil Rights Act in 1972 declared such discrimination to be illegal. Two years later, the Women's Educational Equity Act sought to diminish gender stereotyping and ameliorate females' career opportunities. A 1992 study of the condition of education for girls by the American Association of University Women (AAUW) suggested policy options for action by federal, state, and local agencies of education that would improve females' vocational and professional aspirations, self-esteem, and performance in mathematics and the sciences.[112] Criticism of the AAUW's study denies the validity of the information at its base, and suggests that the policy options recommended by the women's organization should be ignored.[113]

Full Inclusion of Students Who Are Physically Challenged Public Law 94-142 (The Education for All Handicapped Children Act of 1975) was the fulfillment of a social policy that mandated the provision of educational services for young people with various physical, mental, and emotional disabilities equal to those for nondisabled students. Controversy over this policy option centered on the financial expense engendered by the services to be provided, as well as their compulsory nature.[114] Fifteen years later, in 1990, the Individuals with Disabilities Education Act (IDEA) ushered in the policy of full inclusion in the school environment for students with physical challenges. It brought to an end the labeling of students with physical, mental, and emotional challenges, as well as the segregation of those students in separate classrooms in the public schools.

The movement to inclusive schools requires suitable resources and services to be granted for the law's target clientele. Advocates of full inclusion believe that it is the right of students with physical challenges to be educated with their nondisabled peers, and that they can benefit from being part of the regular classroom's least restrictive environment.[115]

Skeptics of the full-inclusion policy, such as American Federation of Teachers President, the late Albert Shanker, take issue with a policy that places "all students with disabilities into general education classrooms without regard to the nature or severity of the students' disabilities, without regard to the ability to behave and function appropriately in a regular classroom, without regard to the educational benefits they derive, and without regard to the impact that inclusion has on the other students in the class."[116] Shanker acknowledged the anticipated savings that administrators expect to accrue from the use of full-inclusion placements, even though the large amounts of money needed to carry out this educational program might not be forthcoming. He highlighted, too, the fact that special education advocates are not satisfied with full inclusion as a permanent policy option, but prefer a trial period to ascertain how well students will adjust, moving the students out of full inclusion if it does not work for them.

RECOMMENDATIONS FOR THE TWENTY-FIRST CENTURY

As the last decade of the twentieth century comes to a close, there is a tendency for people in all parts of society to prognosticate about what the future holds for American education. This section is divided into two parts. The first part considers five categories of recommendations selected from the writings of people immersed in issues of political economy and education. The author supports these recommendations. The second part focuses on the author's recommendations for the implementation in the nation's schools of curricula that emphasize diversity, global education, and civic education for the twenty-first century.

SELECTED RECOMMENDATIONS FOR EDUCATION IN THE TWENTY-FIRST CENTURY

Technological and telecommunication changes will affect education on a nationwide level in the next century. In preparation for that time, decisions about the attitudes, knowledge, and skills that will be required of Americans of all ages, all socioeconomic categories, all ethnic backgrounds, and both genders need to be made by educational policy makers at local, state, and national levels.

Recommendation 1: Focus on the Student to Improve the Status Quo in Education   William E. Klingele favors the formation of "a community of learning impactors," collaborating fully to concentrate on the student.[117] These impactors (educators, media, government, business, public and private agencies, and parents/caregivers) should deliver a continuous and collaborative effort to increase students' learning achievement. Conventional wisdom on the educational reform of American public schools has targeted teachers as the cause of educational decline in students' achievement scores. The teacher alone cannot be blamed for environmental factors external to the schools, which mitigate students' achievement.

Recommendation 2: Create High-Quality Standards for Student Achievement   In order to preclude a rush toward alteration of curriculum, assessment, professional development, and teacher education, states should create academic standards and assessment tools to drive the direction of school reform. This recommendation for rigorous academic standards is visible in the most recent trend in school reform, and has received national, bipartisan support.[118] Goals 2000 legislation, Title I (formerly Chapter 1), and the March 1996 policy statement of the Second National Education Summit espoused the formulation of (1) academic standards for worldclass learning achievements among American students, and (2) assessment tools to measure students' progress toward those standards. The American Federation of Teachers supports standards that are grounded in the core disciplines, are rigorous and world class, evaluate performance, include multiple performance levels, combine knowledge and skills, guide instruction, and are written clearly to understand expectations.[119]

Recommendation 3: Utilize the Education Dollar to Increase Its Productivity and to Fulfill Educational Reform Goals   Odden and Hanushek both agree about the constraints in raising student achievement levels without increasing real dollar expenses. The former believes that the policy and education system need to be nudged to reallocate funds to the strategies that work, and target additional money to underfunded areas (e.g., preschool, kindergarten, tutors, professional development, and rampant fiscal inequalities).[120] Ineffective utilization of public education funds, according to Hanushek, needs to be set at the doorsteps of school administrators who do not (1) monitor their schools' programs; (2) monitor the effectiveness of the use of their schools' resources; and (3) provide incentives for improved schooling and higher student performance.[121]

Recommendation 4: Provide Equal Education for Limited English Proficient (LEP) Students   Five steps could ensure that LEP students are ready to meet common content standards and can reach goals set for world-class achievement, according to Denise McKeon: (1) School and district officials need to make a systematic examination of academic programs open to LEP students; (2) TESOL and access standards need to be used as guidelines for school personnel to review approaches to educating LEP students; (3) state and school officials need to ensure the presence of English as a Second Language (ESL) and bilingual educators on the professional teams that develop curriculum frameworks; (4) state and district officials need to discuss alternative ways to judge the performance of LEP students; and (5) state and district officials need to support the development of standards for English as a Second Language, to ensure that instructors are highly skilled and content standards are created.[122]

Recommendation 5: Educate Students for the Workforce in the Twenty-First Century   Robert Reich, Secretary of Labor in the first Clinton administration, suggested that students need "a formal education that will refine four basic skills: abstraction, system thinking, experimentation, and collaboration."[123] By contrast, Jeremy Rifkin foresees the creation of millions of new jobs in the civil sector, among those nonprofit organizations that serve Americans in local neighborhoods and communities.[124] He favors the incorporation of service learning in the curriculum as an opportunity for American educators to address the challenge of preparing students for their role as civil sector workers in the information age. Service learning allows youngsters to participate in the community, counteracting their feelings of alienation, detachment, and aimlessness. It fosters a sense of personal responsibility, accountability, self-esteem, and leadership, as well as encouraging creativity, initiative, and empathy among participating students. Inclusion of service learning in the curriculum will garner public support derived from a long-standing American tradition of community service. Rifkin's idea is to incorporate into the civil sector of society those workers who no longer are needed in the market and government sectors, thereby enabling those workers to create social capital. Curriculum trends in the 1990s reflect new interest in the creation of social capital, as evidenced by the presence of service learning in the schools.[125]

CURRICULA THAT FOCUS ON DIVERSITY, AND GLOBAL
AND CIVIC EDUCATION FOR THE TWENTY-FIRST CENTURY

As we identify the possibilities of the cyberfuture, we can act to make them happen or prevent them from happening. And we can acquire useful insights into the enormous opportunities and challenges that lie ahead.[126]

Worldwide communication, transportation, and economic networks provide global interface for all of the planet's diverse populations in their nested local, national, and international political divisions. Human concerns about the fundamental issues of housing, nutrition, health, education, employment, justice, and peace are universal. Global demographic shifts within and among countries, as well as heightened worldwide ethnic awareness, are connected to the changing nature of the American population.

Demographic projections that point to a shift away from ethnic European dominance make it imperative for the American educational system to be infused with curricula components that are multicultural, global, and civic in focus. Opportunities must be provided for the nation's youngsters to become proficient in the attitudes, knowledge, and skills that will prepare them for the multiple challenges of the twenty-first century. "Multiculturalism, globalism, and civism, properly conceived, are necessarily conjoined as complementary components of a liberal education in preparation for democratic citizenship."[127]

American society is based on a democratic view of pluralism in which all people have equal opportunity and protection under the law. Curriculum that is multicultural will enable students to be cognizant of the attributes, needs, and citizenship responsibilities of diverse populations within the broader American society. Also, it will promote the values of a democratic society in its respect for the individual, enhancement of all students' self-image and ability to see themselves in the curriculum, fostering acceptance and understanding of differences as "legitimate and empowering," and "moving people beyond the separations that exist to a new culture."[128]

Edward Cornish's "futuribles" need to be taken into account when planning for curriculum that is global.[129] If American children of the twenty-first century are expected to be full participants in the world, it is vital that the schools provide curriculum that has much greater global knowledge than what currently exists. The components of global education include world travel and the study of foreign languages, political geography, world history, anthropology, sociology, social studies, world literature, world music, world art, and the world's religions.[130] A globally educated person, proficient in global competencies, has (1) broad knowledge of world cultures, (2) deep knowledge of another culture, (3) fluency in another language, and (4) a sense of responsibility toward the establishment of global stability, justice, and peace. Future actualization of the U.N. motto "Think globally, act locally!" will depend on people's utilization of a global education content base to solve local and national social, economic, and political problems.

American educational institutions, along with the family, religious and community groups, government, business, and labor groups sustain the historic onus for imparting civic competence and responsibility to our population. It is the schools, however, that carry "the central role."[131] It has been recognized since the founding of the nation that education has a civic mission: to prepare informed, rational, humane, and participating citizens committed to the values and principles of American constitutional democracy.[132] National Goal number three, embedded in the 1994 Educate America Act, projects the year 2000 as a time by which "All students will leave grades four, eight, and twelve having demonstrated competency over challenging subject matter, including ... civics and government ... so that they may be prepared for responsible citizenship, further learning, and productive employment.... All students will be involved in activities that promote and demonstrate ... good citizenship, community service, and personal responsibility."[133] Cornish's choice of "futuribles" about government highlights the importance of emphasizing civism in American education for the twenty-first century.

The prospect of an increasingly "complex, fractious, and interdependent world" of the twenty-first century warrants the revival of the concept of "civic virtue."[134] This idea incorporates civic dispositions that are conducive to "the healthy functioning of the American constitutional democracy," which encompasses civility (e.g., respect, civil discourse), individual responsibility, self-discipline, civic-mindedness, open-mindedness, compromise, toleration of diversity, patience and persistence, compassion, generosity, and loyalty to the nation and its principles.[135] A second component of civic virtue is a commitment to the "fundamental values and principles essential to the preservation and improvement of the constitutional order" through popular sovereignty and the components of constitutional government (e.g., rule of law, separation of powers, checks and balances, minority rights, civilian control of the military, separation of church and state, and federalism).[136]

CONCLUSIONS

American public education is closely connected to the economic and political/governmental structure of the nation. Consequently, the schools are viewed as conduits through which American youth is prepared for a variety of responsibilities and duties within the nation's pluralistic, entrepreneurial, and democratic society.

The goals of American public education historically have been the subject of public discussion. Controversy between the supporters of various interpretations of the public good still is present among societal and educational policy makers. Traditionalist and progressivist viewpoints about which interests the schools should serve are played out in the design, implementation, and assessment decisions that are made about the public schools' structure, organization, and curriculum.

Historically, American public schools have been influenced by the views of political economists, who believe that the schools should be based on the business model, measuring student achievement as the result of the schools' productivity. This notion connects national economic development and growth to a workforce prepared by the schools to contribute to American business being competitive on a world-class level.

American public schools are challenged by society's loss of confidence in their ability to educate students for their responsibilities as adults in a nation and world that increasingly are impacted by changes in technology/telecommunications, demographic movements, and environmental and ecological conditions.

All students in the nation's public schools do not receive consistent high-quality education. There are variables (e.g., property-tax funding, class size, teacher/student ratios, age and condition of school buildings, currency of textbooks, professional expertise of administrators and teachers, a community's socioeconomic class, parental involvement, states' support, and federal intervention) that operate to produce educational inequities.

School reform for the past fifteen years has focused on restructuring school organization, curriculum revision and infusion of education that is multicultural, developing alternate and improved procedures for teacher preparation, adding rigor to teacher certification standards, re-creating student-centered forms of instruction, devising methods for authentic performance tasks and assessment linked to academic standards, and providing opportunities for parental choice in selecting their children's educational institutions.

The twenty-first century will continue to be fraught with challenges for the nation's public schools. Recommendations for meeting those challenges are being provided by a variety of interest groups in society: business leaders, parents, teacher organizations, state governors, federal officials, university and think-tank policy makers, and religious organizations. Where are the voices of the students?

NOTES

1. See Center for Civic Education, *National Standards for Civics and Government* (Calabasas, CA: Center for Civic Education, 1994), p. 153, and Articles I through VII of the Constitution of the United States of America for specifics of the federal system.
2. José A. Cardenas, "Political Limits to an Education of Value: The Role of the State?," in John I. Goodlad and Pamela Keating, eds., *Access to Knowledge, An*

Agenda for Our Nation's Schools (New York: College Entrance Examination Board, 1990), p. 275.

3. Joe Spring, *American Education*, 6th ed. (New York: McGraw-Hill, Inc., 1994), p. 194.
4. Allan C. Ornstein and Daniel U. Levine, *Foundations of Education*, 5th ed. (Boston: Houghton Mifflin Company, 1993), p. 7.
5. Ibid., p. 230.
6. Ibid., p. 200.
7. Cardenas, p. 275.
8. "New Federalism" refers to the policy followed by President Ronald Reagan in the 1980s to reduce the national government's funding, activities, and regulations in several sectors of society, including education. New Federalism was based on the belief that the national government had overstepped its boundaries and sought to return to the states their responsibility for education, as implied in the Tenth Amendment.
9. Ornstein and Levine, p. 226.
10. Spring, p. 5.
11. Charles F. Bahmueller, general ed., *Civitas: A Framework for Civic Education* (Calabasas, CA: Center for Civic Education, 1991), pp. 361–378.
12. Ibid., p. 362.
13. Ibid., pp. 362–363.
14. *Education Week* is an excellent source of information about congressional actions having to do with educational issues.
15. Bahmueller, p. 376.
16. There is a multitude of publications that focus on the history of immigration to the United States. One book in particular recounts the story in an especially poignant manner: Alan M. Kraut, *The Huddled Masses: The Immigrant in American Society, 1880–1921* (Arlington Heights, IL: Harlan Davidson, Inc., 1986).
17. Bahmueller, p. 26.
18. Jack L. Nelson, Stuart B. Palonsky, and Kenneth Carlson, *Critical Issues in Education* (New York: McGraw-Hill, Inc., 1990), p. 3.
19. Ronald C. Doll, *Curriculum Improvement: Decision Making and Process*, 8th ed. (Boston: Allyn & Bacon, 1992), pp. 24–27.
20. Nelson, Palonsky, and Carlson, p. 23.
21. Ibid., pp. 24–25.
22. Ibid., pp. 26–28.
23. Doll, pp. 9–16.
24. Howard D. Mehlinger, "School Reform in the Information Age," in *Phi Delta Kappan*, February 1996, p. 402.
25. Alan J. DeYoung, *Economics and American Education: A Historical and Critical Overview of the Impact of Economic Theories on Schooling in the United States* (New York: Longman, Inc., 1989), p. 24.
26. Bahmueller, p. 185.
27. Doll, p. 9.
28. DeYoung, p. 47.
29. Joel Spring, "Foreword," in Alan J. DeYoung, *Economics and American Education: A Historical and Critical Overview of the Impact of Economic Theories on Schooling in the United States* (New York: Longman, Inc., 1989), p. xi.
30. DeYoung, p. 64.
31. Ibid., p. 66.
32. Ibid., pp. 88–89.
33. Ibid., p. 102.
34. Ibid., p. 105.

35. Ibid., p. 105.

36. Spring in DeYoung, p. xi.

37. James Moffett, "On to the Past, Wrong-Headed School Reform," in *Phi Delta Kappan*, April 1994, p. 587.

38. DeYoung, p. 3.

39. Moffett, p. 587.

40. "The Unfinished Agenda," in *Education Week*, April 27, 1988. Some of the most notable reports during that five-year period included: "Academic Preparation for College: What Students Need to Know and Be Able to Do" (1983); "Educating Americans for the 21st Century" (1983); "High School: A Report on Secondary Education in America" (1983); "A Place Called School" (1984); "Horace's Compromise: The Dilemma of the American White House" (1984); "High Schools and the Changing Workplace: The Employer's View" (1984); "Reconnecting Youth: The Next Stage of Reform" (1985); "Tomorrow's Teachers" (1986); "James Madison High School: A Curriculum for American Students" (1987); and "New Voices: Immigrant Students in U.S. Public Schools" (1988).

41. Marian Wright Edelman, "Investing in Our Children: A Struggle for America's Conscience and Future," in *USA Today Magazine*, March 1993, pp. 24–26.

42. National Center for Children in Poverty, *Five Million Children: A Statistical Profile of Our Poorest Young Citizens* (New York: Columbia University, 1990).

43. Michael S. Knapp, Brenda J. Turnbull, and Patrick M. Shields, "New Directions for Educating the Children of Poverty," in *Educational Leadership*, September 1990, p. 4.

44. James P. Comer, "Educating Students outside the Mainstream," in *Agenda: America's Schools for the 21st Century*, Winter 1992, pp. 26–28.

45. Jeannie Oaks, *Voices from the Field: 30 Expert Opinions on America 2000. The Bush Administration Strategy to 'Reinvent' America's Schools* (Washington, DC: The William T. Grant Foundation Commission on Work, Family, and Citizenship and the Institute for Educational Leadership, 1991).

46. Michael S. Knapp and Patrick M. Shields, "Reconceiving Instruction for the Disadvantaged," in *Phi Delta Kappan*, June 1990, pp. 753–758.

47. Comer, note 44.

48. Douglas J. Besharov, "New Directions for Head Start," in *The World & I*, January 1992, pp. 515–531.

49. Comer, note 44.

50. Besharov, note 48.

51. National Center for Children in Poverty, note 42. The Center was established in 1989 to strengthen programs and policies for poverty-level children and their families.

52. Ibid.

53. Marge Scherer, "On Savage Inequalities: A Conversation with Jonathan Kozol," in *Educational Leadership*, December 1992/January 1993, p. 7.

54. National Center for Children in Poverty, note 42.

55. Scherer, note 53.

56. Jonathan Kozol, "Let's 'Throw' Money at the Pentagon and Allocate It to Education," in *Virginia Journal of Education*, October 1992, pp. 19–22. Kozol is a former teacher and author of *Savage Inequalities: Children in America's Schools* (New York: Harper Perennial, 1991) and *Amazing Grace* (New York: Crown Publishers, Inc., 1995).

57. Edelman, note 41.

58. Comer, note 44.

59. Denise McKeon, "When Meeting 'Common' Standards Is Uncommonly Difficult," in *Educational Leadership*, May 1994.
60. National Association of Bilingual Education, "Census Reports Sharp Increase in Number of Non-English Speaking Americans," in *NABE News*, Volume 16, Number 6, 1993, pp. 1 and 25.
61. U.S. Department of Education, *The Condition of Bilingual Education: A Report to the Congress and the President* (Washington, DC: U.S.D.O.E., 1992).
62. McKeon, pp. 46–48.
63. Ibid. See "Programmatic Deficiencies"; "Teacher Preparation Deficiencies"; and "Assessment and Debates Over Standardized Tests."
64. Joel Spring, *American Education*, pp. 160–161.
65. Ibid., p. 161.
66. Arthur G. Wirth, *Education and Work for the Year 2000, Choices We Face* (San Francisco: Jossey-Bass Inc., 1992), p. xvi.
67. Ibid., p. 69.
68. Jeremy Rifkin, "Rethinking the Mission of American Education: Preparing the Next Generation for the Civil Society," in *Education Week*, January 31, 1996, p. 44.
69. Edward Cornish, "The Cyber Future: 92 Ways Our Lives Will Change by the Year 2025," in *The Futurist*, January-February 1996, pp. 1–15.
70. Wirth, pp. 6–7.
71. Ibid., pp. 97–98.
72. W. Norton Grubb, "The New Vocationalism: What It Is, What It Could Be," in *Phi Delta Kappan*, April 1996, p. 535.
73. Howard D. Mehlinger, "School Reform in the Information Age," in *Phi Delta Kappan*, February, 1996, p. 405.
74. Ibid.
75. Wirth, p. xvi.
76. Rifkin, note 68.
77. "Will Schools Ever Get Better? Enrollments Are Up, Money Is Tight—But There's Hope," in *Business Week*, April 17, 1995, pp. 64–68.
78. Allan Odden, "Productive Discussions about the Education Dollar," in *Education Week*, February 7, 1996, p. 56.
79. Eric A. Hanushek, "Making America's Schools Work, This Time Money Is Not the Answer," in *The Brookings Review*, Fall 1994, pp. 10–13.
80. Odden, p. 56.
81. Ibid. The reports were issued by the Consortium for Policy Research in Education, the Consortium on Productivity in the Schools, and the Economic Policy Institute.
82. Ibid., p. 44.
83. Elaine Warrick-Harris, "Year-Round School, The Best Thing Since Sliced Bread," in *Childhood Education*, Annual Theme Issue (Wheaton, MD: The Association for Childhood Education International, 1995), pp. 282–287.
84. *Brown* v. *Board of Education* (1954).
85. *Griffin* v. *School Board of Prince Edward County* (1964) and *Alexander* v. *Holmes County Board of Education* (1969).
86. *Serrano* v. *Priest* (1971).
87. Orenstein and Levine, pp. 245–248. *San Antonio Independent School District* v. *Rodriguez* (1973); *Rose* v. *Council for Better Education* (1989); *Englewood Independent School District* v. *Kirby* (1989); and *Abbott* v. *Burke* (1990).
88. Bahmueller, p. 369.
89. Moffett, p. 586.

90. National Education Goals Panel, 1994, p. 13.

91. Ibid., pp. 8–11.

92. Jonathan Alter, "Busting the Big Blob: Can White Guys in Suits—Governors and CEOs—Finally Beat Back the Educrats?," *Newsweek*, April 9, 1996, p. 40.

93. Paul Gray, "Debating Standards: Politicians and Business Executives Again Try to Fix Public Education," *Time*, April 8, 1996, p. 40.

94. Ibid.

95. "Text of Policy Statement Issued at National Summit," *Education Week*, April 3, 1996, p. 13.

96. Ibid.

97. Peter Applebome, "Education Summit Calls for Tough Standards to Be Set by States and Local School Districts," *The New York Times*, March 27, 1996, p. B9.

98. "Text of Policy Statement Issued at National Summit," p. 13.

99. Ibid.

100. Ibid.

101. Moffett, p. 586.

102. Archer and Walsh, p. 12.

103. Ibid. Comment made by David Turner, the executive director of the Illinois Principals Association.

104. Tom Watkins, "Other Voices, People Are Talking about Public Charter Schools: Guest Opinion," in *The Public Charter, A Newsletter about Michigan's Public School Academies*, Central Michigan University, Winter 1996, p. 3.

105. Orenstein & Levine, pp. 406–407.

106. James William Noll, Introduction to "Should Multiculturalism Permeate the Curriculum?," in *Taking Sides: Clashing Views on Controversial Educational Issues*, 8th ed. (Guilford, CT: Dushkin Publishing, 1995), p. 82.

107. James A. Banks, "Multicultural Development, Dimensions, and Challenges," *Phi Delta Kappan*, September 1993.

108. Bahmueller, pp. 252–253.

109. Arthur M. Schlesinger, Jr., *The Disuniting of America: Reflections on a Multicultural Society* (New York: W. W. Norton & Company, 1992); Bahmueller, p. 253.

110. Linda Chavez, "Demystifying Multiculturalism," *National Review*, February 21, 1994.

111. Bahmueller, p. 253.

112. American Association of University Women, *How Schools Shortchange Girls: A Study of Major Findings on Girls and Education* (Washington, DC: AAUW, 1992).

113. Rita Kramer, "Are Girls Shortchanged in School?," *Commentary*, June 1992.

114. Noll, Introduction to "Is Full Inclusion of Disabled Students Desirable?," in *Taking Sides: Clashing Views on Controversial Educational Issues*, 8th ed., (Guilford, CT: Dushkin Publishing, 1995), p. 198.

115. Jean B. Arnold and Harold W. Dodge, "Room for All," *The American School Board Journal*, October 1994.

116. Albert Shanker, "Where We Stand on the Rush to Inclusion," *Vital Speeches of the Day*, March 1, 1994.

117. William E. Klingele, "Shifting the Target of Educational Reform," *Educational Horizons*, Summer 1994, pp. 196–201.

118. Matthew Gandal for the American Federation of Teachers (AFT), "Not All Standards Are Created Equal," *Educational Leadership*, March 1995, pp. 16–21. This document was written by the Educational Issues Department of the AFT as a guide for states committed to the task of setting high-quality standards for student achievement.

119. Ibid.

120. Odden, p. 44.

121. Hanushek, note 79.
122. McKeon, pp. 48–49.
123. Wirth, p. 69.
124. Rifkin, note 68.
125. Ibid.
126. Cornish, p. 10.
127. John J. Patrick, "Multiculturalism, Globalism, and Civism in American Education: Connections and Contradictions among Three Trendy Ideas." Lecture delivered on August 10, 1995, at the Harvard Graduate School of Education Institute, "Writing, Reading, and Civic Education."
128. K. Hanson, "Multicultural Education as Democratic Education," in *Women's Educational Equity Act Publishing Center Digest* (Newton, MA: Educational Development Center, Inc., 1992), p. 3.
129. Cornish, note 69.
130. Joel A. Barker, "Preparing for the Twenty-First Century: The EFG Experiment," *Educational Horizons*, Fall 1994, pp. 12–17.
131. Bahmueller, p. 4.
132. Center for Civic Education, p. v.
133. Ibid.
134. Bahmueller, p. 11.
135. Ibid., pp. 13–14.
136. Ibid., pp. 14–15.

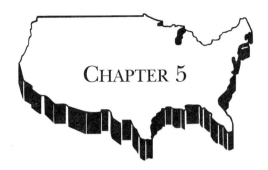

CHAPTER 5

A PROPERTY RIGHTS APPROACH TO ENVIRONMENTAL QUALITY

JAMES A. THORSON

The environment and the economy seem to be at the opposite ends of the spectrum. However, we cannot separate economics from the environment. Economics is concerned with the allocation of scarce resources among alternative ends. A clean environment is a scarce resource since we have less clean air and water than we desire. We can only have a cleaner environment if we are willing to pay for it. The optimal policy will attain the desired level of environmental quality at the lowest cost.

This chapter examines the role of property rights in the environmental problem. A firm will pollute the air or water because the cost of polluting to the firm is small. A firm that generates sulfur dioxide because of its production process will bear only a small fraction of the cost of pollution. The individuals who live downwind from the firm have to bear part of the cost. Much of this cost is not denominated in dollar terms. If smoke from a factory distorts your view of a valley, this is difficult to measure because views of valleys are not traded on an open market. However, you are clearly made worse off. However, suppose that we allocated property rights to clean air. For example, we could give the homeowners the right to clean air, and therefore the only way that the firm could pollute the air is if the residents allowed them to. The likely result would be that the only way that residents would allow the factory to pollute the air is if they are compensated in some way. This compensation would be determined through bargaining between the firm and the residents.

In many situations, the location of firms that generate pollution is the result of bargaining between communities and firms. This bargaining typically occurs through local public officials. However, these local officials are influenced by the preferences of their constituents. One example of this bargaining occurs when a nuclear power plant or a landfill needs a suitable location. If the decision is made on a local level, the plant or the landfill will find a home only if the residents of the community agree to it. The question is, "What sort of bargaining takes place and what compensation is required to allow the obnoxious land use to be located in a community?"

This chapter is organized as follows. First, the historical approach to the problem of environmental quality will be discussed. Second, the property rights approach will be considered relative to the other methods of dealing with this problem. The third section looks at the policy options associated with the property rights approach. The fourth section incorporates all of the benefits and the problems of the property rights approach to make policy recommendations for the twenty-first century. The final section is the conclusion.

THE HISTORICAL APPROACH TO ENVIRONMENTAL QUALITY

To examine the problem of environmental quality, we need to figure out how to determine the optimal amount of pollution. Let's start with the question: What is the optimal amount of pollution? Many people would answer zero, since any pollution makes us worse off. However, the optimal level of pollution is not necessarily zero, since just as pollution has a cost, reducing pollution has a cost as well. For example, one way to reduce the amount of air pollution is for everyone to sell their car for scrap metal. This would definitely reduce the amount of air pollution, but it would only occur at a very high cost. We would have to find some other means of getting to and from work, shopping, and other activities. The important point here is that we want to minimize total costs. If the gain from reduced pollution is exceeded by the cost of reducing pollution, then we can hardly say that society is better off.

The reason we have pollution is that we receive benefits from the activities that generate pollution. For example, let's take the problem of finding a location for a nuclear power plant. The reason we build nuclear power plants is that they provide cheap electricity. If another form of electrical generation could provide us with the electricity at a lower production cost, we would be using that method of production. The problem, however, is that the costs of pollution are not included in the total cost of production. Therefore, we need to find a means of including the pollution costs as part of the total production costs to the firm.

The historical method of dealing with the problem of pollution is through regulation. This regulation can occur on several levels. On a federal level, the government can set limits on the amount of pollution that a firm can produce. In addition, the state can also set limits on the amount of pollution that can be generated. Local government can often control whether a firm is allowed to locate in its jurisdiction.

The problem with the direct regulation approach is that it is not a very efficient method of altering the production costs of the firm. If a firm is producing below the limit set by the government, it will have no incentive to reduce its level of pollution. For example, many states require emissions tests for automobiles. If a car meets the standard, the owner has no incentive to reduce emissions further. In addition, once the firm reaches the limit, the cost of additional pollution effectively becomes infinite, since the firm cannot produce beyond this amount. The problem that the direct regulation approach neglects is that different firms may have different costs of reducing pollution. For example, some firms could reduce their level of pollution at very little cost. Others will find it very costly to reduce the level of pollution. Under regulation, we allow both firms to produce the same level of total output; however, this might not be the solution that minimizes the total amount of pollution.

A related question can be raised that asks, "What are the factors that have caused policy makers to become more interested in alternatives to regulation in recent years?" There are two factors that have contributed to the movement away from direct regulation. First, manufacturing employment has stagnated since the 1970s, and manufacturing employment has been particularly hard hit by environmental regulations. Second, policy makers have become increasingly aware of the potential benefits of deregulation in recent years. Therefore, the movement away from direct regulation in the area of environmental quality is seen as the next logical step.

One reason for the shift toward more market-based methods is that the cost of direct regulation in terms of economic activity and jobs has become more apparent in recent years. In the first two decades after World War II, the level of government regulation regarding environmental matters increased significantly. However, at the same time, the economy was expanding rapidly as well. Therefore, direct regulation may have reduced economic activity relative to the market-based methods, but this was offset by the fact that the economy as a whole was expanding. In particular, manufacturing employment increased from approximately 14 million in 1950 to 20 million in 1970. Therefore, when manufacturing jobs are increasing, voters may be less concerned that the regulations have only slowed the growth of manufacturing jobs, not caused a reduction in the actual number of jobs. In addition, voters tend to be less concerned about jobs as a political issue during times of economic growth.

However, during the 1970s the economy experienced two major recessions and the job outlook for many types of workers became gloomy. This was particularly the case in the manufacturing sector of the economy. The manufacturing sector is particularly hard hit by environmental regulations, so a large fraction of job losses is likely to occur in this sector. When manufacturing jobs are becoming scarcer, policy makers have an incentive to look for methods of improving environmental quality that have a smaller effect on economic activity and employment. Between 1970 and 1995, manufacturing jobs decreased from 20 million to 18.5 million. Therefore, the balancing of economic as well as environmental interests has become more important as a political issue in recent decades.

The second reason for the movement away from direct regulation is the fact that policy makers have become more aware of the benefits of markets and competition in recent years. This awareness started with the deregulation efforts initiated by the Carter administration in the 1970s. Several industries were deregulated, including the trucking industry, the airline industry, and the natural gas industry. In many cases, consumers were found to be better off under deregulation than they were in the era when these industries were regulated. This is because competition serves as a form of regulation. For example, suppose that we are concerned with the quality of bread produced by bakers in a given area. One way to ensure that the bread meets a particular standard is to regulate the quality of bread, and have the government inspect the loaves that are produced in order to make sure that they meet the standard. On the other hand, if there are several producers of bread, competition will ensure that the bread produced meets the minimum standards set by consumers. If one firm produces low-quality bread, consumers will look for substitutes and the firm will sell less bread. Therefore, competition gives the firm an incentive to produce quality bread.

This example can be easily extended to the environmental problem. The reason we have too much pollution is because firms have little incentive to reduce the amount that they generate. Direct regulation puts a limit on the amount of pollution that a firm can generate; however, there is no incentive for firms to reduce pollution below that amount. The alternatives suggested in this chapter change the incentives faced by firms. Under direct regulation, a firm can emit pollution with no opportunity cost if it is below the allowable limit. However, if we move toward more market-oriented methods of regulating environmental quality, then pollution will have an opportunity cost to the firm and firms will have an incentive to look for ways to reduce pollution.

Two alternatives have been suggested to reduce the incentive problem caused by regulation. First, the government could impose a tax on the amount of pollution produced by the firm. This would force the firm to consider the cost of the pollution, as well as the cost of eliminating the pollution. Firms that have a low-pollution abatement cost would tend to reduce the level of pollution rather than pay the tax. Firms with higher costs would pay a larger amount in taxes. A similar proposal was used during the recent health care debate. One of the proposed means of financing health care reform was a cigarette tax. There were two reasons for this (besides the fact that it would generate additional government revenue). First, smokers tend to have more health problems, so it would be a way of attacking the rising cost of health care due to the behavior of smokers. In addition, it would encourage some smokers to quit, since they wouldn't value the right to smoke at the new higher price. Therefore, we would have fewer health problems in the future because of the tax.

The second alternative to the incentive problem is to allow transferable pollution permits. In this situation we determine the optimal amount of pollution, and we give firms the right to generate that much pollution. This could be the same amount allowed under direct regulation, or it could be a lower amount. However, the firms can also trade their right to pollute. Therefore, firms with low-pollution reduction costs will tend to sell off their permits in the market, while those with high costs will purchase those permits. The major difference between these two programs is in the distribution of benefits. Under the tax proposal, the government benefits from the additional tax revenue generated. Therefore, some economists have suggested a pollution tax as a method of reducing the budget deficit. With the permits system, we have a transfer of resources from firms with high-pollution abatement costs to firms with low-pollution abatement costs. In each case, both the tax and the transferable permits force firms to consider the cost of pollution.

One of the reasons that environmental agencies have preferred direct regulation is that the implementation and monitoring costs tend to be smaller. A regulatory agency can determine a standard and then develop a system to monitor compliance much more easily than coming up with a tax or permit system. If a tax is imposed on the amount of pollution generated, then the agency needs an accurate method of measuring the amount of pollution produced. In addition, it also may need people to collect the tax and to deal with firms that are not in compliance. Sometimes, this can be easily accomplished by a tax on a polluting input. For example, if we are concerned with the amount of pollution that is generated from automobiles, we could impose a tax on gasoline. An increase in the price of gasoline would increase the cost of driving and therefore encourage people to drive less.

CHALLENGES, OPPORTUNITIES, AND CONSTRAINTS: AN INTRODUCTION TO THE PROPERTY RIGHTS APPROACH

An alternative to direct regulation is to assign property rights to resources, such as clean air and water, and allow the opposing parties to engage in trade. For example, if a local government owns the property rights to the clean air above the town, a factory can enter the town and start polluting only if the town allows it to. However, if the town allows the firm to produce, it is only likely to do this if it receives compensation for the pollution that it must then endure.

The cornerstone of the property rights approach is the Coase theorem, which was presented by Ronald Coase in his article "The Problem of Social

Cost."[1] Prior to Coase, the conventional wisdom was that the only way to deal effectively with the problem of negative externalities was either direct regulation or some other form of government intervention in the marketplace, such as a pollution tax. Coase suggested that we do not always need government intervention to deal with the problem of externalities. Sometimes private bargaining between individuals and firms may achieve the same result.

What Coase suggested was that if bargaining costs were zero, it would not matter who was assigned the property rights and we will get the optimal amount of pollution. This means that if we give the firm the right to pollute, or the residents the right to breathe clean air, as long as bargaining costs are zero, we will get the same result. Each situation will result in the optimal amount of pollution.

For example, suppose there is a steel mill that produces pollution as a by-product of its output. In addition, we have a group of residents who live near the steel mill who are made worse off by the pollution generated by the firm. We will also assume that none of the residents works in the steel mill, so that the residents do not get any direct benefit from the presence of the steel mill.

If the firm produces steel, there are benefits and costs that need to be addressed. First, the benefit to the firm of producing another unit of steel is the additional profit that the firm receives. Profit is likely to increase with output up to a point. At some point, the cost of producing another unit of steel exceeds the additional revenue that the firm receives, therefore the firm would not want to go beyond this point. In addition, the increase in profit is likely to decline with the amount of output produced. However, the pollution is a negative externality, which means that the firm does not have to bear the entire production cost. The cost of pollution is shared with the residents who live near the plant.

The cost of pollution is difficult to measure, since, as stated previously, pollution is not traded in an open market. However, this problem is not unique to the property rights approach; regulators also have to determine the cost of pollution. There are ways that we can get an approximation of the cost. One method is through the housing market. There have been several studies that have examined the effects of pollution on housing prices. The studies found that the price of housing was significantly lower in areas with higher pollution. If a family is looking to purchase a house, and they have two similar choices with one difference—house A is in a polluted neighborhood and house B is in a neighborhood with cleaner air—the only way to induce a family to accept house A is if the price is lower.

In this example, we will assume that the cost of pollution is measured by the decrease in the value of housing due to pollution. The cost of pollution increases with the amount of pollution produced. Let's start with assigning the property rights to clean air to the households that live near the plant. Therefore, the marginal cost of pollution is upward sloping. In addition, the amount of pollution is directly related to the amount of output produced. If there is no bargaining, the households will want a level of output equal to zero, since any output produces pollution, which decreases the value of their homes. With bargaining, it would be possible for the firm to compensate the homeowners for the damage that it causes.

Now suppose that we give the property rights to the air to the firm, so the firm has the right to pollute the air if it desires. In the absence of bargaining, the firm is going to produce to the point where the marginal benefit is zero. However, at some point the marginal cost to homeowners may exceed the additional profit to the firm. Suppose that the additional profit that the firm makes is equal to $100, but the value of the housing stock decreases by $1,000. If the firm is interested in maximizing profits, as long as the homeowners can offer more than $100, the firm will be better off not producing that level of output. In addition, as long as the firm accepts a price that is less than $1,000, the residents are better off making the payment.[2]

Now the first objection that many people will have to this analysis is on the question of why we would ever want to give the property rights to the firm in the first place. Shouldn't clean air be a right for all of the residents of a community? The answer may well be yes, but the Coase theorem suggests that there is no *a priori* reason why we should grant the property rights to households for any efficiency reasons. That is, as long as bargaining costs are zero, we will get the same level of output, no matter who owns the property rights. In most cases, the government does grant the property rights to environmental quality to the residents of a jurisdiction, not to firms. However, there are exceptions. One example is right-to-farm laws. In many urbanizing areas there is a conflict between farmers and the new residents who are moving into the community. These new residents often seek to place limitations on the type of agricultural activities that are permitted. This occurs because certain agricultural activities, such as pig farming, carry with them large negative externalities. However, state governments have in many instances enacted laws that give farmers the right to continue their agricultural activities. The context of this in terms of the Coase theorem is best stated by William Fischel:

> If a factory is made to reduce its smoke, its owners (and perhaps employees and consumers) will be harmed. If the owner is not made to reduce the smoke, the people who breathe the smoke will be harmed. I have always had a hard time selling this idea to my students, but now I have it on the authority of the Council on Environmental Quality that people who spray chemicals and drive loud machines are the victims of the people who want to use the air for breathing and the early hours for sleeping. Some polluters, it seems, are more equal than others.[3]

One problem that plagues the Coase theorem is the assumption that bargaining costs are zero. If there are a large number of people who live near the steel mill, the cost of making a bargain with each of them may be quite large. Where bargaining costs are high, government intervention may be justified. However, it may then be the government that is bargaining with the firm, so much of the Coase theorem is still applicable. One of the benefits of a representative form of government is that bargaining costs are lower than they would be if every voter were allowed to vote on all of the public policy issues facing a state or the nation.

Although most of the bargaining relative to environmental matters is done between firms and some level of government, it is clear that there are trade-offs. For example, suppose an electric utility is looking for a site to locate a nuclear power plant. The potential danger from living next to a nuclear power plant is a negative externality that will be of concern to the residents of the community. In addition, since most communities can enact fairly powerful zoning laws, in the absence of state or federal intervention, the local community can prevent a nuclear power plant from locating within its jurisdiction. In this case, how will a nuclear power plant find a suitable location? The answer is that it will need to compensate the residents for the right to locate in the community. This compensation may take many forms. For example, a nuclear power plant may increase property-tax revenues, while requiring very little in additional local public services. Therefore, the property tax rate that the homeowners pay will fall, or the level of local public services may increase.

There are, however, some objections to bargaining between firms and the government. One is that the regulatory power of the government is one of the police powers of the state, and these powers should not be bought and sold. For example, if the government sells an exception to a regulation, why doesn't the government take this a step further and sell permits that give drivers the right to disobey speed limits in the jurisdiction? As Fischel suggests, a unit of government that starts selling off exceptions to regulations to the highest bidder, may actually appear to be more like a protection racket than an institution whose purpose is to provide for the public good.[4]

The courts have tended to strike down regulations whose sole purpose is to raise revenue from individuals and firms. However, there are many cases where there are either explicit or implicit transactions between individuals and firms. The transactions tend to be allowed if they relate to the externality caused by the individual or firm. For example, many towns have impact fees that a developer must pay when building new houses in a town. The impact fee is used to offset the increase in municipal services consumed by the new residents. However, the courts have been leery of accepting bargaining between developers and towns where the compensation is not related to externality caused by the development. An example of this is the U.S. Supreme Court decision *Dolan v. Tigard* (1994), where one of the requirements for a plumbing supply store to get a zoning change was to allocate part of its land for open space and a bicycle path. The Supreme Court held that in bargaining between individuals and the local government, the government must demonstrate a "rough proportionality" between the harm caused by the activity and the requirements that the government places on the individual or the firm. The point here is that there are many cases where transactions between individuals and the government occur, and as long as the transactions relate to the externality caused by a firm's activity, the courts tend to uphold such transactions.

Even if bargaining is allowed to occur, there are other problems with bargaining to deal with an externality problem. These include the excessive entry problem, strategic bargaining, and wealth effects from the initial distribution of property rights.

Let's consider the first problem, excessive entry. Suppose that a town pays a firm not to produce steel in its jurisdiction. The question that can be asked is, "What would stop other firms from entering the town in order to receive payments from the town not to produce?" In a similar fashion, suppose that the homeowners own the property rights to clean air and therefore are receiving compensation from the firm for the pollution that it produces. What prevents new individuals from moving into the town to receive payments from the firm as well?

The answer to this question lies in one of the fundamental assumptions of the Coase theorem, which is that property rights must be fully assigned. Therefore, if the firm owns the right to pollute the air, then only the firm has the right to pollute the air. The only way that a new firm can come in and receive payments is if it buys the property rights from the existing firm. Similarly, the only way that a new household can receive payments from the firm is if it purchases the right to clean air from an existing resident of the town.

In practice, property rights tend to run with the land in the town. Suppose that we have a town that is centered around a large lake. In addition, there are homes built around the lake, and the only way to access the lake is to purchase a home. In this case, the value of the access to the lake will be capitalized into the price of the home when it is sold. Therefore, any benefit from access to the lake will be offset by the increase in the price of the home, which eliminates the excessive entry problem.

Another problem with bargaining to deal with externality problems is strategic bargaining. Let's go back to the discussion of the bargaining between the homeowners and the steel mill. Assume again that for some level of output the additional profit to the firm is $100, and the additional cost to the homeowners is $1,000. Suppose that the firm knows the cost to the homeowners of the additional pollution. What is to prevent the firm from trying to convince the homeowners that it will accept nothing less than the full $1,000 benefit to the homeowners as compensation for the decision not to produce? In addition, why would the homeowners be willing to pay any more than $100 since that is the cost of lost profits to the firm? The answer here is that one of the assumptions of the Coase theorem is that there are zero transaction costs.

This assumes that both parties have all relevant information in the transaction. The firm knows that the homeowners benefit by $1,000, and the homeowners know that the firm is better off by $100 if it produces. However, the difference in valuation would appear to give some room for strategic behavior. The solution to this problem depends on the assignment of property rights. In addition to assuring that property rights are exclusively assigned, there needs to be a rule by which the property rights are protected. There are three different rules that can be used. These are property rules, liability rules, and inalienability.

The last rule is the easiest to deal with. Inalienability means that the property rights cannot be exchanged, which eliminates the need for bargaining. Direct regulation, such as limits on the amount of pollution that can be put into the air or water, is an example of this. If the government tells me that my car must meet certain emissions standards, my car must meet the standard or I cannot drive it. I do not have the alternative of bargaining with the state to purchase the right to drive my polluting car.

A liability rule requires payment to the owner of the entitlement when that entitlement is violated. If the state owns the right to clean air and I choose to drive around in my polluting car, then I must compensate the state for the damage that I create. In our case of the steel mill and the homeowners, the homeowners demanding clean air are infringing on the property rights of the firm and are, therefore, liable for the lost profits to the firm, which is $100. Under a liability rule this valuation must be made by a neutral third party. Therefore, the firm cannot hold out for $1,000 since that is not the harm to the firm.

The final alternative is the property rule. The property rule allows the owner of the entitlement to refuse to accept any offer made. In this case, the firm can refuse anything less than $1,000. Therefore, this is the amount that the firm will receive, since the firm will not accept any less, and the homeowners will not offer any more. Therefore, in this case the firm receives the maximum that the homeowners are willing to pay.

Another problem with the property rights approach is the wealth effect. In our initial discussion of the Coase theorem it was stated that it doesn't matter who the property rights are assigned to; we get the same level of pollution in either case. The problem here is that property rights are valuable. Therefore, those who receive the property rights find that their wealth has increased, which may in turn affect their demand for environmental quality. As stated earlier, amenities such as clean air or access to a lake tend to be capitalized into the value of residential housing. Therefore, when the housing values increase, the homeowner's wealth increases, which increases the demand for clean air. This would result in a lower level of pollution allowed by the households.

If we look at the location of firms that generate pollution we see that they are often located in areas with a larger concentration of poor people.

One reason for this location pattern is that the poor are often more willing to accept the firm in its jurisdiction, since they may be more likely to benefit from the additional jobs created. The demand for environmental quality tends to increase with income.

The presence of the wealth effect does not reduce the effectiveness of the property rights approach; it just implies that the results may depend on how the property rights are initially distributed. If we allocate the property rights to the homeowners, we are likely to have less pollution than if the property rights are allocated to the firm. Therefore, when determining the costs of pollution and the benefits of pollution reduction, we need to take into consideration who actually owns the property rights and how this would affect each party's valuation of environmental quality.

POLICY OPTIONS: THE CURRENT DEBATE

We have examined the property rights approach on a theoretical level. The next step is to see how well the property rights approach can work in practice. After all, if a theory cannot be implemented, it has little value for policy purposes. The question to be addressed is, "What options do policy makers have when trying to implement the property rights approach, and how do they compare to the current system?" The criteria that we will use to evaluate the property rights approach is to examine its costs relative to the benefits that it generates. The benchmark in the analysis is the traditional method of using regulation to deal with environmental problems. We will explore whether the property rights approach can decrease the level of pollution at a lower cost than the more traditional approach of direct regulation. The property rights approach will be examined on two levels: (1) on a national level, to determine whether emissions trading is a more efficient solution than direct regulation; (2) on a local level, to see how bargaining between firms and communities deals with the externality problems that can occur when certain undesirable elements, such as an airport or a landfill, move into a town. We will examine what kind of trading takes place, and to what extent it deals with the problem of externalities.

On a national level, probably the best example of the property rights approach is the use of emissions trading. Under this scheme, each firm in an industry is given a fixed level of pollution that it is allowed to generate. This may be the same as the maximum that would be allowed under direct regulation. However, the big difference between the direct regulation and emission permits alternatives is in the cost of pollution under each system. Under direct regulation, the marginal cost to the firm of generating pollution below the allowable level is zero. However, under the emissions permits program, the cost of generating pollution is the value of the right to emit that unit of pollution. Therefore, if the cost to the firm of reducing pollution is less than the value of the permit, then the firm would be better off reducing its pollution and selling off the permit in the market. In addition, under the direct regulation scheme, the marginal cost of generating pollution beyond the allowable limit (assuming full compliance) is infinite, since the firm does not have ability to purchase the right to pollute more. However, under emissions trading, the cost to the firm of generating more pollution is just the price of the additional permits needed. Therefore, the firm will increase the amount of pollution it generates if the cost of reducing pollution exceeds the price of the permits.

In both cases, the total amount of pollution is the same, since we have assumed that the government has given each firm the amount of permits equal to the amount of pollution that could be generated under direct regulation. However, under the emissions trading program, the cost of reducing pollution to the firms must be no more than under direct regulation, and may well be lower. The pollution reduction costs can be no more than under the direct regulation program, since in order for permits to be traded there must be some gain for the firms involved. If there are no gains from trade, the result will be the same as under direct regulation.

One problem that must be considered when implementing an emissions trading program is the size of the transaction costs involved. The transaction costs include the cost of matching up the buyers and sellers of the permits. The higher the transaction costs, the lower will be the gains from the emissions trading program. One particularly important problem that has to be dealt with is the high start-up costs of the program. To start an emissions trading program, a market must be developed where one doesn't exist. In addition, it may take some time before contracts become standardized between firms, which also increases the transaction costs.

An emissions trading program can have up to four different elements: netting, offsets, bubbles, and banking. Netting occurs when a firm starts a new process in a plant that generates a new source of pollution. The firm is allowed to generate the additional pollution if it reduces pollution by a similar amount from some other source in the plant. Therefore, the net effect of the new process is that it generates zero additional pollution. This is often referred to as *internal trading*, since the entire transaction occurs within the firm. The largest number of emissions permit transactions has occurred through netting. One reason for this is that the transaction costs for trading in the firm are small.

Offsets pertain to "non-attainment areas," which are areas that have a level of pollution that exceeds federal standards. The federal government allows no additional pollution in these non-attainment areas, but a new source is allowed if pollution is reduced by a greater amount elsewhere in the area. There are two ways in which the offsets can be obtained. First, the firm can reduce pollution from one of its other plants in the area, which is another form of internal trading, discussed in the previous paragraph. It can also purchase pollution permits from other firms, or through external trading. In the case of offsets, approximately 90 percent of the transactions occur through internal trading. This suggests that transaction costs play an important role in the emissions trading process.

The next part of the emissions trading program is bubbles, which looks at the entire pollution generated by either a plant or all of the plants owned by the firm that are located in a given area. A firm may generate several different types of pollution and the bubble policy looks at the sum of pollution from all sources. If one type of pollution exceeds regulations, the firm can compensate by reducing pollution from other sources. For example, if the firm increases its emissions of sulfur dioxides, it can offset this by decreasing its emissions of some other pollutant, such as carbon monoxide. In this case, the total amount of pollution generated by the firm stays constant. In the case of bubbles there have been relatively few transactions. The majority of these transactions have been internal.

The final part of the emissions trading program is banking. Banking deals with the generation of pollution over time. If a firm reduces its pollution generated this year, it can increase the amount of pollution that it generates in future years. Therefore, if a firm has a slow year and generates less pollution than the law allows, it may then increase the pollution it generates when the demand for its product increases. In addition, the firm is allowed to sell the pollution permits that it banks. For example, a firm may reduce its pollution this year, but not sell off its permits until some time in the future. However, there have been relatively few transactions in the banking program, so the long-run effect has yet to be seen.

To analyze the effect of the emissions trading program, two methods will be used. First, the cost savings from each element of the program will be examined. Then, the effect on the level of environmental quality will be addressed.

The effectiveness of the various elements of the emissions trading program is examined by Robert Hahn.[5] The largest cost savings come from the netting and the bubbles programs. It is estimated that netting reduces costs to firms by between $525 million and $12 billion. There has been little empirical evidence on the effectiveness of the offset program, but Hahn estimates that the reduced costs would be in the hundreds of millions. The bubbles program has saved firms over $400 million. There has been little cost savings from banking, however, because there have been few transactions in this area.

Although there have been significant cost savings due to the implementation of the emissions trading program, there has been little change in the overall level of environmental quality. The reason for this is that firms have either decided to use their emissions permits or sell them off to other firms that then use them. Therefore, the level of pollution in the aggregate has stayed relatively stable. The way to reduce the level of pollution is to reduce the number of permits available. However, the Environmental

Protection Agency (EPA) has been relatively slow in changing the total level of permits allowed. One of the problems here is that there has been relatively little trading between firms because of the high transaction costs involved. It may be less costly to reduce the number of permits allowed, once a more explicit market in the permits develops.

One way of lowering the transaction costs is to develop a standardized contract. For example, the Chicago Board of Trade recently received permission from the Commodities Futures Trading Commission (CFTC) to trade futures contracts in sulfur dioxide emissions. This will have two effects on the transaction costs.

First, a standardized contract will decrease the cost of the transaction because it will reduce the negotiating time necessary to come to an agreement. For example, there is less information about the selling price of new cars than there is about the selling price of stock in the company that makes the cars. The stock prices are published daily, which gives the buyers and sellers useful information. If I know that the going price for a share of stock is $35, then I have little incentive to offer $40. However, when it comes to the buying and selling of new cars, there is less information available about the selling price. Car dealers are not required to disclose the price at which each car was sold. Therefore, the typical way of gathering information about the price is to go from dealer to dealer. This however, increases the transaction costs.

Second, the futures market will increase the information about the going price of the right to emit sulfur dioxide. One prediction by economists at the EPA is that the going price of the right to emit one ton of sulfur dioxide would be between $100 and $400. One important factor that will determine the success of this program is whether the Chicago Board of Trade generates enough interest in its efforts to make trading the contract profitable. In the absence of an external market, information about the prices at which the permits are exchanged is much more difficult to come by, which in turn increases the transaction costs.

The preceding analysis has demonstrated that there are significant cost savings when transferable emissions permits are implemented as a policy tool to deal with the problem of air pollution. However, this policy has had little effect on the overall level of environmental quality. This can be changed by varying the number of permits that the government initially distributes to firms. One problem is the high transaction costs involved in permit trading. This is confirmed by the fact that the overwhelming majority of transactions takes place within the same firm. Once explicit markets are developed to trade emissions permits, the number of external transactions is likely to increase significantly. When the number of external transactions increases, the cost savings to firms should increase significantly as well.

So far, we have analyzed how the property rights approach is useful in dealing with national environmental problems. We can also examine its usefulness on the local level. A local environmental problem affects only the residents and firms in the immediate vicinity. For example, a major airport will generate noise pollution, which will make the people who live in the immediate area worse off; however, those who live far away from the airport suffer little negative effects.

The property rights approach is particularly useful in this case, since local governments often have broad powers to regulate the location and the activities of firms that generate negative externalities. In many cases, they can block the location of the firm entirely, or at least ensure that the firm compensates the jurisdiction for the negative externalities that are created. For example, a store such as Wal-Mart may want to locate in a town. However, the store will draw shoppers from other towns, which will increase the congestion the town faces. One way the town can deal with the increased congestion is to require the store to expand the road to the store, or to put in traffic lights as a way to reduce the problem of congestion. This clearly is an example of a town that owns the property rights to the store's location. The only way the firm can locate in the town is if it compensates the town for the negative externalities it generates.

The primary power of the town comes from its power to implement zoning regulations. Zoning ordinances transfer large amounts of property rights to land from landowners to the local government. The three rights that all landowners have include (1) the right to sell the land, (2) the right to rent the land to others, and (3) the right to exclude others from the land. If any of these rights are violated, then the regulation is considered a "taking" under the Fifth Amendment to the Constitution and compensation is due the landowner. However, the landowner does not necessarily have the right to allocate the parcel of land to its most profitable use. For example, suppose that I own a parcel of land in a residential neighborhood. The most profitable use for that land may be to build a 24-hour convenience store on the property. However, the community can use the zoning ordinance to prohibit that land use, since the convenience store is likely to make some of my neighbors worse off due to the increased traffic that would be generated.

A zoning ordinance is not the only method that residents of a community can use to deal with land-use conflicts. The city of Houston does not have a zoning ordinance and has consistently voted one down each time it comes up for referendum. One reason for the absence of the zoning ordinance is that there are a variety of private covenants that regulate land use. For example, a buyer of a single-family home may find that the deed restricts him or her from converting the land to commercial use. This way a private agreement accomplishes the same task as the zoning ordinance. The majority of towns have zoning ordinances, primarily because of the higher transaction costs of private agreements. As was stated earlier, the transaction costs are likely to increase as the population increases, so zoning is a cheaper substitute for most suburbs and large cities.

The courts have been fairly lenient toward towns in their implementation of zoning laws. The primary requirement is that the zoning ordinance must serve some public purpose. For example, a zoning ordinance may restrict the development of retail stores to reduce the problem of congestion. A common strategy in some suburbs is to declare that one of the goals of the zoning ordinance is to preserve the rural character of the community. This is usually viewed by the courts as a legitimate public purpose, and the suburbs are allowed to require large minimum lot sizes in order to restrict the development of multifamily housing. A zoning ordinance must serve some public purpose, but there is no requirement that the benefit of the ordinance exceed the cost.

Since the zoning ordinance gives a large part of the property rights to the community, this becomes particularly important when it comes to non-residential land use, since most firms generate some negative externality that the town can object to. Therefore, the community can use its zoning power to exact concessions from the firm if it is a significant generator of pollution. In this case, the only way a firm can find a suitable location is if it compensates the town for the negative externalities that it generates. The firm is looking for the community that charges the lowest price for the privilege of location. The question we can ask here is, "What influences the price that communities will charge for the right to locate in the community?"

The largest problems occur when compensation is not allowed to be given to the community where the offending land use is located. One example of this is when the state or local government attempts to find an appropriate site for a new landfill or a new prison. In many cases the state will determine where the facility will be located and the community will have little say in the matter. In this situation, the facility tends to be located in areas where the voters have little political power. The residents may be against the facility in their neighborhood, but they may not have enough influence to prevent it.

The degree of opposition to the location of nondesirable facilities such as landfills and prisons has been studied by Thomas Rasmussen.[6] He examined which factors are most likely to cause significant opposition to these types of facilities, and tested three hypotheses.

The first hypothesis is that when the degree of risk associated with a project is perceived to be low, the opposition from potential neighbors and residents of the town is likely to be weak. For example, if confronted with a choice between a shopping center and a landfill, there will probably be less opposition to the shopping center. Both the shopping center and the landfill may generate negative externalities. The shopping center may generate additional congestion. However, there is less risk associated with the shopping center than with the landfill. In addition, firms that are attempting to locate a land use that generates negative externalities may be inclined to offer to make modifications in the project that would reduce the risk.

The second hypothesis is that if there is a large economic benefit to be gained from the project, the opposition to the project is likely to be weak. This is just another way of saying that if people are compensated for the negative externalities that they must bear, they are more likely to accept them. For example, a town in suburban Chicago proposed building an incinerator for municipal garbage because the property tax base would increase significantly. The larger the economic benefits, the more likely the residents are to accept the negative externalities.

The last hypothesis that Rasmussen proposed is that the degree of opposition to a facility is likely to be weak when the population density of the community is low. One reason for this is that fewer neighbors mean lower bargaining costs. When bargaining costs are lower, the likelihood of reaching an agreement increases. In addition, when there are fewer residents, the economic benefits per capita may be higher, which would increase the probability of the firm and the town coming to an agreement.

The data used in the analysis came from 33 proposed sites for prisons and waste disposal facilities. Each of these was featured in the *New York Times* between 1987 and 1990. The results were for the most part consistent with the preceding hypotheses.

For testing the first hypothesis, the amount of risk was measured by the type of facility. Prisons are generally considered less risky than waste disposal facilities. Therefore, prisons should have less opposition. The results showed that 84 percent of landfills had strong local opposition, while only 36 percent of prisons had strong local opposition. One problem with this analysis is that it ignores any variation in risk between different types of facilities. For example, the risk is likely to be higher for a landfill that stores nuclear waste than for a landfill that serves primarily municipal waste. In addition, a minimum-security prison may pose less risk than a maximum-security prison, due to differences in the type of criminals that are housed in each.

The second hypothesis is strongly supported by the data. In 94 percent of the cases where economic benefits are not available, there is strong opposition to the facility. When economic compensation is available, there is strong opposition to the facility in only 31 percent of the cases. In addition, there is some variation in the economic benefits associated with waste-disposal facilities and prisons. The economic benefits of prisons tend to be much higher than of the waste-disposal facilities.

One question that needs to be addressed here is how opposition to a project will vary with income and economic benefits. We can hypothesize that towns with a higher level of income are likely to be less concerned with economic benefits (or demand a larger level of benefits) than lower-income communities. If the demand for environmental quality increases with income, then we would expect lower-income communities to place a higher value on the existence of economic benefits.

The final hypothesis is that the population density of a community influences the degree of opposition. For projects that were attempting to locate in high-density areas, 85 percent had high levels of local opposition. However, the results were mixed for low-density communities. In these communities 50 percent had strong local opposition, and 50 percent had weak local opposition.

The previous analysis has some important implications for policy makers. First, residents do pay attention to the benefits and costs of new firms and government facilities locating in their community. Residents are concerned about negative externalities, but they appear to be more concerned with facilities such as landfills, which may pose a health risk. Second, although residents are concerned about negative externalities, they may be willing to endure some such externalities if they receive compensation for the inconvenience. Therefore, compensation is an important component when attempting to site an undesirable land use. In addition, firms are often willing to make investments to reduce the negative externalities or the risks associated with the land use. However, these payments are less likely to be made if the residents do not own the property rights to environmental quality. Therefore, the initial assignment of property rights may be important.

The effect of negative externalities on housing prices is often an important factor when residents of a community are deciding whether to allow a firm to locate in the community. For example, there is much literature that examines the effect of air pollution on property values. The results generally show that higher amounts of air pollution are associated with lower property values. This follows from economic theory, since a house that is located in an area with pollution is probably less desirable, and a consumer is less likely to accept a less desirable house unless the price is lower. However, we may find a study that shows that proximity to an undesirable land use has little or no effect on the value of housing. Does this suggest that the market does not take into account the reduction in environmental quality? The answer is, not necessarily, since it may be that the owners of the undesirable land use may have compensated the surrounding residents for the inconvenience that they are forced to live with. If this compensation is large enough, it may offset the negative effect of the undesirable land use.

Consider the example of the location of a nuclear power plant. On the one hand, there is a very large amount of risk associated with living in a town that has a nuclear power plant in its jurisdiction. However, there are also benefits that may accrue to the community. For example, the plant may be a very large part of the community's property tax base and may pay for a large share of the property tax bill for the community. Therefore, the property tax rate may be lower in the community than in the surrounding towns. The reduction in the property tax rate may offset the risk associated with a nuclear power plant. In addition, the power plant may generate employment, which may bring additional benefits to the community. Therefore, if the benefits of the nuclear power plant exceed the cost of the additional risk, housing values may increase rather than decrease.

One problem with using zoning as a method to deal with environmental problems is interjurisdictional spillovers. If a community allows a nuclear power plant to be located within its boundaries, it may get the fiscal and other benefits, but the surrounding towns get the risk with little of the benefits. Therefore, the surrounding towns are likely to be opposed to such a project because the net benefit that they receive from the project will be minimal or even negative. For example, suppose a town wants to allow an incinerator to locate in its boundary because of fiscal gain. However, suppose that it decides to locate the incinerator on the edge of town, upwind from the main residential areas of the town. In this case, the town is trying to gain the fiscal benefits of the project, but passing off some of the costs to other communities.

There are several methods that can be used to deal with the spillovers. These include nuisance rules, tax-base sharing, and forbearance. A nuisance rule says that the town is liable for any damages that it imposes on the surrounding towns. Another approach is to have the surrounding communities share the tax base to the offending land use. In this case, the surrounding communities share in the fiscal benefits from the offending activity. Finally, using the forbearance approach, communities arrive at mutually satisfying agreement. William Fischel suggests that in rural areas, neighboring towns are not necessarily eager to impose costs on their neighbors.[7] Therefore, interjurisdictional spillovers are likely to be kept to a minimum. He suggests mutual-aid agreements for fire and police protection as an example of a town's concern for the well-being of its neighbors.

RECOMMENDATIONS FOR THE TWENTY-FIRST CENTURY

The final question that needs to be addressed is what recommendations can be made to policy makers for future environmental policy. The past few years have seen a gradual movement away from the command-and-control method of dealing with environmental problems to more market-oriented methods. There are several areas that need to be addressed in order to ensure that market-oriented methods work more efficiently.

The first recommendation deals with the problem of transaction costs. Suppose that we develop an emissions permit scheme where each firm is given permits equal to the amount of pollution that can be generated under direct regulation. If the transactions costs are high enough, there may be no gains available from trade. Therefore, the result would be no different than if we used a system of direct regulation. One important part of transaction costs that needs to be addressed is information costs. An impediment to trade is linking up buyers with sellers.

To see this problem, consider the transaction costs involved in the sale of two different assets. Suppose that you wish to sell a home worth $100,000, and you also wish to sell $100,000 worth of stock. To sell the stock, the transaction costs are likely to be approximately $500 (the actual commission will vary from firm to firm) and the transaction will be completed quickly. For a stock that has a large volume, such as the stock of AT&T or General Motors, the entire trade may take place in less than a minute. However, the transaction costs on the sale of the house is much larger. The brokerage commission will be approximately 6 percent of the selling price, or about $6,000. In addition, there are other costs that the seller of the house might have to bear, such as taxes on the house transaction or attorney fees. Also, in addition to the higher sales commission, it usually takes a much longer time to find a buyer for the house. Finally, when a buyer is found and an agreement is reached, it usually takes several weeks for the transaction to be completed, due to the time necessary to arrange for financing and perform a title search.

There are two primary reasons for the increased time it takes to sell a house versus the time necessary to sell a block of stock. The first reason is that stock certificates are homogeneous. When I buy 100 shares of stock, I don't care who the previous owners of the shares were because each share will give me the same benefit. Houses, on the other hand, are more heterogeneous. Individuals have different preferences, so two different houses are likely to give the consumer different levels of satisfaction. There is also concern about the quality of the house. Two similar houses may have different levels of quality, and therefore potential buyers will take some time to determine the quality of the house.

The second reason why it takes less time to sell stock is that in the stock market, information about the sales price of the stock is easy to obtain. If I want to sell 100 shares of stock, it is easy for me to find out the price the last buyer paid per share. Information is available on the price that houses sell for, but it is more costly to obtain. Another problem is that, again, housing is heterogeneous. Even if the sale price of each home were widely known, it would still take some time to interpret the data because of the variation in the features of different houses.

This has two important implications for the trading of emissions permits. First, since transaction costs tend to decrease as the homogeneity of the product increases, there needs to be some mechanism to provide relatively standard contracts for the right to pollute. In addition, information about the prices of permits should be widely available. The objective here is to get the firm to consider the cost of pollution when making business decisions. Under the old scheme of regulation, the cost of pollution is zero, as long as the firm is below the maximum allowable limit of pollution. Therefore, in this case, the firm has no incentive to reduce the amount of pollution it generates. The use of transferable pollution permits increases the cost of pollution to the firm. If the firm is below the allowable limit, it now bears a cost of generating pollution. The cost to the firm is the revenue that it would generate by selling its permits in the market. However, if information about the going price of a permit is not widely available, the firm may not realize the opportunity that it is giving up. As a result, it may be less likely to consider the value of permits in its decision making.

The use of futures markets can be very beneficial both in providing standardized contracts and distributing information about price. For example, consider the case of a futures market in corn. Farmers are better off with a futures market in corn, even though they may never use the market directly to sell their corn. In general, a very small percentage of buyers of futures contracts actually take delivery of the product. A farmer may decide to sell corn to the local mill, but the pricing information gained from the futures market will help the farmer determine whether or not the mill is offering a fair price.

Another benefit to implementing an emissions trading program is that firms can gain by reducing their pollution level. Therefore, it increases the demand for products that can be used to reduce pollution. In this case, we may get new firms entering the pollution-control industry. This increased entry into the industry could have two effects in the long run. First, increased competition would lower the price of pollution-control equipment, which would increase the number of firms that use such equipment. Second, increased entry into this industry could increase the amount of innovation and technological change in pollution control.

An example of this can be seen in the computer industry. In the early 1970s computers were very expensive, so the number of firms that bought and used computers in their daily operations was quite small. However, in the late 1970s personal computers were introduced into the market. Since this time there have been two major changes in the computer industry. First, the number of firms in the industry increased rapidly. In the early 1970s the industry was dominated by large firms such as IBM and Digital Equipment. In the 1980s, as personal computers increased in popularity, a large number of small firms entered the market. Along with the increase in the number of firms was a rapid increase in innovation in the industry. With the increases in innovation, personal computers became more effective substitutes for mainframe computers, which have traditionally been used by large businesses. Second, the price of computers has dropped rapidly, even though the quality has improved. The result is that the use of computers has increased dramatically, since there is a large gain to be had by increasing the number of computers used by businesses.

CONCLUSION

This chapter has shown that there can be significant efficiency advantages when moving from a command-and-control approach to more market-oriented approaches. The main benefit of the market-oriented approaches is that they force firms to consider the cost of the pollution that is generated as a result of the production process. The problem with direct regulation is that it allows no consideration of the fact that there may be gains from trade. Finally, the market-oriented approaches allow firms to profit from reducing their level of pollution. This gives firms an incentive to find new ways of reducing the amount of pollution that they produce.

NOTES

1. Ronald H. Coase, "The Problem of Social Cost," *Journal of Law and Economics* 3 (October 1960), pp. 1–44.
2. What the actual payment will be will depend on several factors, including which side has the greater bargaining power. The effect of bargaining power is beyond the scope of this chapter.
3. William A. Fischel, "The Urbanization of Agricultural Land: A Review of the National Agricultural Lands Study," *Land Economics* 58 (May 1982), pp. 236–259.
4. William A. Fischel, *The Economics of Zoning Laws: A Property Rights Approach to American Land Use Controls* (Baltimore, MD: Johns Hopkins University Press, 1985).
5. Robert W. Hahn, "Economic Prescriptions for Environmental Problems: How the Patient Followed the Doctor's Orders," *Journal of Economic Perspectives* 3 (Spring 1989), pp. 95–114.
6. Thomas H. Rasmussen, "Not in My Backyard: The Politics of Siting Prisons, Landfills, and Incinerators," *State and Local Government Review* 24 (Fall 1992), pp. 128–134.
7. Fischel, *The Economics of Zoning Laws.*

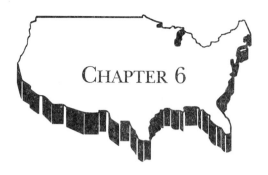

CHAPTER 6

THE NEW IMMIGRANTS

KUL B. RAI AND JOHN W. CRITZER

Since the end of the 1960s, America has seen an explosion in the number of Asian and Latin American immigrants coming to the United States. This influx, both legal and illegal, has produced concerns among many Americans about the impact of immigration on the economy and American culture. Such concerns are not new, as America is a nation of immigrants and policy debates have always centered on the latest group of arrivals. Policy debates and laws on immigration have in great part been shaped by economic factors, race and ethnic issues, and foreign policy.

HISTORICAL BACKGROUND

Both George Washington and Thomas Jefferson believed that immigration would promote America's economy. Washington wanted to attract the wealthy and the skilled to this country, while Jefferson believed that those from the Mediterranean area would benefit America. Yet each had reservations about immigration: Washington was concerned about assimilation of those immigrants who clustered together and retained their former language and customs; Jefferson feared that immigrants who had been ruled by monarchs might find it difficult to adjust to our representative form of government.[1] Neither, however, favored restrictions on immigration.

    The United States experienced its first wave of immigration from 1820 to 1880, which brought more than 10 million people who came mostly from Britain, Ireland, Germany, and to a lesser extent, Scandinavia. During this period, America was rapidly moving from a rural small-town environment to an urban industrial one, and these changes often brought dislocation, hardship, and the need to blame someone. Irish immigrants were singled out because of their religion and their poverty (most had fled Ireland to escape its economic hardship caused in part by a potato famine). Discrimination came primarily in the form of employment. Many job advertisements often included the words: "No Irish Need Apply."[2]

This anger toward newly arriving immigrants led some to organize and seek political action. In 1849, the Know-Nothing Party, which opposed immigrants and Catholics, emerged in New York. Membership was open only to native-born Protestants. When asked their opinion, party members were instructed to reply: "I know nothing."[3] In 1856, the party ran former President Millard Fillmore as its presidential candidate. He lost.

THE ACT TO ENCOURAGE IMMIGRATION OF 1864

During the American Civil War, manpower shortages resulted in the passing of the Act to Encourage Immigration, also known as the Contract Labor Act of 1864, which permitted employers to pay the passage of immigrants who signed contracts to repay these costs. After the war, organized labor blamed the ensuing unemployment on the Act and was able to have it repealed in 1868. The actual practice was not banned until the passage of the Alien Contract Law in 1885.[4]

The 1885 Act and many others were the result of Chinese immigration. The influx of the Chinese was stimulated by the California Gold Rush in 1848. Chinese immigrants also served as contract laborers for the building of the Transcontinental Railroad. Their willingness to accept low wages increased their opportunities to find employment but often under adverse working conditions. Just as there had been anti-Irish riots during the 1840s, anti-Chinese riots occurred in the West during the 1870s and the 1880s.

THE CHINESE EXCLUSION ACT OF 1882

Pressure by labor organizations, the belief that the Chinese could not be assimilated into American society, and racism led to passage of the Chinese Exclusion Act of 1882, which initially stopped Chinese immigration (except for brides), for a ten-year period. This act was extended until its repeal in 1943, primarily as a symbolic gesture to China, one of our allies during World War II.

Japanese immigrants, who were also willing to work for low wages, began replacing Chinese immigrants. Some Japanese immigrants found success as farmers. Their success led the California legislature in 1913 to pass a law restricting land ownership by Japanese immigrants. Steps were also taken at the federal level to discourage and ultimately discontinue Japanese immigration. Japanese entry into the United States was barred from Canada,

Hawaii, and Mexico in 1907 by President Theodore Roosevelt. The so-called Gentlemen's Agreement of 1907–08 led to the cessation of Japanese emigration to the United States. The ban on Japanese immigration, enacted by Congress in 1924, was not lifted until 1952.

The Philippines, acquired by the United States after the Spanish-American War of 1898, was also a source of Asian immigration. Extensive immigration from the Philippines was halted in 1934 through legislation that created a 50-visa quota per year for Filipinos. This quota was increased to 100 in 1946 when the Philippines was given its independence.

THE IMMIGRATION ACTS OF 1882 AND 1891

During this period, Congress became actively involved in developing laws that placed greater restrictions on immigration. First, in order to control the flow of immigration, Congress passed the Immigration Act of 1882, which restricted immigration by individuals with criminal records, mental problems, and those who might need public assistance. A fifty-cent tax on each immigrant entering the United States was also established. Second, concerns about the enforcement of immigration laws led to the passage of the Immigration Act of 1891. A new Bureau of Immigration was created in the Treasury Department to establish complete federal responsibility for immigration laws, thereby eliminating enforcement by the states.

This agency was changed to the Bureau of Immigration and Naturalization in 1906 to reflect its new responsibility. It was made part of the Department of Labor in 1914 and its duties split between two bureaus, one for immigration and the other for naturalization. Both agencies were merged in 1933, creating the Immigration and Naturalization Service (INS). Prior to World War II, the INS was moved to the Department of Justice due to national security considerations.

A second wave of immigration from 1880 to 1920 would bring 23.5 million to the United States, primarily from Southern, Central, and Eastern Europe. These immigrants were mostly Italians, Greeks, Poles, Hungarians, Ukrainians, and other Slavs who concentrated in urban areas upon arrival. Like the first wave, immigrants in the second wave found work in the changing urban industrial environment. This steady supply of labor kept wages low, which permitted the accumulation of capital to foster more industrial development. In turn, the need to reduce costs led to greater use of technology, which resulted in fewer jobs.

Along with concern over jobs, other factors contributed to a major call to limit immigration, especially from Central, Eastern, and Southern Europe. Questions emerged about whether this latest group of immigrants could be assimilated into American society, as they appeared to maintain their customs and traditions longer than previous immigrant groups. In addition, their religions—Jewish, Catholic, and Eastern Orthodox—raised concerns among some Americans.[5]

Another factor that influenced the call for immigration restriction was that in some big cities, such as Boston, Chicago, and New York, political machines emerged that utilized immigrant votes to maintain a political system that was usually quite corrupt.

A literacy test bill passed by Congress was vetoed by President Cleveland in 1896. Labor organizations and groups that supported immigration restriction favored the test, while business groups wishing to maintain a steady flow of workers and keep wages low opposed the legislation. After a number of failed attempts, a literacy test bill was adopted over President Wilson's veto in 1917, requiring immigrants to pass a test in their own language for admittance.

Foreign policy considerations have also played a part in producing calls for tougher immigration laws. During the 1790s, in the aftermath of the French Revolution, legislation to deal with aliens who might commit treason was passed.[6] In the early part of the twentieth century, the Russian Revolution of 1917 and the fear of communism led many to call for greater restrictions on immigration. Some business groups, which had previously favored maintaining a free flow of immigrant workers, joined with labor and other groups committed to stopping immigration.

THE EMERGENCY IMMIGRATION RESTRICTION ACT OF 1921

A quota of 357,803 immigrants per year was established by the Emergency Immigration Restriction Act of 1921. The quota system, based on the 1910 census, primarily benefited countries in Northwestern Europe and to a lesser extent those in Southeastern Europe, but severely restricted immigration from Asia, Africa, and Oceania.[7] This law, however, was altered rather quickly as anti-immigration sentiments produced a demand for even tougher restrictions.

THE NATIONAL ORIGINS ACT OF 1924

The National Origins Act passed in 1924 set a yearly ceiling of 150,000 immigrants, along with a quota system to be established in 1927—although the work was completed in 1929. A provision to allow only those who could be naturalized to enter the United States was written to specifically deny immigration to the Japanese. This action was supported by the 1790 naturalization law that restricted citizenship to whites only.[8] To control the flow of immigrants, a new regulation was adopted requiring American consulates to issue visas against established quotas. Country of birth, rather than residence, was used to establish nationality.[9]

This act produced major regional distinctions in the flow of immigrants. The new system, which was based on the national origins of immigrants from countries that were more numerous in the U.S. population, favored those from Northern and Western Europe over those from Central, Eastern, and

Southern Europe. The flow of immigration declined in the following years due to the national origins system and the Great Depression of the 1930s. Immigrants within the Western Hemisphere had not been restricted in the 1924 legislation. The growth of illegal immigration from Mexico emerged as an issue in the 1920s; however, restrictions were not forthcoming, as south-western agricultural interests effectively lobbied against such legislation in order to maintain a free flow of cheap labor.

The rise of Nazism in Germany during the 1930s raised the issue of refugee status. The strict quotas of the National Origins Act of 1924 placed severe limitations on those who wished to aid the growing number of refugees. A bill to permit 20,000 German-Jewish children into the United States in 1939 died in Congress as the restrictive goals of a tight immigration policy were maintained. The Roosevelt administration, "applying its own interpretation," admitted a large number of refugees.[10]

During World War II, growers were successful in gaining legislation set-ting up the *Bracero* Program, which permitted Mexicans to temporarily enter the United States to work in agriculture. Extended until 1964, this program was finally terminated by the Kennedy administration. A program to tem-porarily bring British West Indians to the United States was also started in 1943. This program has been changed over the years, but currently continues under legislation passed in 1986.

Once the United States was brought into World War II in 1941 with Japan's bombing of Pearl Harbor, over 110,000 Japanese Americans were interned in camps, as they were considered a threat to national security. This program, which cost almost $250 million, was approved by the Supreme Court in 1944.[11]

THE MCCARRAN-WALTER ACT OF 1952

The continuation of the national origins policy created a number of inequal-ities. For example, some countries, such as Great Britain, did not make use of their yearly quotas, while southern European countries like Italy were swamped with requests, and Asian countries were unable to permit any emi-gration. These inequalities were among the many factors that led to a call for immigration reform.[12] The passage of the McCarran-Walter Act of 1952, how-ever, did not alter the basic policy, although one major change was the grant-ing of 156,700 quotas per year for the Eastern Hemisphere. The lifting of racial restrictions on citizenship benefited those Japanese already living in America. A preference system was developed that included a category for those with special training, education, or abilities.

One major component of this legislation, which was defeated, was employer sanctions for hiring illegal aliens from Mexico. While the Act did make it a crime to harbor or bring into the country illegal aliens, the so-called Texas Proviso was added to the law, exempting U.S. employers who employed illegal aliens. Action to halt the flow of illegal immigration was taken in 1954 with a major sweep by the INS that led to the repatriation of nearly one million Mexicans.[13]

Refugees due to wars and the threat of communism led to concrete action by Congress. Prior to this period, actions were usually temporary or limited. For example, after World War II President Truman brought a number of refugees into the country through unused quotas. Congress in the late 1940s did pass legislation that created a commission to deal with the issue of refugees and allowed some countries to use future quotas for refugees, but this policy was terminated in 1957. However, the issue of handling refugees grew as the threat of communism became a major policy concern. President Eisenhower's pressure for reform resulted in the Refugee Act of 1953, which permitted refugees from Europe and China to enter the United States. Soviet repression of the Hungarian Revolution in 1956 led Eisenhower to utilize the "parole" provision of the McCarran-Walter Act of 1952 to bring a large number of Hungarians into this country. This provision was to be used by the attorney general to "parole" aliens on an individual basis into the United States "for emergent reasons or for reasons deemed strictly in the public interest."[14] In practice such "parole" was granted collectively rather than individually, and assisted those fleeing communism. "Parole" status was used from 1959 to 1962 to grant entrance to Cubans fleeing Fidel Castro's Communist Cuba.

It had become quite clear in the early 1960s that a new law dealing with immigration was needed. Prior to his death, President Kennedy submitted a reform package to Congress with the intent of abolishing the national origins system, promoting family reunification, and giving priority to immigrants with needed skills to enter this country.[15]

Immigration policy from the first wave, starting in 1820, to 1965 was often shaped by the need for labor to aid in the expansion of the U.S. economy, but racial and ethnic prejudice—especially against the Irish, Italian, and Asians—also led to call for immigration reform. In addition, foreign policy concerns about the Cold War between the United States and the Soviet Union led presidential actions to bend the regulations to bring in refugees from Communist countries.

CHALLENGES, OPPORTUNITIES, AND CONSTRAINTS

Over four million immigrants were admitted into the United States during the period 1921–30. The immigration flow was even greater in the first two decades of this century. Such massive immigration into the United States did not again take place until the decade of 1971–80, when nearly 4.5 million immigrants settled in the country. That figure jumped to over 7 million during 1981–90 and is likely to increase even further in the last decade of the century. Immigration laws passed since 1965 are responsible for the increase in the number of immigrants entering the United States. More important, the new immigrants have changed the demographic face of the United States.

THE IMMIGRATION ACT OF 1965

The civil rights movement of the 1950s and 1960s and the resultant legislation passed by Congress in the mid- and late 1960s to end race- and gender-based discrimination in employment, housing, voting, and other areas had made the McCarran-Walter Act of 1952 anachronistic. President Lyndon Baines Johnson succeeded where Presidents Truman and Eisenhower had failed. In 1965 Congress passed the Immigration Act, first proposed by John F. Kennedy in 1963, abolishing the national origins quotas for immigration. The new law also abolished the restrictive immigration zone for the 19 Asian countries created by the 1952 law. The total number of immigrants to be admitted under the 1965 Act was set at 290,000. Of these immigrants, 120,000 were to come from the Western Hemisphere and 170,000 from the Eastern Hemisphere.

The two hemispheres were treated differently for many years after the passing of the 1965 law. While in the Eastern Hemisphere, a system of seven preference categories was created that determined the order in which prospective immigrants were to be preferred for admission into the United States, and a ceiling of 20,000 was set for an individual country, the rule for immigrants from the Western Hemisphere was first-come first-served. In 1976 an amendment to the 1965 law passed by Congress extended the preference system to the Western Hemisphere and also imposed a ceiling of 20,000 per country from this hemisphere.[16] Another amendment, passed in 1978, removed the distinction between the two hemispheres for the purpose of immigration and created a worldwide ceiling of 290,000 immigrants.[17]

While the 1952 law had provided first preference for the highly skilled immigrants and their spouses and children, the 1965 law gave first preference to the unmarried adult children of U.S. citizens. The 1965 law did make provision for members of professions, scientists, and artists of exceptional ability in the third preference, and for skilled and unskilled workers in occupations for which labor was in short supply in the United States in the sixth preference (labor certification was required for this category). The preference categories in both laws did not affect the immediate-family reunification principle, a central concern of the lawmakers. The 1965 law, however, gave higher priority to family reunification than the 1952 law. Immediate family members of U.S. citizens, spouses, minor children and parents in the 1965 law, but not the 1952 law, were excluded from the numerical ceiling.

The 1965 law also gave special attention to refugees from Communist countries and the Middle East, and set aside 17,400 visas out of the total 290,000 for them. With the passing of the Refugee Act in 1980 (the Refugee

Act is discussed in the next section), this preference category was eliminated. Another noteworthy feature of the 1965 law applied to rich immigrants who could not otherwise qualify. Anyone investing $40,000 in a business in the United States qualified under "nonpreference," which was essentially an additional preference category.

Although national origins quotas and the discriminatory provisions of the 1952 law against Asians in the 19 countries making up the so-called Asia-Pacific triangle were abolished, the intent of the 1965 law was to retain the racial/ethnic composition of the United States.[18] Senator Edward Kennedy, who was floor manager of the 1965 immigration bill, pointedly said that the ethnic mix of the country was to be retained and that immigration reform would "not inundate America with immigrants from any one country or [from] the most populated and economically deprived nations of Africa and Asia."[19] His brother, Attorney General Robert Kennedy, was precise and expected no more than 5,000 Asian-Pacific immigrants "in the first year and 'no great influx after that.'"[20] Many other political leaders, including President Johnson, had similar views on the new law. There seemed to be an understanding that the law would help reduce the backlog of applicants from Southern and Eastern European countries—such as Italy, Poland, Greece, and Portugal—which in comparison to Britain, West Germany, and Ireland, had low immigration quotas.

The 1965 law did help immigrants from the targeted European countries for a decade.[21] Unexpectedly, it also brought large numbers of Asians and Latin Americans to the United States, who became the predominant new immigrants by the end of the 1970s. Thus, annual immigration from Mexico increased from 37,969 in 1965 to 52,096 in 1979.[22] The increase from the Asian countries during this period was even more spectacular. The number of Indian immigrants jumped from 582 in 1965 to 19,708 in 1979, of Korean immigrants from 2,165 to 29,348, and those from China, Taiwan, and Hong Kong from 4,769 to 30,180.[23]

The unexpected consequences of the 1965 law were produced by a number of factors, notably family reunification.[24] The family reunification principle helped immigrants bring relatives, who in turn sponsored more relatives, thus starting a continuous chain of migration. Other major factors were the Cold War and labor needs, including the demand for professionals. The effort to challenge the Soviet Union led to increases in the number of refugees from Cuba, Nicaragua, Vietnam, Cambodia, Laos, and ultimately from the Soviet Union and Communist China. An increasing number of people seeking asylum also led to unanticipated growth. The demand for professionals in areas such as medicine, nursing, and engineering, and for skilled as well as unskilled labor, further contributed to the rise of immigration into the United States. In addition, the greed of some corporations and individuals and the lack of effective laws and adequate border patrols increased the numbers of illegal immigrants.

THE REFUGEE ACT OF 1980

Prior to the 1965 law, which created the seventh preference for refugees, this group of immigrants was ignored by the immigration laws. Refugees were admitted on an *ad hoc* basis, a system that for the most part continued until the passage of the Refugee Act of 1980.[25] The seventh preference of the 1965 law was responsible for admitting 130,000 refugees by 1980. However, a much larger number of the refugees were allowed to stay in the United States under the "parole" authority given to the attorney general by the 1952 law, which continued after the passage of the 1965 law. This authority continued to be exercised primarily to admit refugees from such Communist countries as Hungary, Cuba, Vietnam, Cambodia, Laos, and China. It is estimated that "by 1980, 99.7 percent of the more than one million refugees admitted under the parole system were from countries under Communist rule."[26]

The intent of the Refugee Act of 1980 was to transform that *ad hoc* refugee policy into a permanent one and to stem the massive influx of refugees. Bill Ong Hing argues that "a major catalyst for the new refugee law was a disturbing anxiety felt by some members of Congress that thousands of Southeastern Asians would destabilize many communities."[27] The refugee law restricted the parole authority of the attorney general in admitting refugees and required the president, after consulting with Congress, to determine annually the ceiling for refugees. The 1965 law's restrictive ideological definition of a refugee was broadened to include any one who could not return to his or her country of nationality because of "persecution or well-founded fear of persecution." Such persecution or the fear thereof could be based on a person's "race, religion, nationality, membership in a particular social group, or political opinion."[28]

The Refugee Act of 1980 did not succeed in controlling the admission of refugees. John Crewdson comments: "...as Congress was to discover repeatedly..., most recently with the Refugee Act of 1980, legislating immigration curbs and halting immigration are two very different things."[29] According to the INS, during the 1980s the admission of refugees into the United States varied between 67,000 in 1986 and 231,700 in 1980.[30] In the early 1990s the number of refugees admitted annually stayed well over 100,000.[31] Most of the refugees in the 1980s and the early 1990s came from East Asia, Eastern Europe, the Soviet Union, and Cuba. In other words, refugees from the Communist countries continued to be favored despite the repeal of the 1965 law's seventh preference.

THE IMMIGRATION REFORM AND CONTROL ACT OF 1986

The Immigration Reform and Control Act (IRCA), passed in November 1986, increased the number of new immigrants by providing legal status to qualified illegal aliens in the country. Although a large number of illegal aliens apprehended by the INS continue to be Mexican citizens, illegal immigrants increasingly have come from other countries as well. Because of the proximity to the United States, Latin American countries are still the most important sending countries of undocumented immigrants. Many in this category, however, now come from Asia—notably China, India, the Philippines, and Pakistan—and even from Europe—particularly Italy and Poland. According to some estimates, as many as 10 percent of the 7.3 million Asians counted in the 1990 census are probably undocumented.[32]

Illegal immigrants have been welcomed by some employers, primarily in agriculture but also in industry—notably garment sweatshops. Some affluent Americans have also sought them for cheap household help. These employers have exploited illegal workers by paying them the lowest possible wages and providing no benefits. Congress implicitly was a party to such exploitation, since until 1986 it did not provide penalties for employers hiring illegal workers. The greatest penalty used against illegal employees has been deportation or rather the end—at least for the time being—of the dream to seek a better life.

The debate preceding the passage of the 1986 law often focused on the lack of control by the United States of its borders and the inordinate number of illegals crossing these borders. Some estimates of the illegals ran as high as 12 million, but the U.S. Bureau of the Census considered the number to be 2 to 3 million.[33] The 1986 law's primary objective was to stem the tide of illegal immigrants by granting amnesty to those qualified among them and by punishing employers who would continue to hire illegals. Amnesty was made available for all those who could document residence, albeit unlawful, in the United States before January 1, 1982, and for those who could prove their work record of at least 90 days in seasonal agriculture during the period May 1985–May 1986. The law also provided amnesty for some other aliens and contained guidelines to prevent discrimination against newly legalized immigrants.[34] A larger-than-expected number of aliens, particularly those employed in seasonal agriculture, applied to avail themselves of amnesty. Most of these applicants won permission, becoming legal residents of the United States.

Most scholars of immigration maintain that the 1986 law did little to reduce the entry of illegal immigrants, and that instead it helped to increase the number of legal immigrants. Based on the data of aliens apprehended, prepared by the INS, Vernon Briggs argues that "despite the enactment of IRCA, there are few signs that illegal immigration to the United States abated … indeed, every indication is that the illegal immigration is again [following a brief respite as a result of IRCA] flourishing."[35] Apparently, fear of civil and criminal penalties has not deterred employers from hiring cheap illegal labor, nor have the borders been controlled by the available police force.

INS data reveal that the number of legal immigrants admitted during fiscal year 1989 was 1,090,924, as compared to 643,025 the previous year.[36] The increase clearly was the result of the 1986 law. The impact of IRCA in increasing new immigrants was even more evident by 1990 and 1991. In 1990, of the total 1,536,483 immigrants admitted, 880,372 were due to IRCA and in 1991, of the total 1,827,167 immigrants, 1,123,162 gained admittance under this law.[37]

THE IMMIGRATION ACT OF 1990

The Immigration Reform and Control Act and the Refugee Act were in part responses to the recommendations of the Select Commission on Immigration and Refugee Policy. The Select Commission, appointed by President Jimmy Carter in 1978 under a directive by Congress, had made over 100 recommendations, recognizing the need for continued immigration, but suggesting only modest increases in the number of immigrants. The two major laws of the 1980s were piecemeal, the first on refugees and the second on illegal aliens. Continuing this approach, Congress created a category of Amerasian immigrants in 1988. Children fathered by American soldiers in Vietnam were admitted, along with their mothers and other siblings, "giving 37,658 such persons immigrant status from 1989 through 1991."[38] (The admission of Amerasians continued after 1991.) The piecemeal approach to immigration was abandoned by Congress in 1990 when it passed a comprehensive statute on the subject. The Select Commission's report also had an impact on this law.

The large number of immigrants admitted in the 1980s and the changing demographic composition of the United States provided an impetus for the passage of the 1990 law. Many in the country felt that the economy could not absorb the increasing number of new immigrants. Some also objected to the changing demographic composition of the nation. Most of the new immigrants were now coming from Asia and Latin America—not Europe, the traditional source of immigrants. Vernon Briggs estimates that "only about 10 percent of immigrants were coming from Europe, the continent that had dominated earlier mass immigrant flows."[39] Some groups wanted to stop the flow of all nonwhite immigration; however, they were small in number and did not have much political clout. The conservatives in power, led by President George Bush, considered immigration essential for the continued prosperity of the country. They were, however, prepared to devise ways to increase European immigration. In addition, a consensus had been reached that despite immigrants' contribution to America, their flow was high and a realistic cap was needed on their numbers.

The Immigration Act of 1990 became effective on October 1, 1991, and limited the total number of new immigrants to 700,000 per year in fiscal years 1992–94 and to 675,000 thereafter. The emphasis on family reunification remained a central feature of immigration. Family immigration was, however, limited to 520,000 annually for the first three years and to 480,000 after that. No limit was placed on the number of spouses, children, and parents (of those at least 21 years of age) of U.S. citizens. In addition, four family-sponsored preferences were created for admission of (1) unmarried sons and daughters of U.S. citizens; (2) spouses and unmarried children of permanent resident aliens; (3) married sons and daughters of U.S. citizens; and (4) brothers and sisters of U.S. citizens. The annual number of immigrants under these four preferences was not to go below 226,000. If that appeared to be a possibility, since the number of immediate relatives (spouses, children, and parents) granted visas the preceding year was to determine a current year's number of family-sponsored visas by subtracting the former from the total for family reunification, the overall cap for immigration was to be "pierced." Critics point out that the piercing provision made the cap on immigration meaningless. Since the number of refugees (and those seeking political asylum) is determined annually, they too were to be admitted in addition to the overall ceiling, adding several thousand more residents in the United States.

A second provision in the 1990 law concerns employment-based visas. The 1965 law used two preferences—third for professionals and sixth for other workers—and allowed a total of 54,000 such immigrants (including immigrants' spouses and children) annually. The 1990 law increased the number of work preferences to five and the number of such admittable workers (and their spouses and children) to 140,000. The highest (first) preference went to priority workers (and their families) with extraordinary ability and national and international recognition in their respective areas. Other (lower) preferences were reserved for professionals with advanced degrees, skilled and needed unskilled workers, "special" immigrants such as ministers of religion and foreign medical graduates, and investors who spent at least $1 million in an urban area or at least half a million in a rural area and created ten or more jobs.

A new feature of the law was 40,000 visas (55,000 starting with fiscal year 1995) for "diversity" immigrants. These visas were for immigrants from countries "adversely affected" by the 1965 law and were to be allocated by a lottery system. A list of 34 countries—a majority of them European—considered "adversely affected" was prepared. The Irish lobby in Congress succeeded in reserving 16,000 of the 40,000 such visas for immigrants from Ireland. A new list of countries to provide "diversity" was to be prepared periodically, based on immigration trends of the recent past.

Another new aspect of the 1990 law is the authority given to the attorney general to grant a temporary "safe haven" to undocumented aliens in the United States from selected countries fleeing an armed conflict or a natural disaster. Protected status for such individuals would include permission to work during their stay in the United States. The law singled out citizens of El Salvador who were in the United States and permitted them to stay for up to 18 months.

Although the flow of immigrants stipulated by the 1990 law has been comparable to that of the preceding ten years or so (excluding immigrants under the IRCA), it has been higher than during the 1960s and 1970s. One scholar estimates that immigrants as well as refugees and those seeking asylum in the 1990s "will double the annual yearly average of newcomers compared to the twenty years between 1961 and 1980."[40]

In addition to an anticipated 800,000 legal immigrants, 300,000 illegal immigrants have been entering the United States annually since the passage of the 1990 law. Increased numbers of legal and illegal immigrants are now also coming from the former Communist countries, notably Russia. Such an inflow of immigrants has created a public outcry against both types of newcomers. California's voters expressed their anti-immigrant sentiments by approving Proposition 187 in 1994, which attempted to deny benefits, including public education, to illegal immigrants. This Proposition, however, was immediately challenged in court. At about the same time a Federal advisory commission, chaired by the late Congresswoman Barbara Jordan of Texas, recommended reduction in the number of legal immigrants and proposed measures to control illegal immigration.

Congress responded to such sentiments by passing changes in immigration and welfare laws in 1996. The number of legal immigrants permitted to enter the United States was left untouched, thanks to the influence of pro-immigration lobbies. However, income requirements for the sponsors of immigrants were introduced and most welfare benefits, such as Supplemental Security Income, food stamps, and Medicaid, would be unavailable to legal immigrants until they become citizens. Measures passed to reduce illegal immigration included increasing the number of border patrol agents, providing more employees to the Immigration and Naturalization Service for investigating the smuggling and employment of illegal immigrants, and making deportation of illegal immigrants (and in some cases of legal immigrants) easier.

NEW IMMIGRANTS' IMPACT ON AMERICAN SOCIETY

New immigrants have changed the demographics of the United States. In the censuses undertaken before 1980, the major race groups counted were white and black. When any other groups, such as Native Americans, Japanese, Chinese, and Filipinos were counted, as in the censuses of 1960 and 1970, they were placed along with "all other" groups in the "other races" category. In 1960 the white and black populations were 158.83 million and 18.87 million, respectively, and other races were 1.62 million (see Table 6.1). When Hispanics and Asians were counted as separate categories for the first time in 1980, their numbers had increased to 14.6 million and 3.6 million, respectively, out of a total population of 226.6 million. Hispanics increased by nearly 8 million and Asians (and Pacific Islanders) by almost 4 million in the next ten years. As shown in Table 6.1, Hispanic and Asian populations in the United States are expected to continue to grow at a high rate in this decade and through the first half of the next century. This projection is based on the assumption that current immigration trends and birth rates will continue.

TABLE 6.1   CHANGING DEMOGRAPHICS
IN THE UNITED STATES (POPULATION IN MILLIONS)

YEAR	WHITE	BLACK	HISPANIC	ASIAN	NATIVE AMERICAN	OTHER RACES	TOTAL
1960	158.83	18.87	NCS	NCS	NCS	1.62	179.32
1970	177.75	22.58	NCS	NCS	NCS	2.88	203.21
1980	180.91	26.14	14.61	3.56	1.33		226.55
1990	188.30	29.27	22.34	7.00	1.80		248.71
2000 (Proj.)	196.70	33.83	30.60	11.58	2.10		274.81
2050 (Proj.)	201.84	80.68	57.32	38.77	4.08		382.69

"Native American" category consists of American Indians, Eskimos, and Aleuts.

NCS: Not Counted Separately.

In 1980, 1990, 2000, and 2050 statistics, whites, blacks, Asians, and Native Americans are "not of Hispanic origin."

Other races counted in 1960 and 1970 are included in later years in the Hispanic, Asian, and Native American categories.

Source: U.S. Bureau of the Census.

The U.S. Bureau of the Census has prepared extensive tables of almost 400 pages on the characteristics of the foreign-born population in the United States.[41] Since most of the foreign-born population consists of new immigrants, these data are of interest to us. The data reveal, for example, that in 1990 the foreign-born population in the United States was 19.8 million, women somewhat outnumbering men, and the median age for this population was 37.3 years.[42] Of the 15.3 million 25-years-and-older foreign-born residents, 3 million were high school graduates and almost as many had college or graduate degrees.[43] Labor force characteristics of the foreign-born population indicate that 7.8 percent were unemployed, and those employed held jobs in all facets of industry, agriculture, and service occupations, as well as in the armed forces and other areas of the public sector.[44] As many as 2.4 million of the 10.7 million employed 16 years and over held jobs in high-status managerial and "professional specialty" occupations.[45] The median household income of the foreign-born was $28,314, and families with incomes below the poverty level were 14.9 percent.[46] A comparison of such characteristics of the foreign-born with those of the total population of the United States is provided in Table 6.2.

TABLE 6.2   CHARACTERISTICS OF THE FOREIGN-BORN
AND THE TOTAL U.S. POPULATION, 1990*

CHARACTERISTICS	FOREIGN-BORN	TOTAL POPULATION
Media Age	37.3	32.8
Median Household Income	$28,314	$29,943
Families Below Poverty Level	14.9	10.7
Unemployment Rate	7.8	5.5
Managerial & Professional Specialty	22.4	26.0
High School Graduates	19.6	30.0
College Degree Holders	11.6	13.1
Advanced Degree Holders	8.8	7.2

*All statistics except median age and median household income are in percentages. For unemployment rate and managerial and professional specialty occupations, those 16 years of age or older are considered. For education statistics, those 25 years of age or older are considered.
Sources: U.S. Bureau of the Census, *1990 Census of Population: The Foreign-Born Population in the United States; Statistical Facts;* and *U.S. Bureau of Labor Statistics.*

The foreign-born population is somewhat older than the total population, which is to be expected since children are a relatively small proportion of the number of immigrants. Overall, the foreign-born are less educated, except at the graduate level where they surpass the total population. Their unemployment and poverty rates are higher than those of the total population; their median household income is lower. The proportion of the foreign-born employed in the high-status managerial and professional category lags behind that of the total population.

There are some striking differences in these characteristics between the foreign-born of different regions and different countries. Asians in general are better educated and more affluent than Latin Americans. Of the Asians, the Japanese, Chinese, Koreans, Filipinos, and Indians (sometimes called Asian Indians) are the most advanced groups in education, employment, and income. The Vietnamese, Laotians, and the Cambodians do rather poorly in comparison to other Asians.[47]

The massive flow of immigrants, largely from the less developed countries of Asia and Latin America, has presented certain challenges, opportunities, and constraints for American policy makers and American society as a whole. We will consider three aspects of such challenges, opportunities, and constraints: public reaction to the new immigrants, the impact of immigration on the economy, and the effect of the growing demographic diversity on the stability and future of society.

Public reaction to immigrants throughout American history has never been warm; rather, it has been hostile or indifferent. Public opinion data as well as historical research confirm this viewpoint.[48] Very few Americans have ever been in favor of increasing immigration levels. Those supporting such increases have generally been less than 10 percent of the total population.[49] While in some years a majority of respondents in public opinion polls have wanted fewer immigrants than were admitted at the time, in most years those holding such a viewpoint have formed a substantial plurality instead of a majority.[50] A minority of the American public has desired no change in the number of immigrants admitted and some do not hold any opinion on this issue.[51]

Some interest groups are openly hostile to the new immigrants from Asia and Latin America.[52] They argue that those immigrants take away jobs from native-born Americans, become a burden on the system through welfare and other programs, increase the country's population at unacceptable rates, deplete the country's resources, and adversely affect the environment. A commonly held perception is that the new immigrants are economic refugees fleeing the poverty of the Third World. While there is some truth to this argument, it is also true that a large number of such immigrants are highly qualified workers and are responsible to a considerable degree for the continued prosperity of the United States. Portes and Rumbaut state that "the proportion of professionals and technicians among occupationally active immigrants consistently exceeds the average among U.S. workers."[53] Furthermore, recent evidence reveals that the new immigrants are less likely to be on welfare than native-born Americans.[54]

Critics of immigration are concerned about the adverse impact of immigration on the American economy. Vernon Briggs has argued that

> the nation's immigration policy remains highly mechanistic, legalistic, nepotistic and inflexible. It is essentially a political policy. Its design continues to reflect a disregard for the economic transformation that is restructuring U.S. employment patterns and reconstituting the labor force.[55]

Briggs' argument appears convincing in view of the facts that the immigration laws of 1965 and 1990 considered family reunification as the dominant goal, the 1980 law disregarded the job skills of refugees, and the 1986 law granted amnesty to illegal aliens based on their entry into the United States prior to a certain date or employment in seasonal agriculture. However, a comparison of the data on the characteristics of the new immigrants and the total U.S. population previously presented provides rather weak evidence in support of such an argument.

While immigrants of the pre-1965 period brought substantial diversity to the country, the diversity of the new immigrants is far more apparent and has a greater potential for destabilizing American society than did the differences of European immigrants. The immigration policy of the pre-1965 period was designed primarily for European immigrants whose racial and cultural differences from native-born Americans were not as marked as are those of the new immigrants. As a result, assimilation of European immigrants into society was a relatively painless matter and occurred without any major social upheavals. Assimilation of the new immigrants into society appears to be harder, in part because of their different skin color and in part because of their conspicuous cultural differences—especially language and religion.

New immigrants present challenges for policy makers to devise methods to positively utilize the diversity of newcomers and at the same time maintain the unity of American society. These challenges also provide opportunities for policy makers to tap into the skills of the new immigrants and enrich society with greater cultural diversity than in earlier periods. Such challenges and opportunities create some major constraints for policy makers and society. First, there is the cost of dealing with cultural diversity. Schools and colleges are increasingly incorporating cultural diversity courses into their curriculums. The introduction of these courses is often done by ignoring some other component of the curriculum that may be critical for students seeking jobs in the highly competitive world economy. On the other hand, given the increased globalization of the marketplace, learning about the diverse cultures of the world provides opportunity to reward individuals both culturally and economically. Diversity, however, carries an inherent risk of separateness. The unity that society had earlier experienced because the immigrants and their children had stressed oneness rather than separateness may be jeopardized. Thus, it is a major challenge for educators to provide students with an understanding of other cultures while at the same time promoting the unity of our society. Finally, diverse societies are seldom peaceful. The diversity of groups and their unwillingness to overcome the perception of separateness have destabilized many societies in the world. Therefore, the greatest challenge presented by the new immigrants to our national and local political leaders is to devise ways to accept diversity while maintaining unity.

POLICY OPTIONS: THE CURRENT DEBATE

Current policy debates about the effectiveness of our immigration policy focus on the impact of immigration on the economy, illegal immigration, bureaucratic and legal reforms, economic assistance to sender countries to reduce immigration flows, bilingual policy, and political power. Various ethnic groups, civil liberties organizations, and business groups support or oppose the options for change.

THE IMPACT OF IMMIGRATION ON THE ECONOMY

One of the most critical debates about immigration is whether increased immigration helps or hinders the American economy. Julian L. Simon argues that increased immigration will benefit America.[56] Increasing the flow of skilled immigrants to the United States, according to Simon, would expand technological advancement, increase the labor supply, provide needed workers who will pay taxes that will reduce the deficit and support retirees on Social Security, enhance American competitiveness in the world, increase America's image abroad, and give new entrants the opportunity to "enjoy the blessings of life in the United States."[57] Various business publications, including *Forbes* and the *Wall Street Journal*, have run editorials calling for increased or open immigrant policies as well.[58] Vernon Briggs, who favors placing limits on the flow of immigration, in examining this issue argues that

> precisely at the time ... that the nation needs a more highly skilled and better educated labor force, its immigration policy is pouring large numbers of unskilled, poorly educated workers with limited English-speaking ability into the central cities....[59]

Employment opportunities for these poorly educated and often unskilled workers, however, may exist in the major cities in the United States. According to Saskia Sassen-Koob, recent changes in the global economy that include the mobility of capital, firms, and labor, along with the decline of the manufacturing sector and in turn middle-income employment, have produced new growth centers based on services in major cities such as New York and Los Angeles.[60] Service industries create technical and professional positions with high pay, but also low-paying jobs such as janitorial and errant services, which are filled by immigrants. In addition, legal and illegal immigrants also find work in the new "sweatshops," companies that produce legal goods such as garments, furniture, and electronics, but pay below the minimum wage and fail to meet other legal work standards.[61]

Other studies that have examined the impact of immigration on the U.S. economy show that the effect on jobs has been minimal and usually related to specific industries.[62] Thomas Muller argues that many new immigrants, especially Asians and Cubans, have become entrepreneurs, revitalizing small family-owned retail stores and various services.[63] He goes on to suggest that such new business enterprises stimulate local economies, creating jobs for both immigrants and native workers and enhancing regional and global competitiveness.[64]

While Julian Simon argues that immigration levels should be increased to enhance the American economy, and Thomas Muller suggests that increased new immigrants have already had a positive impact, Vernon Briggs maintains that immigration policy should be reformed to deal with changes in the U.S. economy. He favors Congress setting a yearly immigration ceiling that would serve as a target. The actual flow of immigrants coming into this country would be set according to whether or not their skills were needed to strengthen our economy. This policy option, however, according to Briggs, would meet with opposition from various groups that favor the current system of family reunification.[65] Opposition might also come from groups that prefer a continuing flow of unskilled immigrants who would be willing to work for low wages.

ILLEGAL IMMIGRATION

Stopping illegal immigration was the major justification for the Immigration Reform and Control Act of 1986 (IRCA). Results about the effectiveness of this program, however, have been mixed, as employer sanctions have not halted the flow of illegal aliens.[66] The issue of employer sanctions was a major controversy in passage of the IRCA. Fear of increased discrimination against Hispanics led a number of Hispanic organizations and the American Civil Liberties Union to oppose employer sanctions. Employer groups also opposed the sanctions because of paperwork requirements and the involvement of employers in immigrant regulation.[67] Growers were especially concerned about this issue. Although the final version of the IRCA did include employer sanctions, it also included special rules to permit illegal aliens who had worked in seasonal agriculture to obtain permanent resident alien status.

One possible step to strengthening employer sanctions is through an employment or identification card that is difficult to counterfeit.[68] To be effective, all Americans would be issued a picture identification card. This could be costly, and many Americans would be concerned about giving the federal government the power to monitor the movement of people, gain access to employee records, and perhaps violate individuals' privacy. On the other hand, if this card was difficult or costly to manufacture, it could serve as an effective tool to reduce illegal immigration.

BUREAUCRATIC AND LEGAL REFORMS

Strengthening the power of the INS could also produce better results. Vernon Briggs argues that placing the INS in the Justice Department has meant that immigration is often a low priority, and that congressional committees tied to Justice have produced a highly legalistic immigration policy. He recommends returning the INS to the Labor Department so that its work can be tied more closely to economic and labor issues.[69] The INS could also be strengthened by adding additional staff and increasing its funding. Illegal immigration could be further reduced by giving jail sentences to illegal aliens. This policy, however, would put added pressure on an already overcrowded prison system.[70] Another possibility is to create a system of fines for illegal immigrants to decrease the incentive to enter the United States.[71]

SENDER COUNTRIES

Another possible means of curtailing the flow of illegal aliens is to assist with the economic development of sender countries.[72] Such attempts as the North American Free Trade Agreement could help stimulate the economy of Mexico and reduce the desire to seek better economic opportunities in the United States. This approach, however, may simply provide some individuals with new skills, who will then enter this country seeking a better standard of living.[73]

The issue of refugees also raises important policy options. Now that the Cold War has ended and communism exists in only a few countries, it is time to rethink our refugee policy. During the Cold War, individuals fleeing Communist Cuba were normally granted "parole status" and permitted to enter this country, while individuals fleeing from Haiti were denied entrance. In 1994, President Clinton discontinued this policy toward Cuban refugees.

Steps to encourage refugee resettlements in areas close to the sender countries could be taken. Vernon Briggs favors tying refugee admissions to total admissions in order to control the flow of immigrants coming into this country.[74] This measure would be controversial as it would mean that increased refugee admissions would have to be offset by reducing family-reunification admissions. Further, he argues the federal government rather than state and local communities should bear the cost of taking care of these refugees.

BILINGUAL POLICY

Another major issue is the impact of the immigrant languages on American culture. Benjamin Franklin wrote during the colonial period about his fear that the massive flow of German immigrants would alter the language and culture of the new Pennsylvania colony.[75] Thus, from the beginning of America there has been controversy surrounding the impact of other languages on culture, customs, and education.

In order to assist the children of new immigrants in the learning process, a number of groups have supported bilingual education in the schools. Supporters of bilingual education also believe that bilingual instruction helps maintain an immigrant's cultural tradition. Critics, such as Nathan Glazer, argue that it does little to increase academic achievement or promote future economic benefits for the students, and hinders assimilation into American culture.[76] While schools should permit all students to learn about various cultures and languages, immigrants do need to learn English as their primary language in order to find economic well-being within the United States.

Many of those who favor bilingual education also support bilingual ballots and electoral information as well as the use of additional languages by government officials. Opposition, however, has emerged with the formation of a number of groups who favor only the use of English. A constitutional amendment has been considered by Congress, and a number of states have passed "official English" initiatives. The issue of bilingualism raises important questions about the relationship of the new immigrants to American society and shows how immigrants and opposition groups place pressure on the political system.

POLITICAL POWER

The new immigrants also have the potential for changing politics by altering the political influence of various groups. Blacks who have recently gained power, especially in urban areas, may find their strength eroding as Asian and Latin American immigrants become naturalized and vote. As the majority of Hispanics tend to reside in urban areas, this is where the shift is more likely to take place. However, studies about Hispanic political behavior show low levels of voter turnout.[77] Research on why these levels exist include high political cynicism and alienation, registration and voting barriers, and low socioeconomic status.[78] Within the various groups that make up the Hispanic population, political parties' support varies, as Cuban Americans tend to be Republicans, while Mexican Americans and Puerto Rican Americans tend to be Democrats, although they do tend to favor voting for Republican presidential candidates.[79] Low participation rates are also found among Asian Americans who as a group, especially Chinese Americans, tend to be Republican.[80]

One possible way in which minorities can gain political power is through the formation of political coalitions by blacks, Asian Americans, and Hispanic Americans—similar to the coalitions of white ethnics during the urban machine era that developed during the late nineteenth century in cities such as Boston, Chicago, and New York. However, as some scholars have noted, this type of coalition is "largely a myth."[81] Although many urban politicians did receive ethnic support, they tended to reward only a small number with jobs or contracts, while the others received only symbolic representation.[82]

SOCIAL SERVICES

Concern about immigrants also rests on their use of various social services. Only permanent residents and those with refugee status are eligible for welfare, Medicaid, and food stamps; however, these two groups plus asylum applicants and those with temporary protected status are eligible for unemployment insurance, emergency health care, federal housing and education.[83] Illegal immigrants are eligible for emergency health care, public education, and W.I.C. (Women, Infants, and Children—a supplemental food program for mothers with very young children).[84] Children of illegal aliens, born in the United States, however, are U.S. citizens and have the same rights as other U.S. citizens. Concern about illegal immigrants receiving such benefits led Californian voters in the November elections of 1994 to approve Proposition 187, which would require teachers and doctors to deny services as well as report to the authorities suspected violators.[85] This initiative is currently being reviewed by the courts.

The impact of immigration on American society has led many to call for reductions in the flow of immigrants. Some possible measures, such as developing an identification card, raise possible questions about how the rights of native-born Americans might be violated. Other measures, such as expanding border patrols or assisting sender countries, will require additional funding. Implementation of any of these measures is no guarantee that concerns about the economy and various social issues will necessarily change.

RECOMMENDATIONS FOR THE TWENTY-FIRST CENTURY

As indicated in Table 6.1, the United States will enter the next century with a population of 275 million, of which 78 million will be members of minorities. Including refugees and those seeking asylum, the number of legal immigrants admitted annually through the 1990s is likely to be about 800,000. In addition, large numbers of illegal aliens, perhaps 4 to 5 million, will continue to work in the United States, thanks to the demand for cheap labor and the poor enforcement of laws to control illegal immigration. The nagging question will remain: Can America absorb so many immigrants without jeopardizing its affluence and stability? Motivated by our concerns for the country's continued prosperity and stability, we make the following recommendations for U.S. immigration policy in the twenty-first century, or rather the early part of the next century.

Congress should set an annual ceiling of 500,000 immigrants, including refugees and those seeking asylum. The president should have authority to determine each year the number of immigrants within the ceiling. A further directive can be given by Congress to the president that no less than 250,000 (and no more than 500,000) immigrants are to be admitted.

We believe that it is unrealistic to expect a ceiling lower than 500,000. The pressure for family reunification will remain, and it will not be possible for Congress to say that immigrants are welcome but not their spouses, children, and parents. It is practical, however, to reduce the number of other relatives of immigrants who are currently admitted under the family-sponsored four preference categories. It is also feasible to admit fewer refugees and those seeking asylum. After all, the Cold War has ended, so a major pressure for admitting refugees has disappeared. Many countries, however, particularly in the Third World, will continue to experience sporadic unrest, causing a large exodus of people across borders. The United States should accept some of these refugees out of compassion, but other countries should also display such compassion. Other countries also have an obligation to do their share in granting political asylum to those fleeing their native lands due to fears of political or religious persecution.

While family reunification will continue to be a major guiding principle of immigration policy, employment-based immigration should be accorded higher priority than at present. Furthermore, although we can use highly qualified immigrants to boost the economy, the policy of the nation should not be that of dependence on immigrants for this purpose. We are not suggesting that immigration of highly qualified immigrants be halted at any time. We do recommend, however, that the number of such immigrants be kept to a minimum, closer to the limit of the 1965 law than the 1990 law, and that greater attention be given to the development of the country's own human resources.

On illegal immigration, the official policy will remain what President Clinton said in a news conference: "We must say no to illegal immigration so we can continue to say yes to legal immigration."[86] However, the policy must be enforced with adequate funding for increasing the border patrol and, equally important, with the cooperation of farmers, businesses, and individuals who hire illegals. It is naive to expect that employers of illegal aliens will have a change of heart overnight. Therefore, we propose that a system of limited temporary work permits be devised to attract needed labor from abroad. We further suggest that the number of legal immigrants permitted from Mexico, the greatest source of illegal immigrants, be increased on the condition that Mexico also control its borders with the United States.

We finally recommend that cultural diversity be accepted with certain limits so that the United States will remain united and stable. We support the concept of English as the official language, including for purposes of instruction, and consider using two or more languages in instruction or other areas potentially detrimental to the unity of society. We do appreciate the need of immigrant children to acquire proficiency in English as rapidly as possible. Therefore, we recommend increasing funds to improve immigrant children's proficiency in English. We believe in cultural diversity and expect immigrants to remain proud of their heritage. While schools and colleges should teach students about the contributions of different cultural groups, we favor that steps be taken to increase unity and assimilation rather than separateness and divisiveness. Only then can we compete with other countries in the twenty-first century and remain prosperous, stable, and united.

NOTES

1. Thomas Muller, *Immigrants and the American City* (New York: New York University Press, 1993), pp. 19–20.
2. Michael C. LeMay, *From Open Door to Dutch Door: An Analysis of U.S. Immigration Policy Since 1820* (New York: Praeger Publishers, 1987), p. 25.
3. Ibid., p. 32.
4. Vernon M. Briggs, Jr., *Mass Immigration and the National Interest* (Armonk, NY: M. E. Sharpe, Inc., 1992), pp. 49–50.
5. LeMay, pp. 38–39.
6. Muller, p. 21.
7. LeMay, p. 82.
8. Benjamin B. Ringer and Elinor R. Lawless, *Race-Ethnicity and Society* (New York: Routledge, 1989), p. 110.
9. LeMay, p. 87.
10. Ibid., p. 95.
11. See ibid., pp. 97–99.
12. Ibid., p. 98.
13. Mark J. Miller, "Never Ending Story: The U.S. Debate over Illegal Immigration," in Gary P. Freeman and James Jupp, eds., *Nations of Immigrants: Australia, the United States, and International Migration* (Melbourne, Australia: Oxford University Press, 1992), p. 56.
14. See Bill Ong Hing, *Making and Remaking Asian America Through Immigration Policy, 1850–1990* (Stanford, CA: Stanford University Press, 1993), p. 124.
15. John F. Kennedy, *A Nation of Immigrants*, Rev. and enlarged ed. (New York: Perennial Library, [1964], 1986), p. 103.
16. Briggs, pp. 113–116.
17. Ibid., p. 114.
18. The 1952 law permitted only 2,000 immigrants annually from the triangle countries, with a quota for each of them out of this total.
19. Hing, p. 40.
20. Ibid., pp. 39–40.

21. David M. Reimers, "An Unintended Reform: The 1965 Immigration Act and Third World Immigration to the United States," in George E. Pozzetta, ed., *Contemporary Immigration and American Society* (New York: Garland Publishing, Inc., 1991), pp. 373–374.

22. Ibid., p. 364. These are unpublished data prepared by the U.S. Immigration and Naturalization Service (INS).

23. Ibid. These too are unpublished INS data.

24. Briggs, pp. 121–177.

25. The Information Series of Current Topics, *Immigration and Illegal Aliens: Burden or Blessing?* (Plano, TX: Information Aids, Inc., 1987), p. 38.

26. See Hing, p. 124.

27. Ibid.

28. Ibid., p. 127.

29. John Crewdson, *The Tarnished Door: The New Immigrants and the Transformation of America* (New York: Times Books, 1983), p. 92.

30. See Briggs, p. 127.

31. Ibid.

32. See Hing, p. 112.

33. Alejandro Portes and Ruben G. Rumbaut, *Immigrant America: A Portrait* (Berkeley: University of California Press, 1990), p. 222.

34. For a detailed discussion of this law, see Briggs, pp. 156–163.

35. Ibid., p. 162.

36. *INS Fact Book: Summary of Recent Immigration Data*, March 1993, p. 13.

37. Ibid., p. 14.

38. Lawrence H. Fuchs, "An Agenda for Tomorrow: Immigration Policy and Ethnic Policies," *The Annals of the American Academy of Political and Social Science*, November 1993, p. 173.

39. Briggs, p. 168.

40. Fuchs, p. 174.

41. U.S. Bureau of the Census, *1990 Census of Population: The Foreign-Born Population in the United States* (Washington, DC, 1993).

42. Ibid., p. 1.

43. Ibid., p. 129.

44. Ibid., p. 193.

45. Ibid.

46. Ibid., p. 257. Income statistics are for the year 1989.

47. See Susumu Awanohara, "Asian Americans Come of Age Politically: Spicier Melting Pot," *Far Eastern Economic Review*, November 22, 1990, pp. 30, 32.

48. Rita Simon, "Old Minorities, New Immigrants: Aspirations, Hopes, and Fears," *The Annals of the American Academy of Political and Social Science*, November 1993, pp. 61–73.

49. Ibid., p. 63. Also see "Americans Feel Threatened by New Immigrants: Fear Effects of Too Much Cultural Diversity," *The Gallup Poll Monthly*, July 1993, p. 3.

50. See Rita Simon, p. 63, and *The Gallup Poll Monthly*, pp. 2–3.

51. Ibid.

52. Some of these groups represent labor, some demand limits on immigration based on their perception of fairness, and others are openly racist and favor white-only immigrants. For a discussion of "current anti-immigration sentiments," see Rita Simon, especially pp. 68–73.

53. Portes and Rumbaut, p. 10.

54. See "Immigrants and Welfare: The Myth of the Parasites," *U.S. News and World Report*, October 3, 1994, p. 38.

55. Briggs, p. 233.

56. Julian L. Simon, "The Case for Greatly Increased Immigration," *The Public Interest*, No. 102, Winter 1991, pp. 89–103.
57. Ibid., p. 90.
58. See Muller, p. 293.
59. Briggs, p. 228.
60. Saskia Sassen-Koob, "Capital Mobility and Labor Migration," in Steven E. Sanderson, ed., *The Americas in the New International Division of Labor* (New York: Holmes and Meier, 1985), pp. 226–251.
61. Ibid., p. 238. Also see Saskia Sassen, "The Informal Economy," in John H. Mollenkopf and Manuel Castells, eds., *Dual City: Restructuring New York* (New York: Russell Sage, 1991), pp. 79–102.
62. Peter J. Dawkins, William Foster, Lindsay Lowell and Demetrios G. Papademetriou, "The Microeconomic Analysis of Immigration in Australia and the United States," in Freeman and Jupp, eds., *Nations of Immigrants: Australia, the United States, and International Migration*, pp. 111–128.
63. Muller, pp. 126–137.
64. Ibid., pp. 136–143.
65. Briggs, p. 247.
66. Miller, p. 65.
67. Ibid., p. 61.
68. Ibid., pp. 67–68.
69. Briggs, pp. 82–83.
70. Muller, p. 313.
71. Briggs, p. 253.
72. Ibid., p. 253.
73. Muller, pp. 315–316.
74. Briggs, p. 254.
75. Muller, pp. 221, 223–224; Ronald J. Schmidt, "Language Policy Conflict in the United States," in Crawford Young, ed., *The Rising Tide of Cultural Pluralism: The Nation-State at Bay?* (Madison: The University of Wisconsin Press, 1993), p. 74.
76. See Muller, p. 232.
77. For a discussion of Hispanic voting behavior, see Paula D. McClain and John A. Garcia, "Expanding Disciplinary Boundaries: Black, Latino, and Racial Minority Group Politics in Political Science," in Ada W. Finifter, ed., *Political Science: The State of the Discipline II* (Washington, DC: American Political Science Association, 1993), pp. 247–279.
78. Ibid., p. 261.
79. Ibid., p. 263.
80. Ibid., p. 268.
81. Rodney E. Hero, *Latinos and the U.S. Political System* (Philadelphia: Temple University Press, 1992), p. 133.
82. Ibid.
83. In 1996 Congress voted to eliminate most welfare benefits for the noncitizen legal immigrants.
84. Sam Howe Verhovek, "Stop Benefits for Aliens? It Wouldn't Be That Easy," *The New York Times*, June 8, 1994, pp. A1, B10.
85. Kenneth B. Noble, "California Immigration Measure Faces Rocky Legal Path," *The New York Times*, November 11, 1994, p. B20.
86. "Clinton Announces Policy on Illegal Immigration," *Congressional Quarterly*, July 31, 1993, p. 2982.

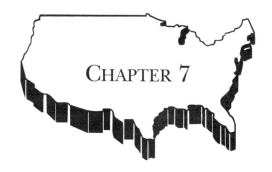

AMERICA AND THE ELECTRONIC REVOLUTION

ROBERT S. WORKMAN (WITH MARIBEL M. BEST)

INTRODUCTION

This chapter deals with the dynamic field of new electronic devices available to and usable by laypeople. This field changes quite literally month to month, week to week and even day to day; constant change and development is the rule rather than the exception. The end result, for example, of the U.S. Telecommunications Act of 1996, which attempts to deal with part of this revolution, cannot be foreseen (more about the Act follows). The Federal Communications Commission is in the long-term process of writing new and revising old regulations to conform to the new Act. After the entire U.S. telecommunications industry—the leading force on the globe—is covered by the new rules, it will still be many years before the net success or failure of the 1996 Act will be discerned.

Rather than the usual books or journal articles, the reader will note that sources for this chapter are heavily weighted toward weekly and monthly commercial publications on telecommunications and the electronic revolution and the most up-to-date textbooks, plus radio and TV interviews. There is even a massive 800-page monthly catalog that is replete with up-to-date review articles on the newest advances.

The dynamic nature of change in the electronic field is such that much of what is written here may be obsolete by the time these pages fall into the reader's hands. Thus, this chapter should be read as a snapshot of the electronic revolution as of February 1997, when it was completed.

A CAVEAT

The reader should bear carefully in mind that even the most advanced hardware and software are subject to all sorts of problems. Hardware failure and glitches in functioning are certainly widely known, and software errors and omissions are common enough so that all providers offer some type of technical advice by telephone—some of which is available twenty-four hours a day, seven days a week. That providers find it necessary to do this would lead one to believe that not everything works all the time or always the way it is supposed to. The point is, claims for capabilities of hardware and/or software must be taken with a grain of salt—not everything performs as expected. Lastly, so-called "vaporware" (promised future hardware or software of significant capability that never in fact appears) is not unknown in the electronic industry.

THE PROBLEM OF CHANGE

"We could not have predicted any of it," so said Herman Goldstein, a coinventor of the first fully electronic calculating machine, ENIAC, in an interview fifty years after the event. Thus, one of the founders of modern computers indicated that the scientists of 1946 had no idea what effect their new machines would have on the history of human development.[1]

"Some are predicting that the opening of the year 2000 will wreak a kind of havoc that can be exceeded only by the electromagnetic pulse of a nuclear attack: computers around the world crashing to a halt or, even worse...."[2]

Both paragraphs above refer to the 50-year period of 1946–96. While in 1946 no one could have figured out what influence an electronic computer would have on society, by the end of that period, computers had become so important to the technologically advanced countries of the world that a rather simple-minded error, made in the 1960s for encoding dates, could cause catastrophic problems at the turn of the century at the worst or cost billions of dollars to prevent at the very least. It seems that in initially writing software for dates to be stored in computer memories, the programmers dropped the two initial digits of "19" for twentieth century dates and thus created the so-called "Millennium Bug"—nobody looked ahead to the year 1999 and beyond. Thus, in the year 2000, that year becomes 00, or for the computer, 1900, and all interest, age, expiration date, life insurance, etc., calculations could go into a tailspin. It is true that old lines of code could be retired or replaced before 2000 but "some software will turn out to be *very* expensive to fix, because the millennium problem is hard wired in chips."[3]

How could it be that something just over fifty years old could become so imbedded in the fabric of the modern states that errors in it could cause chaos?

This problem of the effects of change and development has been approached by philosophers, social scientists, and others over the millennia of recorded history. Religious thinkers have tried to make sense of history (human social development) by trying to discern whether it is linear and steady-state, linear and always advancing from the lesser to the greater/the lower to the higher, or even cyclical in nature. Buddhism takes the latter view, finding existence to be an endless cycle of *samsara*: birth, suffering, death, and rebirth—unless you can find a way out of the cycle. Some Judaic thinkers find history as a linear development until the Messiah comes, while Christians say the entire line of history—now that the Messiah has come for them—is toward His Second Coming and the Final Judgment on the Human Race. In the nineteenth century, Georg F. V. Hegel found meaning in the development of a "spirit" through the ages (which was not the monotheistic God of Islam, Judaism, or Christianity), from the less complex to the more complex by means of a "dialectical" process. The secular philosophers, Karl Marx and Fredrick Engels, threw out Hegel's "spirit" and replaced it with a dynamic inherent in the nature of material existence, and that part of existence that dealt with human history was thought by them to go through distinct epochs or stages.

For thinkers trying to make sense of where humans came from and where they are going, Marx's stages made sense, especially since they were, in part, based on what was known of human history. Marx and Engels pointed out that clearly there was a prehistoric period of human existence—that is, before written records. Today, using the latest scientific evidence, we may say that modern human beings, *Homo sapiens sapiens*, have existed for some 200,000 years. Written records began some 6,000 years Before the Present Era (BPE), and these records are associated with agricultural societies that began about 10,000—plus or minus—BPE. For Marx and Engels, in the nineteenth century, and twentieth century Marxists of all sorts, the earliest human society was that of hunting and gathering or "Primitive Communalism." Settlement into agricultural communities was seen as a major revolution in human existence—a "First Wave" of change—a fact that very few social scientists deny today. Marx and Engels next go off into arguments about slavery, feudalism, and class warfare, which need not concern us here. Finally, they examined the change from agricultural to industrial society, something that began in Great Britain in the eighteenth century, a huge "Second Wave" of change that totally modified the societies of the advanced countries of the world. A very simplified example of this is the fact that at the time of the American revolution, the American population was about 95 percent connected with agriculture and 5 percent with other activities, while today only 5 percent—more or less—is connected with agriculture.

This same gigantic change is going on throughout the world. It is generally supposed that the industrial revolution has been completed in the advanced countries and that they are now in the postindustrial stage. Marx and Engels believed that the "Third Wave" of change would be in social structure, in that socialism would come into existence, to be followed by communism and a full-scale egalitarian society.

Post–World War II thinkers in the West, while rejecting the ideological content of Marxism, did accept the stages of development idea as being in accordance with the known facts of history: Hunting and gathering did give way to agriculture (and civilization), agriculture has now taken second place to industry in the advanced countries, and the rest of the world is following along the same route. The idea of a socialist-communist third wave of Marx is now dead, with the collapse of the Communist system, but there is something new and exciting going on in the postindustrial states that may be, in fact, another huge wave of change.

A new group of professional prognosticators has come into existence whose purpose is to outline and explain the changes that have and are taking place in the societies of the advanced countries in general, and the United States (as the country on the leading edge of change) in particular.[4] Some (Peter Drucker et al.) have found change in a revolution in management; others in consumerism. However, the most influential discussants in the dialogue about the future—John Naisbitt (*Megatrends*),[5] Alvin and Heidi Toffler (inventors of their own "Three Waves" theory),[6] and Nicholas Negroponte (*Being Digital*)[7]—find the wave of change in widely available advanced technology. Whole organizations too, such as the Institute for the Future in Menlo Park, California, have come into the prediction business.

There is no doubt that many significant changes are taking place in the advanced societies of the globe: sexual, religious, social, economic, etc. But it is our thesis that the wave, or stage theory, of history has great value, and that what is happening today in electronic technology is the underlying force in human social change today: This force is driving what is called a "paradigm shift" in the same way that the change took place from the hunting-and-gathering model of society to the agricultural one and then to industrial society. This does not mean that this paradigm shift is taking place everywhere all at one time, anymore than the agricultural or industrial shift did. After all, hunting and gathering still exists in parts of South America, Africa, Asia, and on a few islands (especially New Guinea). It is clear too that many areas of the globe have yet to start industrializing or are still in the process. We are concerned here with the advanced countries of the world in Western Europe, Asia, and North America, especially the United States which is the bellwether of world change. We are not concerned with technology used in production or in military affairs (see Chapter 9, "American Force Posture for the Twenty-First Century"), but rather that which affects the "cognitive elite"—that group of people who have at least a decent high school education or a college degree, where computer literacy is required. Certainly one of the great problems of the future will be to see that all people capable of using the new technology will have access to it. What would or should happen to those incapable of understanding and using modern technology or to those societies that cannot supply to their citizens the training and equipment required, is not something that will be discussed here.

THE COMPUTER AGE BEGINS

The computer age began in 1946, and at that time both the hardware (the physical equipment itself) and the software (the encoded directions telling the equipment what to do) were in the hands of scientists. There was no thought of making the power of computers available to laypersons who were neither scientists nor engineers; however, that is what happened within a half century.

Computing, or calculating, of course, goes far back into human history, developing from a prehistoric notched counting stick that may have been used for counting from 30,000 BPE, to a "counting board" of 3,000 BPE and to an *abacus* of 2,000 years ago.[8] Chinese, Hindus, Arabs, and more recently, Europeans, successively became interested in numbers in calculations and their application to scientific problems.[9] In the nineteenth century, Professor Charles Babbage of the University of Cambridge, England, who is considered the founder of the modern computer, began the construction of a mechanical calculatory device which, if it could have been constructed *precisely* as planned, would have worked. Simultaneous with Babbage's work was that of his colleague, Augusta Ada Byron, who prepared the first programming for Babbage's so-called "Analytical Engine."[10]

The pressure of the constitutional requirement to count the U.S. population every decade caused the first fully functioning calculator to be invented in the late 1880s. This time electricity drove the mechanism rather than a hand-crank.[11] Its inventor, Herman Hollerith, formed the Tabulating Machine Company in 1896, which was combined in 1911 into the Computing Tabulating-Recording Company and then, in 1924, the firm became the world-famous International Business Machines (IBM) corporation.[12]

Mechanical calculators, even if driven by electric power, have many distinct disadvantages: slowness, mechanical wear and tear, size and weight, and inability to transfer data. Thus, it was only when electronic means were used that a really useful computer became possible. The first fully electronic calculator was the ENIAC (Electronic Numerical Integrator and Calculator) which had 18,000 vacuum tubes and miles of electric wires. It was huge—eight feet high by eight feet long—used 174,000 watts of power, weighed 30 tons, and frequently burned out tubes.[13] Its immediate predecessor, the "Harvard Mark I," built in 1944, used electromechanical means, thus it was a hybrid bridge between mechanical and electronic calculating. Some would say this was the first electronic computer.[14]

In order to produce answers, the computer needed to be told what to do in a machine language using an agreed-upon binary code. A binary piece of information is made up of bits that are either 0 or 1—that is, a digital code. Today this method of encoding a machine includes not only numbers but also all information a computer uses.[15] Historians of electronic computing generally recognize five generations of development to date. The *First Generation* (1951–1958) includes the first commercially sold computer, UNIVAC

(Universal Automatic Computer), which was the successor of ENIAC, and which still depended on the vacuum tube. These tubes, resembling light bulbs, frequently blew out and generated a lot of heat. The *Second Generation* of computers (1959–1964) addressed this problem by converting to the newly invented transistor, a small solid-state device that operated coolly and quickly without warm-up, and which used a lot less electricity. The *Third Generation* (1965–1971) came about when "integrated circuit" chips were introduced. These chips are generally made of the cheap and widely available substance silicon, which will conduct electricity if specially prepared, or "doped." The generally used term for a doped chip is "semiconductor," and the industry of that name is a multi-billion-dollar global one today. The *Fourth Generation* (1971–present) is based on the advanced use of semiconductor chips called microprocessors.[16] "Computers today are 100 times smaller than those of the first generation, and a single chip is far more powerful than ENIAC."[17] We may add here the *Fifth Generation* of computing, which began in 1975 with the development of the first microcomputer. Personal computer sales began in earnest in 1980.

THE PERSONAL COMPUTER

Before 1975 computers had evolved into several types: *supercomputers*, the largest, quickest, and most expensive machines for specialized tasks like defense, space travel, and weather forecasting, in which very large amounts of data needed to be processed and analyzed quickly; *mainframes*, large-sized, high-speed units for use in big industry and government; and *minicomputers*, middle-sized, moderate speed units for the business industry and educational institutions.[18] However, all these were only usable by highly trained programmers and engineers.

In 1975 the very first desktop (later called personal computer, or PC) was invented by Ed Roberts and called the "Altair 8800." This machine had dials and switches but no screen or keyboard, and thus it was more of a gadget for electronic hobbyists than anything else.[19] Several years later Apple Computer, founded by Steve Jobs and Steve Wozniak, began to sell Apple I and Apple II home personal computers to the general public. However, only when IBM put a PC on the market did the spread of microcomputers really occur. IBM provided a PC frame on which technological improvements could be added as they came along. IBM set the standard for the PC industry, with its eighty-character line screen, full keyboard, and upgradeable memory. The IBM machine was open to anyone who wished to use or add to its capabilities, in contradistinction to the Apple, which was a closely held proprietary operation. Thus, in the long run the IBM-type machine dominated the market, although not necessarily a machine manufactured by IBM itself. A huge cloning (exact copy) industry sprang into existence, along with a wide assortment of software producers and peripherals manufacturers.

The personal computer, or desktop computer (along with its carryable versions—the portable and laptop), is a revolutionary tool in today's manufacturing and communications industries, and in entertainment, the home office, and the home. The PC gives individuals access to information, information processing, and telecommunications that were formerly unavailable to anyone but scientists and advanced military users.

PCs have gone through fundamental changes based on advances in hardware, such as Central Processing Units (CPUs) and peripheral devices, and software, such as operation systems and GUIs (Graphical User Interfaces).

In order to trace the development of PC capabilities and speed, we may follow the changes in the heart of the PC—the CPU—as manufactured by the Intel Corporation, the principal producer and standard setter in the PC marketplace. CPUs are measured in clock speed—that is, the quickness of the manipulation of a data bit (a binary digit—i.e., 1 or 0). The original measurement of speed was in milliseconds (1/1000th of a second); now PCs generally use a microsecond (1/millionth of a second) as the standard (we should note that supercomputers are capable of nanosecond—[1/billionth of a second]—speeds and that picosecond speeds—[1/trillionth of a second]—are anticipated).[20] Further, the speeds are either counted in MIPS (millions of instructions per second processed—a more scientific counting system) or MHz (megahertz)—millions of cycles per second, the popular way of expressing speed.

The first widely used Intel PC chip was the 8086/8088, used by the IBM-XT in 1981, which worked at up to 25 MHz. Then Intel introduced the transitional 80186, which was soon followed by the 80286, to be used in the IBM-AT PC and clones at around 33 MHz. In 1986 the 80386 was first used in the Compaq 386 PC at 50 MHz, while the 80486, introduced in 1988 and popular through the early 1990s, ran at speeds from 25 MHz up to 100 MHz, with a little tweaking and an overdrive processor add-on. In 1992–93, after a false start due to an error in the mathematical coprocessor, the 80586 chip, dubbed the "Pentium" and also known as the P-5, was put on the market at 125 MHz and 133 MHz. Now a P-6 (80686) chip running at 150 MHz or 166 MHz and one at 200 MHz are available.[21] Enorex Microsystems, Inc. is also advertising a 500 MHz digital semiconductor "Alpha" chip. The CPU is attached to the rest of the computer via a data "bus," the electronic pathway to other parts of the computer, which initially allowed 16 bits to travel at one time. This number of bits on the bus moving simultaneously has been increased to 32 and now to 64 bits in the P-5 chip, which allows that chip to actually process data five times as fast as the 486, which used a 32-bit bus.[22]

After the CPU, but before the peripherals, comes the operating system, which tells the computer what to do and how to do it. Without the operating system, a PC is essentially a hunk of metal attached to some silicon and plastic. Some of the people who created good operating systems have become rich—in fact several dozen became millionaires and several even became billionaires—for example, Bill Gates, President of the Microsoft Corporation, is purportedly the richest man on the planet. There are essentially two main PC operating systems in the world today. The lesser and declining one is that of the Apple Computer company, which is used on its Macintosh machine. Only recently has Apple allowed non-Apple companies to use the system. When Apple held its system close to the vest and threatened unlicensed users with lawsuits, only a small amount of software was written for Apple machines. IBM, on the other hand, let its PC go, and clone makers sprang up all over the world, producing millions of low-cost machines needing software. Bill Gates' fledgling Microsoft (MS) corporation wrote the initial software for IBM's Disk Operating System (DOS) with its keystroke method of user interface (the method by which the user communicates with the computer). This was fine but the keystroke method still needed a level of time and training many people were not willing to put in, in order to operate a PC. Apple's Graphical User Interface (GUI) was much more user-friendly, with its mouse point-and-click on icons scheme, now popularly identified as "windows" technology. Microsoft was able to overcome Apple's technical lead in the GUI field with the introduction of its Windows and Windows-95 software operating system, which replaced MS-DOS software.

A basic PC today is made up of the motherboard (the foundation circuitry of the computer), the Central Processing Unit (CPU) or controller chip, memory chips for holding Random Access Memory (RAM) for running programs, and slots for plugging in drives, monitor, keyboard, and other units needed to operate the machine. The drives come in three kinds: the original 5.25" drive for insertion of floppy disks, which presently can hold up to 1.2 megabytes (MB), 3.5" drive for 1.44MB diskettes, and a hard drive. The hard drive, originally holding only a few megabytes of data, may hold up 4 gigabytes (1 = 1 billion bytes; a byte is a string of data bits, usually about 8 bits, representing one data character) of digital information. The hard drive holds the PC's programs. The monitor, a cathode-ray tube, is like a T.V., and it is connected to the main portion of the PC via a cable. It displays what the computer is doing in full color (if one has a color monitor; otherwise the display is black and white or amber and white).

Lately there are several additional options, including a tape backup system and a Compact Disk (CD) drive, which further increase the amount of data that can be compactly handled. Another piece of equipment now rounds out a basic PC setup—the modem (modulator-demodulator), a device for transmitting data over copper wires or via wireless or digital telephones. We will expand on some aspects of this device later.

To run today's fully equipped PC, software is usually Windows-compatible and can operate the following applications: word processing; spreadsheets; database management; graphical applications of all sorts, including Computer-Aided-Design-Computer-Aided Manufacturing (CAD-CAM); and one can do desktop publishing, or use voice telephone, and even videophone via computer or FAX (facsimile) data to other computer users. Thus, a person on his or her own desktop has access to a wide variety of software tools and applications without the necessity of being either a software or a hardware engineer—or, in fact, knowing anything about the fields. Data is also easily transportable via floppy disks or CDs. The modem, moreover, has added a whole new dimension that makes the PC a revolutionary device for the masses. Where, heretofore, each PC and user was a discrete unit, now connections to other computers are possible via a Local Area Network (LAN) or with any other PC on the planet that has a compatible modem via the Internet, a truly remarkable advance.

A network is "a computer system that uses communications equipment to connect to two or more computers and their resources."[23] The biggest of all networks, the Internet, began in 1969 as a method to prevent the Command, Control and Communications (C^3) military system from being knocked out in one nuclear blow. In order to do this, military computers of the DARPA (Defense Advanced Research Projects Agency) system began to be connected by multiple means—networked by various paths. Eventually, other than purely computer data began to be sent along the net pathways, and thus E-mail (Electronic Mail) was born. Then other sets of computers began to be networked and connections between business and universities were added. Eventually the National Science Foundation connected its supercomputers in the 1980s and in 1991 all the various networks were connected in one grand network of networks, and the U.S. government got out of the Internet business entirely.[24] At the same time, the development of the World Wide Web (WWW) occurred at the European Laboratory for Particle Physics (known by its French acronym, CERN). The WWW uses a graphical interface (windows/icons), is interactive (you can "talk back" on it), is nearly all-encompassing and uses hypertext links (you can skip from "page" to "page" on the Web by following certain key words).[25] Using the Internet, one enters the realm of cyberspace (cybernetics = the study of control processes in electronic systems).

Leaving aside the entertainment aspect of cyberspace (games, idle chat, etc.), there is an enormous amount of data on the Net. There are millions of pages (screens) on the Net dealing with nearly every aspect of human life. The key to the revolution is access to this information, and the Net belongs to no one, despite recent government attempts to the contrary (the attempt of the government of the state of Bavaria, Germany, to prevent pornography from coming in; the unconstitutional attempt of the U.S. Congress to censor Internet material;[26] and the People's Republic of China's project to control Internet access),[27] it is open and uncensored for all who are on-line (connected to the Net via modem). As *Time* magazine noted, "surfing the Net" is now a popular activity of millions.[28] A simple example of the usefulness of the Internet would be someone concerned about breast cancer. With judicious use of Internet "search engines" (programs that seek out data specified by the computer operator), an enormous and up-to-date body of data can be located and read.

The battle currently going on in the computer industry over the Internet has also drawn in the telecommunications giants of the globe. The struggle deals with the hardware and software used to gain access to the Internet, and software for use while connected to the Internet.

The initial connection problem lies with the type of modem used and its speed. The first modem widely available operated at 9.6 Kbps (kilobits per second, or thousands of bits per second) via copper telephone wire. It was replaced by 12.6 Kbps, then 28.8 Kbps and now 33.6 Kbps. Standards for a 56 Kbps modem are currently being formulated.

Next, while on-line, one needs a "browser," or software tool, to use the Internet. Microsoft Explorer and Netscape Company's Navigator are in a struggle to produce the most user-friendly and popular browser. Beyond that, there exist "search engines" like Alta Vista, Yahoo, Lycos, and Excite, and so on, which offer to find whatever it is you are seeking on the Net, once you've gotten to the search engine's site (its electronic location on the Internet, also known as the site's URL—Uniform Resource Locator—address).[29]

Once you are connected to the Net, you want to have "content" and a number of companies offer that, such as Microsoft Network, America on Line, Compuserve, Prodigy, and other such services.

At this point, a number of possibilities have arisen for successfully taking advantage of the new technology. Clearly, "virtual communities" can be formed in cyberspace to meet the individual needs of those on-line.[30] Education can be made available to anyone with a modem,[31] and those who have access to the Net and are computer literate will have the advantage over those people or countries who do not. The U.S. federal government[32] and some state governments[33] are actively seeking to ensure Internet connections for public schools because it is perceived that "wondrous things occur when a school is wired to the max."[34] A student, once he or she has learned how to use it, can do research on the Internet.[35]

PROBLEMS

Two major problems, however, have arisen; one technical and one social. The technical one deals with the ability of the medium used (copper wire, fiber, or wireless "air waves") to deliver data to the computer terminal connected to the Net quickly enough, the problem of so-called "downloading" time. The U.S. Congress recently rewrote the 60-year-old telecommunications law by deregulating much of what television, cable television, digital/satellite television, and wireless telephone and telephone services can do.[36] This will cause a great deal of competition among the telephone companies, satellite and cable TV, and wireless services because now all will be able to offer telephone and related services, television, and Internet connections.[37] The problem, as anyone can tell you who has a home PC connected to the Internet via the POTS (Plain Old Telephone System), is "bandwidth"—the capacity of the data link (in this case, wire) to carry data bits to and from one's PC. Even with a 28.8 Kbps or a top-of-the-line 33.6 Kbps modem, home connection to the Internet can be an irksome task due to slowness of data transfer. The famous British international newsmagazine *The Economist* carried a series of business and technology briefs that dealt with this problem starting in May 1996.[38] In brief, *The Economist* outlined four solutions to the bandwidth problem.

The first possibility is the general use of cable modems offered by cable TV systems. This device could transmit data at up to 33,000 Kbps but cable television is, at this point in time, a one-way street, with data coming in and none going out. In order to set up a full-scale cable modem operation, the cable system must be modified at great cost to the company and to the customers. Thus, it is not a feasible alternative to POTS at this time.[39]

The second possibility is to rework the copper wires of the telephone system now in place by using ISDN (Integrated Services Digital Network) technology, which operates at 128 Kbps or ADSL (Asymmetric Digital Subscriber Line) technology. ADSL uses unexploited copper wire capacity at a "very high bit rate" to transmit data from five to six times faster than the currently commercially available fastest 33.6 Kbps rate to as high as 7 Mbps (megabits per second/millions of bit per second). It is estimated that 85 percent of America's current phone lines could support ADSL technology. Unfortunately ADSL capability drops off very rapidly the further one is from the telephone company's switching stations, thus making it none too feasible, at least in the United States, where 50 percent of telephones are too far from company offices to be satisfactorily connected to ADSL.[40] Also, ADSL modems cost $1,500 to $3,000.

The third possibility is wireless connection, the same technology as used in cellular phones and microwave transmission via transmitters, antennae, or satellites. The problem is that wireless transmission is not particularly quick, and would need considerable investment.[41]

The fourth possibility, and the one farthest in the future, would be a globe-girdling set of relatively low orbit satellites that would offer not only worldwide telephone but also Internet connections at 1.5 Mbps. Plans for such satellites foresee launches early in the twenty-first century.[42] In the near future, at least in the United States, the best bets are some sort of boosted POTS system, such as ISDN or ADSL, which uses existing copper wires.

In the long run, the complete rewiring of the telephone system for fiber optics would certainly resolve the bandwidth issue, although it could take as long as three decades to complete. Nicholas Negroponte, in his book *Being Digital*, says that fiber-optic lines are the way to go because they are cheap and can carry the full panoply of multimedia right to the office or home. The advantage of fiber is that "We literally do not know how many bits per second we can send down a fiber." Research seems to show that 1 Gbps (1 gigabit per second/1 billion bits per second) is possible on one fiber the size of a human hair alone, made out of sand (silicon).[43] Imagine what a bundle of fibers could do. We should note that it is likely that there will be alliances in the twenty-first century of TV networks, Internet connectors, and cable TV networks that will change the way multimedia will be delivered.[44]

The darker side of this massive networking is the potential for erosion of privacy and the actual invasion of privacy that can take place. The Internet goes both ways—one contacts a site, but the site can register the contact and make note of it; in fact some sites place "cookies" into the PC to gain data and transmit it back to the Internet site upon the next contact.[45] The possibility of this sort of privacy invasion has been noted by many observers.[46]

In the twenty-first century, citizens of the advanced countries will see a "Radical Transformation of … [the] job market."[47] "[A] software designer in Peoria will be competing with his or her counterpart in Pohang," "bits will be borderless … with absolutely no respect for geopolitical boundaries," while work will be passed around the globe on a twenty-four-hour basis.[48] Because of networking, computers will work both for individuals and in massive parallel processing, for groups.[49] Governments in the twenty-first century will still exist because unification in the face of nationalism will not be possible, but the world will be more transparent and distances will not mean so much.[50] The "information superhighway" talked about in the twentieth century will be built in the twenty-first century,[51] and a true revolution in human society will come about.

BY WAY OF A CONCLUSION

It is obvious from the preceding discussion that there can be no definitive conclusion to this chapter. In the United States, 94 percent of the population is reachable by telephone, the long distance part of which generates $70 billion alone.[52] Because of the Telecommunications Act of 1996, local, long distance telephone, wireless, and cable television companies will find themselves in competition. At this point, computer chip manufacturers are coming up against a barrier because the capacity of a doped silicon surface to be etched by a light beam has been reached. Squeezing more circuits onto a chip will necessitate a new and narrower beam etching method—a beam that can be used in the production of densely etched chips cheap enough for the mass market. Technology does exist, using X-rays perhaps, but costs must be brought down. When this is done, greater advances than can even now be foreseen could take place.[53] The field of extremely small electronic devices, called nanotechnology, which deals with materials down to the molecular level, is only now developing, and it is hard to foresee where it will go.[54]

Other advances in the semiconductor revolution include the use of "smart cards," small plastic cards that have computer chips with data imbedded in them. These cards can store monetary value and personal information. They can also be used as identification devices for telephone, medical data, and bank use.[55] Also, it appears that soon very small "flash cards" for data storage will become available. These solid-state devices can be written on, erased, and rewritten and will have the capacity to carry up to 64 megabytes.[56]

The key question is just what all this will mean in the twenty-first century. Clearly and minimally, U.S. inhabitants who have the desire to make use of the electronic revolution will have at hand some of the most advanced technology on the planet. It can be used for something as simple as a new tool for mass marketing[57] or as complex as the high-speed transfer of data from one corner of the globe to another—or even getting a college degree.[58] With the caveat mentioned in the introduction always in mind, we can nevertheless say that there will be major, and in part unforeseen and unforeseeable, social and even policy changes in the twenty-first century caused by this amazing new wave of change.

Finally, let us take a quick look at what Microsoft Corporation (MS) projects for the year 2000 and beyond. MS predicts that anything electrical could have a computer in it or be attached to one. Thus, there will be a whole new breed of PCs.[59] One new type will be the TVPC, in which television programs, videocassette recorders and players, and the Internet will be interactive. Another type of microcomputer will be the personal digital assistant (PDA), or wallet PC, which will be a portable unit for all telecommunications: voice mail, E-mail, and direct conversation. Next there will be a PC kiosk, like public telephone booths today, where one could videoconference, send Faxes, buy tickets, and send and receive messages. Another possibility will be Simply Interactive PCs, which will be centers for entertainment, communications, and productivity in home and office—a sort of consumer appliance.

The point is that Microsoft is betting on a huge new market in consumer electronics in the twenty-first century.

The preceding having been said, let us end with a few recommendations for government policy.

RECOMMENDATIONS FOR THE TWENTY-FIRST CENTURY

RECOMMENDATION 1

The government should do all in its power to keep an open and competitive worldwide market in electronic technology. The United States, the leader in developing new hardware and software, need not fear fair competition. However, theft of patented software and hardware must be rigorously combated by federal government action.

RECOMMENDATION 2

For the good of national development and security, the states and the federal governments must do all in their capacity to be sure that all Americans have access to computer training and technology.

RECOMMENDATION 3

The 1996 Telecommunications Act must be implemented by establishing the wisest and most competitive regulations possible.

RECOMMENDATION 4

The "information superhighway," and the fiber-optic system needed to support the highway, must be built for the good of the country. All levels of government must assist in facilitating its construction and provide enough "on-ramps" (connections) to serve the public good.

RECOMMENDATION 5

American society and government units must prepare themselves to take advantage of all that the electronic revolution has to offer.

NOTES

1. Interview with Herman Goldstein, on "Morning Edition," *National Public Radio,* February 14, 1996.
2. James Gleick, "Fast Forward, Oh-Oh," *The New York Times Magazine,* June 2, 1996, p. 19.
3. Ibid. Also "The Millennium Bug: 1900," *The Economist,* August 3–19, 1996, pp. 3, 53–54.
4. Michael Krantz, "Cashing in on Tomorrow," *Time,* July 15, 1996, pp. 52–54.
5. John Naisbitt, *Megatrends: Ten New Directions Transforming Our Lives* (New York: Warner Books, 1984).
6. Alvin Toffler (with Heidi Toffler), *Future Shock; The Third Wave; Powershift* (New York: Bantam Books, various dates).
7. Nicholas Negroponte, *Being Digital* (New York: Vintage Books, 1995).
8. Daniel Slotnick, et al., *Computers and Applications* (Lexington, MA: D. C. Heath & Co., 1986), p. 28.
9. Ibid., p. 29.
10. H. L. Capron, *Computers: Tools for a Information Age,* 4th ed. (Menlo Park, CA: The Benjamin/Cummings Pub. Co., 1996), p. B-3.
11. Ibid.
12. Steven Mandell, *Computers and Information Processing* (St. Paul, MN: West Pub. Co., 1989), pp. 31–32.
13. Ibid., p. 34.
14. Slotnick, p. 33.
15. Negroponte, pp. 14–17.
16. Slotnick, pp. 34–42; Mandell, pp. 36–43.
17. Capron, p. B-8.
18. See any glossary of computer terms.
19. Capron, pp. B-2, B-10.
20. Ibid., p. 53.
21. Stephen Plain, "Power Pros—200 MHz Pentium Pros Mean Business," *Computer Shopper: Metro Edition,* July 1996, pp. 130–158.
22. Capron, pp. 53–55 and Glossary.
23. Ibid., p. 126.
24. Richard Smith, et al., *Navigating the Internet,* 3rd ed. (Indianapolis, IN: Sams.Net, 1995), pp. 5–9.
25. Ibid., pp. 264–265.
26. "The Long Arm of Harassment Law," *The New York Times,* July 7, 1996, p. E9.

27. "China's Grip on the Net," *The New York Times*, Feb. 11, 1996, p. E2.
28. *Time*, "Special Issue: Welcome to Cyberspace," Spring 1995.
29. "Techwatch," *Time*, April 15, 1996, p. 80; and J. M. Blocher, et al., *An Interactive Guide to the Internet* (Indianapolis, IN: Que Education and Training Co, 1996), p. 26.
30. Philip Elmer-Dewitt, "First Nation in Cyberspace," *Time*, December 6, 1993, pp. 62–64.
31. Steve Lohr, "When the Alma Mater Ends with 'Edu,'" *The New York Times*, July 7, 1996, p. E2.
32. "Clinton Proposes $2 billion program to connect public schools by computer," *Hartford Courant*, Feb. 16, 1996, p. A15; and "A study finds progress in linking public schools to the Internet," *The New York Times*, Feb. 18, 1996, p. 32.
33. Andrea Zimmerman, "Connecticut Q&A: John B. Larson—Universal Internet Access, Fall of '96," *The New York Times*, July 14, 1996, p. CN5.
34. See note 28, p. 49.
35. Dave and Mary Campbell, *The Student's Guide to Doing Research on the Internet* (Reading, MA: Addison-Wesley Pub. Co, 1995).
36. Edmund L. Andrews, "Congress Votes to Reshape Communications Industry, Ending a 4-Year Struggle," *The New York Times*, Feb. 2, 1996, p. 1.
37. "Technology Brief," *The Economist*, May 11, 1996, p. 72.
38. "War of the Wires," *The Economist*, May 11, 1996, pp. 59–60.
39. *The Economist*, July 6, 1996, p. 72.
40. Ibid., July 13, 1996, p. 88.
41. Ibid., July 20, 1996, p. 69.
42. Ibid., July 27, 1996, p. 70.
43. Negroponte, p. 23.
44. "NBC-Microsoft project meshes TV, cable, Internet," *Hartford Courant*, July 14, 1996, p. G1.
45. "All Things Considered," *National Public Radio*, July 14, 1996.
46. "We Know You're Reading This," *The Economist*, Feb. 10, 1996, pp. 27–28; "Virtual Privacy," *The Economist*, Feb. 10, 1996, pp. 16–17; "Privacy Eroded by Technology," *New Haven Register*, Feb. 20, 1996, p. A10; and Negroponte, p. 227.
47. Negroponte, p. 227.
48. Ibid., p. 228.
49. Ibid., p. 229.
50. Ibid., p. 250.
51. Ibid., pp. 231, 233–240.
52. "All Things Considered," *National Public Radio*, August 1, 1996.
53. Ibid., July 15, 1996.
54. Gary Stix, "Trends in Nanotechnology: Waiting for Breakthroughs," *Scientific American*, April 1996, pp. 94–99.
55. Carol Fancher, "Smart Cards," *Scientific American*, August 1996, pp. 40–45.
56. John Boyd, "New Flash Cards Expected Soon," *The Japan Times Weekly International Edition*, July 15–21, 1996, p. 16.
57. Steve Kemper, "Cyber Selling," *Northeast*, July 21, 1996, p. 7.
58. See note 31, and Emily Weiner, "Classroom Journal: Reflections of an On-Line Graduate," *The New York Times: Education Life* [supplement], section 4A, August 4, 1996, p. 42.
59. "The Future of the PC: How PC Technology Will Change Your Life in the Year 2000 and Beyond," *Microsoft Magazine* June/July 1996, pp. 10–22.

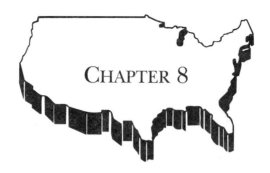

CHAPTER 8

AMERICAN WOMEN
AND THE TWENTY-FIRST CENTURY

ANTONIA C. MORAN

During the twentieth century, women transformed themselves from second-class citizens to nearly full participants in American economic and political life. Legal barriers limiting their access to economic and political power were removed, and new protections for rights created. During the late twentieth century, women moved in great numbers into more highly paid and respected positions in the world of work, entered political life with increasing influence, and engaged their male partners in searching reevaluations of gender roles, marriage, child rearing, and families. Nonetheless, women remain poorer than men, severely underrepresented in positions of power—whether political or economic—and face an ideological backlash. This chapter will examine a wide range of issues affecting women, men, and children. It will focus on women's rights and participation in the spheres of traditional electoral politics, the economy, and the family. The challenge for the next century is to identify the reasons for the continuing differences between men's and women's access to society's resources, and to implement full equalization of rights. On the way to achieving full equality, a new definition of equal rights will be necessary.

HISTORICAL BACKGROUND

The last forty years of the twentieth century were a period of profound social change, particularly for women. It was not the first time in American history, however, that women had moved into public view demanding social, legal, and political change to overcome inequality. There have been three periods when advocacy for women's rights has been successful in changing both legal rules and public attitudes regarding women's appropriate role in society. The first wave of feminism attracted public attention in 1848, when the Seneca Falls Convention released a Declaration of Rights demanding voting rights, and the right to be treated as an adult before the law, particularly in regard to property and child-custody disputes, as well as other legal issues. Interrupted by the Civil War, the first wave regained strength during the late 1800s, when women gained voting rights in several western states, and the National Women's Suffrage Association, led by Susan B. Anthony and Elizabeth Cady Stanton, exemplified the movement.[1]

The second wave of feminism began before World War I, when feminists, picking up the work of their mothers and grandmothers, succeeded in persuading Congress to pass, and the legislatures of thirty-eight states to ratify, the Nineteenth Amendment to the U.S. Constitution, granting women the right to vote.[2] This generation of women and their daughters made a deep and lasting impact on American society. More than ever before, they went to college and entered professions and politics, with many remaining in public life until their retirements during the 1960s. While large numbers of working-class women continued to work for pay as domestic servants, farm laborers, or factory workers, others entered totally new categories of work, as typists and clerical employees. One outward sign of the changes they made in the definition of women's place in society can be seen in the transformation of women's clothing: from whale-boned corsets and long, heavy skirts to short, lightweight dresses permitting easy movement and a modern life.

After the Second World War and full recovery from the Great Depression of the 1930s, public attention turned to restoring American society to a modern version of normality. Men returned to their jobs, and women to their new houses in the suburbs. Women married and had children at a much younger age than in the early years of the century, and the average number of children per family rose to a level resembling pre–World War I rates. Women's participation in higher education dropped significantly.[3] Nonetheless, there remained women activists, particularly among the 30 percent of women who continued to work outside the home. The League of Women Voters, women's clubs, professional women's groups, and women's unions continued to raise the issue of their exclusion from economic and political equality.

Several forces came together simultaneously during the early 1960s to create the third wave of American feminism. The birth control pill was first approved for use in 1960, making a relatively risk-free sexual life before marriage equally available to women and men, creating the sexual revolution of the 1960s and 1970s, and significantly weakening the double standards by which men's and women's sexual behavior had been measured. In 1961, responding to the demands of working women for a reexamination of economic opportunity, President John F. Kennedy appointed a Presidential Commission on the Status of Women, chaired by Eleanor Roosevelt. Its report, issued in 1963, documented the lack of equality for women in the workplace.[4] The civil rights movement, ongoing since the 1950s, introduced several American heroines. Among them were Rosa Parks, who risked life and limb in order to sit down in a bus; Daisy Bates, who led nine Little Rock children through the mobs to integrate the high school; four little girls who died in a bombing of the church where they were attending Sunday School; and Fannie Lou Hamer, who led rural Mississippi sharecroppers into the voting booth. In the late 1960s, the anti–Vietnam War movement produced women activists who rebelled against their exclusion from leadership roles and the attitudes of male leaders. Several books on the condition of women were published, including Betty Friedan's *The Feminist Mystique*, which for the first time identified "the problem that has no name, ... the voice within women that says: 'I want something more than my husband and my children and my home.'"[5] The social ferment begun during this period grew from the achievements of the earlier feminist movements, even if many third wave feminists were unaware of the earlier events.

We will approach the third wave of feminism (1960s–1990s), a period of social change, from two perspectives: first, women at work and in the world; and second, women as individuals and in their private lives. Gains in one area made change in the other possible, or even necessary; ultimately, the two perspectives are deeply interrelated.

In the United States, as in most cultures, wealth is a measure of personal freedom of choice. At the root of women's inequality, including within their personal relationships with men, lies a hard economic fact: Women have less money than men. Working women, painfully aware of the differences between their earnings and men's, advocated for legislative change through their labor unions at the national level. The Presidential Commission on the Status of Women issued its report in 1963, recommending the elimination of pay discrimination by compensating work of comparable worth equally; extension of the Fair Labor Standards Act to unprotected workers, such as domestic and agricultural workers; child care for all income levels; paid maternity leave; improved educational opportunities; equal rights for women to serve on juries and to be adjudged by juries containing women; and elimination of the remaining limits on married women's legal rights. The commission also urged the courts to apply the due process and Equal Protection clauses of the Constitution to statutes that discriminated against women based solely on their sex. In addition, heavily influenced by labor unions' support for protective legislation, the commission did not endorse the Equal Rights Amendment.[6] In the 1960s, a major factor in economic inequality was differential rates of pay. Pay discrimination arose from two circumstances. First, women were simply paid less than men doing the same job, or they did the same work but under a different job title. The title for people who cleaned offices, for example, was either "maid" or "custodian," and "maids" earned less. Second, there were "men's jobs" and "women's jobs," and the men's jobs paid better. In one large telephone company, the executives' chauffeurs (all men) were paid more than women supervising telephone operators (who were also all women).[7] Accountants were men; bookkeepers were women. Work segregation was furthered by the practice of advertising openings under either "Help Wanted: Male" or "Help Wanted: Female" headings until this became illegal in 1972. Pay discrimination was a very real phenomenon: In 1960, women earned 60 cents for every $1.00 earned by men.[8]

Although the Commission recommended that pay rates reflect the comparative value or worth of the jobs people held, Congress explicitly rejected that standard when it passed the Equal Pay Act of 1963. Instead, the Equal Pay Act guarantees equal pay for "equal work on jobs the performance of which requires equal skill, effort, and responsibility...."[9] In practice this meant that pay equalization would only occur within essentially identical job titles. All "custodians" would receive the same pay, but women placed in "maintainer" positions could be paid less. The initial exclusion of domestic workers and farm laborers from the Act's protection meant that occupations in which large percentages of minority women were employed remained outside federal pay regulation until 1972. Moreover, equalizing pay did not help those women who worked in occupations without male workers, such as nursing, or on assembly lines where virtually no men had been hired. Although women were unable to make great gains from Congress in 1963, the following year was a very different story.

After years of increasing civil rights protests, the civil rights march of 1963, and the assassination of President John F. Kennedy, President Lyndon Johnson determined to create a memorial to Kennedy and his own mark on history by the passage of a major civil rights bill. After months of debate, southern members of the House of Representatives, in a last-ditch effort to kill the bill, introduced an amendment to prohibit discrimination on the basis of sex, as well as race. Given the difficulty Congress had experienced in addressing discrimination against women on the job, no one could have predicted that a general prohibition on sex discrimination would be adopted. Congress approved the amendment, however, after a brief floor debate led by women members of the House of Representatives. When the final vote was taken, the Civil Rights Act of 1964 prohibited discrimination in employment on the basis of an "individual's race, color, religion, sex, or national origin."[10] Within months of passage, President Johnson issued Executive Order 11,246, prohibiting all contractors with federal contracts from discriminating in their own and in their subcontractors' employment practices, effectively applying federal employment law to private businesses and ultimately requiring the establishment of voluntary—and sometimes court-ordered—affirmative action plans.[11]

In 1972, the Civil Rights Act was amended to prohibit sex discrimination at any level in educational institutions, and to expand the coverage of the Equal Pay Act. In 1967, the Civil Rights Act had been amended to cover discrimination on the basis of age (people over the age of 40 are members of the protected class).[12] In 1973, discrimination against people with disabilities was also prohibited.[13]

While most people had a fairly clear understanding of what it would mean to end race-based employment discrimination, few could imagine a workplace in which men and women were treated absolutely equally. For example, what was equal treatment for pregnant women? How would equal treatment affect what had appeared to be perfectly voluntary choices, such as women's preferences for work in teaching and nursing, and men's preferences in machinery and transportation? Moreover, both men and women had internalized criteria for quality; most could not imagine a female newscaster or judge who would not be a joke; the phrase "a male nurse" was an oxymoron. Women's rights organizations took a strong position in favor of absolute equality. The problem, however, was enforcement.

Congress had chosen the broadest possible source of authority to prohibit discrimination, basing the Civil Rights Act on the powers given to the legislative branch under the Commerce Clause of the Constitution instead of on the Equal Protection Clause of the 14th Amendment, adopted after the Civil War. This made it possible to place enforcement of the Act in the legal tradition of other business regulations passed by Congress and upheld by the Supreme Court. The language of the legislation makes it an "unfair employment practice," not a violation of equal protection rights, to discriminate in employment decisions.

Within this technical language lies the Congressional intent to enforce the Act by requiring affirmative action. The enforcement mechanism for violations of unfair employment practices had been developed during the 1930s, under the National Labor Relations Act (NLRA). Employers found to have violated that law by firing union activists were required to take corrective action, by identifying union sympathizers (ordinarily prohibited under the NLRA), and hiring those who had suffered discrimination in the past. This "affirmative action" remedy was written into the regulations enforcing the Civil Rights Act for all forms of illegal discrimination, and has been upheld by the Supreme Court in a long line of cases,[14] although it is currently under severe attack from conservative judges at the appellate court level and from the current Supreme Court, particularly in relation to remediation of discrimination based on race. Recent cases have overturned programs under which cities set aside money for minority contractors and legislative redistricting designed to permit the election of minority representatives. At this writing, the 5th Circuit has ruled that all consideration of race in college admissions is unconstitutional, overturning existing Supreme Court decisions in much of the deep South. The Supreme Court is currently waiting for a better case to reconsider this issue at the national level.[15]

Like the National Labor Relations Act, the Civil Rights Act is enforced by an administrative agency, the Equal Employment Opportunity Commission (EEOC), which takes cases both from individuals and from groups of people ("class action" cases). Its orders are enforceable by the federal courts. In addition, complainants are allowed to pursue their own cases in court after a certain period of time. Advocates argue that the EEOC was understaffed from the beginning; its backlog of unresolved cases is in the thousands. Its inability to keep up with its caseload allows the EEOC to decide what kinds of cases it will pursue. Under the Bush administration, Director Clarence Thomas chose to ignore most class action complaints and also most complaints relating to age discrimination.

For women, the Civil Rights Act opened whole new vistas of unimagined opportunity. For example, newspapers were required to abandon their sex-segregated job ads; women could apply for the accountant positions, and not just the bookkeeper jobs. It would no longer be possible for law firms to hire young men fresh out of law school as potential partners, and offer their female colleagues secretarial positions, which was Sandra Day O'Connor's experience after graduating in the top of her class at Stanford. Women and blacks brought class action lawsuits on behalf of all women or African Americans discriminated against by an employer and won. The awards included back pay, promotions, new hires, and multiyear affirmative action plans.

Assisted by public policy guaranteeing equality, women moved into the workforce en masse.[16] Between 1950 and 1994, the percent of women who worked outside the home rose from 34 percent to 59 percent. By 1994, 59 percent of women over 16 worked, with 6 percent holding two jobs. Sixty percent of married women were employed.[17] Women's earnings, which continued to fall compared to men's—from 60 cents to a man's dollar in 1960 to 59 cents in 1970—then rose slowly. Women of color* were earning 42 cents for a man's dollar in 1960; that number rose slightly over the decade. To some extent the decline in women's average earnings was the result of the retirement of the women of the 1920s, whose salaries, while still lower than their male colleagues, were higher than those of entrance-level women.[18] By 1994, three-quarters of women between 25 and 54 were employed and earning 76 cents for every male dollar. This improvement was only partially the result of declining pay discrimination; most was the result of a continuing erosion of men's earnings, rather than increases in women's. The percentage of women with children under 18 who worked rose from 11.9 percent in 1950 to 30 percent in 1980, to 45 percent in 1981 to 70 percent in 1994. Half the women with children less than a year old are now employed. Unemployment rates for women have been slightly higher than for men; the unemployment rates for black men and women are frequently more than double those of whites.

---

*The phrase *women of color* is the author's choice, not the editors'.

Many women work for the personal rewards; others work to raise their families above the poverty level. Only in families with both spouses employed, however, was there an increase in family income from 1973 to 1993.

Race and gender both unify and separate women at work. In spite of the common myth of the black welfare mother, black women have always had a much higher rate of workforce participation than white women. "Liberation" for many black women might have meant the right to stay home with their children, without the stigma or impoverishment of welfare; for white women, it meant having the right to enter the workforce. At the same time, both black and white women's income has always been less than black men's, even when unemployment rates for women were lower. Between 1971 and 1991, black women experienced the highest percent increase in earnings (from a median annual income of $15,845 to $18,720 in constant 1991 dollars); men's median income, although it fell from a high of $32,219 in 1986 to $30,266 in 1991, remained much higher. Black men's income, lower than white men's earnings, was 18 to 30 percent higher than black women's.

Women have increased their participation in previously male dominated professions dramatically; nonetheless, their predominance in traditionally lower paid female professions—such as social worker—remains a contributing factor to lower incomes. The most important factor, however, is lower earnings for women in "pink-collar" positions: clerical work, retail sales, health care, and service-industry positions from which there is little opportunity for upward mobility, unionization, or job security—all traditional factors in increasing income. Moreover, these positions are likely to provide less access to health care or retirement income.

Women rarely achieve top management positions. Recent studies by the U.S. Labor Department have confirmed the existence of "glass ceilings," trapping women in middle levels of management. Labor unions now also refer to "sticky floors," which keep women locked in low-level positions. In August 1991, then-Secretary of Labor Elizabeth Dole released the first Glass Ceiling Report, documenting the effects of sex discrimination in high-level positions, and recommending more affirmative recruitment into these positions. The Report concluded that the glass ceiling was lower than expected; that minorities found the ceiling even lower than white women did; and that when women and minorities were found in higher positions, they were support positions, rather than positions central to the company's business, with reduced opportunities for further advancement. The Report recommended that companies educate their top-level managers about the need for a diverse management, establish affirmative action programs, and comply voluntarily with the Civil Rights Act.[19]

The Civil Rights Act encouraged women to challenge less obvious kinds of workplace discrimination. Laws requiring that pregnant school teachers leave the classroom were overturned, as were airline requirements that stewardesses's jobs be terminated upon marriage. Hiring practices that discriminated against women, such as weight, height, and upper-body strength tests, were revised. Protective legislation that excluded women from night work, or other kinds of jobs that paid more than the jobs women were allowed to hold, was also overturned.

One difficult issue was sexual harassment. Many people—women included—believed that dealing with sexual advances from employers was a normal part of a working woman's life; it came with the decision to leave the safety of private life. If the harassment was serious, women could just quit their jobs. In the 1980s, courts began to find employers liable, under the Civil Rights Act, for the harm suffered by women who had been sexually harassed. Courts had little difficulty finding that employers, who fired workers for refusing to comply with sexual demands, had violated the law, calling this "*quid pro quo* harassment."[20] However, many women argued that they had been harmed by employers who allowed other employees to surround them with sexual innuendo, or that they had been forced to resign to escape an intolerable situation. Courts had begun to recognize that African Americans could be harassed out of a job without the employer making an obviously illegal employment decision, but they had not reached the same conclusion regarding women. Catherine MacKinnon's book, *The Sexual Harassment of Working Women*, published in 1979, gave the phenomenon a name, and proposed a legal framework that the Supreme Court used in *Meritor* v. *Vinson*, holding that employers could be held liable for the existence of "hostile environment" sexual harassment.[21] Public understanding of these issues grew after Anita Hill, an attorney and former employee, told her story of sexual harassment by Clarence Thomas, former director of the EEOC, in Senate hearings on his nomination for Supreme Court Justice in 1991. While the public debated her treatment by an all-male Judiciary Committee, and compared her credibility to Judge Thomas's, all over the country women revealed their secret stories of harassment at work, sometimes unforgiven occurrences of decades past.

Another series of court cases led to a major revision in the laws and practices concerning pensions. Older women were more likely to be poor than men because of pay differentials, interrupted work histories, and because they lived longer. In order to spread their pension benefits over a longer life span, women were given lower monthly benefits, or charged more for an equal benefit. In *Manhart* and *Norris*, the Supreme Court determined that the distinction between potential pension beneficiaries by sex violated the Civil Rights Act, and ordered pension providers to stop setting contribution and benefit rates on the basis of sex.[22]

Women had experienced significant discrimination in access to credit, whether through loans or credit cards. Lenders refused to take into account the wife's contribution to repayment of loans, identifying the borrower as the husband, and denying the wife, even after divorce or the husband's death, credit based on her own income or work history. In 1974, Congress passed the Equal Credit Opportunity Act, permitting women to establish and maintain credit in their own names, and prohibiting discrimination based on sex or marital status.

While the Supreme Court had generally sustained state laws that discriminated on the basis of sex prior to the passage of the Civil Rights Act, during the 1970s it issued a number of 14th Amendment Equal Protection Clause decisions, overturning state statutes that had drawn distinctions between males and females. Justice William Brennan attempted to raise sex discrimination to the level of race discrimination, requiring "strict scrutiny" and a heavy presumption of unconstitutionality. The Court, however, ultimately settled on an "intermediate level" of scrutiny for cases involving classifications by sex. For example, the Court found that government programs that provided different benefits for the spouses of male and female employees were based on outmoded stereotypes, and improperly discriminated against women, but upheld statutory rape statutes against males.[23] Most cases involving sex discrimination currently rely on the Civil Rights Act and its amendments, on state statutes and constitutions, or on institutional policies and collective bargaining agreements.

Between 1965 and 1995, a dramatic shift occurred in women's expectations of their work life. In the 1960s, many young women viewed institutions of higher education as places to find husbands of a better socioeconomic class, and the appropriate outcome of their education to be a "MRS" degree and not employment. To the extent that college meant professional training, it was primarily for teaching and nursing positions, or for secretarial employment. Even working women expected that they would leave the workforce upon marriage or when their first child was born, and not return. Most men were brought up to assume their primary role in life as "provider"; they would be failures as men if their wives were forced into the workplace. Women were not supposed to earn more than their husbands, and a man whose wife did earn more than he did had a hard time facing his male peers. Today, both women and men recognize that women will spend some years employed outside the home, and that many women will aspire to careers equal to or higher paying than the men they marry.

A discussion of women's economic condition would not be complete without consideration of welfare. Five percent of all women, 15 percent of black women and 11 percent of Hispanic women, between the ages of 15 and 64, were on welfare in 1992. For white families with children and a female head of household, the poverty rate was nearly 40 percent; for similar black families, 58 percent, and for Hispanic families of the same description, the rate was 61 percent. The numbers of families on welfare fell during the 1960s and 1970s, but rose through the 1980s and into the 1990s. The economic recovery that began in 1993 has resulted in some reduction in the number of the poor.

Welfare reforms adopted under the Reagan administration removed housing and food subsidies from the working poor, forcing many of these families below the poverty line. Women predominate among those who earn the minimum wage, or who hold part-time jobs, making them far more susceptible to economic fluctuation or impoverishment with the loss of housing or food subsidies. Clearly, employment has not been sufficient to raise many women above the poverty line. The working poor are also less likely to have access to health care (although Medicaid is available to people earning up to 133 percent of the poverty line), and are less likely to have accrued private pensions upon retirement. They are also less likely to be able to afford quality child care. Welfare reform, passed by Congress in 1996, aimed at moving recipients back into the workforce as quickly as possible by denying benefits after a certain period of time, and by requiring training or work in exchange for receipt of benefits, may increase the numbers of vulnerable working poor women with children. The average length of welfare dependence has been between two and three years; reduction of welfare availability to the length of time an average recipient needs will bring real hardship to the most vulnerable members of society: very poor children. Unless welfare reform includes funds for child care, access to Head Start preschool programs, school nutrition programs, and health care for working families too poor to pay for it themselves, whole generations of very young children will be exposed to homelessness, malnutrition, and other forms of physical and psychological deprivation that studies show result in permanent damage to intelligence and mental health.

While there has been some reduction in the difference between men's and women's economic status, neither government, the corporate world, nor education has eliminated discrimination. The rate at which women and minorities have moved into male-dominated, well-paid work has been too slow to be caused by lack of preparation or ability alone.[24] To the extent that the inequity is caused by resistance based on sex discrimination, only some form of external intervention can level the playing field for those who are excluded. To the extent that the differences are caused by women's choices, uninfluenced by coercive cultural expectations of traditional behavior, we must ask why women's preferences, and women's work, provide lower income and less societal recognition than men's.

MAKING CHANGE: CONTEXT, METHODOLOGY, AND CONTENT

As individual women tried to enter or remain in jobs from which they had been excluded, they raised questions about societal attitudes toward women. Would a female newscaster have the same credibility as a man, since deep voices had been associated with credibility for so long? Would women firefighters have the courage and physical strength that men did? Could a woman supervise male employees? Did women have the commitment to become high-quality professionals? (The Boston Symphony Orchestra discovered that women could be accomplished classical musicians when they auditioned new members behind a screen, so that interviewers could not determine their sex.) Did language influence the way we thought about women and men? Did it matter if we called mailmen "letter carriers," or firemen "firefighters"? Could you change the deep-seated, sometimes unconscious prejudices that associated feminine characteristics with weakness, lack of education, superficiality, or emotionalism? Should women aspire to a behavioral or management style that matched the traditional, male standard? What was the appropriate model? What about the old traditions of women's moral leadership? What about pregnancy, child care, and the other family responsibilities that fathers, husbands, and sons were unprepared to assume?

The first challenge was to break down the barriers, and to permit women to participate fully in the public world. Women's advocates agreed that if women wanted to be treated as equals, then they would have to behave as equals. Childbearing, the one real difference between men and women, should be treated as any other medical disability: covered by medical insurance, and with paid medical leave for as long as the woman's physician believed she needed to be out of work for health reasons. Initially, women's advocates believed that if women were given any special consideration for their roles as mothers, they would be reviving the old arguments for protective legislation. Special considerations for working mothers, or "mommy tracks," were viewed by some women's advocates as permission for women to achieve at lower levels than men, and by others as excuses for employers to treat women as less reliable, more expensive, and therefore less desirable employees.

EDUCATION

When women expect to support themselves, they prepare for the job market by going to school. In 1970, 55 percent of white women, 33 percent of black women, and 31 percent of Hispanic women had received 12 or more years of schooling. By 1993, 81 percent of white women, 68 percent of black women, and 55 percent of Hispanic women had completed high school or attended college. Over the same period of time, the number of older women returning to college more than doubled, from 25 percent to 49 percent of women college students.[25] During the same period, the number of eighteen-year-olds decreased, as the baby-boom generation postponed childbearing and average family size declined. The expected decline of the college student population was almost entirely offset by women in their twenties, thirties, and even forties, who returned to college to further their own personal goals and to acquire workforce skills. These women also forced the expansion of programs for part-time students, persuaded institutions to grant academic credit for knowledge that had been acquired outside the classroom, pressured colleges into providing child care, and demanded academic course work that reflected their own experiences as women.

Women students declared majors in disciplines from which they had been excluded in the past. In June 1960, one quarter of the degrees in the biological sciences were awarded to women. Thirty years later, women received half of the undergraduate biology degrees awarded. Similar increases occurred in mathematics and the physical sciences. Business programs awarded 7 percent of their degrees to undergraduate women in 1960, and 47 percent of their degrees to women in 1992. Women rose from 41 percent of the 1960 graduating class in psychology to 73 percent in 1992. In education, English, undergraduate health professions, and the visual and performing arts, women comprised more than half the student body.

By 1992, women outnumbered men among the recipients of postsecondary degrees at every level except the doctoral level. Even here, there was real progress. In 1960, only 1,000 women received Ph.D.s, 11 percent of the total. In 1995, 16,333 Ph.D.s were awarded to women; 31 percent of the degrees awarded in the sciences went to women, and 52 percent of the nonscience degrees.[26] In the years between 1974 and 1992, women law school graduates rose from 11 percent of the class to 42.6 percent, women medical students from 11 percent to 38 percent, and women dentistry students from 2 percent to 32 percent.[27] Nonetheless, the representation of women in college and university faculty remains low: In 1993, only 44 percent of four-year college women faculty were tenured, while 69 percent of their male colleagues were tenured. Women remain clustered in two-year colleges, in the lower ranks of four-year colleges, and in colleges with less prestige. In fact, between 1910 and 1985, the percentage of female college faculty increased by only 8 percent.[28] Progress has been made at the presidential level, however. In 1975 there were only 16 female college presidents of public institutions; by 1992, there were 164. However, only 12 percent of all heads of accredited institutions were women. The gains experienced by women academic employees were the direct result of affirmative action programs, undertaken voluntarily or in the face of court orders.

Underlying these changes was the women's liberation movement, which must be discussed before we move on to other institutional developments.

CONSCIOUSNESS-RAISING

The social change that has just been documented did not occur easily. It required changes in the circumstances of individual lives, and changes in the way individual women (and men) viewed themselves and their roles in the world. Two books are usually given credit for beginning this change. The first, Simone de Beauvoir's *The Second Sex*, a philosophical analysis of women's condition, was of unquestionable importance to women who viewed themselves as intellectuals: The book that shook the suburbs, however, was Betty Friedan's *The Feminist Mystique*.[29]

Many women who read Betty Friedan's exposé of the quiet desperation of the isolated, underemployed, and undervalued suburban housewife recognized their own condition. The book demanded to be talked about. Women gathered in what may have started out as "kaffeeklatsches" but evolved into a mechanism of significant social change: Countless and uncounted small groups of women who met weekly, sometimes for several years, to talk openly about their lives and their feelings, uncovering surprising realities, helping one another transform their lives, and creating the ideology and structure of the women's liberation movement.[30] The "rules" for consciousness-raising were very heavily influenced by another group of women: young women of the left, who came together out of anger over sex discrimination within the antiwar movement, the New Left organizations such as Students for a Democratic Society (SDS), and the civil rights movement. Consciousness-raising occurred without any formal structure or national organization, but was encouraged by new publications and articles in the traditional women's journals, and a set of common rules: Women were free to speak their minds; the group was committed to hearing and respecting each other's words; what was said remained within the group; and there was no hierarchy of organization, or preference given for social status. Suburban housewives and radical college students alike discovered their suppressed anger over exclusion from education, work, respect, and responsibility and realized that they were not just dissatisfied individual social misfits. The act of expression allowed women to identify and to analyze their own lives as part of a patriarchal society in which women were systematically and individually denied equality. Comprehension led to change. As individuals, women reshaped their lives. As groups, they produced books, founded cooperative ventures, developed multiple forms of public advocacy, and supported women who assumed leadership in many arenas, including academic, political, and social change organizations. Among the most important achievements of women's consciousness-raising are the following:

1. The identification and description of women's exclusion and oppression in a male-dominated society. Many women had internalized existing conditions, believing, for example, that only the rarest, and unfeminine, women could be good lawyers, doctors, musicians, leaders, or entrepreneurs. While this was clearly untrue, the work of becoming conscious of one's ability and power was not easy in the face of overwhelming social denial.

2. The identification of "sisterhood": the belief that women shared a common bond, a common strength, that outweighed their differences; and that women had the power to sustain one another as they challenged established rules, attitudes, and exclusionary power structures.

3. The discovery that male dominance in marriage extended to violence; and that some women were in physical and mental danger from abusive husbands. Since the police were rarely helpful, some groups created self-defense programs, including secret hiding places for women and their children (the earliest battered women's shelters), and other forms of intervention.

4.   The discovery that women were receiving poor health care because of inadequate information and paternalistic treatment by male doctors. Women began to demand a role in deciding appropriate treatment for themselves. The Boston Health Collective published *Our Bodies, Ourselves* to disseminate medical information to women. Women's health groups developed safe techniques for early abortions in the years before it became legal for medical professionals to terminate pregnancies.[31]

5.   The discovery that children's schoolbooks were socializing girls to forego education and a public life. Mothers and teachers demanded textbook revision and changes in school curricula.

6.   The demands by women students, faculty, and staff that colleges and universities create women's centers and a women's studies curriculum, hire more women professors and administrators, admit more women students into programs where they were underrepresented, and establish on-site child care.

7.   The creation of women's legal resources concerning issues of divorce law and child custody law, including referrals to attorneys, and creating networks of feminist attorneys.

8.   The provision of financial, legal, and moral support to women in their legal battles for equal pay and equal treatment at work.

9.   The development of new theories of organization, rejecting hierarchy and majority rule for decision by consensus. Women's groups functioned as participatory democracies, explicitly avoiding the creation of formal leadership, and strengthening each woman's individual voice.

10. The beginnings of feminist theory, epistemology, and jurisprudence. Women scholars, confronting the fact that their history, political condition, economic status, and psychological realities had been obscured by academic research but revealed by the process of women telling their stories, developed new theories of knowledge, creating feminist epistemology: the theory that knowledge may best be found by intense attention to individual accounts rather than in quantitative research.[32] Feminist theory has also been applied to literature, history, science, anthropology, sociology, and most other academic disciplines. For many scholars, it has transformed their view of the world, and is currently one of the richest and most rapidly developing areas of academic thought.

Ultimately, women began to talk about politics, bringing to that discussion the issues that had been excluded from public political debate as "private" or "personal." Social policy regarding marriage and child care, access to work, patient's rights, sexual freedom, abortion, and adoption was reexamined, as the presence of discrimination in the law itself was identified. Changes in one's personal life, like changes in working life, required more than consciousness; it frequently required legislative or judicial action. Economic equity required government intervention to assure equal treatment, tax reform to recognize child care expenditures as business expenses, and incentives for employers to recruit and retain women employees. Spousal violence required legislative change to make rape of a spouse an illegal act, and to provide legal recourse to its victims. Congress had opened the door to political change, and women walked through it. The personal and the political were deeply intertwined in the areas of sex, marriage, and the family.

WOMEN, MEN, AND CHILDREN: THE PRIVATE SPHERE

BIRTH CONTROL AND ABORTION

American laws and traditions regarding the relationships between men and women in marriage, sexual behavior, and the custody of children arose from Western European cultures in which women and children were forms of property, necessary for the transmission of wealth from one generation to another. Achievement of equality, however, requires more than eliminating the legal disabilities that limit women's rights to participate as equals in marriage, childrearing, divorce, and child custody. Real equality requires a reconstruction of the roles of men and women within relationships—especially within marriage. While the most onerous legal rules have been repealed, Americans continue to contend with legal and cultural traditions in which women's rights are subservient to men's.

Most American college students of the 1990s are unfamiliar with the "double standards" of sexual behavior that their parents conformed to or rebelled against. Men were expected to have sex, to want to have sex, and to enjoy it—and for some cultural groups, before and outside marriage, as well as within. Sex was a man's legal right in his marriage, and his wife's legal obligation. Women were not expected to want sex, to enjoy it, or to appear to be sexually active. Pregnancy was not shown in movies, or publicly talked about, except with euphemisms. Unmarried women who became pregnant were "fallen" women; if they were young, their parents frequently arranged "shotgun weddings," which were essentially forced marriages. In some states, it was not an illegal homicide if a man killed his wife and her lover on finding them in bed; women had no comparable legal defense. In most states, a history of physical abuse was generally insufficient to exonerate women who killed their husbands.

The "sexual revolution" of the 1960s was a rejection of the double standard, and an assertion of women's right to have and to enjoy sex on the same terms as men had enjoyed it. It was made possible by the release of the Kinsey Report, documenting the existence of women's sexuality; the work of Masters and Johnson, debunking theories of women's "frigidity," and supporting women's rights to sexual pleasure; the invention of a safe, reliable birth control pill; and by women's readiness to explore new forms of freedom and independence.[34] Increased sexual activity, however, carries with it an increased likelihood of pregnancy and sexually transmitted diseases, including AIDS.

Women's increased participation in education and work made the consequences of an unwanted pregnancy even more severe, and existing limitations on the availability of birth control and abortion even more onerous. Laws restricting the distribution of birth control and the availability of abortion, adopted in the late nineteenth century, remained in force in the 1960s and 1970s. In 1962, several states prohibited the distribution of birth control for anything other than health reasons. Many states liberalized their abortion statutes, but full legal abortion was not available anywhere within the continental United States until 1973. But the fact that abortions were illegal did not stop women from having them. Thousands of women died in botched illegal abortions, and many more were permanently injured.

Challenges to state laws prohibiting the distribution of birth control began in the early 1960s, funded in part by the Planned Parenthood Association. The Supreme Court, in *Griswold* v. *Connecticut* and *Eisenstadt* v. *Baird*, significantly expanded the Bill of Rights by identifying an implied right to privacy, entitling married couples—and later, all couples—to determine whether or not to bear children, overturning state limitations on birth control.[34] In *Roe* v. *Wade*, the Court ruled that this privacy right covered the woman's decision, in consultation with her doctor, to terminate a pregnancy.[35] *Roe* balanced the state's right to regulate the woman's health and to protect potential life by dividing pregnancy into three trimesters. In the first trimester, the only right greater than individual privacy is the state's right to protect the woman's health. In the second trimester, the state has increased rights to regulate abortion, because during this period, abortions are more dangerous for the mother than is childbirth. In the third trimester, when the fetus is potentially capable of surviving on its own, the state's right to protect potential life may supersede the woman's privacy right.

Although the Supreme Court has found constitutional protection for a woman's right to decide whether or not to bear a child, and to terminate a pregnancy during its early stages, it has also upheld "pro-childbearing" policies adopted by Congress and state governments. These policies include denial of state and federal funding for abortions, and a wide range of limits on the availability of abortions.[36] Many opponents believed that Roe would be overturned when justices appointed by Presidents Reagan and Bush held a majority in the Supreme Court. Several states adopted extremely stringent limits on abortion with the intention of providing an opportunity for the Court to reverse *Roe*. During the late 1980s, Justice Sandra Day O'Connor provided the critical fifth vote upholding *Roe*, although the case, *Webster* v. *Missouri*, made any public support of abortion illegal in Missouri.[37] Only three years later, in *Planned Parenthood* v. *Casey*, three Republican appointees, Justices Sandra Day O'Connor, David Souter, and William Kennedy, wrote a strong centrist opinion announcing their support for *Roe*, but replacing the trimester system with a "viability" test.[38] Only three justices, Rehnquist, Scalia, and Thomas continue to argue against a constitutional abortion right.

At the same time, organizations such as Operation Rescue have undertaken campaigns designed to dissuade women from terminating their pregnancy, by making visits to targeted abortion clinics so unpleasant, frightening, and even dangerous, that these clinics must organize escorts to walk clients from their cars to the door. Within the past five years, several doctors and staff members have been murdered by antiabortion activists operating without the sanction of mainstream antiabortion groups. The number of communities in which abortions are not locally available continues to rise; 84 percent of counties have no doctor who performs abortions. Only about 12 percent of obstetric and gynecological medical training programs currently require training in abortion methods.[39]

Alternatives to surgical abortion, such as abortion-producing medications, are currently in use in Europe. Some religious organizations, believing that a human being is created at the moment the ovum is fertilized, have opposed the introduction of new birth control methods designed to keep a fertilized egg from implanting in the uterine wall. Hesitancy on the part of manufacturers and government regulators to confront this controversy has delayed the introduction of medications such as RU-486, the French "morning-after" pill, as well as development of safe intrauterine devices, leaving women dependent on surgical abortion for termination of pregnancy, even in the early weeks.

Relatively reliable methods of birth control, when coupled with safe, legal abortions, opened the door to economic opportunity for women. It is not accidental that women who support abortion rights tend to be highly educated and aspire to a life centered on work and professions, while opponents are more likely to be married, and to be homemakers.[40]

DOMESTIC VIOLENCE

The consciousness-raising movement uncovered the existence of violence in the family. Families had been viewed as safe havens, where women were protected and cherished. By the 1970s, the idea that a husband had a right to "discipline" his wife as well as their children was unacceptable to most Americans, and most believed that violence between married couples had become rare. At the same time, women were taught that they were responsible for the quality of family life; if there was a failure, it was the wife's fault. Wives in abusive situations were caught in a classic Catch-22: Violence could only exist in a failed marriage, and a failed marriage was the wife's fault, especially if she had driven her husband to violence; any revelation of her injuries would only demonstrate the immensity of her failure as a wife. Spousal abuse and sexual abuse were a source of immense shame—literally unspeakable—especially when combined with husbands' or fathers' threats of retaliation if the truth were revealed.

Statistics compiled by the American Medical Association (AMA) in 1992 show that an estimated 4 million women are seriously assaulted by male partners each year. According to the AMA, 154 of every 1,000 pregnant women are assaulted during the first four months of pregnancy, and 170 of every

1,000 pregnant women are assaulted in the last five months.[41] Consciousness-raising groups discovered that violence was not only far more frequent than anyone had expected, but that the police routinely ignored women's complaints and requests for help. Even when the police came, they were hindered by existing statutes that did not provide adequate protection for many assault victims. In some states, mere bruises were not enough; broken bones were required. Moreover, prosecutors (overwhelmingly male) were unwilling to bring these cases to trial. According to a 1982 United States Civil Rights Commission report, the odds that a spousal abuse case would get to a court were 100 to 1.[42] Not only were there no shelters for women under attack, but in a culture where people moved away from parents and family, women had lost their traditional source of protection.

The first women's shelters were run by volunteers and funded by private contributions. Federal funds were not made available until passage of the Family Violence Prevention and Services Act in 1984.[43] The following year, after Tracy Thurman's successful $3 million suit against the city of Torrington, CT, police departments began to train officers to recognize and respond to incidents of domestic violence. State legislatures have recently passed anti-stalking laws, giving police legal grounds to arrest people whose behavior is increasingly threatening, before a physical assault occurs.

Wives also reported that they had been raped by their husbands. In most states, forced sex between a married couple was specifically excluded from the statutes defining rape. Marriage was understood to be a contract between a man and a woman: He had an obligation to provide housing, food, and clothing, and a legal right to demand sex. Changing the laws required altering both statutes and attitudes, which was more easily accomplished as it became easier for women to become economically independent. Cases in which rape occurred between a married couple who had been separated for some time contributed to changing public opinion. It is still probably true that only the most egregious cases of marital rape are reported.

Violence against sexual partners has proven to be unexpectedly intractable. Thirty percent of female homicide victims are killed by men to whom they have been married, or to whom they are related.[44] Programs requiring abusers to attend counseling or mediation have frequently failed, partly because they assume equal bargaining power between the husband and wife. Wives may be less powerful for many reasons: less physical strength, less willingness to use violence, the need to protect children, financial dependence, and threats of custody disputes or kidnapping. A wife may also be psychologically undermined by her husband's accusations, and her belief that she is at fault. Many experts now advocate the arrest and incarceration of violent spouses.

Consciousness-raising groups also brought to light another form of domestic violence: the sexual abuse of children. The existence of sexual abuse of children—primarily but not exclusively girls—was revealed as adult women told their own stories and confronted the consequences of these experiences in their lives. For most people, it was difficult to believe that such abuse could happen; many simply denied its existence, even refusing to believe members of their families who described their experiences. In consciousness-raising groups, not only did women listen to one another, but sometimes they confirmed the accounts with stories of their own experiences of incest, discovering that it was far more prevalent than anyone had imagined.

As women began to assert their rights to choose the context in which they lived, many concluded that their marriages were no longer acceptable. While some left marriages because they were violent, others simply left in search of a better life. Both men and women made this choice with increasing frequency, and demanded legal change to make divorce easier.

DIVORCE

The statistics about marriage and divorce can be very misleading. Even though half of all marriages are expected to end in divorce, at any given time most adults are in fact married. The state of being "divorced" (i.e., divorced and not remarried) exists for a relatively short time for most people. In 1993, 56 percent of women and 60 percent of men were married and living with their spouses.[45] Only 9.9 percent of women and 7.6 percent of men were "divorced." The lowest marriage rate was for black men, only 40 percent of whom were married and living with their wives. Black women are more than twice as likely to be divorced than white women, and only 32 percent of them are likely to be married and living with their husbands. The most significant change in family status since 1970 has been the decline in the number of black married couples, from 66 percent of black households in 1970 to 47 percent in 1993. By comparison, the decline for whites has been from 86 percent of white households to 78 percent.[46] In 1970, there were 4.3 million divorced Americans, or 3 percent of the population. By 1994, the number had risen to approximately 9 percent of the population. The increasing numbers of children being raised in single-parent homes have led some conservatives to support proposals to restrict divorce, although none have been adopted at this writing. At the same time, some men have formed organizations whose purpose it is to limit the amount they are compelled to pay in alimony and child support.

Divorce statutes and common law have changed substantially between 1960 and 1996. The changes occurred in two separate categories: the requirements for dissolution, and the financial and childrearing consequences of the divorce. In general, divorce has become easier to obtain, even when one spouse prefers to remain married. Women and their children suffer significant financial loss as the immediate result of divorce, even though both state and national governments have acted to increase the amount of child support fathers provide.

The two most significant changes in divorce law were (1) a provision that a suit for divorce could be granted over the opposition of the other spouse; and (2) the creation of "no-fault" divorce. Old laws required that one party charge the other with causing the marriage to fail—either by adultery or abandonment, for example. Under no-fault divorce, couples prove only that the marriage has broken down irrevocably. Legal changes affecting financial arrangements included making alimony (payments for adult support) available to the spouse who earned less, regardless of gender, and giving the poorer spouse access to pensions. For those wives who had set aside their own careers to put their husbands through college or graduate school, judges treated a larger part of the husband's lifetime income as property acquired during the marriage, and therefore subject to division.

The divorce rate soared, and women's standard of living fell. The most recent conservative estimate is that ex-wives experience nearly a 30 percent decrease in their living standard, while their husbands' income increases by 10 percent.[47] Median family income for white married couples was $43,659 in 1993, for single, white female-headed households, $19,962.[48] For black married couples, median income was $35,181, and for single black women, $11,905. Hispanic families earned $28,454, and single Hispanic women earned $12,047.[49] In the years between 1978 and 1993, when married couples managed to increase their standard of living, generally by having both adults work, the income of single women with children declined, from $15,060 to $13,459 (in constant 1993 dollars). For many women, child support payments have been critical to avoiding poverty. Nonetheless, in 1989, only 57.7 percent of all eligible women were awarded child support, and of those women, only half received the full amount of their award. An additional quarter received only partial payments. In the same year, of those women eligible for child support, 54.4 percent of Hispanic women fell below the poverty line, as did 51.2 of black women, and 35.7 percent of white women. The disproportionate rate of poverty for women with children has led to rising concern about the "feminization of poverty." While during the 1960s, the poorest segment of the population was the elderly, it is now children. Nearly half of all the children in households headed by women are poor. The desire for equality and independence led many women to seek only child support payments, and to take nothing for their own support. For the children of mothers who work part time, or at low-paying jobs, the difference between a middle-class life and one of poverty lies in the child support check.

Both state and federal governments have responded to the problem of "deadbeat dads" by permitting divorced mothers, who are unable to collect court-ordered child support from their former spouses, to receive welfare, while the state takes on the responsibility of enforcement and collection. With the assistance of federal legislation and formal agreements between the states, it is now possible for states to trace absentee fathers anywhere in the United States, and to deduct from their paychecks the money owed. This does little, however, to return the father to his children.

In 90 percent of divorces in which children are involved, the mother retains physical custody. This has not always been the case. In the nineteenth century, fathers had a common-law right to the labor of their children, and women who wanted a divorce usually were forced to leave their children behind. Custody and child support payments were among the major issues of the early women's rights movement. By the 1930s, most courts granted custody to the mother, under the "tender years" doctrine. More recently, the standard has become a placement "in the best interests of the child," permitting fathers to challenge mother's claims. Most parents currently negotiate some form of joint custody, in which they have a shared responsibility until their children reach eighteen. The absence of a legal presumption in favor of the mother means that fathers can and do make custody arrangements part of the legal contest over financial arrangements. Faced with the threat of loss of custody, some mothers accept inadequate support arrangements.

In several well-publicized court battles, women have lost custody of their children when the judge has determined that the father can offer a higher standard of living, or when the mother has had hetero- or homosexual love affairs, or more recently, when a mother would have put her child in day care while she attended college. Men have been fairly successful in court when challenging the award of custody to the mother, winning between one-third and one-half of contested cases.[50]

The basic family unit has changed. It is more likely to have experienced divorce, and remarriage. The traditional nuclear family of two parents and 2.7 children has been replaced in many households by stepparents, visiting noncustodial children, step and half siblings, unmarried adults raising their own or others' children, adult children living at home while looking for work, grandchildren, multiple families avoiding homelessness, unrelated and unmarried older adults sharing living space and expenses, and a wide variety of arrangements driven by lifestyle changes or by the economy.

Among these new families are lesbian and gay couples, some of whom have children. Some of the changes necessary to accommodate these relationships are tax laws recognizing partnerships other than marriage; laws recognizing same-sex partners as eligible to receive health care and pension benefits based on one partner's employment; inheritance, guardianship, and custody laws that recognize the permanence of these relationships; and the establishment of legal rights without requiring private negotiations or allowing other relatives to routinely challenge choices made by the couple. Gay rights advocates argue that "family values" are as important to them as to heterosexual couples.

If old subjects are now coming back in a new guise regarding marriage and divorce, the same is also true of statutory rape laws. Statutory rape is a crime that is defined by the victim's age alone. These laws, prohibiting sex with underage girls (traditionally fifteen or younger), remain on the books even though they have not been enforced. Although the Supreme Court upheld statutory rape laws, states simply stopped prosecuting these cases.[51] As the number of young pregnant teenagers has increased in recent years, statistics showing that the average age of their partners is well over eighteen, with many in their twenties and thirties, have led women's advocates to reconsider these statutes and demand their enforcement. Girls between the ages of eleven and fourteen are unlikely to be acting entirely of their own free will when they are involved with men twice their own age, particularly when they live in ethnic communities in which traditional double standards and men's supremacy prevail. The advantage of prosecuting statutory rape cases is that the girl is not required to bring a charge of rape against the man; her age and her pregnancy are sufficient to establish a violation of the law.

WOMEN IN POLITICS: MAKING THE PERSONAL POLITICAL

Before we pose the question of the appropriate direction for public policy on women's issues, we need to ask why, more than seventy-five years after achieving full voting rights, women remain significantly underrepresented in the political environment.

That women are underrepresented is beyond question. In "The Year of the Woman," 1992, the number of women serving in the U.S. Senate rose to six, with California providing two of those. The number of women in the House of Representatives rose to forty-eight. Considering that women constitute 51 percent of the population, 46 percent of the workforce, and that 62 percent of eligible women vote, 6 percent representation in the Senate and slightly more than 10 percent representation in the U.S. Congress hardly deserve celebration.[52]

There have been some very significant changes, however, primarily in public opinion and in the number of women holding office at the state and local levels. In the 1920s, some women believed it was actually wrong for women to vote.[53] Public opinion surveys between the 1930s and 1970s generally revealed opposition from both men and women to women serving in political office. In the late 1940s, for example, surveys revealed that between half and two-thirds of men and women would not vote for a woman for president, governor, or senator. Nearly 90 percent believed that mayors should nearly always be men. These attitudes began to change only in the late 1960s. By 1991, surveys indicated that nearly 90 percent of the public would vote for a qualified woman for president. Between 1974 and 1991, the proportion of people who believed that men were better suited than women for politics fell from 44 percent to 25 percent.[54]

The number of women holding local office as mayor or city council member more than doubled over the period between 1974 and 1988, but there are almost no communities in which women hold a majority on the council.[55] At the state level, between 1981 and 1995, the number of women legislators rose from 13 percent to 21 percent, doubling the actual number of elected women.[56] There have now been several women governors elected. And of course, Geraldine Ferraro ran as the Democratic vice presidential candidate with presidential candidate Walter Mondale in 1984, becoming the first and only woman to be nominated for this office by a major political party. Recent studies of political party support, campaign fund-raising, and other components of political success indicate that the field is now open for women candidates who choose to run.

The most significant test of women's political power came during the campaign to ratify the Equal Rights Amendment (ERA) to the United States Constitution.[57] Passed by both the House of Representatives and Senate in 1972, the ERA was quickly ratified by twenty-two states. By 1974, the ERA had been ratified in thirty-three of the required thirty-eight states. The anti-ERA forces, led by Phyllis Schlafly, organized a national campaign of letter writing and personal lobbying that proved very successful. Thirteen states attempted to revoke their ratification vote. By the late 1970s, the battle was being waged state by state. When the 1982 deadline for ratification arrived, ERA forces were three states short: In only thirty-five states had the ERA been ratified.

There are many reasons for the failure of the ERA. By the late 1970s, most of women's legal disabilities and inequalities had already been repealed or ruled unenforceable. ERA advocates underestimated how deeply women who had chosen a traditional role as wife and mother believed the ERA would lead to the loss of status and legal rights. Some women questioned whether absolute equality was the correct legal standard; they wondered whether recognition of childbearing and raising—as well as recognition of women's exclusion from the economy—might not require legal distinctions. Finally, the ERA was misrepresented and misconstrued by both its opposition and its advocates. Women on both sides argued its symbolic value and lost sight of the real limits of its reach. For all these reasons—including traditional male opposition—the ERA failed to pass. The campaign, however, had trained and energized women to raise money, campaign, and run for office.

There are many reasons for women's slow entry into partisan politics. Women's responsibilities for child care and homemaking are too time- and energy-consuming for many to participate fully in political life during the years their children are young. Women are only now arriving at the appropriate level in the traditional careers that produce politicians. Many women continue to believe that they will not have the full support of political parties and campaign contributors, although the evidence indicates otherwise. And perhaps more important, women have been more likely to volunteer their time in nonpartisan, issue-oriented organizations, with specific objectives other than personal power (like the ERA and anti-ERA campaigns). This has made them less comfortable with party discipline, and less willing to demonstrate the loyalty that leads to party endorsement. A number of organizations have arisen in recent years with the express goal of identifying and supporting women candidates. They include Emily's List, which provides campaign contributions for Democratic women running primarily for national office; the National Women's Political Caucus, a nonpartisan but pro-choice organization; and NOW PAC, the political arm of the National Organization for Women.[58] Women candidates at the local level differ from men candidates in the greater amount of support they receive from issue-oriented organizations. While studies indicate relatively equal access to traditional means of campaign support, it is clear that women's organizations, nonbusiness issue-based organizations, and nonpolitical organizations tend to provide more support for women than for men. On the other hand, up to now, men have received more support from business organizations—which is where the money is.[59]

The prediction at the time women received the right to vote that women would constitute a special voting bloc was not fulfilled until the Reagan era. In recent years, women have been more likely than men to consider themselves Democrats. In 1992, 36 percent of women identified themselves as Democrats, and only 29 percent of men; 32 percent of women were Republicans, compared to 34 percent of men. This "gender gap" was a major factor in Bill Clinton's election to the presidency in 1992 and his reelection in 1996. The Women's Political Caucus cautions that gender differences may only reflect the life choices of certain women. The gender gap in party affiliation is greater among younger women than older, and also among the educated, where men and women differ by 18 percent.[60] Sue Tolleson Rinehart has concluded that in a system with weak political parties and a weak ideological system, women's "gender consciousness" has begun to, and will increasingly, serve as the predominant determinant of voting and policy choices. Gender consciousness brings women into political life based on a sense of commonality on a range of issues including peace, children, aging, health, environmental, and consumer concerns. Gender-conscious women, whether Democrat or Republican, believe women have a special role and a special voice, bringing nurturance and cooperation to public debate, even if they disagree on basic issues such as abortion, divorce, and family responsibilities.[61]

Several recent studies indicate that late-twentieth-century women politicians do exhibit different voting behavior than men. A study of women in the 103rd Congress (January 1993–January 1995) concluded that they voted differently as a group; made a difference by expanding the debate and shaping the content of legislation; felt a special responsibility to represent women; shared a collective, bipartisan agenda; and were empowered by use of existing Congressional procedures and positions.[62] Sue Thomas, in her study of state legislators, reached similar conclusions, but emphasized an evolving role and sense of purpose for women legislators, as the public increasingly considers women politicians as "normal" and not as outsiders. Thomas points out, however, that political campaigns emphasizing "feminine" qualities or problem-solving abilities of women candidates may backfire when "masculine" qualities, such as toughness and aggressiveness, are perceived to be necessary to the job.[63]

The Future

The removal of formal barriers to participation in the economy, in politics, in education, and in equality in family life have taken us to a critical point. For most of this century the goal of the women's movement was the achievement of equal treatment with men. Now that the legal and political framework has been established for equal opportunity and equal treatment, some important questions remain unanswered: Why does there continue to be an imbalance in men's and women's access to society's resources? What real differences exist between men and women? How significant are they, and how should they be accommodated?

The very use of the word "feminist" to describe the movement for equal rights for women illustrates an internal conflict: Are women the absolute equals of men, or are they "feminine" and different from "masculine"? Third wave feminists initially argued for absolute equality, believing that assertions of difference simply opened the door to a return to the old separation between the public and private spheres, and the assignment of women to the old, limiting roles. By the 1980s, most women's advocates had accepted the necessity of differential treatment for women, when faced with work rules regarding job security for pregnant women or women who had just given birth. Absolutely equal treatment would require women to return to work as soon as their bodies had physically healed from the birth. The psychological cost of this much-too-early separation from an infant soon became apparent. While one approach to childbirth and child care has been to place equal responsibility on both parents, the experiences of working women have made it clear that child care, particularly of very young children, is a woman's issue.[64] Children of divorced parents are far more likely to live with their mothers than with their fathers. Even prison officials have had to accommodate gender differences in child care by creating different visiting rules and community placements for women prisoners who are parents. A woman prisoner who is a mother is frequently the custodial parent of her children. This is rarely true for men prisoners who are fathers.

Where do gender differences begin and end? How much of the differences we observe are imposed, and how much are freely chosen? What kinds of differences enhance individual growth and what kinds are oppressive? Early hopes that parenting could be a truly egalitarian experience have not been fulfilled. Mothers choose their jobs based on work schedule rather than compensation, and are much more likely to miss work because of children's needs. Mothers continue to carry the lion's share of household and child care responsibilities. Some argue that this inequality is a remnant of the old separate spheres rules that deny men full access to their children. Others claim that it reflects the uniquely feminine experience of childbirth and child rearing.

The interest in gender differences has been stimulated by the discovery that many medical, psychological, and philosophical studies—ostensibly designed to uncover facts of human biology and psychology—have been conducted on groups from which women (and minorities) were excluded. When Carol Gilligan discovered that studies designed to illustrate human moral development were based entirely on Harvard students—when the student body was exclusively male—she conducted the same studies on mixed groups, and concluded that girls were more likely to focus on caretaking, while boys were more concerned with moral absolutes.[65] When Congresswomen Pat Schroeder and Olympia Snow discovered that studies of aging, heart disease, and cancer excluded women and women's diseases, they used the Congressional Caucus for Women's Issues to press Congress to pass legislation requiring that federally funded health research include women, and identify the special health needs of women.[66] Attempts to rectify the gaps in knowledge have led to studies of similarities and differences between women and men. For example, new techniques for studying the functioning of the brain now permit examination and comparison of brain structures and functioning; a number of small experiments have been reported to indicate some interesting gender differences.[67]

While some feminists continue to believe that affirmation of gender differences will pave the way for a return to separate spheres for men and women, others have found the discussion of difference to be itself liberating. Deborah Tannen's work on differences in men's and women's use of language has helped explain unintended conflict and misunderstanding between men and women.[68] John Gray's popular books on the different emotional patterns of men and women are widely used to improve personal relationships by recognizing and meeting each other's needs, a counterintuitive process.[69] Some feminists have begun to reexamine fundamental theories of society, human evolution, and community behavior from the perspective of "mothering," suggesting concepts such as mutual dependence, continually changing relationships, and nurturance as substitutes for individualism, static definitions of the human condition, self-reliance, and self-interest.[70] Part of women's oppression, these writers contend, is the devaluing of women's life experience and their special contributions to society. Other feminists argue vehemently that the physical and psychological differences *within* each sex are as great or greater than the differences *between* them, and that "difference theory" is comforting only because it is the old familiar stereotype in modern dress. They caution that any loss of vigilance in the cause of equality leads to backsliding and backlash.

Feminist theory emphasizes that the world is seen differently by people in different situations; that one's own life situation changes over time; that societal distinctions between classes of people lead to oppression by denying access to society's resources; that community and responsibility are as important to social health as independence and self-reliance; and that legal and political systems must accommodate individual (but not socially imposed) difference in order to be just.

In concrete terms, this means that as a society, we must recognize and reverse the increasing impoverishment of children, particularly those in single-parent families, and that equal resources must be expended on the questions affecting men and women differently, such as health research and policy, aging, child care, compensation for work, job security, education, and crime. As individuals, Americans must examine their ideas about gender roles, the meaning of equity and equality, and how these values should be implemented in our public lives.

The United States is already ahead of many other countries in achieving an equal place for women. Men are discovering the long-neglected resources of the community of women; most recognize that a society cannot be strong if more than half its citizens are kept from participating at the highest level of achievement. Women are finally arriving at the places from which they can assure their sisters and daughters an equal chance to exercise their "inalienable right to life, liberty and the pursuit of happiness." The changes of the twentieth century have put us on the threshold of discovering what real equality might be like in the twenty-first century. The protection of these hard-won gains and the implementation of real equality are the tasks of the next generation.

NOTES

1. Some feminists of the 1960s believed they were the second wave of the women's movement. However, recent scholars, including Jo Freeman, now adopt the "three wave" approach in order to adequately recognize the women of the nineteenth century.
2. "The right of citizens of the United States to vote shall not be denied or abridged by the United States or by any State on account of sex. Congress shall have power to enforce this article by appropriate legislation." U.S. Const. Amend. XIX. Ratified August 18, 1920.
3. Barbara R. Bergman, *The Economic Emergence of Women* (New York: Basic Books, 1986), pp. 40–51. The actual number of bachelor's degrees awarded to women rose from 17,000 in 1920 to 104,000 in 1950, and 139,000 in 1960. However, in 1920, only 32,000 men were awarded degrees, while in 1960, 256,000 men were.
4. Sue Heineman, *Timelines of American Women's History* (New York: Roundtable Press/Perigee, 1996), p. 70. Most professional education excluded or severely limited admission of women students.
5. Betty Friedan, *The Feminine Mystique* (New York: W. W. Norton, 1963), quoted in Heineman, p. 71.
6. Individual states and many universities also established commissions on the sta-

tus of women. Their reports varied in quality and content, and observers differed greatly in their opinions of them. On the whole, they avoided making recommendations that would have appeared too radical. Probably their first most significant contribution was the development of statistical proof of the disparity between men and women in almost all areas of legal rights, education, work, and income. The second contribution was entirely inadvertent: At a national meeting of state status-of-women commissioners in 1966, the commissioners, angry at the lack of government enforcement of legal rights, walked out of formal meetings and created the National Organization for Women (NOW), with Betty Friedan as its first president (Heineman, p. 73). Its mission was "to confront, with concrete action, the conditions that now prevent women from enjoying the equality of opportunity and freedom ... which is their right, as individual Americans, and as human beings." Statement of Purpose, quoted in Heineman, p. 73.

The Fair Labor Standards Act established a minimum wage and federal enforcement mechanisms for collection of wages owed to workers. 29 U.S.C. §§215–217.

Prior to 1937, when a major ideological shift changed the Supreme Court's approach to legislation regulating employment conditions, the only state or federal regulations of working conditions that the Court would sustain were those designed to protect women and children from harmful or dangerous work. These protective laws limited hours of work, the weight a woman could be required to lift as part of the job, and so on. Women have been divided over the question of whether these statutes protected their health, or limited their access to higher-paying jobs traditionally held by men.

7. Bergman, p. 84.

8. During the Second World War, when men left their jobs to join the military, Congress adopted legislation prohibiting wage discrimination against women who replaced men at work. The law was intended to protect the wages of men by keeping pay scales high in their absence. This legislation expired in 1948, as men reentered the civilian workforce. Women's pay actually declined for several years.

9. "No employer having employees subject to any provisions of this section shall discriminate, ... between employees on the basis of sex ... by paying wages to employees in such establishment at a rate less than the rate at which he pays wages to employees of the opposite sex ... for equal work on jobs the performance of which requires equal skill, effort, responsibility, and which are performed under similar working conditions, except where such payment is made pursuant to (i) a seniority system; (ii) a merit system; (iii) a system which measures earnings by quantity or quality of production; or (iv) a differential based on any other factor than sex." 29 U.S.C. §206(d)(1)[3].

10. 42 U.S.C. §2000e-2.

11. 30 Fed. Reg. 12319 (1965).

12. 29 U.S.C. §§621–634.

13. 29 U.S.C. §§706, 791, 793, 794, 794a.

14. See, for example, *United Steelworkers* v. *Weber*, 443 U.S. 193 (1979); *Fullilove* v. *Klutznick*, 448 U.S. 448 (1980).

15. *Hopwood* v. *Texas*, 5th Cir. No. 94-50569, issued March 18, 1996; app. den. *Texas* v. *Hopwood*, No. 95-1773. Linda Greenhouse, "Justices Decline Affirmative-Action Case," *The New York Times*, July 2, 1996, p. A12.

16. The term *work* here means employed for pay, or actively looking for employment. Women do, of course, work when they are at home or caring for children. Some women's rights advocates have argued that true equality would mean pay-

ing women for their currently unpaid labor as homemakers, mothers, and care-takers of the elderly.

17. Unless otherwise indicated, statistics cited have been drawn from the series *The American Woman: A Status Report,* issued every two years for the Women's Research and Education Institute. The editors of these volumes have drawn heavily on census data and U.S. Dept. of Labor statistics. Sara E. Rix, ed., *The American Woman: A Status Report; 1988–1989* (New York: W. W. Norton Company, 1988); Sara E. Rix, ed., *The American Woman: A Status Report; 1990–1991* (New York: W. W. Norton Company, 1990); Paula Ries and Anne J. Stone, eds., *The American Woman: A Status Report; 1992–1993* (New York: W. W. Norton Company, 1992); Cynthia Costello and Anne J. Stone, eds., *The American Woman: A Status Report; 1994–1995* (New York: W. W. Norton Company, 1994); and Cynthia Costello and Barbara Kivimae Krimgold, eds., *The American Woman: 1996–1997* (New York: W. W. Norton Company, 1996). Much of the data in the 1996–1997 volume is based on U.S. Census Bureau data collected since 1994.

18. Heineman, pp. 129, 131, 135.

19. Marshall J. Berger, "The Department of Labor's Glass Ceiling Initiative," *Labor Law Journal* (July 1992), p. 421, quoted in J. Ralph Lindgren and Nadine Taub, *The Law of Sex Discrimination,* 2nd ed. (Minneapolis: West Publishing Co., 1993), p. 260.

20. See *Barnes* v. *Costle,* 561 F.2d 983 (D.C. Cir. 1977); and *Tompkins* v. *Public Service,* 568 F.2d 1044 (3rd Cir., 1977).

21. *Meritor Savings Bank* v. *Vinson,* 477 U.S. 57 (1986).

22. *City of Los Angeles Department of Water and Power* v. *Manhart,* 435 U.S. 702 (1978); and *Arizona Governing Committee for Tax Deferred Annuity and Deferred Compensation Plans* v. *Norris,* 463 U.S. 1073 (1983).

23. See *Frontiero* v. *Richardson,* 411 U.S. 677 (1973); and *Michael M.* v. *Superior Court,* 450 U.S. 464 (1981).

24. Men's voices are still perceived as more authoritative; they are preferred for the closing for political advertisements, as well as for many commercials. Shankar Vedantam, "Candidates Turn to Men When Seeking Voices to Get Out the Vote," *The Hartford Courant,* March 21, 1996, p. A8.

25. These percentages are for women 25 and older. Statistics on education are also drawn from *The American Woman* reports, unless otherwise noted.

26. Denise Magner, "Study of 1995 Ph.D.s Finds Record Number of Black Doctorates," *The Chronicle of Higher Education,* June 14, 1996, p. 25.

27. The 1972 amendments to the Civil Rights Act prohibited sex discrimination in education. The numbers of students graduating from professional schools in 1974 reflect the last years of legal limitations on the number of women accepted in professional schools. Until the 1972 changes, the standards for admission for men and women were very different; many men were accepted with academic credentials that would have made them ineligible had they been female. It was affirmative action for men.

28. *The American Woman; 1992–1993,* p. 297. The faculty of teacher training colleges, earlier called "normal schools," had been predominantly female, as had been the faculty of nursing schools. These positions paid less than other college faculty positions; they were, however, the primary academic positions available to women with postbaccalaureate degrees, other than positions at women's colleges.

29. Simone de Beauvoir, *The Second Sex,* H. M. Parshley, trans. (New York: Knopf, 1953), originally published in France in 1949; Friedan, *The Feminine Mystique.*

30. Studies of women's political activity from the 1800s to the present have tended

to show extensive organization outside traditional political structures. In their introduction to *Women, Politics, and Change,* Tilley and Gurin write, "Another apparent continuity in women's politics is the importance of voluntary group involvement outside parties. From the early nineteenth century to the present, women have joined and worked for change through voluntary associations, most often without explicitly partisan goals. In this activity, they pioneered the typically twentieth century political strategy of interest group politics." Louise A. Tilly and Patricia Gurin, eds., *Women, Politics, and Change* (New York: Russell Sage Foundation, 1990).

31. Boston Women's Health Book Collective, *Our Bodies, Ourselves* (New York: Simon & Schuster, 1973).

32. This is a grossly oversimplified explanation of a very complex field of thought, heavily influenced by Marx and Hegel, Foucault, and the French postmodernists, as well as hundreds of contemporary women thinkers.

33. Alfred C. Kinsey, *Sexual Behavior in the Human Female* (Philadelphia: Saunders, 1953); William H. Masters and Virginia E. Johnson, *Human Sexual Inadequacy* (Boston: Little, Brown, 1970).

34. *Griswold* v. *Connecticut,* 381 U.S. 479 (1965) (privacy rights regarding birth control exist between married couples). *Eisenstadt* v. *Baird,* 405 U.S. 438 (1972) (privacy rights regarding birth control exist between all heterosexual couples).

35. *Roe* v. *Wade,* 410 U.S. 113 (1973).

36. *Maher* v. *Roe,* 432 U.S. 464 (1977); *Harris* v. *McRae,* 448 U.S. 297 (1980); *Webster* v. *Reproductive Health Services,* 109 S.Ct. 3040 (1989).

37. *Webster* v. *Reproductive Health Services,* 492 U.S. 490 (1989).

38. *Planned Parenthood of Southeastern Pennsylvania* v. *Casey,* 112 S.Ct. 2791 (1992).

39. Susan Gilbert, "Clinic Violence Sets Off Push for Wider Abortion Training," *The New York Times,* January 11, 1995, p. C11.

40. Barbara Hinkson Craig and David M. O'Brien, *Abortion and American Politics,* (Chatham, NJ: Chatham House Publishers, Inc., 1993), pp. 46, 258. See also Kristin Luker, *Abortion and the Politics of Motherhood* (Berkeley: University of California Press, 1984).

41. *American Woman 1994–1995,* pp. 121–122.

42. Deborah L. Rhode, *Justice and Gender: Sex Discrimination and the Law* (Cambridge, MA: Harvard University Press, 1989), p. 240.

43. Heileman, p. 165.

44. Rhode, p. 237.

45. This difference between women and men is probably the result of the fact that men die earlier than women, leaving significant numbers of unmarried older women. Women outnumber men in the population beginning in the 30–39-year age range; there are more than twice as many women over 80 than there are men.

46. Based on 1992 statistics. *American Woman,* 1994–1995, p. 257.

47. Felicia R. Lee, "Influential Study on Divorce Impact Is Said to Be Flawed," *The New York Times,* May 9, 1996, p. C6. These statistics are revisions of the study *The Divorce Revolution,* by Dr. Lenore J. Weitzman (New York: Free Press, 1985), whose original calculations found an average 73 percent decline for women, and a 42 percent increase for men.

48. This figure includes widows; to the extent that it is depressed by the low pension incomes of the elderly, it exaggerates the difference between married families and single women.

49. *American Woman, 1994–1995,* p. 330.

50. Rhode, p. 156.

51. *Michael M.* v. *Superior Court of Sonoma County,* 450 U.S. 464 (1981).

52. Another woman, Kay Bailey Hutchison, joined the Senate when she won election to the unexpired Senate term of Lloyd Benson from Texas who became Treasury Secretary.

53. Nancy E. McGlen and Karen O'Connor, *Women, Politics, and American Society* (Englewood Cliffs: Prentice Hall, 1995), pp. 60–65.

54. R. Darcy, Susan Welch, and Janet Clark, *Women, Elections and Representation*, 2nd ed. (Lincoln: University of Nebraska Press, 1994), p. 179. See also Nancy E. McGlen and Karen O'Connor, *Women, Politics and American Society* (Englewood Cliffs: Prentice Hall, 1995).

55. Darcy, p. 32.

56. Ibid., p. 52.

57. "Sec. 1. Equality of rights under the law shall not be denied or abridged by the United States or any state on account of sex. Sec. 2. The Congress shall have the power to enforce, by appropriate legislation, the provisions of this article. Sec. 3. The amendment shall take effect two years after the date of ratification." Proposed Amendment to the United States Constitution, Section 1, Senate Joint Resolution 8, Senate Joint Resolution 9 and House Joint Resolution 208, 92nd Cong., 1st Sess. (1971). Approved by a vote of 354 to 23 in the House of Representatives and 84 to 8 in the Senate.

58. "EMILY" stands for the phrase Early Money Is Like Yeast.

59. M. Kent Jennings, "Women in Party Politics" in Tilly and Gurin, pp. 221–248.

60. McGlen, p. 73.

61. Susan Tolleson Rinehart, *Gender Consciousness and Politics* (New York: Routledge, 1992).

62. Debra Dodson, Susan J. Carroll, Ruth B. Mandel, Katherine E. Kleenman, Ronnee Schreiber, and Debra Liebowitz, *Voices, Views, Votes: The Impact of Women in the 103rd Congress* (New Brunswick, NJ: Center for the Woman and Politics, Eagleton Institute of Politics, 1995).

63. Sue Thomas, *How Women Legislate* (New York: Oxford University Press, 1994).

64. The United States Dept. of Labor, when it collects statistics on working parents and children, asks women only about their children. While this avoids the problem of counting children twice, it does little to indicate the impact of child raising on fathers, and confirms the belief that when two parents are employed, the children are the mother's responsibility.

65. Carol Gilligan, *In a Different Voice: Psychological Theory and Women's Development* (Cambridge: Harvard University Press, 1982).

66. Patricia Schroeder and Olympia Snow, "The Politics of Women's Health" in *The American Woman: 1994–1995*, pp. 91–108.

67. See, for example, Simon LeVay, *The Sexual Brain* (Cambridge, MA: MIT Press, 1993).

68. Deborah Tannen, *You Just Don't Understand: Men and Women in Conversation* (New York: William Morrow and Company, 1990).

69. John Gray, *Men Are from Mars, Women Are from Venus: A Practical Guide for Improving Communication and Getting What You Want in Your Relationships* (New York: HarperCollins, 1992); and John Gray, *Men, Women and Relationships: Making Peace with the Opposite Sex*, 2nd ed. (Hillsboro, OR: Beyond Words Publishing Co., 1993).

70. See, for example, Martha Albertson Fineman, *Neutered Mother, The Sexual Family and Other Twentieth Century Tragedies* (New York: Routledge, 1995), among many others.

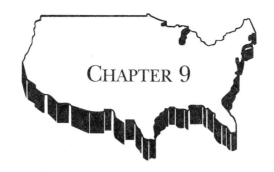

CHAPTER 9

AMERICAN FORCE POSTURE
FOR THE TWENTY-FIRST CENTURY

PAUL J. BEST

INTRODUCTION

The reader may legitimately wonder why a chapter that deals mainly with foreign threats would appear in a domestic politics textbook. The answer is quite straightforward and fourfold. First, the nature and propensity of people and states to take part in aggressive behavior has not changed in recorded history. Second, the necessity of preparing to resist and of actually resisting threats and aggression is among the most fundamental activities of states. Third, North America has never been able to stay out of major modern global conflicts. Fourth, defense policy decisions have important domestic implications.

HUMAN NATURE AND THE RIGHT TO DEFENSE

A persistent tension in human life from the beginnings of recorded history, and surely before that—although we have no written proof—is that between the *ought* and the *is*: what some people think people *ought* to do and what people *really do*. This tension expresses itself especially in the way nations ought to interact and how they really interact. This is the tension between real world (realpolitik) international relations and how theoreticians say these interactions ought to take place.

World religions, whether monotheistic (Islam, Judaism, Christianity) or nontheistic (Buddhism), generally preach that we *ought* to treat our fellow creatures fairly and justly (the norm) *but* we must also deal with the reality of human behavior. For example, Buddhism generally preaches nonviolence and passivity in the face of aggression. However, the destruction of that movement in northern India, when the invading Muslims—who viewed Buddhism as false and perhaps even devil worship—virtually extirpated it, led to some rethinking, as one may suppose, about a right to defense.[1] In the fifth century A.D. St. Augustine, the Christian bishop of Hippo, North Africa, upon observing the effects of the collapse of the Western Roman Empire, started the development of a rationalization for a "just war" of defense, based on Roman law principles.[2] Judaism and Islam, in fact, have never been loath to resort to force too, if defense of the faith can somehow be called upon to justify it. Even those without a clear belief or philosophy usually fall back on the notion of a natural right of self-defense: that every creature has the right to protect its existence from unjust aggression. Very few philosophies require adherents to die when under violent, unjust attack, and those that do are likely to disappear in a hostile world.

It appears, then, at this stage in the history of humankind there will be unjust aggression among people and states because that is what history teaches us. Thus, there will be the necessity to repel unjust attacks.[3] There seems to be no reasonable hope that people are changing for the better in this regard. In fact, the twentieth century has seen the worst years in recorded human history, with World War I and its aftermath carrying off perhaps 50 million, the Soviet "experiment" in itself another 50 million, and China's Great Cultural Revolution causing the loss of millions more. In World War II, all told, maybe 100 million-plus also died. Thus, as a result of these and lesser wars and revolutions, revolts, uprisings, massacres, war-caused famines and plagues, and ethnic cleansings in this century, maybe 300–400 million people died.

One can hope that the propensity of people to use violence might change in the future. In fact, the first and last episodes of a very popular U.S. (and later world-wide), science-fiction television series, "Star-Trek: The Next Generation," dealt precisely with this issue. The first episode takes place about 400 years from now, when the human race is reaching out to the stars by means of faster-than-light spaceships. A ship traveling to Deneb IV is stopped by a superior being and its captain and officers are put on trial as being representatives of a "savage, child race" too dangerous to be allowed free travel in the galaxy. The superior being, "Q," displays before the captain the murderous history of the human race and invites him to refute the charge that the human race is unworthy, but of course the captain cannot defend human history. The best that he can do is say that people have changed for the better, which he eventually proves, Hollywood fashion, by saving a creature that is being misused by others who are nonhumans.[4]

Q returns in the last episode to remind humans that there was no final judgment in the trial, and that the humans, an "inferior ape-like race," continue on trial and that they are even likely to annihilate themselves through stupid mistakes. Thus, this speculation of the future of humans, while initially positive, ends on an ambivalent note when Q says, "the trial never ends."[5]

While we may hope for a better future, we must deal with the reality. One of the founders of modern political science, Thomas Hobbes, believed that in their natural state, people were likely to be constantly at war or preparing for war, and that a social contract needs to be made among people whereby a government or commonwealth is formed so that a ruler could keep his/her citizens in line and could protect them from other people—that is, other states/governments.[6]

THE UNITED STATES NEEDS A STRONG DEFENSE

It is reasonable, and indeed necessary, for American policy makers to act on what is known about people rather than rely on a hope for a betterment of behavior. Based on this, the old Roman maxim "si vis pacem, para bellum— if you wish for peace, be prepared for war" still holds true.

Perhaps before going further, we should dispose of a well-worn myth about the United States and its position on the globe. This myth refers to the possibility that the United States of America could stay out of major global conflicts. It was supposed that the great moats of the Atlantic to the East and the Pacific to the West, plus the frozen Polar zone to the North and the weak and fractionalized groups of islands and Central America to the South, were sufficient to protect a fortress America: Nobody could get to us, and thus we could safely ignore the rest of the world. It would be a very nice, comfortable situation indeed, if it was true. Unfortunately, it never was true. Part of the reason for the establishment of British and French North American colonies was denial (denial of territory to potential opponents) and assistance (a base to assist in fighting enemies). The French colonies were directed mainly against Great Britain, and British colonies helped against France and Spain. Once firmly established, neither the British and French North American colonies nor later the United States and Canada have ever been successful in staying out of major world conflicts—that is, wars fought in modern times by major European powers which had intercontinental ramifications. Referred to here are the major, and even global, wars of the last 500 years, fought among European states after these countries broke out of the isolation of their obscure peninsula on the Eurasian-African land mass and seized control of worldwide sea lanes of communication (SLOCs). The battles for supremacy by Spain, France, Britain, and later Germany had international dimensions and they drew the North American colonies and later the United States and Canada, usually rather early on, into the conflicts.

The titanic seventeenth-century British struggle with Spain was the first wave of global conflict, a sort of "first world war." Later, the eighteenth-century wars (a kind of "second world war") with France, fought from India to Quebec, affected North American colonies in the so-called "French And Indian Wars." In the culmination of the second wave of conflict, Americans were successful in their revolt against Great Britain (the Revolutionary War) because several of the global contenders—France, Spain and even the Netherlands—drew off British power.

The "third world war," also known as the Wars of the French Revolution and the Napoleonic Wars, a twenty-five-year series of battles from Egypt to Moscow, to India and the Caribbean, was echoed in North America in the War of 1812.

Between 1815 and 1914, there were nearly 100 years of general peace; certainly a number of regional European conflicts took place, but none reached a global scale. So, of course, the United States was not drawn into a major struggle, thus strengthening the myth of the splendid isolation of the United States. However, the United States could not stay out of the "fifth world war"—the two rounds of the German attempt in the twentieth century to dominate all of continental Europe, better known as World War I (1914–1918) and World War II (1939–1945). Peripheral to the German second round was the Pacific War, which actually began in 1937 when the Japanese attacked the central area of China. Japan, because of its infamous attack on Pearl Harbor in Hawaii on December 7, 1941, and on the U.S. colony of the Philippines on December 8, 1941, forced the United States, rather unwillingly, into the Pacific War. The Japanese attacks, even though on far outlying U.S. territories and not on the mainland, forever destroyed the feeling of safety felt by most Americans.

From 1942 to 1960, the threat of an attack from the sea or from long-range bombers on the North American mainland was real (though not probable), but stoppable by military means then at hand. From 1960 to the present, the advent of Submarine Launched Ballistic Missiles (SLBMs) and Inter-Continental Ballistic Missiles (ICBMs) has created a situation whereby North America is truly naked to its enemies. There is currently no deployable antimissile system available. Beyond that, the possible stealthy use of weapons of mass destruction against the North American homeland can not be precluded. Thus, reality has to be taken into account, and policy needs to be formulated based on the aforementioned.[7]

The late Aaron Wildawsky and his colleague Max Singer, in their book, *The Real World Order*, recognized the fact of human and state struggle. They noted there has been a change from the former three-world model (*First World* = the technologically advanced, liberal democratic, free-market "Western" states; *Second World* = the Communist-ruled countries; and *The Third World* = everybody else) of the period of East-West struggle (1945–1990) into a two-world paradigm. The new model refers to "Zones of Peace" and "Zones of Turmoil."[8]

The zone of peace includes North America (United States and Canada), Asia (Japan, Australia, New Zealand, and Pacific Ocean islands), and Central and Western Europe. The rest of the world can be considered more or less in the zone of turmoil. The zone of peace is, in fact, the old First World, plus some ex-Communist states in Central Europe (Poland, Hungary, the Czech Republic, Slovakia, Slovenia and possibly the Baltic states of Latvia, Estonia, and Lithuania). The zone of turmoil includes the rest of the old Communist Second World and the whole of the Third World.

Singer and Wildawsky note the following in their study:

1. There is no threat to America as long as the most powerful nations on the planet remain democracies.

2. In the economic sphere, the main rivals of the United States are the European Union and Japan. Therefore it is in U.S. interest to keep international trade as open as possible, and to protect itself from countries or groups of countries trying to create special advantages for their own citizens.

3. The United States ought to participate in joint efforts to limit violence and encourage democracy in the various areas of turmoil, together with the European Union and Japan—which should be treated as equals.

4. The United Nations organization ought to be supported and encouraged, and it should assist in recommendation 3.[9]

Finally, in *The Real World Order*, Singer and Wildawsky conclude the following:

> The United States will need to have a substantial military force that is capable of fighting effectively.... This force should be ready and capable of using our technological ... advantages ... to defeat much larger second-class military forces in the zones of turmoil. We also need ... [an] active defense against potential missile attacks ....[10]

Events are unfolding as this is being written that confirm the necessity of a strong force posture for and a firm defense of the United States in the next century. There are many who wish the United States ill. The 259 people who died in the crash of Pan Am Flight 103 in December 1988, their plane having been blown out of the skies, attest to the existence of real anti-U.S. forces at large abroad. Even at home we have witnessed the World Trade Center bombing and the Oklahoma City tragedy.[11]

The war in Southeast Europe also reminds us of the ugly side of human nature. To quote from a review of recent literature about the collapse of Yugoslavia and the horrors of Bosnia:

> What we are less certain about is the underlying shocking mystery: why do human beings take such great pleasure in killing each other? So far, analyses of the Yugoslav War have not moved us very far in grappling with that fact.[12]

DEFINING THE AMERICAN DEFENSE PERIMETER

In a real sense, the outer limits of U.S. defense interests encompass the whole planet, including the ocean depths and near space, out to about 24,000 miles from the surface, where synchronous orbit satellites are located. This does

not mean that America need concern itself with every part of the globe equally, but rather there are areas of greater and lesser interest.

The Primary Zone of Defense for the United States is North America. For purposes of defense, North America includes *NORAD* (the North American Aero-
Space Defense network, which includes the United States, Canada, and
Greenland), *NAFTA* (the North American Free Trade Agreement, which
includes Canada, Mexico, and perhaps soon several Central American states),
Central America (especially Panama), plus the Caribbean Islands. To the West,
the state of Hawaii, the Commonwealth of the Marianas, the U.S. possessions
of Guam, Wake Island, etc., and U.S. protectorates (Micronesia, Palau, and the
Marshall Islands) should be included in the primary defense zone. For the
twenty-first century, the United States ought to extend its blue water absolute-
defense network out to the crests of the Atlantic Ocean undersea mountain
chain to the East, on a line stretching from the North Pole going to the East of
Greenland down the chain to the Tropic of Cancer. The Western edge of the
perimeter should run from the North Pole to Little Diomede Island to 200
miles beyond the westernmost Aleutian island and the same distance West of
the Marianas, Guam, and Palau, back across the Pacific at the equator, to
Clipperton Island and Panama. This would be the Pacific part of the U.S primary defense zone. On the South, a line from Panama, including the
Caribbean islands, out to the Atlantic Ocean mountains at the Tropic of Cancer
would delineate the southern extent of the primary defense zone. Within this
perimeter/triangle, the situation of non–United States territories would be
decided on by bilateral and/or multilateral treaties. United States protectorates
in the Pacific, Greenland (still partially dependent on Denmark, but having
home rule), and Panama could be offered U.S. statehood under mutually
agreeable conditions, as would the Commonwealths of Puerto Rico and the
Marianas. The situation of British possessions (Bermuda, the British Virgin
Islands, Cayman Islands, and Turks and Caicos), the French islands of St. Pierre
and Miguelon near New Foundland, plus Clipperton in the Pacific and French
Caribbean islands, could also be negotiated, as would the status of American
Samoa in the South Pacific, with its unusual geographic and legal situation.

Greenland, if it wishes to stay separate, ought to be offered membership
in NAFTA. Mexico, on the other hand, ought to be encouraged to join
NORAD and even the North Atlantic Treaty Organization. Mexico has been
too long neglected by U.S. policy makers.[13] U.S. policy makers should also
keep a weather eye on Quebec, which well may soon emerge as the newest
independent state in North America.

The Second U.S. Defense Zone should include the areas covered by the
North Atlantic Treaty Organization (NATO), which already includes the
United States, Canada, Greenland, and most of Western Europe. With the
expansion of NATO on the horizon, it can be expected that much of Central
Europe will be added to NATO's rolls—that is, Poland, Hungary, Slovakia,
the Czech Republic, Slovenia and possibly Latvia, Estonia, and Lithuania.[14]

Thus, NATO will encompass the European states of "Western-Roman" inheritance (Roman Catholic and Protestant religious background), plus Greece and Turkey. This defense zone would also include the Mediterranean Sea and the Atlantic Ocean to the east of the crest of the Mid-Atlantic undersea mountain range, down to the Tropic of Cancer.

The Third U.S. Defense Zone, and not less important than the second, should include Japan, the Republic of Korea (ROK) and the many non-U.S. Pacific Island states—the United States has bilateral treaties with most of these governments. Also included would be the ANZUS (Australia, New Zealand, U.S.) treaty states of Australia and New Zealand. The Philippines could also be included if it were willing to share the defense burdens involved.

The Fourth U.S. Defense Zone would include all of Latin America below Panama, and the dominant institution there should be the Organization of American States (OAS), which includes all of North and South America except Canada and Greenland—these latter two should be encouraged to join OAS.

The rest of the world need not be part of a specific U.S. defense zone, but would be included in parts of current military theaters of operations. The U.S. joint command structure more or less takes much of what has been said above into account. Continental Command (ConCom) covers North America; Southern Command (SouthCom) deals with Central and South America; Atlantic Command (ACom) covers the North and South Atlantic Oceans; European Command (EuCom) handles Central and Western Europe, the Mediterranean Sea and Turkey, Syria, Lebanon, and Israel—plus parts of Africa not in CentCom; Central Command (CentCom) covers the Middle East, including the Arabian Peninsula, Iraq, Iran, the Persian Gulf, plus Egypt, Ethiopia, Sudan, Somalia, and Kenya in Africa; and Pacific Command (PaCom) covers all of the Pacific and Indian Oceans and lands washed by the same, except those in the CentCom area. The interior of Asia—that is, Eurasia (Russia), Central Asia, and Inner Asia—are not specifically designated to any standing joint command of U.S. forces.[15]

The areas of absolute defense, which the United States must defend in order to survive in the twenty-first century include zones 1, 2, and 3. The rest of the joint command areas are in the zones of turmoil in which the United States has interests, but which are not vital to America's survival. (The one exception might be—under current levels of technology—the Persian Gulf region. If, however, other sources of power—say hydrogen—were developed, that area would not be of great interest to the United States.)

Perhaps a few words are in order as to why zones 1–3 are vital to the United States. Zone 1, North America and adjacent waters and islands are vital for several reasons. Initially, denying an enemy access to adjacent waters and lands is important, assuming the solution of the technical problems associated with the development of a theater missile defense system. Sufficient time to activate such a defense—5–10 minutes—would be needed. Allowing an enemy to enter waters to the West of the Atlantic mountain undersea range or to get within the Pacific Ocean and island defense line or into the Caribbean Sea in order to launch an attack would not allow sufficient time to bring defense into play. An attack mounted from outside the primary zone would probably allow sufficient reaction time. It is obvious that a theater ballistic missile defense is needed by the United States, as is complete aerospace defense over the primary zone.[16] Also, stealth attacks coming from sea-based forces could be headed off while well out at sea (a freighter carrying biological, nuclear, or chemical weapons, for example, does not need to come within the twelve-nautical-mile limit of absolute sovereignty in order to go into action). Within the primary zone are sufficient raw materials and natural resources to maintain the whole zone in case of emergency or necessity; this is not to reinstitute a plan for a Fortress America or Manifest Destiny policy but rather to indicate a basic minimum requirement for the country. Also, the Panama Canal will be, for the foreseeable future, a vital link in North American east-west—as well as world—commerce.[17] The United States *must* negotiate with all the principals involved for a fair, doable, durable, and acceptable mutual defense system for the primary zone. Immigration, dual citizenship rights of citizens of all countries in the zone, and offers of U.S. statehood to those areas interested should be pursued with fairness and respect, in order to consolidate this quadrant of the globe into a safe, peaceful, and successful region.

The second U.S. defense zone should be based on a mutual and co-equal relationship with the European Union and NATO, and all the countries that are now or will be members of the EU and NATO. Mutual and reciprocal arrangements for defense, acquisition of weapons (the so-called two-way-street system used by NATO), joint task forces, joint exercises, and joint ventures in other world areas should be expected. Maintaining the deployment of the current 100,000 U.S. Army, Navy, Air Force, and Marine personnel in the European Theater should help to continue to anchor the U.S. defenses to its east.

In the long run, the United States must accommodate itself to two changes now taking place in its relationships to its NATO partners. First, ten of the NATO countries have lately been strengthening the European wing of NATO under the aegis of the WEU (West European Union). The French, after staying away for nearly three decades, have offered to rejoin the joint NATO command structure on the condition that the European Pillar of the Atlantic alliance has more autonomy and that European NATO activities that the United States and Canada do not wish to join could be operated by the WEU using assets lent to it by NATO's North Atlantic Council.[18] Second, the United States must help in deciding on NATO expansion. Much discussion has taken place on this issue, and an enormous amount of literature has been generated.[19] It is expected that NATO will be expanded in the following sequence: Slovenia (the least controversial candidate), then Poland, the Czech Republic, and Hungary, and further in the future, Slovakia and the three Baltic Republics. The situation of the Ukraine is unclear, but there have been reports that Ukraine might, in the long run and assuming its stabilization and Russian acquiescence, also decide to join.[20]

The United States, its NATO partners, NATO candidates, members of the NATO-sponsored "Partnership For Peace program" (PFP), other members of the EU, and neutral European states are joined together within the NACC (North Atlantic Cooperation Council) and the OCSE (Organization for Cooperation and Security in Europe) for the express purpose of allaying the fears of Russia, which is the legal and actual successor of the U.S.S.R. Russia is still a very dangerous actor on the European, Eurasian, and world stage. This problem has been discussed in detail elsewhere[21] but suffice it to say America's force posture has to take into account a resurgence of Russian activity, and be prepared for it.[22]

In any case, in the twentieth century the United States has recognized that control of Western (and Central) Europe by a hostile power is inimical to U.S. interests and, in fact, could be a major factor in the defeat of the United States in a large scale war. Thus it was that the United States came to the aid of the Western democracies in rounds 1 and 2 of the German war for the dominance of the continent, and in 1948 the United States reentered, in the face of the Soviet threat, in order to establish mutual North American and West European defense in the form of the North Atlantic Treaty Organization, the single most important agreement to which the United States subscribes.

Zone 3 began to be important to the United States at the turn of the nineteenth and twentieth centuries when Hawaii was annexed and former Spanish Pacific possessions were seized; however, until 1941 the area took a back seat to other U.S. interests. In World War II, the Pacific was the second important war zone (after Europe), but today there are those who would say that the Asia-Pacific region will be the most important area of interest in the twenty-first century. That region—with its burgeoning industry, rapid economic development, and massive market—has overtaken the European area as the primary market for U.S. raw materials, foodstuffs, industrial products, and services. Thus, the Pacific is an area at least as vital to the United States as Europe. The Pacific defense zone contains approximately 100,000 U.S. armed forces personnel distributed on Hawaii, other Pacific islands, Japan, and the Republic of Korea. The United States also maintains close defense ties with Australia and Singapore, and has forces on Diego Garcia Island in the Indian Ocean.

U.S. FORCE POSTURE FOR THE TWENTY-FIRST CENTURY—CONTEXT

Given the fact of human violence and the necessity to maintain defense perimeters, what sort of a defense posture should the United States have? What sort of a national military policy should there be? By no means is this the first time these sort of questions have been asked. The latest reappraisal of U.S. defense began in the early 1990s, as soon as it became apparent that the U.S.S.R. had really collapsed, and that Russia was no longer an enemy. The massive defense outlays of the Cold War period culminated in the Reagan defense build up of the 1980s, which was the main cause for plunging the United States much deeper into debt—indeed, the debt generated by the Reagan administration was larger than the country had been put under by all previous presidents combined. While it is true that Reagan's policy was in good part the reason for the collapse of U.S.S.R., it nonetheless added several trillions of dollars in unpaid loans to the national debt. The cost of defense was truly crushing, and paying off these loans will take many decades, if not a century. In fact, one commentator became famous for including the United States in his book, *The Rise and Fall of the Great Powers*, fearing that the United States, like other great nations before it, was falling victim to imperial "overstretch."[23]

Thus, in 1991, when the Gulf War ended and the Soviet Union disappeared, President George Bush ordered a complete review of U.S. defense policies and expenditures. Later, the Clinton administration confirmed the reappraisal, and continued much of the Bush administration's drawdown of military forces. We discuss the post–Cold War period as a single unit below.

Bush's Secretary of Defense Dick Cheney and Clinton's Les Aspin looked at the huge and expensive collection of forces marshaled to fight the Soviet Union and its allies across the full spectrum of military conflict—from low-grade chaotic violence to all-out thermonuclear war. This spectrum of conflict had last been looked at in detail in scientific/military literature by Herman Kahn of the Hudson Institute in the 1950s, when he was writing his famous books, *On Thermonuclear War* and *On Escalation*.[24] It was clear that while Kahn's forty-four steps or rungs on the ladder of escalation were still possible, the latter group—those after "the Nuclear Threshold" (steps twenty-one to forty-four)—were less likely to be reached and, below them, on the nonnuclear level, there was no immediate threat.[25] The battle over what was at first called the "Base Force Structure" and later the "Bottom up Review" and now the "Quadrennial Review" of U.S. military assets (which would lead to a drawdown of forces) was fought locally, statewide, nationally—and even internationally, since reductions in funding would affect U.S. allies too. Obviously, there were many areas within the United States where the local economy depended on military expenditures. In southeast Connecticut, for example, reduction in submarine production at the Electric Boat Company—which had, nor could have, no other customer than the U.S. government—had devastating effects throughout the region, as trained workers were laid off and production units closed or consolidated.[26] The national Base Closing Committee stirred up many a hornet's nest when it recommended the closing of hundreds of bases throughout the country. Further, the reductions in personnel and equipment and the defunding of pet

Congressional projects caused many political fights, as legislators attempted to protect constituents' jobs and military funding for their districts and states. These battles are too deep and involved to go into here, but a thorough reading of military literature since 1990 will apprise the reader of the depth and extent of the struggle.[27]

The upshot can be seen in the following tables, which indicate projected force structure components by the beginning of the twenty-first century.

TABLE 9.1   COMPARISON OF FORCE RESTRUCTURING PLANS[28]

	COLD WAR BASE, 1990	PRESIDENT BUSH'S BASE FORCE STRUCTURE, 1993	PRESIDENT CLINTON'S BOTTOM UP REVIEW, 1999
ARMY			
Active divisions	18	14	10
NAVY			
Ship battle forces	546	430	346
Aircraft carriers	15	13	11
Airwings	13	11	10
AIR FORCE			
Active fighter wings	24	16	13
MARINE CORPS			
Active divisions	3	3	3

TABLE 9.2   THE "BOTTOM UP REVIEW":
PERSONNEL END STRENGTH (IN THOUSANDS)[29]

ACTIVE MILITARY	FY93	FY95	FY96	FY97	FY98	FY99
Army	586	510	500	495	495	495
Navy	510	442	426	408	398	394
Marine Corps	183	174	174	174	174	174
Air Force	450	400	396	392	391	390
Total	1,729	1,526	1,496	1,469	1,458	1,453

FY = [Federal] Fiscal Year, in other words, Oct. 1–Sept. 30th.

Conventional and nuclear force levels and their deployment, besides being driven by fiscal and policy decisions, also are influenced by the various treaties the United States entered into with its erstwhile enemy the U.S.S.R. which have been carried forward under the legal successor of the U.S.S.R., the Russian Federation. These treaties are listed in Table 9.3.

TABLE 9.3   MAJOR ARMS LIMITATION TREATIES[30]

TREATY	PROVISIONS	DATE
ABM	essentially prevents deployment of Anti-Ballistic Missile missiles (U.S.S.R.-U.S.A.)	1972
SALT I	a very limited Strategic Arms Limitation Treaty (U.S.S.R.-U.S.A.)	1972
SALT II	a second limitation on strategic weapons (U.S.S.R.-U.S.A.)	1979
INF	eliminated Intermediate-range Nuclear Forces (between 500km and 1,500km range) in the European theater (NATO and Warsaw Pact)	1987
CFE	Conventional Forces in Europe reduced to a low level (NATO and Warsaw Pact) with a 1992 protocol (Russia and NATO)	1990
START I	actual reduction in both strategic launch vehicles and warheads: Strategic Arms Reduction Treaty (U.S.A.-U.S.S.R), signed by Soviet successor states in 1992	1991
START II	further reduction in strategic nuclear forces (Russia-U.S.A.)	1993
Chemical Weapons Convention	bans chemical weapons after 2005 (130 countries)	1993
START III	further reduction in nuclear weapons (under discussion)	1993

FORCES AND DEPLOYMENT:
POLICY RECOMMENDATIONS FOR THE TWENTY-FIRST CENTURY

Given the fact of the end of the Cold War and the necessity to reduce the crushing defense burden the United States was forced to carry, a reduced armed force is a reality for the twenty-first century that cannot be overlooked. Arguments over just what posture the United States should take in the next century seem to be a cottage industry in the last decade of the twentieth century. Books such as *The End of the American Century, Beyond American Hegemony*, and *America as an Ordinary Power* furthered the "declinism" train of thought, while *The Myth of American Decline, America's Economic Resurgence*, and *Bound to Lead* were the retorts of those who think the twenty-first century will be led by the United States.[31] Paul Kennedy, in his *Preparing for the Twenty-First Century*, tries to take a middle-of-the-road approach by outlining what he thinks is coming, and how countries ought to prepare for social, economic, political, demographic, and technical change.[32] Whether one sees a rise or decline or something in between for the United States, it is absolutely clear that America's role in the world will be less than it played in the forty-five years of the Cold War.

Thus, the United States, in order to protect its primary zone of defense, ought to maintain both a sufficient, standing, and ready-to-act armed force, plus a reserve component that can be called to active duty quickly. Exact figures cannot be cited here as to the precise numbers of personnel or amounts of equipment. The professional military is paid to make these assessments, and elected officials ought to act in the best national interest in making final force and personnel decisions.[33] Beyond the standing forces and a ready reserve, the United States must not allow its lead in weapons production to be lost. While it is true that large numbers of advanced aircraft and ships are not needed now, and that the useful lives of inventory weapons can be lengthened by rebuilding and upgrading, nonetheless, while they may be slowed to a crawl, production lines of advanced weaponry must not be stopped. The loss of highly trained projectors and fabricators could be lethal to U.S. defense if and when a major threat requires the restarting of large-scale production. The NORAD (originally North American Air Defense, now North American Aerospace Defense Command) system, a joint U.S.-Canadian organization, ought to be strengthened and reinvigorated. NORAD currently disposes of or has access to an infrared "Surveillance and Warning" satellite system, an on-ground "Ballistic Missile Early Warning [Radar] System" (BMEWS), U.S. Air Force "Space Track" radars around the world, the U.S. Navy "Space Surveillance System," the "Perimeter Acquisition Radar Attack Characterization System (PARCS)," and "Pave-Paws" phased-array radars, plus the "Ground-Based Electro-Optical Deep Space Surveillance System," the "North Warning Radar" system (which is replacing the "Distance Early Warning System"), and miscellaneous other detector and tracking radars.[34] Mexico ought to be invited to join this command in order to take part in North American defense on all azimuths.[35] Further, NORAD should be tasked to expand its operation to include the waters of the U.S. primary defense zone. The U.S. Navy has made nearly all the adjacent waters of North America transparent down to the bottom of the ocean basins. That which travels upon or under these waters will be of interest in twenty-first century defense. The air, space, on-water, and underwater defense of North America ought to be strengthened. To support this, two treaties to which the United States is party—the Law of the Sea and the Anti-Ballistic Missile Treaty—ought to be modified.

In relation to the U.N. Convention on the Law of the Sea, the United States ought to append a stipulation in which it recognizes and supports right-of-innocent passage for all vessels on international waters, but which reserves the right to take action over, upon, or under the sea against any vessel that threatens the security of North America without waiting for it to enter the twelve-nautical-mile zone of absolute sovereignty.[36]

U.S. policy recommendations for the second defense zone include the maintenance of U.S. forces in the NATO area of approximately 100,000 personnel, plus sufficient equipment preplaced for reinforcement purposes. The NATO partners of the United States should be required to bear as exact a proportion of the common defense as the United States does. The days of America carrying a disproportionate share of the costs are gone! NATO should be expanded by early in the twenty-first century to include Slovenia, Slovakia, Poland, Hungary, the Czech Republic, Latvia, Estonia, Lithuania, and any other Western or Central European country that wishes to join.[37] The principal problem of NATO expansion is the Russian Federation. At various times recently, there have been bellows from the Russian bear regarding perceived Western/NATO threats. In order to allay Russian fears, the United States, its NATO partners, and especially Germany ought to construct a non-threatening proposal that would take these fears into account.[38] This would include an agreement not to base large NATO forces on the borders of the Russian Federation or Belarus. The Ukrainian situation has yet to clarify itself, but it would be a matter of very delicate negotiation between Ukraine, NATO, and Russia. In order to prevent any fear of a rapid nuclear strike, INF provisions must be rigorously enforced; however, INF refers only to missiles of intermediate range (500–1500km), and does not include short-range missiles (less than 500km range) or other types of weapons of mass destruction, such as nuclear land mines, artillery shells, and chemical and biological weapons. Perhaps the "Rapacki Plan," a project proposed by the Polish Foreign Minister Adam Rapacki in 1957 to denuclearize Central Europe, could be revived, revised, and put into effect.[39] Russia could also be given some leeway in its Conventional Forces in Europe (CFE) obligations by allowing more conventional forces in its European "Northern Military District" and North Caucasus Military District, especially the latter because of the Chechnyan and other Caucasian military and ethnic problems.[40]

Russia's relation with NATO has been somewhat eased by its participation in the NATO-sponsored North Atlantic Cooperation Council (NACC: pronounced Nak-see) starting from its initial meeting in 1991. The basic idea was to expand or change NATO from an alliance aimed at a specific enemy to a more general security agreement as a whole.[41] Everyday cooperation between NATO and the post-Communist Central and East European states has been concentrated in the "Partnership for Peace" (PFP) program attached to NATO and NACC, and Russia accepted an invitation to join in cooperation and transparency in military affairs.[42] Twenty-seven non-NATO Central and European states have joined the PFP program.[43] The Russian Federation is also a member of the Organization for Security and Cooperation in Europe (OSCE), which includes all of Europe, the United States, and Canada—fifty-four member states altogether. The OSCE is concerned with reducing tensions and enhancing travel, trade, and culture on the European continent.[44]

While things look good in the second defense zone of the United States, nonetheless Russia has many problems, problems that could be resolved in a way antithetical to U.S. and NATO interests. The role of the post-Soviet Russian military has not yet been regularized. Loss of direct control over Central Asia and the Caucasus region grates hard on Russia's martial traditions although Russia does keep soldiers stationed in those areas. Worse, from the point of view of national pride, is the absolute loss of the Baltic states (Latvia, Estonia, and Lithuania) and Ukraine. Belarus, it seems, has been partially recovered by the voluntary reintegration of that state with Russia under the administration of President Aleksander Lukashenka.[45] Ethnic Russians living outside of Russia in the so-called "near abroad"—that is, ex-Soviet territories where Russians immigrated in large numbers in the twentieth century—are under the protection of Russia and its armed forces, at least unofficially. Russia sees former Soviet territories assembled within the Commonwealth of Independent States (CIS) and the Russians living there as a legitimate concern of the Russian Federation. Russians in near-abroad non-CIS states (Ukraine and the Baltic countries) also come under the umbrella of that concern.[46] Beyond that, Russian armed forces have a special role to play vis-à-vis non-Russians (up to 15 percent of the population) within the Russian Federation—note especially the Chechnya situation.[47]

The rise of a Napoleonic figure—the so-called "Man on Horseback"—cannot be precluded in Russia, and the phenomenon of retired General Aleksandr Lebed—who, with no political experience, gained 15 percent of the vote in the Russian presidential election in 1996, and then became the newly re-elected President Boris Yeltsin's National Security Adviser—is the sort of thing that ought to be watched. Russia's military could be a loose cannon, and the possibility of a sudden anti-Western turn in Russia must be taken into account in all U.S. policy decisions about the second zone.[48]

Thus, while Russian interests may be taken into account, the United States by no means should allow Russia to have veto power over American decisions. Like the G-7 economic club where Russia is a sort of honorary eighth member, Russia may be seen as a sort of honorary NATO member, but when it comes to NATO expansion and U.S. vital interests Russia should play no role.

Professor William Wohlforth of Princeton University concludes his nearly thirty-page discussion of "Realism and the End of the Cold War" with a caveat that seems appropriate to quote here:

> This leads to the frankly inductive warning for the West: keep a weather eye on Russia. Russia has often experienced rapid shifts in relative power with dire international consequences. In this century alone, Russia's sudden decline after the 1905 war with Japan and its equally sudden rise in the years before 1914 were important preconditions for World War I; its apparent weakness conditioned the disastrous diplomacy of the 1930s; its sudden rise in apparent power as a result of World War II set the Cold War in motion; its perceived forward surge in the late 1950s and early 1960s set the stage for the dangerous crisis of that era; and its apparent sudden decline in the late 1980s was the catalyst for the greatest upheaval in international relationships in half a century. Russia may be down now, but prudent policymakers should not count it out.[49]

U.S. force posture in the third zone in the twenty-first century ought to consist of essentially what there is at the end of the twentieth century—that is, a forward development of approximately 100,000 air and land forces distributed on U.S. territorial bases in Hawaii, Guam, the Marianas, and on allied territories in Japan and the Republic of Korea. Additionally, Naval personnel and ships are also based, as mentioned previously, at supply and repair stations in Singapore and on the island of Diego Garcia in the Indian Ocean, which is leased from Great Britain and where there are also Air Force personnel. Pacific Command (PacCom), headquartered on Oahu, Hawaii, also controls the Third Fleet which covers the Eastern and Central Pacific, and the Seventh Fleet, which patrols the Western Pacific and the Indian Ocean.[50]

The principal problems in the Pacific theater of operations are those we have with Japan, the People's Democratic Republic of [North] Korea (PDRK), and the People's Republic of China (PRC). In relation to Japan, the United States has borne the burden of Northeast Asian defense for decades. Japan, while an ally, has been given a free ride for quite awhile. Relations between Japan and the United States now must be placed on an equal footing, with both nations carrying their weight in the bilateral alliance.[51] Japan is important in the intersection of the European and Asian interests of the United States—that is, it is in Northeast Asia where Russia and China meet with the United States: the strategic quadrangle. These four interests clash on the Korean peninsula, where two mutually hostile states face each other across a nearly half-century-old armistice line.[52] Japan has a very large "Self Defense" force in the region, which includes a Navy that is tasked to defend the Sea Lanes of Communication (SLOCs).[53] Whether Japan likes it or not, it is a major player in the Pacific region. U.S. bases in Japan ought to be reciprocated with Japanese forces exercising with U.S. forces all over the Pacific and in North America. Recent problems with U.S. bases in Okinawa could be, in part, resolved if all bases in Japan became joint allied bases. Some forward-based U.S. forces should, in part, be repositioned to U.S. territory, namely, Guam and the Commonwealth of the Marianas.

It may also be time for the United States to expand its defense by beginning to establish a comprehensive defense alliance for the G-7 and related countries. Mexico and Canada both have Atlantic and Pacific interests in the same way the United States does; thus a combined NATO and Pacific alliance should be envisioned, with its fulcrum in North America. Such an alliance would encompass nearly all the industrialized liberal democracies on the planet!

In regard to the Republic of Korea (ROK), the necessity of the continuation of a small in-place U.S. trip wire force in South Korea appears unavoidable. Deterrence of a possible People's Democratic Republic of [North] Korea (PDRK) attack is necessary into the foreseeable future. Surely the PDRK will disappear, but when that will occur cannot be specifically identified. The cost will undoubtedly be high, and chaos and massive refugee flows must be anticipated. The United States has a great obligation in relation to the ROK, dating back to the immediate post–World War II errors and omissions. The Korean War itself has yet to end, there is only an armistice that the PDRK is attempting to dissolve.[54] U.S. bases in the ROK ought to be repositioned out of Seoul and Pusan—regardless of the historical reasons for their existence—to places where they are less of a public irritant.

Other U.S. allies in the region, Australia and New Zealand, have regularly operated in conjunction with the United States in military exercises, training, bases, aerospace activities, and so on. The only major problem has been New Zealand's past refusal to admit U.S. Naval ships into its ports if they are nuclear-powered or may be carrying nuclear weapons. The U.S. Navy's policy of neither confirming nor denying the presence of nuclear weapons has not been sufficient for New Zealand, as it has been for other Asian nations with nonnuclear policies. A definitive resolution of this recurring problem should be attempted.

Regarding non-allied Asian states, the Philippines should be called on once and for all to either ally or disavow a U.S. connection. If a formal alliance is reached, the Philippines will sorely need training and equipment for all branches of its armed forces; however, any U.S. bases in the Philippines should be on an equal basis with access, say, to Subic Bay and Cubi Point Air Station, based on joint/bilateral agreements beneficial to both sides. The phenomena of Olongapo City, outside Subic Bay Naval Base, and Angeles, outside of the now defunct U.S. Clark Air Force Base, as true dens of iniquity must not be repeated. Whether the Philippines is to be our partner or not, colonialism is dead. If the Philippines chooses not to ally with the United States, so be it. The current U.S. agreements with Singapore for resupply and repair facilities there, and with Great Britain in regard to the lease of Diego Garcia island for supply, repair, and staging facilities for PaCom and CentCom, seem to be sufficient and ought to be continued well into the twenty-first century.

Southeast Asia is an area of lesser U.S. interest than Northeast Asia and China. However, regardless of what may happen with the Philippines and the current Singapore agreement, there are concerns about Cambodia, Thailand, Malaysia, and Indonesia. These concerns can be addressed in discussion with ASEAN (Association of South East Asian Nations) and in bilateral diplomacy; a special forward U.S. presence in this area does not appear to be needed.[55]

The People's Republic of China has not yet been addressed because the biggest U.S. problem in Asia has been saved for last. The PRC disposes of the largest armed force or rather, armed forces, in East Asia: the People's Liberation Army, commonly referred to in English as the PLA. The approximate force posture in East Asia in 1996 is shown in Table 9.4.

TABLE 9.4

	PERSONNEL	AIRCRAFT	SHIPS
China, People's Republic of	2.2 million (ninety-one divisions)	6,160	1,080 (1.02 million tons)
Taiwan, Republic of China	290,000 (two divisions +30,000 marines)	420	390 (220,000 tons)
North Korea (PDRK)	1 million (twenty-six divisions)	770	630 (87,000 tons)
South Korea (ROK)	550,000 (twenty-two divisions + 25,000 marines)	490	220 (139,000 tons)
Russia (Far East only)	218,000 (twenty-six divisions)	1,000	675 (1.68 million tons)
Japan	151,000 (thirteen divisions)	510	160 (344,000 tons)
United States			
South Korea	27,000 (one division)	90	
Japan	23,000 (one division)	200	
Seventh Fleet			60 (650,000 tons) (+140 aircraft)

Source: *Defense of Japan 1995,* quoted in *Japan Times Weekly International Edition,* January 15–21, 1996, p. 3.

Of course, gross figures do not indicate how ready for use the forces are—for instance, the Russian Navy is reported to be rusting away in port, mainly at Vladivostok.

The PRC is on the rise, no doubt. Its reported rates of economic expansion are high, and the country disposes of atomic and hydrogen weapons, plus short-, intermediate-range, and intercontinental ballistic missiles. The PRC has forced Great Britain out of Hong Kong as of July 1, 1997, and has threatened many times to reunite Taiwan with the mainland soon, and by force if necessary. Beyond that, the PRC appears to be ready for force projection capabilities with the acquisition of aircraft carriers, long-range submarines, and in-flight refueling capacity for its fighters and bombers. The threat of this to-be-acquired capacity has been felt in the South China Sea, where the PRC has claimed sovereignty over islands, reefs, and banks in the face of counterclaims by Taiwan, Vietnam, Malaysia, Brunei, and the Philippines—a very bold assertion already reinforced by naval power and the establishment of permanent bases.[56]

The PRC's military power, power projection capabilities, and will to use force to achieve its foreign policy goals are a major concern for the United States and its allies, and a probable flash point in the first half of the twenty-first century.[57]

Given the aforementioned, what should be the general strategic priorities of the United States in the East Asia/Asia Pacific region for the next century? Here are some possible answers:

1.   Forward deployment of forces should be maintained at a level that makes the United States a credible actor in PaCom's area of concern.

2.   The United States should plan in detail for the various contingencies on the Korean peninsula. War can not be ruled out. The PDRK does occasionally hold out the olive branch and offer to form one state with two systems and to recognize that "Korean reunification can never be achieved by the method of one side forcing its own ideology and social system upon the other."[58] Otherwise "the crucial questions concerning Korean unification are 'when and how,' not 'if.'"[59] Whatever occurs will "present the South with staggering problems in absorbing the North economically and politically."[60]

3.   The relationship of the United States with Japan must be stabilized on the basis of equality in the Pacific theater. Japan, in general, recognizes that the Japan-U.S. security arrangement should be the basis of Japan's Grand Strategy in the twenty-first century and that it should not act unilaterally in the Pacific region—that collective defense is the best way.[61]

4.   Other than the Korean problem, the principal challenge to the United States comes from the PRC. The immediate flash points are in the South China Sea and the straits between Taiwan and the mainland. Other points of contention will undoubtedly occur.[62] The PRC problem will require a long-term U.S. engagement with China, similar to that which it had with the Soviet Union. Whether a policy of "containment" for the PRC will be necessary remains to be seen. "Stripped of its theoretical superstructure,

containment encompasses the complex and shifting assortment of policies through which the United States sought to respond to the Soviet challenge."[63] That we will be replacing *Soviet* with *PRC* in future definitions of
containment seems probable.

The Fourth Zone of U.S. defense, South America, needs little comment.
In fact, it might even be referred to as zone $3\,^1/2$. Since Central America is in
the U.S. primary defense zone we refer here not to all of Latin America, but
to the continent south of Panama and the Caribbean Sea. Forward placement
of any U.S. forces is not anticipated. The OAS and related training of South
American military in the United States, plus American supplies of air and
equipment, appear to be sufficient, and other than denial of bases to a possible enemy, in the area of defense the United States need do no more.

SUMMATION AND A PROJECTION

Preparing for the eventualities of the twenty-first century is not easy but it
must be done. The Vice Chairman of the U.S. Joint Chiefs of Staff, Admiral
William Owens, spoke with Charlayne Hunter-Gault about "Modernizing the
Military" on National Public Television's "Newshour with Jim Lehrer" (March
1, 1996). He said that besides having top-flight, well-trained professional personnel, the driving force in future military conflict will be technology. Within
3 to 5 years, an all-weather view of a battlefield and a region will be available
in real time via satellite. The United States is using and will continue to develop a less-than-brute-force approach. All assets will be brought to bear on an
opponent's forces using stand-off weapons. Precision strikes directed from
video-reconnaissance drones will soon be possible in which smart ballistic
missiles of a 200-mile range can be directed to targets using a mouse pointer
on an IBM Think Pad microminiature computer, and targets can be struck to
an accuracy of a few meters.

In May 1996, Andrew Marshall of the Office of Net Assessments, U.S.
Department of Defense, at a symposium on international security at Yale
University, spoke of "a prospective revolution in military affairs," in which,
within two to three decades, a major revolution in the nature of warfare will
take place. Already, an assault breaker system is partially in place, in which
accuracy independent of range has been achieved, and delivery systems,
smart ammunitions, and sensors—plus quick target acquisition—eliminate a
safe rear zone for an aggressor. Long-range precision strike systems will soon
be deployed, and land- and space-based systems will soon dominate near
ocean areas of countries possessing them. The United States needs to monitor very carefully which countries want to acquire these technologies. Mr.
Marshall, in the question-and-answer period, said that a certain segment of
the PLA's officer corps was currently interested in this revolution in war.

Although the Soviets were the first theorists, in the late 1970s and the 1980s, to write of a revolution in the military, neither their Russian successors nor West Europeans are pursuing the topic.

Unfortunately, however, the lure of technology can be overwhelming. Congress has tried to force the U.S. Air Force to acquire more B-2 supersonic stealth bombers than it wants. The cost of each B-2 is so great—over a half billion dollars per unit—that further acquisition would be a great drain on the declining Air Force budget.[64]

There is no doubt that technology, if properly used, will be decisive in the twenty-first century, *in some conflicts*. Even the notion of a "Twenty-First Century Land Warrior," a "completely new, high-tech soldier" is being discussed.[65] However, *ex post facto*, the "smart" weapons of the highest tech war of the twentieth century, the Gulf War, proved to be less effective than first claimed: 90 percent success rates may well have been only 40 percent—not much different from "dumb" weapons.[66] Too much emphasis on technology will lead us in the wrong direction:

> ...technology is only part of the equation. An effective approach to war must look beyond sensors, munitions and C⁴I [Command, Control, Communications, Computers, and Intelligence], even if these technologies are organized into a "system of systems." Any approach to war that ignores strategy and friction and tempts us to forget that war is waged against an adversary with an active will, is doomed to failure.[67]

Conflict in the future may well be quite different than anticipated. Nanotechnology (extremely small, molecular-sized, machines) could well be developed that would change the whole nature and meaning of aggression. Over a quarter century ago, the famous Polish science-fiction writer Stanislaw Lem started mentioning "synsects" in his works—very small synthetic insects that would function in clouds. One could be attacked and not recognize it, nor be able to identify who launched the attack—such an attack could destroy computers and machinery.[68] In fact, *Scientific American* recently carried a story about how far nanotechnology has developed, and projected a one-to-three-decade development time for usable nanomachines.[69]

In the "less than technologically advanced" category, the United States may be faced with attacks that include biological war and simple smuggled plutonium or uranium bombs.[70]

Unfortunately, in the stealth and terrorism field, the United States has much to blame itself for: The United States trained a large number of fighters in the Afghan war, fighters who now turn their training on the United States and its allies, in the so-called "blow back" effect.[71]

Tom Clancy, an American writer of military-style adventure novels, has certainly brought home to the U.S. reading public the possibility of a stealth nuclear attack by a small group of fanatics in *The Sum of All Fears* (1991), and the threat of a stealthy preparation for war by a large power in *Debt of Honor*

(1994). In the latter, an "attack" begins with the crash of computers running the stock market, which throws the advanced states of the world into a huge economic crisis, and then continues with the threat of an attack on the Primary Zone by stealthily prepared ICBMs with thermonuclear warheads.

While the United States may prepare for a high-tech war that includes an Air Force Information Warfare Center designed to counter hostile hacking into military computers,[72] new aircraft, a new low-profile, on-the-water Navy with arsenal ships, land warfare with pilotless drones, and inexpensive lethal robots, it may be that low intensity, cheap attacks will be the future.[73] A stealthy low-tech attack on a high-cost weapon system—say, a billion-dollar aircraft carrier or bomber—might be a way for an enemy to hurt the United States. Low- or no-tech preindustrial war, as fought in Somalia, where a tribal leader, Mohammed Adid, shunned use of a telephone and instead communicated using sticks beating oil drums, was successful in that situation.[74] In sum then, the United States must be prepared for the full spectrum of conflict, with credible forces that can defend against all who wish the United States ill; anything less than that could be deadly. We may conclude with this quote:

> In order to be successful, any new strategy to use military forces in the post-Cold War world should be undergirded by clear, specific objectives, directed at a genuine, discernible threat, supported by high-quality military forces, assisted, as required, by allies, and it must remain faithful to the prevailing strategic culture.... The absence of a strategy means that the "regret factor" will be very prominent. Perhaps the United States will be lucky, and pessimism will have been wasted. But the words of Douglas MacArthur keep reverberating: "The history of failure in war can be summed up in two words—too late. Too late in comprehending the deadly purpose of a potential enemy; too late in realizing the mortal danger; too late in preparedness; too late in uniting all possible forces for resistance; too late in standing with one's friends."[75]

Clear assessment of danger, correct and timely preparation to avert the danger, and, if necessary, the ability to defend the United States of America from all attacks is what is needed for the twenty-first century.[76]

NOTES

1. Lawrence P. Rockwood [Captain], "Apology of a Buddhist Soldier," *Tricycle: The Buddhist Review*, Spring 1996, pp. 71–76.
2. James T. Johnson and George Weigel, *Just War and the Gulf War* (Washington, DC: Ethics and Public Policy Center, 1991), see section "Justifiable Resort to Force," pp. 20–29.
3. Defense can be at least theoretically passive. See Robert Burrows, *The Strategy of Non-Violent Defense* (Albany, NY: State University of New York Press, 1996).
4. "Encounter at Far Point" episode of "Star Trek: The Next Generation" (1987).
5. "All Good Things" episode of "Star Trek: The Next Generation" (1994).
6. Thomas Hobbes, *Leviathan* (London: Penguin Books, 1981 [first published in 1651]).

7. For a survey of modern global conflict, see Paul Kennedy, *The Rise and Fall of the Great Powers* (New York: Random House, 1987).

8. Max Singer and Aaron Wildawsky, *The Real World Order: Zones of Peace/Zones of Turmoil*, rev. ed. (Chatham, NJ: Chatham House Publishers, 1996).

9. Ibid., pp. 208–219.

10. Ibid., p. 213.

11. Lana Morrow, "Natural Evil or Man-Made?, *Time*, July 29, 1996, p. 88, and Kevin Fedarko, "Who Wishes Us Ill," ibid., p. 41.

12. Gale Stokes, John Lampe, and Dennison Rusinow, with Julie Mostov, "Instant History: Understanding the Wars of Yugoslav Succession," *Slavic Review*, Spring 1996, Vol. 55, No. 1, p. 160.

13. See "Emerging Mexico: A Special Issue," *National Geographic*, August 1996.

14. See Jeffrey Simon, *NATO Enlargement: Opinions and Options* (Washington, DC: National Defense University, 1995).

15. "U.S. European Command (EuCom)," *Joint Force Quarterly: A Professional Journal*, Summer 1996, pp. 28–29.

16. See Robert G. Bell, "Ballistic Missile Defense," *Strategic Forum*, July 1995.

17. Victor Krulak, *Panama: An Assessment*, (Washington, DC: United States Strategic Institute, 1990).

18. "NATO Acquires a European Identity," *The Economist*, June 8, 1996, pp. 51–52.

19. A whole "not for attribution" symposium on "NATO Expansion: Opinions and Options" was held at the U.S. National Defense University on April 24–25, 1995, in Washington, DC. Two books came out of the National Defense University's Institute for Strategic Studies at the same time: Jeffrey Simon, *Central European Civil-Military Relations and NATO Expansion*, McNair Paper 39, p. 157; and James W. Morrison, *NATO Expansion and Alternative Future Security Alignments*, McNair Paper 40, p. 171. The papers of the conference were published in September 1995, under the editorship of Jeffrey Simon, as *NATO Enlargement: Opinions and Options*, also published by the National Defense University. In 1993 the same editor had already published a compilation of opinions under the title of *NATO: The Challenge of Change*, also from NDU.

20. Polish Press Agency, "Ukraina tez chce do NATO (Ukraine also wishes to join NATO)," in *Nowy dziennik*, June 7, 1996, p. 16.

21. Paul J. Best, "American Policy toward East Europe," in Kul B. Rai, David F. Walsh, and Paul J. Best, *America in the 21st Century: Challenges and Opportunities in Foreign Policy* (Upper Saddle River, NJ: Prentice Hall, 1996).

22. See also Paul J. Best, "Mikhail Gorbachev, Boris Yeltsin, and the Democratization of Russia," in David F. Walsh, Paul J. Best, and Kul B. Rai *Governing through Turbulence: Leadership and Change in the Late Twentieth Century* (Westport, CT: Praeger Publishers, 1995).

23. Paul Kennedy, note 7.

24. Herman Kahn, *On Thermonuclear War*, 2nd ed. (New York: The Free Press, 1960); and Herman Kahn, *On Escalation: Metaphors and Scenarios*, rev. ed. (Baltimore, MD: Penguin Books, 1965).

25. Kahn, *Escalation*, pp. 94–195.

26. Joan B. Petro [official of the town of Waterford, CT, near the New London-Groton submarine production facilities], unpublished report, "Results of United States Military Downsizing in Southeastern Connecticut," Nov. 17, 1994.

27. For examples, see "Situation Reports: Congress/Administration" and "Congressional Watch," sections of *The Armed Forces Journal International*, published monthly in Washington, DC, since 1863.

28. Terry Dresbach [Captain, U.S. Marine Corps], unpublished report, "The Bottom Up Review and Military Draw-Down," November 21, 1994. His sources

were Caspar W. Weinberger, "Winning Two Wars—or Losing One," *Forbes*, October 11, 1993, p. 35; and J. E. Livingston [General], "Marine Reserve Force and the Marine Corps Message," professional correspondence, April 24, 1994, pp. 15–18.

29. Dresbach, note 28; Livingston, note 28; and *The Military Balance 1993–1994* (London: The International Institute for Strategic Studies, 1993), pp. 13–29.

30. See up-to-date international relations textbooks, especially John T. Rourke, *International Politics on the World Stage*, 4th ed. (Guilford, CT: Dushkin Publishing, 1993), Chapter 14: "International Security: Alternative Approaches" (pp. 390–430). Page 403 has a complete table of arms control treaties.

31. Paul Kennedy, *Preparing for the Twenty-First Century* (New York: Random House, 1993), p. 291.

32. Ibid.

33. Detailed and authoritative statements on worldwide military personnel and equipment are available annually from *The Military Balance*, published by The International Institute for Strategic Studies in London, England.

34. *The Military Balance 1995–1996*, p. 24.

35. For further discussion, see Michael Dziedzic, "NAFTA and North American Security," *Strategic Forum*, January 1995.

36. Ann Hollick, "Ocean Law: Senate Approval of the U.N. Convention," *Strategic Forum*, August 1995.

37. See Jan Zielonka, "Security in Central Europe," *Adelphi Paper* No. 272, Autumn 1992.

38. See Charles L. Barry and Lennard Souchon, eds., *Security Architecture for Europe* (Washington, DC: National Defense University, 1994).

39. See James Ozinga, *The Rapacki Plan* (Jefferson, NC: McFarland and Co., 1989).

40. See "Territory of the Former Soviet Union and its neighbors showing existing military deployment and CFE Treaty limits" [MAP], The International Institute for Strategic Studies, 1995; and "Outflanked: Conventional Forces in Europe," *The Economist*, June 8, 1996, p. 52.

41. Charles Kegley and Eugene Wittkopf, *World Politics: Trend and Transformation*, 5th ed. (New York: St. Martin's Press, 1995), p. 482.

42. "Russia and NATO: A Partnership for a United and Peaceful Europe," *NATO Review*, August, 1994, pp. 3–6.

43. Jeffrey Simon, "Partnership for Peace: Guaranteeing Success," *Strategic Forum*, September 1995; and *CSCE Digest*, June, 1996, p. 8.

44. To keep track of and encourage OSCE development, the United States has its own Commission on Security and Cooperation in Europe (CSCE) in Washington, DC, which publishes the monthly bulletin *CSCE Digest*.

45. Andrzej Nowosad, "Aleksander Lukashenka Zamyka Granice: Bialorus za Zelazna Kurtyna" (Aleksander Lukashenka Closes the Border: Belarus behind the Iron Curtain), *Nowy dziennik*, June 21, 1996, p. 1.

46. See "Special Focus on Russia and Its 'Near Abroad,'" *Jane's Intelligence Review*, Vol. 6, No. 12, December 1994; and "Russian Soldiers in the 'Near Abroad,'" *The Economist*, December 10, 1994, p. 55.

47. See Henry R. Hutlenbach, "Russia's 'Nearer Abroad' Inside the Federation: The Eleven Theses on Nationalities," *Analysis of Current Events*, June 1993.

48. See Richard F. Staar, *The New Military in Russia: Ten Myths Shape the Image* (Annapolis, MD: Naval Institute Press, 1996); and James Brusstar and Ellen Jones, *The Russian Military's Role in Politics* (Washington, DC: National Defense University, McNair Paper No. 34, 1995).

49. William C. Wohlforth, "Realism and the End of the Cold War," *International Security*, Vol. 19, No. 3, (Winter 1994/95), p. 129.

50. *The Military Balance 1995–1996*, pp. 30–31.
51. Patrick Cronin, "The U.S.-Japan Alliance Redefined," *Strategic Forum*, May 1996; Patrick Cronin and Ezra Vogel, "Unifying U.S. Policy on Japan," *Strategic Forum*, November 1995; and Yoshio Karita, "Japan-U.S. Partnership for a more substantial leadership in the coming century," *Japan Info*, August/September 1996, p. 1.
52. Shim Jae Hoon, "Silent Partner" [Russia in Korea], *Far Eastern Economic Review*, Jan. 5, 1995, pp. 14–15; and Michael Mandelbaum, ed. *The Strategic Quadrangle: Russia, China, Japan and the United States in East Asia* (New York: Council on Foreign Relations, 1995).
53. "A Survey of Japan's Tomorrow," *The Economist*, July 13, 1996, p. 8.
54. Ahn, Byung-joon, "Korea-U.S. Alliance toward Unification," *Korea Focus on Current Topics*, Vol. 4, No.2, March–April 1996, pp. 5–15.
55. See Michael Everett, "Multilateralism in Southeast Asia," *Strategic Forum*, June 1995; and Michael Everett and Mary Sommerville, *Multilateralism Activities in South East Asia* (Washington, DC: National Defense University, 1995).
56. Richard Hull, "The South China Sea," *Strategic Forum*, February 1996.
57. Takahiko Ueda, "Some fear, others dismiss China's threat potential," *The Japan Times Weekly International Edition*, January 15–21, 1996, p. 3; Ron Montaperto, "China as a Military Power," *Strategic Forum*, December 1995; and Tetsushi Kajimoto, "Defense Report Voices China Concerns," *Japan Times Weekly International Edition*, July 29–August 4, 1996, p. 1.
58. Song Thae Jun, "Best Way for Korean Reunification," *The Pyongyang Times*, July 13, 1996, p. 7.
59. Hans Binnendijk, "U.S. Strategic Objectives in East Asia," *Strategic Forum*, March 1996, p. 3.
60. Ibid., p. 4.
61. See Toshiyuki Shikata on Japan's "Grand Strategy in the Succeeding Era" in Michael Bellows, ed., *Asia in the 21st Century: Evolving Strategic Priorities* (Washington, DC: National Defense University, 1994), pp. 55–70.
62. See section entitled "U.S. Security: Interests and Challenges" in Douglas Stuart and William Tow, "A U.S. Strategy for the Asia Pacific: Building a multipolar balance-of-power in Asia," *Adelphi Paper*, No. 299, 1995, pp. 28–49.
63. See John O. Iatrides, "Containment [of the USSR]" in *Encyclopedia of U.S. Foreign Policy* (New York: Council on Foreign Relations, Oxford University Press, 1997).
64. See "A Focus on the Continuing B-2 Debate," *Strategic Review*, Vol. 24, No. 1 (Winter 1996), pp. 6–20; and Jeffrey Record, "The Never-Ending Bomber Debate," *Strategic Review*, Vol. 23, No. 4, Fall 1995, pp. 7–15.
65. See *Armed Forces Journal International*, issue on "Twenty-First Century Land Warrior: A Whole New Breed," February 1995.
66. Tim Weiner, "Smart Weapons Were Overrated, Study Concludes," *The New York Times*, July 9, 1996, p. 1; and Tim Weiner, "Selling Weapons: Stealth, Lies and Videotape," *The New York Times*, July 14, 1996, p. E3.
67. Mackubin Thomas Owens, "Editorial: Planning for Future Conflict: Strategy vs. 'Fads,'" *Strategic Review*, Vol. 24, No. 3, Summer 1996, p. 6.
68. See especially Stanislaw Lem, *The Invincible* (New York: Ace Books, 1973) for a full novelistic approach to nanotechnology.
69. Gary Stix, "Trends in Nanotechnology: Waiting for Breakthroughs," *Scientific American*, April 1996, pp. 94–99.
70. Richard Danzig, "Biological Warfare: A Nation at Risk—A Time to Act," *Strategic Forum*, No. 58, January 1996.
71. Philip Shenon, "Holy War Is Home to Haunt the Saudis," *The New York Times*, July 14, 1996, p. E3.

72. Richard Behar, "Who's Reading Your E-Mail?" *Fortune*, February 3, 1997, p. 58; see also Chapter 7 in this text, "America and the Electronic Revolution."

73. Gary Stix, "Trends in Defense Technology: Fighting Future Wars," *Scientific American*, December 1995, pp. 92–98.

74. Ibid., p. 98.

75. Roger Barnett, "The Sinews of National Military Strategy," *USSI Report* (Washington, DC: January 1994) United States Strategic Institute, p. 26.

76. Annual assessments of threats and the means to avert these threats can be found in *Strategic Assessment 1995: U.S. Security Challenges in Transition; Strategic Assessment 1996: Instruments of U.S. Power; Strategic Assessment 1997: Flashpoints and Force Structure*, and succeeding years, published by the Institute for National Strategic Studies, National Defense University. See also the *Strategic Survey* and *Military Balance* annuals issued by the [London] International Institute for Strategic Studies; and the various *Jane's* annuals on all aspects of military hardware.

Specific studies (which may or may not become annuals or be updated), such as Zalmay Khalilzad, *Strategic Appraisal 1996*, Project Air Force, The Rand Corporation; and Charles Kegley and Gregory Raymond, *A Multi-Polar Peace: Great Power Politics in the Twenty-First Century* (New York: St. Martin's Press, 1994) should also be consulted.

Former Secretary of Defense Caspar Weinberger has also published his views about the future in *The Next War* (Washington, DC: Regnery Publishing, 1997). In 470 pages, with illustrations, the former Secretary, along with the Hoover Institution's Peter Schweizer, tackles the question of defense planning. See review by former Secretary of the Navy James Webb in *The New York Times Book Review*, January 5, 1997, p. 23.

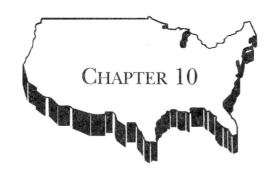

CHAPTER 10

IS THE AMERICAN
DEMOCRATIC SYSTEM PREPARED
FOR THE TWENTY-FIRST CENTURY?

RUSSELL G. FRYER

INTRODUCTION

Is the American national government prepared for the twenty-first century? Is a constitutional-legal-political system erected in the late eighteenth century, when America was a predominately rural society with a population of less than 4 million (including a million African slaves), capable of meeting the challenges and problems of the twenty-first century? Some would argue that the nation has enjoyed remarkable vitality, stability, and prosperity in over 200 years, with the original framework of government intact. Separated powers, federalism, the Bill of Rights, a powerful independent judiciary, popular sovereignty, and competitive party politics have ensured both democracy and reasonably effective governance. However, many Americans at the present time—perhaps a majority—feel that weakness, inadequacy, and decline have set in over recent decades, and this country seems to be losing its capacity to govern itself, especially when it comes to national problem solving. If this is indeed the case, perhaps it will require major surgery to heal the patient, and it is unclear whether or not the inherited system can be reformed and revitalized to deal with the changing world of the present and future.

In broad terms, the American system of government may be evaluated according to the following criteria:

1. Accountability—the relationship between democratic ideals, or values, and operating political reality. If liberty, equality, and justice are still looked upon as the pillars of a democratic ethos, then how are these ideals presently faring in the nation?

2. Effectiveness—are problems being addressed and dealt with in a way that is more likely than not to advance the public good?

3. Responsiveness—is government, especially in Washington, sufficiently reflective of the needs, aspirations, and well-being of more than 250 million citizens?

Admittedly, such criteria are at best vague and immeasurable, but to the extent that the American system can be assessed, identifying major areas of weakness and strength can help to illuminate the actual performance characteristics of the American political system and establish the basis for a national debate on the adequacy of American democracy. Recent critical studies of American politics have identified specific practical conditions that are undermining the performance of the political system in the areas of accountability, effectiveness, and responsiveness. These include individual failures of leadership and judgment—from the president on down, institutional weakness and malfeasance—especially involving Congress and executive departments, and the domination of the political process by organized special interests, which increasingly appear to favor minority economic interests over the majority interest. In addition, the huge expense for both incumbents and challengers of running for high office politicizes and personalizes policy making to such an extent that there is a diminishing prospect that nationalism will triumph over parochialism.[1]

According to defenders of the current system, in the worst of times significant numbers of voters finally get fed up with "politics as usual" and decide it is time to "throw the rascals out," instituting a political upheaval that transforms party control of Congress or the presidency. Many believe that this is what happened in the 1994 Congressional elections which allowed the Republicans to become the majority party by a wide margin after forty years as the minority party in the House of Representatives. This would appear to reinforce the notion of a self-corrective political system. Yet such a conclusion may be premature. There is still the matter of divided government—different parties controlling the executive and legislative branches—and a public mood that distrusts most politicians, both political parties, and government in general.[2] It is, therefore, not clear whether recent electoral and political changes will enhance the accountability, responsiveness, or effectiveness of the American political system. Given the data suggesting relative economic decline and the presence of severe political cleavages in American society, the evidence may point more to accelerating decline than to economic and political renewal.[3]

This chapter will argue that the American democratic system is unprepared for the twenty-first century. It will review criticisms of American political culture, political institutions, and political processes from a wide range of sources and perspectives. The argument can be simply stated. Current American political culture emphasizes the norms of self-interest, economic acquisitiveness, and greed, while ignoring community and national interests. It no longer offers adequate solutions to such problems as urban decay, growing inequality, racial and gender discrimination, and diminishing economic opportunities. Similarly, it contains no prescriptions or guidelines for how American society should proceed in the twenty-first century. American political institutions are uncoordinated, antiquated, redundant, conflictual, and excessively sensitive to special interests. The governmental system, based on eighteenth and nineteenth century political principles of separation, division, and decentralization, has proven unable to deal legislatively or administratively with pressing national problems. Finally, the current political process displays an excessive preoccupation with narrow self-interest, excessive partisanship, and the influence of money. Since the process is viewed as increasingly irrelevant to real problem solving by the general public, it is experiencing a loss of legitimacy.

Throughout the chapter, attention will be given to the political values that constitute the core of America's democratic political beliefs. Historically, these values have been the source of both the strengths and weaknesses of the American conception of democracy, and it will be argued that they hold the best hope for the rejuvenation of the American political system in the twenty-first century. A review of the major criticisms of American democracy is a timely exercise, not only to challenge any existing complacency about America's present condition, but also because these arguments are central to the developing national debate on the proper political and economic course of action for the twenty-first century.

THE CASE AGAINST THE AMERICAN POLITICAL SYSTEM

Is America losing its capacity to govern itself? Every major political institution—the presidency, Congress, the party system, the regulatory agencies, the judiciary, interest groups—and the electorate has manifested a serious and debilitating loss of legitimacy and effectiveness over the past several decades. Opinion polls reveal the growing disenchantment, even cynicism, that the general public presently directs at the political system—not to mention individual political leaders.[4] Economic weakness and growing inequality, political weakness and policy failure, social confusion and divisiveness are commonplace complaints. In the conduct of foreign affairs, despite being the only remaining military superpower, the United States has to compete for influence and ascendancy with a growing number of small and large states.[5]

Heading the list of concerns is how often the entrenched vested interests win and the public interest loses, even when a president or majority of Congress feels otherwise. Old laws granting favors to special interests have become virtually institutionalized, and cannot be repealed even if no longer justified in any national interest sense. In a system where majority rule is weak, minority veto power usually carries the day. Every government program has a constituency and encounters lobbying efforts that make it difficult if not impossible to dislodge the program or make it more accountable. In addition, most legislators have favorite state and local programs, which they seek to maintain and enhance, even when the president or congressional leadership would prefer to eliminate them for budgetary reasons. Books by journalists and scholars pour off the presses, detailing and explaining the source of the problem. Jonathan Rauch has recently made the following argument in his book, *Demosclerosis: The Silent Killer of American Government:*

> The proliferation and professionalization of interest groups and lobbies over the last three decades represents a deep and fundamental change in America's social structure.... The fact is that all groups, without exception, claim to be serving some larger good, and almost all believe it. And all groups, without exception, are lobbying for more of whatever it is that members want, generally at some expense to nonmembers. By the same token, every single law, regulation, subsidy, and program creates losers as well as winners, and whether you think justice is served depends on who pays when the bill arrives.[6]

The increasing influence of special lobbies is a major contribution to uncontrollable budget deficits, as spending outpaces revenues, fees for services rendered by professional lobbyists or consultants are inflated, and entitlements benefit many but not everyone equally. Voters are in revolt against rising taxes and the rising costs of government, but don't want to give up any of their own desired benefits, whether or not justified in the larger scheme of things.

A common criticism is that politicians no longer serve the institutions they were voted into office to represent, but have become excessively dependent both on the outside special interests that keep the money flowing into campaign coffers, and on the elites that know how to manipulate the system for financial gain. As a result, institutions have become captive to special interest favoritism, and have lost their effectiveness. Kevin Phillips has made the following observation about the basic institutions of American democracy in his book, *Arrogant Capital:* "Once ingredients of its youthful success, [they] are becoming weak foundations in its old age, while the grass roots of America have been losing national influence to a permanent political interest-group and financial elite located in Washington, New York, and other centers."[7] Although the author's plea for a renewed populism (more participatory democracy) may offer a corrective to the situation, critics may question the readiness or ability of such a vast electorate to arrive at a reasonable consensus on the best course of action for dealing with such complicated and controversial problems.[8]

Theoretically, the president can push forward an agenda for change, but he or she is likely to get considerable resistance from Congress, and, at best, achieve only partial victories even when his or her party is in power. In the conduct of foreign affairs, a contemporary president seems to have more power than accountability. On the other hand, in the exercise of domestic economic policy making, a president in many instances has greater responsibility than actual power to get things accomplished. Despite the enormous potential power of the presidency, there exist formidable institutional, partisan, and ideological constraints on that power to accomplish or initiate change.[9] The public, however, continues to harbor very high expectations regarding presidential leadership, which are quite unrealistic given the diminished ability of any president to command a coalition of support for his or her policies. There is clearly a growing gap between the person and the office, between campaign promises that help get a candidate elected and the actual ability to govern and deliver on campaign promises.[10]

Congress as an institution is diffuse, conflictual, and inefficient, thanks to the competing claims of parochial constituencies, special interest campaign contributors, and the constant concern about reelection, especially for two-year term Congresspersons.[11] While four-year governorships are now the rule, there seems little prospect that this will happen for House members.

Dwight Eisenhower, John Kennedy, Lyndon Johnson, and Jimmy Carter are the only presidents since Franklin Roosevelt who have enjoyed the luxury of not having the opposition party control the legislative branch in part or for the entirety of their respective terms. Some scholars have argued that divided government has made little difference regarding the output of legislation, but this says little about the substantive aspects of legislation and problem solving.[12] Divided government (different parties controlling the White House and Congress) makes cooperation, coordination, and effective decision making between these two main political branches of government much more difficult to achieve. Even when a president's party controls both popularly-elected political branches, there is no notable improvement in the prospects for effective governance.[13] Constituency, partisanship, and ideology outweigh national interest concerns on most issues of public policy, increasing the odds that special interests will triumph over the public interest, and that minority veto power will defeat the majority will, leading to the politics of deadlock and paralysis.[14]

Agency and departmental bureaucracies, as well as state and local governments, have primary responsibility for the implementation of programs and policies. This participation exacerbates the prospects for delay, redirection, and manipulation of the intentions of law makers, as agencies allocate funds and interpret rules, laws, and regulations. Money appropriations in the pipeline can take an inordinate amount of time to get applied to the policy or program, breeding waste and mismanagement. So-called empire building is virtually a bureaucratic necessity, and in times of budget cuts and tight budgets, it is a constant struggle to keep tabs on expenditures and make sure the tax dollar is well spent. Good intentions have to contend with the vagaries and uncertainties of so many agencies with "pieces of the action." In fact, the sheer size and complexity of most government programs, coupled with the huge amounts of money usually involved, inhibit the fixing of responsibility for mistakes and failures, or even the ability to monitor them.

The American judicial system is a far cry from what is expected of it—from the standpoint of the democratic values of equality, equity, and respect for individual rights and dignity. It is experiencing overburdening and adversarial pressures to a degree that undermines the values it espouses. Litigation, next to the lottery, has become the average American's best prospect for getting rich. Lawyers do well, by and large, while everyone else involved in the criminal justice system suffers indignity, wasted time, and questionable justice, whether because of the heavy reliance on plea-bargaining deals or on settlements that are either monetarily outlandish or unfair to one or both parties involved.[15]

The total prison population has passed the 1 million mark for the first time in American history, and at least 40 percent of inmates were convicted of drug-related crimes. The constant bickering over the death penalty, mandated sentencing, and early prison release because of space problems continues unabated. The cost of all this to taxpayers is escalating and means less money for dealing with other problems.

A "gun culture" and the fact that there are more guns in private hands than adult people in this country today stand as stark testimony to one of the most egregious failures of American civilization. Fear of criminal assault afflicts everyone, some more than others depending on where one lives. There is no relief in sight, and apparently no way of achieving more effective gun control, even if it were feasible and desired by a majority of Americans, which is probably the case.

The role of the media to observe, report, and criticize has led to an avalanche of negative publicity directed at public officials who show the slightest vulnerability (personal indiscretions, misstatements, weakness, etc.) so that positive accomplishments get undermentioned, underreported, and frequently ignored. Speculation, premature disclosures of "leaks," and personal attacks have become more prominently featured than straight news reporting on talk shows, especially by some columnists and by special feature investigative reporters. Tabloid journalism is more popular than ever, and celebrities in all areas of life are fair game for having their most intimate and private affairs exposed to the public with or without supporting documentation.[16]

Perceptions tend to define reality for most people. People prefer to be told what to think, feel, and blame rather than do the hard work of challenging, analyzing, and thinking through difficult issues. In effect, the power of the media to make or break the reputations of public officials has significantly increased, and "reversals of fortune" seem to be more interesting to people than reasonable attempts to keep personal and public roles separate.[17]

STRUCTURAL INADEQUACIES OF THE AMERICAN POLITICAL SYSTEM

Although many critics blame individuals—from the president on down—for the inadequacies, failures, and weaknesses of American government, the real cause may be the system itself, the inherited structure set forth by the constitutional-legal system and the ongoing political-institutional processes. Many arguments have been advanced documenting this situation, but two points have received special attention. First, although the separation of powers or checks and balances ensures democratic pluralism and accountability in theory, it does little to prevent systemic abuses of power. The Vietnam War decision making under President Lyndon Johnson, the Watergate involvement of President Richard Nixon, and the Iran-Contra affair under President Ronald Reagan stand as testimony to this reality. Each of these historic episodes cost immense sums for investigation and adjudication, and contributed to the undermining of confidence in the system for many Americans. They have also left the capacity of the system to fix responsibility for such significant leadership failures very much in doubt. Second, federalism, or the distribution of responsibility, authority, and power between the central government and fifty state governments, has experienced an imbalance that has grown worse over time. This imbalance is the result of the expansion of national government intrusion into peoples' lives through laws, regulations, restrictions, combined with the growing discrepancy from one state to another in the ability to deal with demands for services.

In some respects, the state that one lives in is more important for one's well-being than the fact one is a citizen of the United States. Believers in more "grass-roots democracy," or "bringing government closer to the people," have a strong champion in Republican party conservatism. It remains to be seen, however, whether this approach will provide better results than tackling problems nationally in the interest of uniformity and equity, and whether federal government resources geared to a progressive income tax system are not better than the regressive taxes and the limited resources most states have.[18]

Major studies have attributed the current problems in the political process to the prevailing system of political values. A renowned political scientist, Robert A. Dahl, has put the case this way:

> Out of our past we have inherited ways of thinking about ourselves that condemn us to try too much and accomplish too little. We fail not so much because our aspirations are too high but because they conflict; and within ourselves, too, we are conflicted in ways we do not fully recognize. In this sense our consciousness, both individual and collective, distorts our understanding of ourselves and our possibilities.... Yet there is this strong bias against majorities in the political system the framers helped to create. Because they succeeded in designing a system that makes it easier for privileged minorities to prevent changes they dislike than for majorities to bring about the changes they want, it is strongly tilted in favor of the status quo and against reform. In their effort to protect basic rights, what the framers did in effect was to hand out extra chips in the game of politics to people who are already advantaged, while they handicapped the disadvantaged who would like to change the status quo. From a moral perspective, the consequences seem arbitrary and quite lacking in principled justification.[19]

Dahl believes that five historical "commitments" have generated intense value conflicts that will threaten to tear the system apart if a better way is not found to reconcile these divergent views of American democratic governance. He identifies these commitments as (1) the primacy of individual rights; (2) democracy rather than republicanism or equality as a substantive ideal; (3) private enterprise capitalism; (4) welfare statism; and (5) internationalism and America's role as a major world power.[20] Unfortunately, these commitments are not easily harmonized, and conflicts generated by social change, power, and ideological developments have severely weakened the capacity of the system to deal effectively with the increased demands placed upon it. In Dahl's view, an anti-majoritarian structure inhibits the democratic functioning of American government. Economic advantage gets translated too quickly into political advantage. The separation of powers, so vital to democratic pluralism and accountability, has not prevented institutional abuses of power, and has weakened governmental performance. Hierarchies of power, especially bureaucratic power, are undermining democratic responsiveness and efficiency.

James L. Sundquist has long been one of the strongest advocates of facing up to structural inadequacies in the American system. He states his case as follows:

> The problem of the U.S. government will not be solved by anything so simple as a change in leadership—or a return to office of the incumbent leadership, depending on one's preference. The American governmental system has built-in structural features that have always presented severe difficulties for any president who would provide the sought after leadership. But deep-seated trends have been, and are, at work that will make effective government even more difficult to attain in the future than it has been in the past.[21]

According to Sundquist, this ongoing crisis of weak government exhibits the following symptoms: (1) disintegration of the party system, displaced by personality and media politics; (2) the democratization of the presidential selection process, which favors less experienced and politically weaker candidates; (3) the growing power of Congress that is a check on presidential abuse of power, but at the expense of effective government; and (4) the pervasive deterioration of administrative competence throughout the system, partly because of a lack of stable professionalism and political manipulation of the civil service.[22] As a result of these factors, although we expect and demand so much of the president as the initiator and coordinator of public policy and the focal point of national interest, there is neither the constitutional nor practical power to legitimize a president's authority. So much power is shared and dispersed among competing power centers that minority veto power is a more realistic expectation than responsiveness to majority rule wishes.

THE DECLINING LEGITIMACY OF THE AMERICAN POLITICAL SYSTEM

Increasing numbers of citizens now believe that America is losing the capacity to govern itself. It is frequently alleged that corruption permeates the entire system. Despite the fact that much of it is not, strictly speaking, illegal, it is not immune to exposure, investigation, and a semblance of accountability.[23] The legitimacy of the system is eroding, and the growing estrangement between the general public and its representatives bodes ill for both democracy and effective government. In addition, the growing intensity of partisan, ideological, and ethnic/racial cleavages in the political culture exacerbates national divisions.[24] The sheer size and complexity of American government may be a good part of the problem. No one is really in charge and no one knows how to monitor and fix responsibility when things start to go wrong, especially with respect to abuse of power and malfeasance.

Many fear that public officials who do care about doing what's right will be politically destroyed by a system where the rewards and punishments are askew. The American ideology of self-interest and individualism still has a stranglehold over politics and government, leaving little room for a real sense of social responsibility and public service.

Correcting the most serious abuses of power and democratic failure is both a collective and individual responsibility of ordinary citizens, public officials, and civil servants. In theory America is a self-corrective system; at least serious problems are usually addressed and something is done to alleviate them. Historically, America has been a success story among the nations of the world, but it may well be ill-equipped to deal with the challenges of the twenty-first century unless there are significant institutional reforms and a marked shift away from minority, special-interest power and toward majority, public-interest politics.

Even though Americans still can claim to enjoy living in the strongest democracy in the world, the performance level of American government is widely perceived to be rapidly deteriorating. Opinion polls verify this when people are asked how they feel about the presidency and Congress as institutions of government in general. At a time when we Americans need more from government in the way of security, liberty, and equality, an antigovernment animus is sweeping the country. Confidence in democracy as a system may be as strong as ever, but confidence in elected officials and specific institutions is probably as low as it can get in the late twentieth century. It speaks loudly for the position that American national government is not prepared to enter the twenty-first century as presently constituted. Whether this is a failure primarily of the American people or the operations of government itself is an open question.

On the positive side, however, the following should be noted:

1. There exists a broad-based commitment to democratic norms and values, even when actual governance falls short of the mark.

2. America is a society rich in resources, diversity, and economic strength, despite the uneven impact these advantages have upon the general populace.

3. America still expends more money, time, and energy attacking problems than any other country, and even when the results are dismal, the effort continues.

4. The 1994 election, which gave Republicans control of the House of Representatives for the first time in forty years and simultaneous control of the Senate, is a rare occurrence that may result in a real housecleaning and diminish the role and power of intrusive government. Whether this will lead to greater equity and democracy, however, is an open question.[25]

5. American volunteerism is still alive and well, including people helping others in need at individual and community levels and through charitable contributions. It remains to be seen whether this can be translated into better problem solving and less wasteful, less corrupt government.

MONEY AND POLITICS

There is a huge gray area of ethical ambiguity and uncertainty regarding interest-group influence peddling and public officials who are supposed to be concerned about the larger public interest in the representation of their constituencies. Conflicts of interest, which may not be illegal but are often unethical, seem endemic to American government and politics. Despite legal restrictions on the amount of individual and political action committee (PAC) contributions to politicians running for office or reelection, the loopholes are so prominent that groups can successfully evade them. At all times, incumbents have one eye focused on big campaign contributions when they have to vote on issues of public policy, and the public interest more often than not loses out to special-interest politics.[26] In addition, some critics allege that there is a conflict of interest inherent in the fact that many politicians come from a legal background and work for law firms both before and after leaving office. The increased dependence of the public sector on consultants with the right contacts further adds to the loss of control by public officials. The term, "being in bed together," is commonly used to describe Washington power and politics. Top public officials, top media individuals, and the elites of various institutions, instead of displaying the expected adversarial and critical roles, frequently participate in an "incestuous" relationship of personal attachment, friendship, and mutual benefit regardless of the public good.[27] One can also question how impartial, critical, and reliable the top media people can be, given this rather common phenomenon in Washington. This is an especially important issue since democracy depends on a reasonably objective and free press, which may not always be the case in actuality.

Obviously, money can bring influence over the political agenda. It is clear today that huge sums are needed for successful political campaigns, leaving less room for simply doing the public's business. Legislators frequently complain they spend as much or more time soliciting funds for future campaigns than on anything else. Large corporations literally buy their way into the process to assure that their primary interests are served by governing officials in both branches of the government—executive and legislative—regardless of party affiliation. They occasionally lose, but mostly they win, if not by getting what they want, then by preventing measures that they don't want from being enacted.[28]

Millions of Americans, possibly more than half the population, receive subsidies from government of one sort or another, including welfare benefits, Social Security payments, agricultural subsidies, business-corporate subsidies, and special tax breaks. Meanwhile, it is a generally accepted fact that one out of five children lives in poverty—the prime breeding ground for future crime and welfare dependency. The maldistribution of wealth in this country is greater than anywhere else in the advanced industrialized world, and this is the end result of public policies, ideological convictions, and the fact that most Americans who are reasonably well-off are not as concerned as they might be about the existing distribution of wealth or government benefits.[29] Because of the steady cumulative rise in the cost of living, which wages and salaries rarely cover adequately, the young generation is hit hardest by the increasing economic inequity.

Finance capitalism has always been in competition with industrial capitalism in America, but in earlier periods finance capitalism took a back seat to productive capitalism. This seems to have changed in the 1980s and continues to change in the 1990s. Today big companies buy up, absorb, or eliminate smaller companies simply to inflate the value of stocks, with no regard for the products, jobs, and communities that are affected.[30] Everyone winds up losing, except top executives, lawyers, and a select number of stockholders. This is capitalism without a social conscience or democratic grounding.

Ironically, instead of contributing to America's growth and productivity, there is a side to capitalism that undermines it, as Kevin Phillips maintains in his book, *Arrogant Capital*:

> For most firms, federal debt has meant gravy, not hardship. Wall Street profited enormously during the era of huge deficits from 1982 onwards. What at first made the 1980s golden was tax cuts, deregulation, and declining inflation. But by the early 1990s, trading in U.S. government debt and assorted speculative derivatives had become the new framework of unprecedented profits at many of New York's most famous investment firms. Which brings us to an important corollary of financialization: As massive debt becomes a major national problem, it also becomes a major financial opportunity and vested interest.[31]

Felix G. Rohatyn, a highly respected economic analyst, reinforces this point:

> The big beneficiaries of our economic expansion have been owners of financial assets and a new class of highly compensated technicians working for companies where profit-sharing and stock ownership was widely spread.
>
> What is occurring is a huge transfer of wealth from lower-skilled middle-class American workers to the owners of capital assets and to the new technological aristocracy.
>
> As a result, the institutional relationship created by the mutual loyalty of employees and employers in most American business has been badly

frayed.... These relationships have been replaced by a combination of fear for the future and a cynicism for the present as a broad proportion of working people see themselves as simply temporary assets to be hired or fired to protect the bottom line and create 'shareholder value.'[32]

THE ISSUES OF TRUST AND ACCOUNTABILITY

Official secrecy, misrepresentation of facts, and self-serving distortions of the truth seem to be all too common today in national government. Who or what institutions can you trust to tell the truth? In his book, *For the President's Eyes Only: Secret Intelligence and the American Presidency from Washington to Bush*, Christopher Andrew argues, for instance, that the CIA has recently been concerned with putting a spin on information that kept the public in the dark about what was really happening in the Soviet Union and elsewhere. The inflated estimates of the Soviet economy and military capability for decades might be a case in point, bolstering the exorbitant funding requests of such agencies as the Defense Department. Manipulating public opinion at the expense of the truth seems common no matter which political party is in power in Washington.[33]

The essence of democratic accountability is that the means matter as much as the ends to be pursued. When power is employed to subvert means in deference to ends, no matter how apparently worthy, democracy is at risk. This happened repeatedly during the Cold War era under the rubric of anti-communism. The illegal and undemocratic abuse of power tended to be justified as long as it advanced America's Cold War agenda, despite sometimes dubious grounds for doing so. The American dilemma is the need to keep democratic values, norms, and traditions in reasonable alignment with the reality of politics, society, and economics. Many Americans feel that America has become a weak government but remains a strong democracy. Others feel it is becoming a weaker democracy, while the government is too strong.[34]

Today there is growing evidence that American government is an anachronism. It is the only political system in the world, democratic or non-democratic, that is not based on executive supremacy. In democratic regimes, reinforced by relatively strong national party systems, some form of majority-rule democracy is in effect in which there is considerable integration of authority and power for policy enactment that requires only majority parliamentary backing. Although it is true that all governments today are weak and inadequate when it comes to dealing with current problems—especially fiscal ones—the public sector is in a stronger position than the private sector in setting national priorities and implementing policies. America may well be an exception where there is nobody really in charge because the system itself militates against coordinating power and authority.[35] The federal system exacerbates the problem of the decentralization of power. Fifty state governments and countless smaller units of government all have pieces of the action—no program, policy, or planning can dispense with the intricate, cumbersome, and uneven distribution of power and authority within the American system on multiple levels. There is no way this will ever change, and perhaps this is just as well. It accommodates the great size and diversity of the country and makes American democracy more responsive to the people. But at the same time it makes government less manageable, and inhibits any coherent effort to deal with problems on a national basis.[36]

Would it be possible to achieve a system of executive and national government ascendancy without destroying democratic accountability and the inherited constitutional system? Giving the president a line-item veto over appropriation bills (with some restrictions) is a first step. But Congress, especially the Senate, would have to eliminate, or revise, procedural roadblocks that favor the minority over the majority, such as the Senate filibuster, riders to amendments in the Senate that are substantively different from the original legislation, and a laundry list of parliamentary delaying tactics. This would not involve structural change, just the willingness of Congress to shift some power to the president and curb its appetite for safeguarding minority veto power.[37]

American democracy is in crisis, not only because government is losing legitimacy in the eyes of its own citizens and in regard to institutional performance, but because it lacks a means of identifying the public interest and then acting in accordance with such a concept.[38] The ability of political leaders and institutions to speak for the public interest has greatly diminished over time. Note the failure of health care reform in the 103rd Congress, crime bills and drug enforcement that cost the taxpayers billions of dollars but don't seem to alleviate the problems, and welfare reform that neither saves money nor strengthens the "safety net" for the truly needy. W. J. Stankiewicz, in his work, *Aspects of Political Theory*, makes this point:

> So long as government was viewed as a merely regulatory body for maintaining peace and order, all that was expected from a truly democratic government was an inability to act other than through set procedures, in line with an established code and in a strictly limited area. The least government was the best. But the demands for an active rather than passive government could, with the necessary qualification that the action must not be simply in the government's own interest or that of interest groups alone, have created the need for a more adequate definition of public interest; and the need is becoming more and more obvious as the demands upon government grow.[39]

There has always been a defect in the classical liberal view of people that has contributed to the problem of defining the public interest. Traditionally, Protestant individualism, Lockean-Jeffersonian-Madisonian constitutionalism, and the capitalist emphasis on the virtues of property and acquisitiveness have made the private sector superior to the public sector, and the self more important than society in American historical consciousness. As a result, the unhindered, minimally regulated, pursuit of self-interest has been the corner-stone of the American attitude toward government. The transformation of lib-eralism in the twentieth century, as a consequence of the New Deal tradition's response to economic crisis, moderated, but did not repudiate, this basic atti-tude toward government. So there has never been much support for the beneficent state or the spirit of self-sacrifice for the larger good. Conditions did permit some modification of the excessive strain on the institutional and social structure until recently, thanks to the abundance of land and resources open to use and exploitation. Now that relative scarcity is once more the order of the day, with increased demands on government and curtailed revenue sources, there is less that can be expected in this regard, and the scales are tip-ping decisively toward an antigovernment bias. This benefits Republican party conservatives as the longtime standard bearers of less government.[40]

There are three major problems hindering agreement on the public interest in American society. First, there is a conflict between equally basic ends—liberty and equality—with any policy decision likely to sacrifice one for the other. Second, there is the question of which institution of government—the presidency, Congress, or the Supreme Court—should be given the pri-mary responsibility and authority for determining what is in the public inter-est. Third, there is the structural diversity and cultural pluralism that accom-pany the division of power among different levels of government. Taken sep-arately, each poses formidable barriers to an effective means of arriving at the public interest. Taken together, they favor systemic stability over needed insti-tutional reforms.[41]

Economically, the growing inequality in America among the various income strata—especially the shrinking of the middle class and the persis-tence of poverty—fuels the prospect of social unrest and high crime rates. When coupled with the structural economic changes that dry up the avail-ability of entry-level and unskilled jobs, the gulf between the better-off and poor keeps widening.[42] Expansion of the middle class has been the great suc-cess story of America throughout much of the twentieth century, and if this ceases to be the case in the next century, it will have dire consequences for the nation's health and well-being.[43] This disturbing trend is already in evi-dence, and policy decisions in Washington do not lend encouragement to the possibility that this condition will be arrested and reversed. In fact, it may be getting progressively worse as the loss of welfare benefits, health care cov-erage, and economic opportunity hurts those at the lower rungs of the socioeconomic system, while those in the upper-middle-class and wealthy segments of society prosper, but in diminishing numbers proportionate to the population as a whole.

Socioculturally, a "crisis of authority" can be viewed as widespread con-fusion of values whereby truth and falsehood, good and evil, appropriate and inappropriate behavior become meaningless distinctions.[44] Whether or not there is a positive side to a culture that promotes personal liberation from discriminatory social sanctions—and a case can be made that the present is preferable to the past in this respect—there are very real dangers for a society that permits itself to sacrifice reasonable standards on the altar of unrestrained freedom. Once this road is traveled to its farthest point, authoritarian solutions to the problem of growing disorder become a possible alternative.

Politically, a "crisis of authority" occurs whenever people lose control of their government in democracies. This seems to be happening in America, as demands on government escalate and financial resources contract. Instead of benefits going to those who pass "the means test of need," they end up in the hands of those who are in the strongest position to help themselves by virtue of greater economic resources and political clout. Eventually, less equality and more socioeconomic stratification will produce an intolerable strain on the democratic fabric, tearing society asunder. Sociologist Amitai Etzioni offers this comment on what may be happening as a consequence of these developments:

> The private self and the public self in the American persona have split off from each other—with possibly serious consequences for the nation. Privately, many people feel quite self-confident, optimistic about their future, able to cope, satisfied, even happy. But when they view their public life, as members of a national community, they are quite pessimistic; they tend to see themselves as incompetent, dissatisfied, and unable to master the future. The private self, whose identity lies in personal pursuits, from work to family, and the public self, built around one's role as a member of the public, the community, the nation, are out of kilter.[45]

Some critics see the situation as Hobbes triumphing over Locke. In the Hobbesian view of people, society, and the state, people's irremediable egoism, aggressiveness, and selfishness require a strong central authority to prevent violence, anarchy, and the breakdown of society. The only way of safeguarding individualism is by delegating responsibility for one's individual well-being to an all-powerful ruler or central authority. In contrast, in the Lockean view of people, society, and the state, the good of the individual is promoted by limiting the power of government through institutional and constitutional means. Thus, political democracy becomes the basis of ensuring greater socioeconomic progress. But if this should fail to materialize, at least to the degree necessary for a balanced and stable political economy, then Hobbes, not Locke, becomes a more realistic guide for the preservation of a seriously weakened democratic system.[46]

THE RISE AND FALL OF THE TWO-PARTY SYSTEM

Even though the framers of the Constitution, without exception, distrusted organized political parties and made no provision for them in the Constitution, parties evolved early during the nation-building period, first around strong opposition leaders—namely Thomas Jefferson and Alexander Hamilton—and later as ongoing institutions mediating between rulers and the ruled.[47] Although third parties sometimes emerged to play an important role in electoral politics, the state-by-state, "winner-take-all" electoral college system severely inhibited third party candidates from capturing the presidency. Eventually, the Republican and Democratic parties, highly decentralized on national, state, and local levels, acquired a distinctive political coloration by appealing to different segments of the populace and vying for the temporary support of "independent" voters, a growing element of the electorate in recent years.

Despite the incidence of one-party dominance in the nation, states, regions, and localities, competition between major party candidates was a regular feature of the political landscape, and provided a considerable degree of stability in a pronouncedly heterogeneous society. As evidence accumulates that the party system no longer commands the confidence or allegiance of increasing numbers of voters, there is a strong suspicion that one of the instrumentalities of American democracy is in deep trouble.[48] Summarizing traditional ideologies of Republicans and Democrats, Stanley B. Greenberg, in his book, *Middle-Class Dreams: The Politics and Power of the New American Majority*, puts it this way:

> Modern America has been shaped by two dominant political visions of the nation's promise: a top-down view that placed its faith in a business-led prosperity and a bottom-up view that championed and advanced the common person. The top-down view held that business leadership and entrepreneurial values would bring change, growth, and general well-being. The bottom-up idea held that people had to be protected or assisted so they could prosper as the country changed and that their rising standards of living was the measure of the nation's success. Each vision represented a kind of compact that honored certain values and behavior and created certain obligations that in turn allowed ordinary people to order their lives and maintain their faith in the country.[49]

Today it would appear that neither major party has the ability to create a meaningful majority of followers, and the result is uncertainty, disorganization, and possibly political and economic decline. As the politics of personality displaces the politics of party in the national arena, every election is up for grabs, with no road maps or real continuity regarding policy and leaders. Fragmentation of power, combined with disenchantment with politicians and bureaucrats and a growing sense of alienation between the people and their elected representatives, characterizes the American political scene. It mirrors the intensified social cleavages among groups—especially a growing separation between black and white Americans, manifested by the recurring attacks on affirmative action, busing, the welfare system, and disruptive protest incidents.

As the middle class turns against the former alliance of the Democratic party leadership between the intelligentsia and underclass because of the perceived high levels of taxation, it similarly disapproves of the takeover by the religious right of the social-moral issue agenda of the Republican party. There is widespread distrust and opposition to both traditional parties. Institutional weakness and instability would be a high price to pay for these developments.

It appears that race has become the wedge issue that is creating divided loyalty and allegiance with the two major parties. The evidence is mounting that too many white Americans fear black Americans, and black Americans distrust white Americans, regardless of individuals and circumstances.[50] While the Republican party attracts the allegiance of a few African Americans (mostly successful ones), the Democratic party remains the haven of lower-class and middle-class African Americans, along with other minority groups. Moral issues have also had a divisive effect on the two parties. The so-called "Christian Right," led by televangelist Pat Robertson, media expert Ralph Reed, and the perennial presidential candidate, Patrick Buchanan, seems to hold strong sway over Republican party national candidates for public office, compelling them to take the "right stand" on such issues as the right to life, opposition to gun control, capital punishment, and opposition to "liberal permissiveness" on other social-moral issues.[51] Despite the fact that polling results invariably indicate that the majority of the American public disagrees with the neoconservative position on all these issues, and gaining the nomination can be a detriment to winning broader support for gaining the presidency, Republican party candidates for president have felt constrained from forcefully advocating more moderate positions on the majority of such issues.

In effect, as we head into the twenty-first century, it appears for the time being that the politics of divisiveness, partisanship, and ideological cleavage not only splits the major parties' normal constituencies, but also makes it less likely that a consensus for policy and decision can emerge that will strengthen rather than weaken public interest politics. This development, if it persists, bodes ill for both American government and democracy.

DILEMMAS OF LIBERALISM VERSUS CONSERVATISM

Along with partisan politics, the most salient aspect of American politics and government is the perennial contrast between liberal and conservative solutions to problems. A major split between Democratic and Republican party politicians is as much ideological as strictly partisan, especially over budgetary matters and the proper role of government. While Republicans think in terms of deregulation, smaller government, reduced social services, and advancing economic growth tied to unfettered private enterprise capitalism, Democrats are more inclined to favor equality and policies that help the economically less advantaged segments of the population, making government a significant actor in the process. Today, however, neither paradigm seems capable of solving the nation's problems or attracting the support of a majority of the electorate. E. J. Dionne, Jr., in his impressive book, *Why Americans Hate Politics*, pinpoints the recent failures of liberal and conservative political philosophies designed to strengthen democratic governance:

> Our system has become one long-running advertisement against self-government.... Because of our flight from public life, our common citizenship no longer fosters a sense of community or common purpose.... Most of the problems of our political life can be traced to the failure of the dominant ideologies of American politics, liberalism and conservatism.... We are suffering from a false polarization in our politics, in which liberals and conservatives keep arguing about the same things when the country wants to move on.[52]

While these ideological movements are good at opposing each other, neither is capable of gaining sufficient popular support in developing solutions to problems, as both are experiencing internal contradictions. Each would increase the role of government via mandated spending while also reducing government via downsizing and cutting selective programs. Conservatives want less governmental interference in the political and economic realms, but more regulation over social and moral behavior. Liberals want less government interference in regard to social and moral behavior, but more regulation of political and economic affairs. The incoherence of these incompatible value orientations only breeds confusion and political impotency.[53]

Of course, it may well be that the cause of this failure reflects a deeper cultural source: the tendency of Americans to want to better themselves at others' expense and, if necessary, a willingness to engage in fierce struggle for narrowing and scarcer resources.[54] Solutions defy reasonable debate and agreement, or as Dionne states, "our political culture encourages us to run away from solutions."[55] The politics of compromise has given way to the politics of divisiveness, and the center of the political spectrum, where most Americans can be found, offers little in the way of solid footing, and resembles more a quagmire of sinking confidence in the system.

In spite of the much heralded Republican "contract" with the American people announced on the eve of the 1994 Congressional elections, under the guidance of Speaker of the House Newt Gingrich of Georgia, there has been little improvement in the nation's capacity to pull itself together and move forward in a positive way. The prolonged 1995–96 federal budget stalemate between the president and Congress exemplifies this extremely wasteful and costly situation. Conservatives are united in what they are against—liberal permissiveness—but divided on what they are for—policies that might achieve a viable vision of the public good, not just politically, but for society and the economy. Liberals are divided into pragmatists (e.g., President Bill

Clinton) and ideologues (e.g., elements of the intellectual elite). Neither faction has sufficient broad-based support to command the allegiance of a liberal constituency for needed reforms that would establish a means test for entitlements like Social Security and Medicare, while strengthening the safety net for those who cannot make it in a changing society and economy.

Both political movements, conservatism and liberalism, are bankrupt, but as E. J. Dionne maintains, there is nothing available to replace them as road map and guide to a better future. Again, Dionne effectively summarizes this development:

> The great American middle felt cheated by our politics for most of the last thirty years. In liberalism it saw a creed that demeaned its values; in conservatism it saw a doctrine that shortchanged its interests. To engage members of this broad middle, liberals must show more respect for their values, and conservatives must pay more heed to their interests.[56]

DEMOCRACY AND SELF-INTEREST

It is a well-known fact that the liberal foundations of American democracy drew heavily upon the political theories of Montesquieu, Hobbes, and Locke, thinkers who to various degrees postulated individual self-interest as the primary or exclusive motivating force in political behavior.[57] As mediated by Jefferson, Madison, and Tocqueville, this view of self-interest was translated into a broad—rather than narrow—understanding of self-interest. In other words, self-interest need not be just selfishness; it could also encompass other-regarding, altruistic, idealistic motivational modes. Enlightened self-interest, to use Tocqueville's term, could be considered the grounding of democratic politics, as opposed to narrow, selfish, egotistical self-interest.[58] If individual character is highly developed and ethically based, and circumstances provide leeway for acting responsibly, selflessly, and prudently, then chances are the results will be more beneficial for the larger public interest. If, however, individual character is weak and circumstances favoring opportunism, aggrandizement, and selfishness are strong, then the individual is likely to be out for one's self more than one's public responsibility. It may not be possible to predict in advance for any individual which choice will be made, but when character rises above circumstances, prospects are good that it will strengthen democratic values.[59]

The times can also affect which concept of self-interest is adopted. When competition, conflict, and scarcity are rampant, the adoption of enlightened self-interest over narrow self-interest is less likely. Also, the prevailing political environment can have great influence. If reputation and success are measured by who you know and what you can do for certain special interests, then the narrow concept of self-interest is sure to dominate. If, however, a person can make a successful political career by keeping one's personal integrity intact—unfortunately a declining possibility today—then the larger public good is more likely to be benefited. Citizens in a democracy have a responsibility that few seem to accept: that is, to evaluate candidates for public office on the basis of character rather than superficial attributes of personality. It is never easy to make accurate and objective assessments of anybody's character, especially public officials. Yet it needs to be attempted. Democracy ultimately stands or falls on the capacity of citizens to make good judgments about who is selected to govern them.[60]

SCARCITY AND NEED

Raising the financial resources to accomplish what needs to be done to improve the infrastructure, solve social problems, and maintain an enormous military organization is an increasingly difficult task for governments at all levels, especially given the growing popular demand that budgets be reduced or balanced. Expectations and demands on government continue to expand, while the willingness to support government via taxation is diminishing. The result is that governments cannot cope with the demands placed upon them by a growing population and by world power responsibilities. It is doubtful that reduced spending on specific programs and entitlements will ever keep up with increasing demands on governments to deal with national needs.

Scarcity and need are increasingly obvious conditions in the United States today. Indebtedness, deficits, and borrowing against the future to meet present needs have turned the United States into a vulnerable, weakened, and uncertain giant.[61] The era when the American people and officials had the wealth and resources to accomplish any goal is over, perhaps forever. The United States is increasingly being forced by history and events to join the rest of the world, where growing scarcity is the rule, not the exception. The reverse was once the case for the U.S. economy, especially in the twenty-five or so years following the end of World War II, but no longer. Limiting wants, instead of expecting more and better, has definitely become a necessity even for the wealthiest nation on earth.[62]

This means that many big-ticket items like space exploration, agricultural subsidies, welfare, Social Security, and medical care—not to mention the military establishment and government operations—will have to be curtailed in order to achieve a better balance between expenditures and revenues. Cost cutting, improved efficiency, and more careful attention to national priorities will have to come into play. Otherwise, the United States will enter into permanent decline relative to the other advanced industrial nations that have recognized the need to do exactly that, even if it means some reduction in consumerism and living standards generally. There is no more urgent problem facing this country than deficit reduction and the return to fiscal responsibility. The longer this problem is put off or evaded, the worse will be the damage to America's reputation and standing. The political will to change exists, but results are largely inadequate and disappointing. Politicians still practice "politics as usual," despite the rhetoric of change. Taxes keep taking a bigger proportion of everybody's income, even in the face of prospective federal tax decreases, and the system remains blatantly inadequate, unfair, and unpopular. Until this matter is effectively dealt with, everybody will suffer, and the country will languish in economic turmoil and political paralysis.

THE FUTURE OF AMERICAN DEMOCRACY

It is possible America will continue to grow as one of the world's greatest economic and political powers, achieving improved living standards for a majority of its people and exercising more influence in the world than any other state.[63] Yet a strong military capability and overall strong economy may not compensate for political weakness and financial irresponsibility. American democracy is in deep trouble. At a time when so many nations that have never known democracy—most importantly the former Communist states—are rushing to transform totalitarian-authoritarian regimes into democratic-capitalistic ones, America no longer offers a good model of democratic constitutionalism and governance. The maldistribution of income and wealth in this country is growing, and the opportunity to acquire a piece of the American Dream is a receding mirage for too many of us.[64] In the view of E. J. Dionne, Jr., "American politics is mired in recrimination and accusation ... [and] the result, across the spectrum, is a political war of all against all."[65] The incidence of democratic civility is at an all-time low, and criminality, drugs, addiction of all sorts, and random violence have become scourges of society.

It is frequently alleged that Americans don't care enough about the public sphere or the requirements of social responsibility.[66] Even as equality and nondiscrimination have become official policy, and are legally enforced, the quality of life in America for a growing number of citizens has notably declined. Many believe that America is becoming a less humane, less tolerant, and less responsible society. The homicide rate, gun culture violence, growth of homelessness, teenage unwed pregnancy, and the terrible cost of addiction testify to this condition. The power of money may have displaced the power of democracy in motivating Americans to "ask not what they can do for their country but what they can do for themselves," to reverse John Kennedy's famous rhetoric. As necessary as money is to the good life, it should not be an end in itself. More and more, for too many people, the end seems to justify any means.

Ironically, it may be the case that as America became stronger as a state, it became weaker as a civilization. This condition needs to be corrected. There will have to be a stronger across-the-board commitment to democratic values of freedom, equality, tolerance, and justice. The formal trappings of democracy are not enough. Democracy has to become institutionalized as a way of thinking, a way of deciding, and a way of acting. Citizens have to do more than pay it lip service. It has to be practiced on a wide scale.[67]

A massive transformation of values in the direction of real democracy within the populace will have to take place before political reform can begin to take hold. There is also the specific problem of what kind of changes should be instituted to make the American government and political system function more effectively. Peter F. Drucker has summarized the need for change as follows:

> The civilian part of the U.S. government has outgrown its size and outlived its policies.... In fact there is no point in blaming this or that president for the total disarray of our government today. It is the fault neither of the Democrats nor of the Republicans. Government has outgrown the structure, the policies, and the rules designed for it and still in use.[68]

Surely the central problem of democracy is to find a way to transcend interest-group, special-interest, and parochial (community, regional, and state) concerns so that some conception of the 'common good' can be translated into public policy.[69]

There is no question that Americans have always been skeptical of government's ability to solve problems that might otherwise be left to private initiative. Certainly the cumbersome separation of powers, the checks and balances, and the multiple centers of power—the features that make the American system unique—testify to this point. Historically, they have permitted a wide range of views, interests, and values to infuse the decision-making process, surely a requirement for a genuine democracy. Despite the frequent delays, stalemates, and diluted compromises, the system has been responsive to the wide range of diverse and complex interests that exist in American society. Still, an increasingly urgent question remains today: Can this nation continue to afford such a slow, deliberate, and inconclusive political process, given the scope, immensity, and seriousness of the problems and challenges facing it now and in the future? From the perspective of this chapter, the answer is no, but a pragmatic and realistic approach that accepts a role for government in solving the nation's problems, as well as the possibility that significant constitutional and political change may have to be undertaken, offers the best hope for the twenty-first century.

NOTES

1. See Kevin Phillips, *Arrogant Capital: Washington, Wall Street, and the Frustration of American Politics* (Boston: Little, Brown, 1994).
2. See Christopher Lasch, *The Revolt of the Elites and the Betrayal of Democracy* (New York: W. W. Norton, 1995).

3. See Jean Bethke Elshtain, *Democracy on Trial* (New York: HarperCollins Basic Books, 1995).

4. See Susan Herbst, *Numbered Voices: How Opinion Polling Has Shaped American Politics* (Chicago: University of Chicago Press, 1993).

5. See Donald Snow, *National Security: Defense Policy for a New International Order,* 3rd ed. (New York: St. Martin's Press, 1995).

6. Jonathan Rauch, *Demosclerosis, The Silent Killer of American Government* (New York: Times Books, 1995), p. 47.

7. Phillips, pp. xii, 113.

8. See William A. Henry III, *In Defense of Elitism* (New York: Doubleday, 1994).

9. See James L. Sundquist, *Constitutional Reform and Effective Government* (Washington, DC: The Brookings Institute, 1986).

10. See H. Mark Roelofs, *The Poverty of American Politics: A Theoretical Interpretation* (Philadelphia: Temple University Press, 1992).

11. Hedrick Smith, *The Power Game: How Washington Works* (New York: Ballantine Books, 1988).

12. See David R. Mayhew, *Divided We Govern: Party Control, Lawmaking, and Investigations 1946–1990* (New Haven: Yale University Press, 1991).

13. See David Lazare, *The Frozen Republic: How the Constitution Is Paralyzing Democracy* (New York: Harcourt, Brace & Co., 1996).

14. See Kevin Phillips, *Boiling Point: Democrats, Republicans, and the Decline of Middle-Class Prosperity* (New York: Harper Perennial, 1993).

15. See Philip K. Howard, *The Death of Common Sense* (New York: Warner Books, 1996).

16. See James Fallows, *Breaking the News: How the Media Undermine American Democracy* (New York: Pantheon Books, 1996). See also Ronald Kessler, *Inside the White House: The Hidden Lives of the Modern Presidents and the Secrets of the World's Most Powerful Institution* (New York: Pocket Books, 1995).

17. See Gertrude Himmelfarb, *The De-Moralization of Society: From Victorian Virtues to Modern Values* (New York: Alfred A. Knopf, 1995).

18. See Mickey Kaus, *The End of Inequality* (New York: HarperCollins Basic Books, 1992).

19. "On Removing Certain Impediments to Democracy in the United States," *Political Science Quarterly,* Spring 1977, p. 6.

20. Ibid., pp. 7–8.

21. "The Crisis of Competence in Our National Government," Political Science Quarterly, Summer 1980, p. 183.

22. Ibid., p. 185.

23. See Arthur M. Schlesinger, Jr., *The Disuniting of America: Reflections on a Multicultural Society* (New York: W. W. Norton, 1993). See also Philip M. Stern, *The Best Congress Money Can Buy* (New York: Pantheon Books, 1988); Katherine S. Newman, *Declining Fortunes: The Withering of the American Dream* (New York: HarperCollins Basic Books, 1993); and James B. Stewart, *Blood Sport: The President and His Adversaries* (New York: Simon & Schuster, 1996).

24. See Jeffrey C. Goldfarb, *The Cynical Society: The Culture of Politics and the Politics of Culture in American Life* (Chicago: University of Chicago Press, 1991). See also Andrew Hacker, *Two Nations: Black and White, Separate, Hostile, Unequal* (New York: Charles Scribner's Sons, 1992); and Stephen L. Carter, *The Culture of Disbelief: How American Law and Politics Trivialize Religious Devotion* (New York: HarperCollins Basic Books, 1993).

25. Ed Gillespie and Bob Schellhas, eds., *Contract with America* (New York: Times Books, 1994).

26. See Amitai Etzioni, *Capital Corruption: The New Attack on American Democracy*

(New York: Harcourt Brace Jovanovich, 1984). See also Jeffrey H. Birnbaum, *Lobbyists: How Influence Peddlers Get Their Way in Washington* (New York: Times Books, 1992).

27. See Alan Ehrenhalt, *The United States of Ambition: Politicians, Power and the Pursuit of Office* (New York: Times Books, 1992).

28. William Greider, *Who Will Tell the People: The Betrayal of American Democracy* (New York: Simon & Schuster, 1992).

29. See John Kenneth Galbraith, *The Culture of Contentment* (Boston: Houghton Mifflin Co., 1992).

30. See James Ring Adams, *The Big Fix: Inside the S&L Scandal* (New York: John Wiley & Sons, 1991). See also James B. Stewart, *Den of Thieves* (New York: Simon & Schuster, 1991).

31. Phillips, *Arrogant Capital*, p. 107.

32. Quoted in A. M. Rosenthal's column, "American Class Struggle," *The New York Times*, Tuesday, March 21, 1995, p. A21.

33. See Christopher Andrew, *For the President's Eyes Only: Secret Intelligence and the American Presidency from Washington to Bush* (New York: HarperCollins, 1995).

34. See Jane J. Mansbridge, ed., *Beyond Self-Interest* (Chicago: University of Chicago Press, 1990). See also Theodore J. Lowi, *The End of the Republican Era* (Norman: University of Oklahoma Press, 1995).

35. See Valerie Bunch, *Do New Leaders Make a Difference?* (Princeton, NJ: Princeton University Press, 1981). See also Elizabeth Drew, *Showdown: The Struggle Between the Gingrich Congress and the Clinton White House* (New York: Simon & Schuster, 1996); and William E. Hudson, *American Democracy in Peril: Seven Challenges to America's Future* (Chatham, NJ: Chatham House Publishers, 1995).

36. See Judith E. Gruber, *Controlling Bureaucracies: Dilemmas in Democratic Governance* (Berkeley: University of California Press, 1987).

37. See H. Mark Roelofs, *Ideology and Myth in American Politics: A Critique of a National Mind* (Boston: Little, Brown, 1976).

38. See Michael J. Sandel, *Democracy's Discontent: America in Search of a Public Philosophy* (Cambridge: Harvard University Press, 1996). See also Samuel P. Huntington, *The Promise of Disharmony* (Cambridge: Harvard University Press, 1981).

39. W. J. Stankiewicz, *Aspects of Political Theory: Classical Concepts in the Age of Relativism* (London: Collier Macmillan, 1976), p. 33.

40. See James Lincoln Collier, *The Rise of Selfishness in America* (New York: Oxford University Press, 1991).

41. See Robert A. Dahl, *Democracy and Its Critics* (New Haven: Yale University Press, 1989).

42. See Todd Gitlin, *The Twilight of Common Dreams: Why America Is Wracked by Culture Wars* (New York: Henry Holt & Co., 1995).

43. See Michael B. Katz, *The Undeserving Poor, From the War on Poverty to the War on Welfare* (New York: Pantheon Books, 1989).

44. See Robert Hughes, *Culture of Complaint: The Fraying of America* (New York: Warner Books, 1994).

45. "America's New Split Personality," *Psychology Today*, October 1978, p. 17. See also Amitai Etzioni, *The Spirit of Community: The Reinvention of American Society* (New York: Simon & Schuster Touchstone Book, 1993); and Amitai Etzioni, *The Moral Dimension: Toward a New Economics* (New York: The Free Press, 1988).

46. C. B. Macpherson, *The Political Theory of Possessive Individualism* (New York: Oxford University Press, 1962).

47. See Leonard Lurie, *Party Politics: Why We Have Poor Presidents* (New York: Stein & Day, 1980).

48. See Robert Kuttner, *The Life of the Party: Democratic Prospects in 1988 and Beyond* (New York: Viking, 1987). See also James MacGregor Burns, *The Power to Lead: The Crisis of the American Presidency* (New York: Simon & Schuster, 1984); and Michael Kelly, "The Political Scene: Uninvited Guests," *The New Yorker*, March 11, 1996, pp. 58–62.

49. Stanley B. Greenberg, *Middle-Class Dreams: The Politics and Power of the New American Majority* (New York: Random House Times Books, 1995), p. 8.

50. See Cornel West, *Race Matters* (New York: Vintage Books, 1994).

51. See *Political Science & Politics,* publication of the American Political Science Association, Vol. XXVIII, No. 1, March 1995, special issue articles on "The Christian Right and the 1994 Elections."

52. E. J. Dionne, Jr., *Why Americans Hate Politics* (New York: Simon & Schuster, 1991), pp. 10–11.

53. See Grant McConnell, *Private Power & American Democracy* (New York: Alfred A. Knopf, 1966).

54. See Philip Slater, *A Dream Deferred: America's Discontent and the Search for a New Democratic Ideal* (Boston: Beacon Press, 1991).

55. Dionne, p. 21.

56. Ibid., p. 345.

57. See David W. Minar, *Ideas and Politics: The American Experience* (Homewood, IL: The Dorsey Press, 1964).

58. See *Democracy in America,* various editions available.

59. See Robert M. Bellah, et al., *The Good Society* (New York: Alfred A. Knopf, 1991). See also James Q. Wilson, *On Character* (Washington, DC: The American Enterprise Institute Press, 1995).

60. See Charles Murray, *The Pursuit of Happiness and Good Government* (New York: Simon & Schuster, 1988).

61. See Paul Kennedy, *The Rise and Fall of the Great Powers: Economic Change and Military Conflict from 1500 to 2000* (New York: Vintage Books, 1989).

62. See Christopher Jencks, *Rethinking Social Policy: Race, Poverty and the Underclass* (New York: Harper Perennial, 1993).

63. See Robert J. Samuelson, *The Good Life and Its Discontents: The American Dream in the Age of Entitlement 1945–1995* (Times Books, 1995); and Dennis H. Wrong, *The Problem of Order: What Unites and Divides Society* (New York: The Free Press, 1994).

64. See Barbara Ehrenreich, *Fear of Falling: The Inner Life of the Middle Class* (New York: Harper Perennial, 1990).

65. See E. J. Dionne, Jr., *They Only Look Dead: Why Progressives Will Dominate the Next Political Era* (New York: Simon & Schuster, 1996).

66. See Ralph Ketchum, *Individualism and Public Life: A Modern Dilemma* (New York: Basil Blackwell, 1987). See also Robert H. Wiebe, *Self-Rule: A Cultural History of American Democracy* (Chicago: University of Chicago Press, 1995); and James A. Morone, *The Democratic Wish: Popular Participation and the Limits of American Government* (New York: Basic Books, 1990).

67. See Benjamin Barber, *Strong Democracy: Participatory Politics for a New Age* (Berkeley: University of California Press, 1984).

68. Peter F. Drucker, *Managing in a Time of Great Change* (New York: Truman Tally Books/Dutton, 1995), pp. 290–291.

69. See John Patrick Diggins, *The Promise of Pragmatism: Modernism and the Crisis of Knowledge and Authority* (Chicago: University of Chicago Press, 1994).

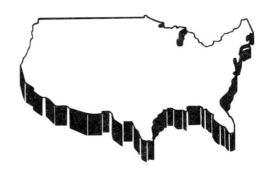

INDEX